The CAR Book

2015

by
Jack Gillis

and
Amy Curran
Peter Kitchen

with
Richard Eckman

Foreword by
Clarence Ditlow
Center for Auto Safety

A Center for Auto Safety Publication

D0520273

ACKNOWLEDGMENTS

Co-author Peter Kitchen once again managed and organized this 35th edition of *The Car Book*. It is a monumental effort as literally thousands of data points go into compiling the book and all of its ratings. For 24 years, Amy Curran has been expertly preparing all the graphics necessary to clearly present the data, managing the logistics necessary to get a printed book in the hands of the public, and keeping the project on track. This year, Richard "Ricky" Eckman provided excellent research and data analysis. Thanks to Amy, Peter, and Ricky, consumers have the information they need to make a smart, sensible new car choice.

As has been the case for 34 years, this year's edition would not have been possible without the essential contributions from Clarence Ditlow and the staff of the Center for Auto Safety, including Michael Brooks and Jon Robinson.

As always, the most important factor in being able to bring this information to the American car buyer for 35 years is the encouragement, support, and love from my brilliant and beautiful wife, Marilyn Mohrman-Gillis. For her and four terrific children–Katie, John, Brian and Brennan–I am eternally grateful.

—*J.G.*

As Always,
for Marilyn &
Katie, John, Brian, and Brennan

---

35 YEARS!

During the 35 years that *The Car Book* has been published, it has been accompanied by a variety of auto-related consumer guides including *The Used Car Book* 1988-2002; *The Truck Van and 4x4 Book* 1991-1999; *The Value and Luxury Car Books* 2000; *How to Make Your Car Last Forever* 1987; *The Armchair Mechanic* 1988; and, *The Car Repair Book* 1991. In all, we've produced 65 auto-related books along with another 8 consumer guides. In recognition of 35 years of publications, I want to honor and thank the legions of people who have helped make these books possible. The number of books each person worked on follows their name.

Coauthors:

Ailis Aaron 14, Deirdre Aaron 2, Ivy Baer 1, Scott Beatty 12, Ashley Cheng 11, Amy Curran 47, Richard Eckman 1, Dabney Edwards 2, Jay Einhorn 6, Alisa Feingold 16, Karen Fierst 34, Brennan Gillis 1, Brian Gillis 1, John Gillis Jr. 1, Katie Gillis 2, Eric Glenn 1, Eli Greenspan 1, Daniel Gustafson 4, Ben Hardaway 3, David Iberkleid 3, Tom Kelly 2, Peter Kitchen 3, Nicole Klein 3, Seth Krevat 3, Mike McQuiller 1, Julia Redmon 5, Virginia Redmon 1, Jerilyn Saxon 7, Evan Shurak 2, Andrew Siegel 1, Julie Beth Wright 4.

Contributors:

Stephanie Ackerman 7, Jim Armstrong 1, Stu Armstrong 1, Anu Ashutosh 2, Chris Atkinson 1, Judith Bailey 3, Jessica Baldwin 1, Debra Barclay 11, Jennifer Barrett 3, Ben Becker 2, Carol Berger 1, Nancy Berk 2, Kristin Beyard 1, Debbie Bindeman 15, David Biss 4, Michael Brooks 11, Elizabeth Brown 2, Joe Bruha 1, Kevin Busen 1, Martha Casey 9, Andrew Chap 1, Jeff Clark 1, David Cokely 1, Susan Cole 24, Jennifer Cook Mirabito 1, Alan Coombs 1, Ben Crenshaw 1, Caroline Cruz 1, Jim Cullum 5, Brad Daniels 1, Jennifer Davidson 2, John DeCicco 2, Joe DeGrande 1, Cheryl Denenberg 7, Pat Donlon 6, Rosemary Shahan 3, Bill Earp 1, Marshall Einhorn 2, Morshed El Hag 6, Mari Beth Emigh 1, Jerret Engle 3, Meaghan Farrell 1, Barry Fierst 9, Eyal Fierst 4, Matthew Figueroa 1, Anne Fleming 1, Nicole Freydberg 1, Edna Friedberg 3, Grant Gasson 1, Sherrie Good 4, Christy Goodrich 1, Carolyn Gorman 12, Nancy Green 7, Sharon Guttman 3, John Guyton 1, Kim Hazelbaker 11, Karen Heckler 5, Vico Henriques 6, Maggie Herman 3, Kaz Hickok 4, Ann Himmelberg 1, Neene Hirata 2, Susan Hoffmann 1, Bill Hogan 1, Bryan Hoopman 1, Dan Howell 1, Mizuho Ikeuchi 1, Mark Jacobson 1, Richard Jester 1, Alisa Joaquin 3, Evan Johnson 7, Steve Julius 3, Irvine Kaplan 2, George Kaveney 1, Al Kettler 1, Mike Kido 4, Lisa Kitei 3, Michael Kott 3, Stuart Krichevsky 45, Bill Kumbar 3, Sonia Kundert 1, Christopher Lank 1, Ann Lavie 10, Elaine Lawless 1, Ed Lewis 3, David Lewkowict 3, Shelley Liebman 3, Mary Kay Linge 1, Faith Little 5, Lou Lombardo 3, Ann Lyons 1, Roger MacBride Allen 2, Joel Makower 3, James Marshall 4, Patricia McCullen-Noettl 1, Kathy Melborn 2, Cristina Mendoza 6, John Michel 9, Cynthia Miller 1, Trina Mohrbacher 1, Rick Morgan 2, Stephanie Narva 6, Debra Anne Naylor 1, David Noettl 3, John Noettl 24, Karen Noettl 5, Steven Noettl 7, Bill North-Rudin 6, Phil Nowicki 15, Ted Orme 1, Stephanie Ortbals 3, George Ottoson 1, Pete Packer 15, Wendy Pellow 2, Mary Penrose 1, Elisa Petrini 1, Fran Pflieger 1, Torryn Phelps 2, Sarah Phillips 3, Laura Polachek 3, Carol Pollack 1, Wayne Powell 3, Bryan Pratt 2, Stephen Quine 1, Toufic Rahman 6, Tammy Rhodes 1, Jennifer Rieder 2, Sara Roberts 2, Jon Robinson 4, Sara Roschwalb 3, Jill Rosensweig 2, Harriet Rubin 4, Beth Schelske 1, Susan Schneider 3, Roger Scholl 1, Lois Sharon 1, Jerry Sheehan 1, Anne Marie Shelness 1, Russell Shew 16, Amy Shock 4, David Smith 1, Malcolm Smith 2, Steve Smith 4, Sherri Soderberg Pittman 4, Beverly Southerland 1, Tanny Southerland 1, Erika Sova 3, Karen Steinke 2, Martin Thomas 2, Susan Tiffany 1, Stephanie Tombrello 2, Barbara Tracey 2, Keren Trost 1, Buddy Vagoni 1, Jon Vernick 1, Darlene Watson 1, Elaine Weinstein 2, Ray Weiss 11, Clay White 1, Donna Whitlow 1, Teresa Wooten-Talley 8, Ken Wright 2, Susan Beth Wright 1, Peter Zetlin 1.

CLARENCE DITLOW

When regulators sleep and auto companies place profits over safety, safety defects pile up. The record 60 million vehicles recalled in 2014 resulted from Congressional hearings and Justice Department criminal prosecutions exposing a deadly mass of concealed by the auto industry. From the Corvair in the 1960s through Ford Pinto and Firestone 500 tires in the 1970s, GM pickup sidesaddle gas tanks in the 1980s, Ford Explorer rollover in the 1990s, Toyota unintended acceleration and Jeep gas tanks in the 2000s and now GM ignition switches and Takata airbags, the auto companies concealed defects to avoid recalls and save money. Toyota bragged that it saved a $100 million by avoiding a sudden acceleration.

After each of the defects, Congress held hearings and gave the National Highway Traffic Safety Administration (NHTSA) new authority to regulate the auto industry which NHTSA failed to use. NHTSA Administrator David Friedman told Congress he was unaware the agency had subpoena authority it was used so infrequently.

But Congress has not given NHTSA the two things it needs most - adequate funding and criminal penalties against auto companies for failing to comply with the Safety Act. Unlike other federal regulatory agencies, NHTSA does not even have its own vehicle research and test facility. Its annual vehicle safety budget is a puny $134 million - less than 50¢ per vehicle on the road. The budget for finding defects and ordering recalls is even smaller - less than 10¢ per vehicle.

Since passage of the National Traffic and Motor Vehicle Safety Act in 1966, industry lobbyists blocked the passage of criminal penalties for executives who knowingly violate the Safety Act. The prospect of going to jail will change corporate behavior far quicker than a large fine.

Over time NHTSA has become captured by the industry it regulates. The early NHTSA aggressively litigated defects cases to obtain recalls and caught most defects early in the life of a vehicle. Few employees went to work for or came from the regulated auto industry. The last tough NHTSA Administrator was Joan Claybrook who the auto industry called the Dragon Lady for her stringent enforcement of the Safety Act in the late 1970s.

Beginning in the 1980s, top NHTSA officials left to become consultants, lawyers, or expert witnesses for the auto industry. The list reads like a who's who of Administrators (Diane Steed, Jerry Curry, Sue Bailey and David Strickland), Chief Counsels (Erika Jones, Jacqueline Glassman and Paul Rice) as well as numerous Associate and Deputy Administrators (William Boehly, Kenneth Weinstein, Barry Felrice and Robert Sheldon).

The revolving door swings both ways. Today's NHTSA is populated by employees from industry. Some like Ms. Glassman come from industry and go back to industry. Imbued by industry influence, the culture of NHTSA has become one where the agency views industry as its constituents, not the public it's supposed to

protect. Only a complete change of culture at NHTSA, closing of the revolving door, passage of criminal penalties, and adequate funding for the agency will prevent future record recalls as auto makers will always place profits over safety and innovation.

Until NHTSA changes its culture to protecting the public, the 2015 Car Book is the average consumer's answer to finding a new car that has the advanced safety features like lane departure, radar braking and adaptive cruise control, active pre-crash safety and automatic crash notification that will be options only on some models. Use *The Car Book* and its new comprehensive crash safety rating to buy a car that's going to protect you in a crash. Use *The Car Book*'s Safety Chapter to find out all the optional safety features and which models have them when you buy a new vehicle. Your buying decision not only may save your life but also sends a message to automakers not to withhold vital safety features.

By using *The Car Book* to buy a safer car, you have taken an important first step toward your personal vehicle safety and helping the Center for Auto Safety reach our Vision of Zero Traffic Deaths by 2050. The next step is to support the Center for Auto Safety which works every day on your behalf to ensure that all Americans ride in safe and reliable vehicles. Go to our Website www.autosafety.org and find out how you can support the Center and have CAS be your safety and lemon insurance.

JACK GILLIS

2014 was a difficult year for the U.S. auto industry. With more recalls than any other year in history, consumers may be a bit wary of the new models. The good news? There are plenty of good choices among the 2015 models—if you know what to look for!

Amazingly, the is the 35th year we've been bringing consumers the information they need to make a smart and safe choice among the new vehicles. While the driverless car is still a few years down the road, many of today's new cars have a variety of highly technical crash avoidance systems. From automatic breaking to lane changing and self-parking, the many new and life-saving features that were previously only available on high priced cars are becoming available on vehicles the rest of us can afford.

Not only is the vehicle getting better, so is the buying experience. More and more dealers are abandoning the difficult netotiation process in favor of a straightforward posted price. So with lots of new electronics, improved safety features, and some improvements in the showroom, *The Car Book* is ready to guide you to a great new 2015 vehicle!

Working closely with the Center for Auto Safety's Clarence Ditlow and his staff, as we have for 35 years, my goal is to sift through the myriad of government and industry data on cars and present the information so you can actually use it. Thirty-five years ago, *The Car Book* was the first publication to give consumers the ability to make an informed choice on one of the most important and complex items that they will ever purchase. Today, thanks in large part to the efforts of the Center for Auto Safety in Washington, DC, our mission has never wavered.

This past year, the Center's Clarence Ditlow has been the primary advocate who has brought media, consumer and Congressional attention to the many serious auto defects that have been in the news. His efforts have saved lives and brought about important changes in auto company practices and government regulations.

In setting out to change the way people buy their cars, *The Car Book* was able to change the way car companies made them.

In keeping with *The Car Book*'s philosophy of making it as easy as possible to identify the truly good performers in the government crash tests, we provide a unique Car Book Combined Crash Test Rating which combines all of the complex government testing into a simple, straightforward number. In addition, we take the step of comparing the vehicles on a relative basis to each other so you can easily tell the best performers from the worst.

Unfortunately, not all 2015 vehicles have been crash tested. While we (and you!) look forward to the day when all of your choices have been tested, our safety ratings will provide a good indication of which cars can be expected to best protect you.

Before *The Car Book*, consumers had no idea which warranties were better, what you could expect to pay for typical repairs, which cars cost the most and least to insure, or how they stacked up in government complaints. Now you have this information all in one place.

Our exclusive car-by-car ratings at the end of the book provide an overview of all the criteria you need to make a good choice. Here, you'll be able to quickly assess key features and see how the car you're interested in stacks up against its competition so you can make sure your selection is the best car for you.

Even though the choices get better each year and safety is improved, it's still a challenge to separate the lemons from the peaches. There are notable differences in how cars protect you in a crash, how much they cost to maintain, the benefits of their warranties, and how far they'll go on a gallon of expensive gasoline. Nevertheless, if you use the information in *The Car Book*, there is no reason why your next car should not last at least 150,000 miles.

Our "Showroom Strategies" section will give you the keys to getting the best deal. In spite of all the new car technology and the Internet, the fundamentals of buying a good, safe, reliable car remain the same: do your homework; shop around; and remember that car dealers need you more than you need them!

The information in *The Car Book* is based on data collected and developed by our staff, the U.S. Department of Transportation, and the Center for Auto Safety. With all of this information in hand, you'll find some great choices for 2015.

—Jack

USING THE BUYING GUIDE

T he "Buying Guide" provides a quick comparison of the 2015 cars in terms of their safety, warranty, fuel economy, complaint rating, and price range—arranged by size class. To fully understand the information in the charts, it is important to read the related section in the book.

Overall Rating: This shows how well this car stacks up on a scale of 1 to 10 when compared to all others on the market. Because safety is the most important component of our ratings, cars with no crash test results at printing are not given an overall rating.

Combined Crash Test Rating: This indicates how well the car performed in the government's frontal and side crash test programs compared to this year's vehicles tested to date. See page 18 for details.

Warranty Rating: This is an overall comparative assessment of the car's warranty.

Fuel Economy: This is the EPA city/highway mpg for, what is expected to be, the most popular version of each model.

Complaint Rating: This is based on complaints received by the U.S. Department of Transportation. If not rated, the vehicle is too new to have a complaint rating.

Price Range: This will give you a general idea of the "sticker," or suggested retail price.

Indicates a *Car Book* Best Bet. See page 13.

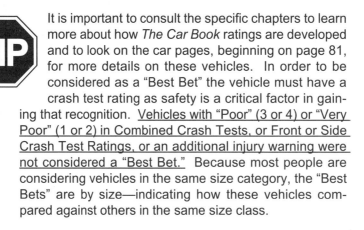

ABOUT THE CAR BOOK BEST BETS

It is important to consult the specific chapters to learn more about how *The Car Book* ratings are developed and to look on the car pages, beginning on page 81, for more details on these vehicles. In order to be considered as a "Best Bet" the vehicle must have a crash test rating as safety is a critical factor in gaining that recognition. <u>Vehicles with "Poor" (3 or 4) or "Very Poor" (1 or 2) in Combined Crash Tests, or Front or Side Crash Test Ratings, or an additional injury warning were not considered a "Best Bet."</u> Because most people are considering vehicles in the same size category, the "Best Bets" are by size—indicating how these vehicles compared against others in the same size class.

Vehicle	Page #	Overall Rating	Combined Crash Test Rating	Warranty Rating	Fuel Economy	Complaint Rating	Price Range
Subcompact							
Chevrolet Sonic	119	9	Very Good	Good	25/35	Average	$14-$21,000
Chevrolet Spark	120	5	Poor	Good	30/39	Very Poor	$12-$27,000
Fiat 500	134	2	Very Poor	Poor	27/34	Very Poor	$16-$26,000
Ford Fiesta	142	2	Poor	Poor	27/37	Very Poor	$14-$21,000
Honda Fit	152	6	Very Good	Very Poor	33/41		$15-$20,000
Hyundai Accent	155	5	Very Poor	Very Good	26/37	Good	$14-$17,000
Hyundai Veloster	162	6	Average	Very Good	27/36	Very Poor	$17-$23,000
Kia Rio	178	5	Very Poor	Very Good	27/37	Very Good	$13-$18,000
Kia Soul	181	7	Very Good	Very Good	23/31	Poor	$15-$35,000
Mazda MX-5 Miata	202			Very Poor	21/28	Very Good	$23-$32,000
Mini Cooper	211			Very Good	28/37	Poor	$20-$36,000
Mini Countryman	212			Very Good	27/34	Very Good	$22-$35,000
Mitsubishi Mirage	214	3	Very Poor	Very Good	37/44	Average	$12-$15,000
Nissan 370Z	217			Very Poor	19/26	Average	$29-$49,000
Nissan Versa	230	2	Very Poor	Very Poor	31/40	Good	$11-$16,000
Scion xB	237			Very Poor	22/28	Good	$16-$17,000
Smart ForTwo	238			Poor	34/38	Average	$13-$25,000
Toyota Prius C	252	5	Very Poor	Very Poor	53/46	Very Good	$19-$24,000
Toyota Yaris	260	5	Poor	Very Poor	30/36	Very Good	$14-$17,000
Volkswagen Beetle	261	3	Poor	Poor	25/33	Average	$20-$31,000
Compact							
Acura ILX	81	7	Average	Poor	24/35	Very Good	$27-$31,000
Audi A3	86	5	Good	Average	24/33		$29-$47,000
Audi A4	87	6	Average	Average	22/31	Good	$35-$45,000
BMW 3 Series	94	9	Good	Very Good	23/35	Average	$32-$49,000
BMW 4 Series	95			Very Good	23/35	Good	$40-$56,000
Buick Verano	106	9	Good	Good	21/32	Average	$23-$29,000
Cadillac ATS	107	9	Good	Very Good	21/33	Very Poor	$33-$51,000
Chevrolet Cruze	114	8	Good	Good	26/38	Average	$17-$25,000
Chevrolet Volt	125	8	Poor	Good	35/40	Very Poor	$34-$34,000
Dodge Dart	131	5	Good	Average	24/34		$16-$22,000
Fiat 500L	135			Poor	22/30	Very Poor	$19-$24,000
Ford C-MAX	136	5	Poor	Poor	42/37	Very Poor	$24-$31,000
Ford Focus	144			Poor	27/40	Very Poor	$16-$39,000

Vehicle	Page #	Overall Rating	Combined Crash Test Rating	Warranty Rating	Fuel Economy	Complaint Rating	Price Range
Compact (cont.)							
Honda Civic	149	6	Poor	Very Poor	30/39	Very Good	$18-$27,000
Hyundai Elantra	156	6	Average	Very Good	28/38	Average	$17-$22,000
Infiniti Q60	164			Good	19/27	Very Good	$40-$62,000
Kia Forte	176	5	Poor	Very Good	25/36	Very Poor	$15-$21,000
Lexus CT	186			Average	43/40	Average	$32-$32,000
Lexus IS	190	5	Average	Average	21/30	Poor	$36-$63,000
Mazda Mazda3	199	5	Average	Very Poor	30/41	Good	$16-$26,000
Mercedes-Benz C-Class	203			Poor	22/31		$38-$62,000
Mercedes-Benz CLA-Class	204			Poor	26/38	Very Poor	$29-$47,000
Mitsubishi Lancer	213	2	Very Poor	Poor	26/34	Average	$17-$40,000
Nissan Leaf	222	2	Very Poor	Very Poor	126/101	Very Poor	$29-$35,000
Nissan Sentra	228			Very Poor	30/39	Average	$15-$19,000
Scion FR-S	235	3	Poor	Very Poor	25/34	Good	$24-$31,000
Scion tC	236	5	Average	Very Poor	23/31	Very Good	$19-$20,000
Subaru BRZ	239	2	Poor	Very Poor	25/34	Poor	$25-$29,000
Subaru Impreza	241	4	Poor	Very Poor	28/37	Good	$18-$24,000
Toyota Corolla	249	8	Good	Very Poor	27/36	Very Good	$16-$22,000
Toyota Prius	251	4	Poor	Very Poor	51/48	Very Poor	$23-$34,000
Volkswagen Golf	263			Poor	26/36		$17-$29,000
Volkswagen Jetta	264	5	Good	Poor	23/34	Average	$17-$31,000
Intermediate							
Acura RLX	84			Poor	20/31	Very Poor	$48-$60,000
Acura TLX	85			Poor	24/35		$30-$44,000
Audi A5	88			Average	22/31	Very Good	$40-$56,000
Audi A6	89	7	Good	Average	18/27	Good	$44-$62,000
BMW 5 Series	96	8	Average	Very Poor	23/34	Poor	$49-$66,000
BMW 6 Series	97			Very Good	17/25	Very Good	$76-$97,000
Buick Regal	105	6	Average	Good	19/31	Very Good	$29-$39,000
Cadillac CTS	108	10	Good	Very Good	18/29	Average	$45-$69,000
Chevrolet Camaro	111	7	Very Good	Good	18/27	Average	$23-$72,000
Chevrolet Corvette	113			Good	16/29	Poor	$53-$63,000
Chevrolet Malibu	117	7	Good	Good	25/36	Average	$22-$30,000
Chrysler 200	126	8	Good	Average	23/36		$21-$30,000
Ford Fusion	145	4	Average	Poor	22/34	Poor	$22-$36,000
Ford Mustang	146			Poor	19/28		$23-$46,000
Honda Accord	148	7	Good	Very Poor	27/36	Average	$22-$35,000
Hyundai Sonata	160	8	Very Good	Very Good	25/37		$21-$29,000
Infiniti Q50	163			Good	20/29	Good	$37-$48,000

Vehicle	Page #	Overall Rating	Combined Crash Test Rating	Warranty Rating	Fuel Economy	Complaint Rating	Price Range
Intermediate (cont.)							
Infiniti Q70	165			Good	18/24	Very Poor	$49-$67,000
Kia Cadenza	175			Very Good	19/28	Very Poor	$34-$43,000
Kia Optima	177	7	Average	Very Good	23/34	Average	$21-$35,000
Lexus GS	188			Average	19/29	Very Good	$48-$61,000
Lincoln MKZ	196	4	Average	Good	18/27	Average	$35-$37,000
Mazda Mazda6	201	4	Average	Very Poor	26/38	Very Poor	$21-$29,000
Nissan Altima	218	5	Average	Very Poor	27/38	Poor	$22-$31,000
Nissan Maxima	223	1	Very Poor	Very Poor	19/26	Good	$31-$34,000
Subaru Legacy	242	7	Very Good	Very Poor	26/36		$21-$29,000
Subaru Outback	243	7	Very Good	Very Poor	25/33		$24-$32,000
Toyota Camry	248	7	Good	Very Poor	25/35	Good	$22-$31,000
Toyota Prius V	253	8	Good	Very Poor	44/40	Very Good	$26-$30,000
Volkswagen CC	262			Poor	22/31	Average	$32-$43,000
Volkswagen Passat	265	5	Good	Poor	24/36	Poor	$21-$35,000
Volvo S60	268	10	Very Good	Good	25/37	Good	$33-$46,000
Volvo V60	269			Good	25/37		$35-$48,000
Large							
Audi A7	90			Average	18/28	Average	$65-$72,000
BMW 7 Series	98			Very Good	17/25	Good	$74-$141,000
Buick LaCrosse	104	8	Very Good	Good	18/28	Good	$33-$40,000
Cadillac XTS	110	9	Very Good	Very Good	18/28	Average	$44-$69,000
Chevrolet Impala	116	6	Good	Good	18/28	Very Poor	$26-$35,000
Chrysler 300	127			Average	19/31	Poor	$30-$48,000
Dodge Challenger	129	5	Good	Average	19/30		$26-$57,000
Dodge Charger	130			Average	19/31	Very Poor	$26-$43,000
Ford Taurus	147	4	Good	Poor	19/29	Good	$26-$40,000
Hyundai Genesis	157	7	Very Good	Very Good	18/29		$34-$51,000
Lexus ES	187	7	Average	Average	21/31	Very Good	$37-$40,000
Lincoln MKS	194	5	Good	Good	19/28	Average	$40-$47,000
Mercedes-Benz E-Class	205	4	Poor	Poor	20/29	Very Good	$51-$102,000
Mercedes-Benz S-Class	210			Poor	17/26	Good	$94-$222,000
Tesla Model S	245	10	Very Good	Good	88/90		$71-$105,000
Toyota Avalon	247	7	Good	Very Poor	21/31	Poor	$32-$41,000
Minivan							
Chrysler Town and Country	128	3	Very Poor	Average	17/25	Poor	$29-$39,000
Honda Odyssey	153	7	Good	Very Poor	19/28	Average	$28-$44,000
Kia Sedona	179			Very Good	18/24		$25-$39,000
Mazda Mazda5	200			Very Poor	21/28	Average	$21-$24,000

Vehicle	Page #	Overall Rating	Combined Crash Test Rating	Warranty Rating	Fuel Economy	Complaint Rating	Price Range
Minivan (cont.)							
Nissan Quest	226			Very Poor	20/27	Poor	$26-$43,000
Toyota Sienna	256	3	Poor	Very Poor	18/25	Poor	$28-$46,000
Small SUV							
Acura RDX	83	8	Very Good	Poor	19/27	Average	$34-$39,000
Audi Q3	91			Average	20/28		$32-$38,000
Audi Q5	92	4	Poor	Average	20/28	Very Good	$38-$54,000
BMW X1	99			Very Good	22/32	Good	$30-$38,000
Buick Encore	103	10	Good	Good	23/30	Good	$24-$30,000
Cadillac SRX	109	8	Good	Very Good	17/24	Average	$37-$51,000
Chevrolet Trax	124	7	Good	Good	24/31		$20-$26,000
Ford Escape	138	5	Average	Poor	22/31	Poor	$23-$31,000
Honda Crosstour	150			Very Poor	19/28		$27-$37,000
Honda CR-V	151	6	Average	Very Poor	26/33	Average	$22-$29,000
Hyundai Tucson	161	5	Very Poor	Very Good	21/28	Good	$21-$27,000
Jeep Cherokee	169	4	Average	Average	21/28	Very Poor	$22-$30,000
Jeep Compass	170			Average	20/23	Poor	$18-$27,000
Jeep Patriot	172			Average	20/23	Poor	$16-$26,000
Jeep Renegade	173			Average			
Jeep Wrangler	174			Average	17/21	Very Poor	$22-$35,000
Kia Sportage	182	5	Average	Very Good	21/28	Very Good	$21-$29,000
Land Rover Rnge Rvr Evoque	184			Poor	21/30	Good	$41-$58,000
Lexus NX	191			Average	22/28		$39-$41,000
Lincoln MKC	193	5	Poor	Good	19/26		$33-$35,000
Mazda CX-5	197	5	Very Good	Very Poor	26/32	Very Poor	$21-$29,000
Mercedes-Benz GLA-Class	206			Poor	24/32		$31-$48,000
Mercedes-Benz GLK-Class	208			Poor	18/25	Poor	$37-$39,000
Mitsubishi Outlander Sport	216	4	Poor	Very Good	25/32	Very Good	$19-$24,000
Nissan Juke	221			Very Poor	26/31	Very Good	$20-$30,000
Porsche Macan	233			Average	17/23		$49-$72,000
Subaru Forester	240	2	Average	Very Poor	24/32	Poor	$22-$33,000
Subaru XV Crosstrek	244	5	Average	Very Poor	26/34	Very Good	$21-$29,000
Toyota RAV4	254	4	Poor	Very Poor	22/29	Very Good	$23-$29,000
Volkswagen Tiguan	266	1	Very Poor	Poor	21/26	Poor	$25-$39,000
Mid-Size SUV							
Acura MDX	82	6	Good	Poor	18/27	Very Poor	$42-$56,000
Audi Q7	93			Average	16/22	Good	$47-$64,000
BMW X3	100	8	Average	Very Good	21/28	Good	$38-$45,000
BMW X5	101	6	Good	Very Good	18/27	Poor	$53-$69,000

Vehicle	Page #	Overall Rating	Combined Crash Test Rating	Warranty Rating	Fuel Economy	Complaint Rating	Price Range
Mid-Size SUV (cont.)							
Chevrolet Equinox	115	2	Very Poor	Good	22/32	Poor	$24-$33,000
Dodge Journey	133			Average	17/25	Very Poor	$19-$30,000
Ford Edge	137			Poor	/		$28-$39,000
Ford Explorer	140	3	Good	Poor	17/23	Poor	$30-$42,000
GMC Terrain	115	3	Very Poor	Average	22/32	Good	$26-$37,000
Honda Pilot	154	2	Very Poor	Very Poor	17/24	Good	$29-$41,000
Hyundai Santa Fe	158			Very Good	18/25	Very Poor	$30-$36,000
Hyundai Santa Fe Sport	159	7	Average	Very Good	20/27		$24-$33,000
Infiniti QX60	166			Good	19/26	Very Poor	$42-$46,000
Infiniti QX70	167			Good	16/22	Very Good	$45-$47,000
Jeep Grand Cherokee	171	3	Average	Average	14/20	Very Poor	$29-$64,000
Kia Sorento	180	4	Good	Very Good	20/27	Very Poor	$24-$41,000
Land Rover Rnge Rvr Sport	185			Poor	14/19	Very Good	$63-$93,000
Lexus RX	192	6	Average	Average	18/24	Very Good	$40-$48,000
Lincoln MKX	195	5	Very Poor	Good	17/23	Good	$39-$48,000
Mazda CX-9	198	1	Very Poor	Very Poor	16/22	Average	$29-$36,000
Mercedes-Benz M-Class	209	5	Very Good	Poor	17/22	Very Good	$49-$98,000
Mitsubishi Outlander	215	4	Average	Very Good	24/29	Very Poor	$23-$28,000
Nissan Murano	224			Very Poor	21/28		$29-$40,000
Nissan Pathfinder	225			Very Poor	19/26	Very Poor	$29-$43,000
Nissan Rogue	227	2	Very Poor	Very Poor	25/32	Good	$22-$29,000
Nissan Xterra	231			Very Poor	15/20	Poor	$23-$31,000
Porsche Cayenne	232			Average	17/24	Very Good	$61-$113,000
Toyota Venza	259	3	Average	Very Poor	20/26	Good	$28-$39,000
Volkswagen Touareg	267			Poor	17/23	Poor	$44-$64,000
Volvo XC60	270	9	Very Good	Good	17/24	Average	$36-$50,000
Large SUV							
Buick Enclave	102	7	Very Good	Good	17/24	Poor	$38-$49,000
Cadillac Escalade	122			Very Good	14/21		$71-$82,000
Cadillac Escalade ESV	121			Very Good	14/20		$74-$85,000
Chevrolet Suburban	121	5	Average	Good	15/22		$47-$64,000
Chevrolet Tahoe	122	6	Good	Good	16/22		$44-$62,000
Chevrolet Traverse	123	7	Very Good	Good	17/24	Average	$30-$43,000
Dodge Durango	132	2	Average	Average	14/22	Very Poor	$30-$43,000
Ford Expedition	139	7	Very Good	Poor	15/20	Good	$38-$60,000
Ford Flex	143			Poor	18/25	Poor	$31-$44,000
GMC Acadia	123	6	Very Good	Average	17/24	Poor	$33-$49,000
GMC Yukon	122	5	Good	Average	14/21		$46-$65,000

Vehicle	Page #	Overall Rating	Combined Crash Test Rating	Warranty Rating	Fuel Economy	Complaint Rating	Price Range
Large SUV (cont.)							
GMC Yukon XL	121	4	Average	Average	14/20		$49-$68,000
Infiniti QX80	168			Good	14/20	Very Good	$63-$66,000
Land Rover Range Rover	183			Poor	14/19	Very Poor	$83-$135,000
Lexus GX	189			Average	15/20	Good	$49-$60,000
Lincoln Navigator	139	9	Very Good	Good	15/20	Very Good	$61-$67,000
Mercedes-Benz GL-Class	207			Poor	17/21	Good	$63-$119,000
Nissan Armada	219			Very Poor	13/19	Poor	$38-$53,000
Toyota 4Runner	246	3	Very Poor	Very Poor	17/21	Very Good	$33-$43,000
Toyota Highlander	250	7	Very Good	Very Poor	18/24	Very Good	$29-$49,000
Toyota Sequoia	255			Very Poor	13/17	Good	$44-$64,000
Compact Pickup							
Chevrolet Colorado	112			Good	20/27		$20-$34,000
GMC Canyon	112			Average	17/24		$20-$37,000
Nissan Frontier	220			Very Poor	15/21	Average	$17-$35,000
Toyota Tacoma	257	1	Very Poor	Very Poor	16/21	Good	$20-$37,000
Standard Pickup							
Chevrolet Silverado	118	7	Very Good	Good	16/22	Average	$26-$51,000
Ford F-150	141			Poor	17/23		$25-$54,000
GMC Sierra	118	6	Very Good	Average	16/22	Poor	$26-$53,000
Nissan Titan	229			Very Poor	12/17	Poor	$29-$43,000
Ram 1500	234	3	Average	Average	13/19	Poor	$24-$49,000
Toyota Tundra	258	3	Average	Very Poor	13/17	Very Good	$29-$47,000

BEST BETS

T he following is our list of the highest rated vehicles in each size category. The ratings are based on expected performance in nine important categories–Combined Crash Rating, Safety Features, Rollover, Preventive Maintenance, Repair Costs, Warranty, Fuel Economy, Complaints, and Insurance Costs–with the heaviest emphasis placed on safety. (See box on previous page.)

CHEVROLET SONIC
SUBCOMPACT

Combo Crash Tests 9	Warranty 7
Safety Features 9	Fuel Economy 8
Rollover 5	Complaints 5
PM 8	Insurance 1
Repair Costs 10	**OVERALL RATING. . . 9**

Page 119

KIA SOUL
SUBCOMPACT

Combo Crash Tests 9	Warranty 10
Safety Features 4	Fuel Economy 6
Rollover 4	Complaints 3
PM 4	Insurance 3
Repair Costs 9	**OVERALL RATING. . . 7**

Page 181

BMW 3 SERIES
COMPACT

Combo Crash Tests 7	Warranty 9
Safety Features 9	Fuel Economy 6
Rollover 8	Complaints 5
PM 9	Insurance 8
Repair Costs 3	**OVERALL RATING. . . 9**

Page 94

BUICK VERANO
COMPACT

Combo Crash Tests 8	Warranty 7
Safety Features 10	Fuel Economy 5
Rollover 4	Complaints 6
PM 8	Insurance 5
Repair Costs 7	**OVERALL RATING. . . 9**

Page 106

CHEVROLET CRUZE
COMPACT

Combo Crash Tests 8	Warranty 7
Safety Features 9	Fuel Economy 8
Rollover 7	Complaints 5
PM 5	Insurance 1
Repair Costs 8	**OVERALL RATING. . . 8**

Page 114

TOYOTA COROLLA

COMPACT

Combo Crash Tests 8
Safety Features 2
Rollover 6
PM 10
Repair Costs. 9
Warranty. 2
Fuel Economy. 9
Complaints 9
Insurance 1
OVERALL RATING. . . 8

Page 249

CADILLAC CTS

INTERMEDIATE

Combo Crash Tests 8
Safety Features 8
Rollover 8
PM 10
Repair Costs. 4
Warranty. 9
Fuel Economy. 3
Complaints 6
Insurance 10
OVERALL RATING. . 10

Page 108

CHRYSLER 200

INTERMEDIATE

Combo Crash Tests 8
Safety Features 6
Rollover 7
PM 6
Repair Costs. 9
Warranty. 5
Fuel Economy. 7
Complaints . . . . –
Insurance 3
OVERALL RATING. . . 8

Page 126

HYUNDAI SONATA

INTERMEDIATE

Combo Crash Tests 9
Safety Features 5
Rollover 7
PM 2
Repair Costs. 9
Warranty. 10
Fuel Economy. 8
Complaints . . . . –
Insurance 3
OVERALL RATING. . . 8

Page 160

VOLVO S60

INTERMEDIATE

Combo Crash Tests 9
Safety Features 10
Rollover 8
PM 9
Repair Costs. 7
Warranty. 8
Fuel Economy. 8
Complaints 7
Insurance 5
OVERALL RATING. . 10

Page 268

BUICK LACROSSE

LARGE

Page 104

Combo Crash Tests	9	Warranty	7
Safety Features	9	Fuel Economy	3
Rollover	6	Complaints	7
PM	5	Insurance	5
Repair Costs	4	**OVERALL RATING**	**8**

CADILLAC XTS

LARGE

Page 110

Combo Crash Tests	10	Warranty	9
Safety Features	8	Fuel Economy	3
Rollover	6	Complaints	5
PM	10	Insurance	8
Repair Costs	2	**OVERALL RATING**	**9**

HYUNDAI GENESIS

LARGE

Page 157

Combo Crash Tests	9	Warranty	10
Safety Features	6	Fuel Economy	3
Rollover	8	Complaints	–
PM	3	Insurance	3
Repair Costs	4	**OVERALL RATING**	**7**

LEXUS ES

LARGE

Page 187

Combo Crash Tests	6	Warranty	6
Safety Features	9	Fuel Economy	5
Rollover	7	Complaints	9
PM	7	Insurance	5
Repair Costs	1	**OVERALL RATING**	**7**

TESLA MODEL S

LARGE

Page 245

Combo Crash Tests	9	Warranty	8
Safety Features	10	Fuel Economy	10
Rollover	10	Complaints	–
PM	–	Insurance	5
Repair Costs	–	**OVERALL RATING**	**10**

TOYOTA AVALON

LARGE

Page 247

Combo Crash Tests	7	Warranty	2
Safety Features	8	Fuel Economy	5
Rollover	7	Complaints	4
PM	8	Insurance	8
Repair Costs	4	**OVERALL RATING**	**7**

HONDA ODYSSEY

MINIVAN

Page 153

Combo Crash Tests	8	Warranty	1
Safety Features	7	Fuel Economy	4
Rollover	5	Complaints	5
PM	6	Insurance	10
Repair Costs	9	**OVERALL RATING**	**7**

ACURA RDX

SMALL SUV

Page 83

Combo Crash Tests	9	Warranty	4
Safety Features	5	Fuel Economy	4
Rollover	4	Complaints	6
PM	8	Insurance	10
Repair Costs	7	**OVERALL RATING**	**8**

BUICK ENCORE

SMALL SUV

Page 103

Combo Crash Tests	8	Warranty	7
Safety Features	10	Fuel Economy	6
Rollover	3	Complaints	7
PM	8	Insurance	8
Repair Costs	8	**OVERALL RATING**	**10**

CADILLAC SRX

SMALL SUV

Page 109

Combo Crash Tests	7	Warranty	9
Safety Features	7	Fuel Economy	2
Rollover	3	Complaints	6
PM	10	Insurance	8
Repair Costs	6	**OVERALL RATING**	**8**

CHEVROLET TRAX

SMALL SUV

Page 124

Combo Crash Tests 8	Warranty 7
Safety Features 9	Fuel Economy 6
Rollover 2	Complaints . . . .–
PM . . . .–	Insurance 5
Repair Costs . . . .–	**OVERALL RATING. . . 7**

BMW X3

MID-SIZE SUV

Page 100

Combo Crash Tests 6	Warranty 9
Safety Features 9	Fuel Economy 5
Rollover 3	Complaints 8
PM 10	Insurance 8
Repair Costs 3	**OVERALL RATING. . . 8**

HYUNDAI SANTA FE SPORT

MID-SIZE SUV

Page 159

Combo Crash Tests 6	Warranty 10
Safety Features 5	Fuel Economy 4
Rollover 4	Complaints . . . .–
PM 4	Insurance 8
Repair Costs 8	**OVERALL RATING. . . 7**

VOLVO XC60

MID-SIZE SUV

Page 270

Combo Crash Tests 9	Warranty 8
Safety Features 9	Fuel Economy 2
Rollover 3	Complaints 6
PM 9	Insurance 10
Repair Costs 7	**OVERALL RATING. . . 9**

BUICK ENCLAVE

LARGE SUV

Page 102

Combo Crash Tests 9	Warranty 7
Safety Features 7	Fuel Economy 2
Rollover 3	Complaints 4
PM 6	Insurance 10
Repair Costs 3	**OVERALL RATING. . . 7**

CHEVROLET TRAVERSE

LARGE SUV

Page 123

Combo Crash Tests 9	Warranty 7
Safety Features 7	Fuel Economy. 2
Rollover 3	Complaints 5
PM 6	Insurance 10
Repair Costs. 5	**OVERALL RATING. . . 7**

FORD EXPEDITION

LARGE SUV

Page 139

Combo Crash Tests 10	Warranty 3
Safety Features 5	Fuel Economy. 1
Rollover 2	Complaints 7
PM 4	Insurance 10
Repair Costs. 8	**OVERALL RATING. . . 7**

LINCOLN NAVIGATOR

LARGE SUV

Page 139

Combo Crash Tests 10	Warranty 8
Safety Features 5	Fuel Economy. 1
Rollover 2	Complaints 10
PM 7	Insurance 8
Repair Costs. 8	**OVERALL RATING. . . 9**

TOYOTA HIGHLANDER

LARGE SUV

Page 250

Combo Crash Tests 9	Warranty 2
Safety Features 8	Fuel Economy. 3
Rollover 3	Complaints 10
PM 9	Insurance 8
Repair Costs. 2	**OVERALL RATING. . . 7**

CHEVROLET SILVERADO

STANDARD PICKUP

Page 118

Combo Crash Tests 9	Warranty 7
Safety Features 6	Fuel Economy. 2
Rollover 3	Complaints 5
PM 5	Insurance 10
Repair Costs. 6	**OVERALL RATING. . . 7**

CRASH TESTS

Safety is likely the most important factor that most of us consider when choosing a new car. In the past, evaluating safety was difficult. Now, thanks to the information in *The Car Book*, it's much easier to pick a safe vehicle. The bottom line: For the greatest protection, you'll want the maximum number of safety features (See Safety Checklist, pages 78-79) and good crash test results (the following tables).

A key factor in occupant protection is how well the car protects you in a crash. This depends on its ability to absorb the force of the impact rather than transfer it to the occupant. In 2011, the government began a new crash test program with more sophisticated dummies, additional test measurements, and a small female dummy.

In the frontal test, the vehicle impacts a solid barrier at 35 mph. In the side test, a moving barrier is crashed into the side of the vehicle at 38.5 mph. A second side test, new in 2011, simulates hitting a tree or roadside pole by smashing a vertical pole into the driver side door at 20 mph. The only occupant in this side pole test is a small female dummy in the driver seat.

The new dummies measure impact on a different scale from previous tests, and the new test measures neck injuries and chest deflection which were not included in the previous tests. These new test results cannot be compared with older results.

Not all 2015 vehicles have undergone the new tests. The good news is that by carrying forward previous tests from cars that haven't changed, we have results for 125 2015 models. The bad news is that there are 74 models for which we don't have crash test results.

How the Cars are Rated: The combined crash test ratings are based on the <u>relative</u> performance of the vehicles tested to date using the new test. *This is a big difference from the government's "star" program.* Rather than large groups of undifferentiated vehicles in the government's star ratings, *The Car Book* rates them from best to worst. This means that those manufacturers really working on safety, each year, will rise to the top.

The first column provides *The Car Book's* Combined Crash Test Rating. The cars are rated from 10 Best to 1 Worst. The front is weighted 60%, the side 36%, and the pole test 4% with results compared among all new 2015 crash tests to date.

Next are the individual front and side tests. Again, relative to all other 2015 vehicles tested, we indicate if the vehicle was Very Good, Good, Average, Poor or Very Poor. For side tests, the cars are rated separately from the trucks. Because of their construction the dynamics of a side test are different in cars and trucks.

The next five columns indicate the likelihood of the occupant sustaining a life-threatening injury. The percent likelihood is listed for the driver and front passenger in the front test, the driver and rear passenger in the side test, and the driver in the side pole test. Lower percentages mean a lower likelihood of being seriously injured. This information is taken directly from the government's analysis of the crash test results.

USING CRASH TEST DATA

One of the most important results of our being the first to publish crash test data, and later develop our relative comparative ratings, is that it has put enormous pressure on the manufacturers to improve. Whereas years ago, when competition was based soley on style and horsepower, thanks to *The Car Book*, today's manufacturers are feverously competing on safety features. While the most important factors in evaluating the safety of today's vehicles are crash test performance and advanced safety features, size and weight do play a role. It is important to compare vehicles in the size classes that follow. For example, in a frontal collision between a subcompact and SUV rated 'Very Good," you'll be better off in the SUV. Nevertheless, selecting the best performers in whatever size class you are buying, is fundamental to protecting yourself. And remember, these tests are conducted with fully belted dummies, if you are not wearing your safety belt, then test results do not really apply.

CRASH TESTS

Crash Test Performance (10=Best, 1=Worst)	Combined Car Book Crash Test Rating	Test Type	Car Book Crash Test Rating-Index (Lower numbers are better)	Likelihood of Life Threatening Injury				
				Front Fixed Barrier		Side Moving Barrier		Side Pole
				Front Driver	Front Pass.	Side Driver	Side Pass.	Pole Driver
Subcompact								
Chevrolet Sonic	9	Front	Very Good-166	8.7%	8.7%			
		Side	Good-113			7.0%	4.6%	7.1%
Chevrolet Spark	3	Front	Poor-228	13.6%	10.7%			
		Side	Poor-147			9.2%	6.8%	5.6%
Fiat 500	1	Front	Very Poor-256	11.4%	16.0%			
		Side	Poor-148			5.3%	8.0%	15.8%
Ford Fiesta[1]	3	Front	Average-199	8.2%	12.8%			
		Side	Very Poor-381			11.3%	31.5%	3.6%
Honda CR-Z		Front	Very Poor-265	10.4%	18.0%			
		Side				19.1%		6.5%
Honda Fit	9	Front	Good-175	9.2%	9.1%			
		Side	Very Good-85			6.8%	2.5%	3.5%
Hyundai Accent[2]	2	Front	Poor-209	9.2%	12.8%			
		Side	Very Poor-234			8.6%	17.0%	4.3%
Hyundai Veloster	5	Front	Average-205	12.4%	9.2%			
		Side	Average-131			6.9%	7.8%	1.5%
Kia Rio[3]	1	Front	Very Poor-230	10.8%	13.7%			
		Side	Very Poor-177			13.5%	7.0%	3.5%
Kia Soul	9	Front	Good-180	7.6%	11.2%			
		Side	Very Good-81			4.7%	4.0%	2.6%
Mitsubishi Mirage	2	Front	Poor-218	12.6%	10.5%			
		Side	Very Poor-169			7.4%	9.8%	9.6%
Nissan Versa	1	Front	Very Poor-295	12.2%	19.7%			
		Side	Very Poor-256			16.4%	13.5%	4.7%
Nissan Versa Note	2	Front	Very Poor-329	15.9%	20.2%			
		Side	Poor-136			8.9%	6.4%	2.8%
Scion iQ	1	Front	Very Poor-258	12.1%	15.6%			
		Side	Very Poor-294			14.8%	18.7%	6.7%
Smart ForTwo Electic Drive		Front	Very Poor-253	13.9%	13.2%			
		Side	No Index-			7.0%		16.2%
Toyota Prius C[4]	2	Front	Poor-215	12.2%	10.5%			
		Side	Very Poor-239			14.8%	12.0%	8.1%
Toyota Yaris	3	Front	Poor-217	9.9%	13.1%			
		Side	Poor-159			7.3%	8.7%	10.1%

[1,2,3,4] Additional Injury Potential: Due to the intrusion of the left rear door during the side impact test, the interior door panel struck the torso of the rear passenger dummy, causing a high lower spine acceleration. High lower spine accelerations, in excess of 82 g's, indicate a higher likelihood of thoracic injury.

CRASH TESTS

Crash Test Performance (10=Best, 1=Worst)	Combined Car Book Crash Test Rating	Test Type	Car Book Crash Test Rating-Index (Lower numbers are better)	Likelihood of Life Threatening Injury				
				Front Fixed Barrier		Side Moving Barrier		Side Pole
				Front Driver	Front Pass.	Side Driver	Side Pass.	Pole Driver
Subcompact (cont.)								
Volkswagen Beetle	4	Front	Poor-216	9.6%	13.2%			
		Side	Average-125			7.3%	6.0%	5.3%
Compact								
Acura ILX	5	Front	Average-193	9.3%	11.0%			
		Side	Poor-139			8.0%	5.2%	13.9%
Audi A3	7	Front	Average-197	11.2%	9.6%			
		Side	Good-113			7.0%	5.1%	4.2%
Audi A4	6	Front	Good-178	9.5%	9.1%			
		Side	Poor-152			12.8%	4.8%	3.8%
BMW 3 Series	7	Front	Average-194	11.6%	8.9%			
		Side	Good-108			7.9%	4.3%	2.3%
Buick Verano	8	Front	Average-196	9.4%	11.2%			
		Side	Very Good-65			3.9%	1.7%	9.0%
Cadillac ATS	8	Front	Very Good-162	8.2%	8.7%			
		Side	Poor-138			7.5%	7.4%	4.8%
Chevrolet Cruze	8	Front	Good-176	8.2%	10.2%			
		Side	Average-114			7.1%	4.8%	6.7%
Chevrolet Volt	4	Front	Poor-205	8.8%	12.9%			
		Side	Poor-141			7.9%	7.9%	2.0%
Dodge Dart	8	Front	Good-188	9.2%	10.6%			
		Side	Very Good-78			4.1%	4.1%	2.4%
Ford C-MAX	4	Front	Poor-224	10.9%	12.9%			
		Side	Average-119			6.2%	5.7%	8.1%
Honda Civic	4	Front	Poor-209	11.1%	11.0%			
		Side	Average-118			5.6%	6.5%	5.7%
Honda Civic Coupe	2	Front	Poor-217	11.1%	11.9%			
		Side	Very Poor-166			7.2%	10.8%	3.5%
Hyundai Elantra	5	Front	Average-199	9.7%	11.3%			
		Side	Poor-146			12.0%	3.9%	7.8%
Kia Forte	3	Front	Poor-208	10.1%	11.9%			
		Side	Poor-156			9.0%	8.4%	2.7%
Lexus IS	6	Front	Poor-226	10.8%	13.2%			
		Side	Very Good-85			5.4%	3.2%	5.9%
Mazda Mazda3	6	Front	Good-185	8.5%	10.9%			
		Side	Average-119			11.5%	2.4%	2.8%

CRASH TESTS

Crash Test Performance (10=Best, 1=Worst)	Combined Car Book Crash Test Rating	Test Type	Car Book Crash Test Rating-Index (Lower numbers are better)	Likelihood of Life Threatening Injury				
				Front Fixed Barrier		Side Moving Barrier		Side Pole
				Front Driver	Front Pass.	Side Driver	Side Pass.	Pole Driver
Compact (cont.)								
Mitsubishi Lancer	2	Front	Poor-214	9.4%	13.3%			
		Side	Very Poor-199			4.0%	16.4%	5.6%
Nissan Leaf	1	Front	Very Poor-229	9.2%	15.1%			
		Side	Very Poor-215			5.6%	17.0%	5.0%
Scion FR-S	4	Front	Average-195	10.1%	10.5%			
		Side	Very Poor-166			15.6%	4.0%	3.3%
Scion tC	6	Front	Average-201	9.1%	12.1%			
		Side	Good-89			2.7%	6.1%	4.0%
Subaru BRZ	4	Front	Average-195	10.1%	10.5%			
		Side	Very Poor-166			15.6%	4.0%	3.3%
Subaru Impreza	4	Front	Very Poor-240	12.1%	13.6%			
		Side	Good-96			6.0%	2.4%	12.8%
Toyota Corolla	8	Front	Good-187	8.1%	11.6%			
		Side	Very Good-87			3.1%	5.1%	6.6%
Toyota Prius	4	Front	Poor-227	11.4%	12.8%			
		Side	Average-114			5.1%	5.7%	10.0%
Volkswagen Jetta	7	Front	Average-200	10.0%	11.1%			
		Side	Very Good-78			4.2%	3.9%	3.8%
Intermediate								
Audi A6	8	Front	Very Good-163	9.3%	7.7%			
		Side	Average-115			8.1%	3.9%	7.0%
Audi Allroad	6	Front	Good-178	9.5%	9.1%			
		Side	Poor-152			12.8%	4.8%	3.8%
BMW 5 Series	5	Front	Very Poor-233	13.1%	11.7%			
		Side	Very Good-85			8.4%	0.8%	5.5%
Buick Regal	6	Front	Average-199	9.9%	11.1%			
		Side	Average-116			4.1%	7.8%	4.3%
Cadillac CTS	8	Front	Good-184	8.1%	11.2%			
		Side	Good-102			6.9%	3.3%	7.9%
Chevrolet Camaro	10	Front	Very Good-171	9.6%	8.3%			
		Side	Very Good-66			5.7%	1.5%	3.2%
Chevrolet Malibu	7	Front	Average-198	10.1%	10.7%			
		Side	Good-111			5.6%	6.1%	4.1%
Chrysler 200	8	Front	Good-173	8.3%	9.9%			
		Side	Average-116			4.7%	7.0%	5.9%
Ford Fusion	6	Front	Good-176	7.5%	10.9%			
		Side	Very Poor-195			18.4%	5.0%	2.8%

CRASH TESTS

Crash Test Performance (10=Best, 1=Worst)	Combined Car Book Crash Test Rating	Test Type	Car Book Crash Test Rating-Index (Lower numbers are better)	Likelihood of Life Threatening Injury				
				Front Fixed Barrier		Side Moving Barrier		Side Pole
				Front Driver	Front Pass.	Side Driver	Side Pass.	Pole Driver
Intermediate (cont.)								
Ford Fusion Energi	8	Front	Very Good-154	7.3%	8.7%			
		Side	Poor-158			14.6%	3.6%	4.7%
Honda Accord	7	Front	Average-201	11.0%	10.2%			
		Side	Very Good-60			3.4%	2.9%	2.6%
Honda Accord Coupe	9	Front	Very Good-169	8.7%	8.9%			
		Side	Good-104			2.9%	7.7%	3.0%
Hyundai Sonata	9	Front	Very Good-147	7.5%	7.8%			
		Side	Average-114			5.8%	6.2%	4.6%
Hyundai Sonata Hybrid	7	Front	Average-197	8.9%	11.9%			
		Side	Good-103			7.6%	2.6%	9.2%
Kia Optima	6	Front	Good-174	8.6%	9.6%			
		Side	Very Poor-167			16.8%	2.0%	7.9%
Lincoln MKZ	6	Front	Good-176	7.5%	10.9%			
		Side	Very Poor-195			18.4%	5.0%	2.8%
Mazda Mazda6	6	Front	Average-201	9.5%	11.7%			
		Side	Good-96			8.2%	2.5%	3.5%
Nissan Altima	6	Front	Very Good-165	7.2%	10.0%			
		Side	Very Poor-189			17.7%	4.4%	4.9%
Nissan Maxima	1	Front	Very Poor-297	11.1%	20.9%			
		Side	Very Poor-168			15.6%	4.0%	4.3%
Subaru Legacy	10	Front	Very Good-161	8.9%	7.9%			
		Side	Very Good-80			3.3%	4.7%	4.0%
Subaru Outback	10	Front	Very Good-161	8.9%	7.9%			
		Side	Very Good-50			2.9%	1.9%	4.0%
Toyota Camry	7	Front	Average-195	11.2%	9.4%			
		Side	Good-107			6.1%	3.8%	11.3%
Toyota Prius V	7	Front	Poor-211	10.3%	12.0%			
		Side	Very Good-70			4.3%	1.5%	10.5%
Volkswagen Passat	8	Front	Very Good-155	7.7%	8.5%			
		Side	Poor-137			13.1%	2.7%	3.9%
Volvo S60	9	Front	Very Good-158	8.3%	8.2%			
		Side	Average-119			9.8%	3.7%	3.2%
Large								
Buick LaCrosse	9	Front	Very Good-169	7.9%	9.8%			
		Side	Good-112			5.7%	4.9%	10.5%
Cadillac XTS	10	Front	Very Good-160	7.6%	9.1%			
		Side	Good-88			4.2%	4.3%	6.7%

CRASH TESTS

Crash Test Performance (10=Best, 1=Worst)	Combined Car Book Crash Test Rating	Test Type	Car Book Crash Test Rating-Index (Lower numbers are better)	Likelihood of Life Threatening Injury				
				Front Fixed Barrier		Side Moving Barrier		Side Pole
				Front Driver	Front Pass.	Side Driver	Side Pass.	Pole Driver
Large (cont.)								
Chevrolet Impala	7	Front	Good-173	7.5%	10.6%			
		Side	Poor-142			10.1%	6.1%	2.9%
Chevrolet Impala Limited	4	Front	Average-194	8.4%	12.0%			
		Side	Very Poor-230			22.8%	4.7%	5.0%
Dodge Challenger	7	Front	Average-204	11.7%	9.8%			
		Side	Very Good-56			4.7%	1.4%	2.6%
Ford Taurus	7	Front	Very Good-164	8.4%	8.7%			
		Side	Poor-154			8.3%	8.3%	5.8%
Hyundai Genesis	9	Front	Very Good-153	7.7%	8.3%			
		Side	Good-108			10.9%	0.9%	6.5%
Lexus ES	6	Front	Good-187	9.7%	9.9%			
		Side	Average-134			11.7%	2.9%	6.9%
Lincoln MKS	7	Front	Very Good-164	8.4%	8.7%			
		Side	Poor-154			8.3%	8.3%	5.8%
Mercedes-Benz E-Class	3	Front	Very Poor-265	13.7%	14.8%			
		Side	Average-116			2.2%	6.7%	17.8%
Tesla Model S	9	Front	Good-180	9.4%	9.5%			
		Side	Very Good-58			3.5%	1.5%	7.9%
Toyota Avalon	7	Front	Average-193	10.4%	9.9%			
		Side	Good-91			6.2%	2.3%	10.2%
Minivan								
Chrysler Town and Country	2	Front	Poor-207	11.2%	10.7%			
		Side	Very Poor-152			7.4%	8.8%	5.5%
Honda Odyssey	8	Front	Good-187	9.9%	9.8%			
		Side	Very Good-57			2.9%	2.3%	5.6%
Toyota Sienna	4	Front	Very Poor-234	8.4%	16.4%			
		Side	Good-59			3.3%	2.7%	3.6%
Small SUV								
Acura RDX	9	Front	Very Good-149	7.0%	8.5%			
		Side	Average-76			3.5%	3.0%	9.6%
Audi Q5	3	Front	Very Poor-230	14.6%	9.9%			
		Side	Average-74			2.7%	4.4%	4.9%
Buick Encore	8	Front	Very Good-165	8.3%	9.0%			
		Side	Average-66			3.3%	3.0%	5.4%
Cadillac SRX	7	Front	Good-191	8.6%	11.4%			
		Side	Average-67			2.7%	1.7%	14.8%

CRASH TESTS

Crash Test Performance (10=Best, 1=Worst)	Combined Car Book Crash Test Rating	Test Type	Car Book Crash Test Rating-Index (Lower numbers are better)	Likelihood of Life Threatening Injury				
				Front Fixed Barrier		Side Moving Barrier		Side Pole
				Front Driver	Front Pass.	Side Driver	Side Pass.	Pole Driver
Small SUV (cont.)								
Chevrolet Trax	8	Front	Very Good-165	8.3%	9.0%			
		Side	Average-66			3.3%	3.0%	5.4%
Ford Escape	6	Front	Average-202	10.2%	11.2%			
		Side	Good-60			2.0%	3.5%	5.0%
Honda CR-V	5	Front	Average-199	9.5%	11.5%			
		Side	Average-73			3.1%	3.9%	5.7%
Hyundai Tucson	1	Front	Very Poor-230	11.4%	13.1%			
		Side	Very Poor-104			8.6%	2.3%	7.5%
Jeep Cherokee	6	Front	Poor-228	11.2%	13.1%			
		Side	Very Good-45			3.2%	1.7%	1.6%
Kia Sportage	5	Front	Good-185	8.9%	10.5%			
		Side	Very Poor-101			7.7%	3.5%	3.3%
Lincoln MKC[5]	3	Front	Poor-213	8.9%	13.7%			
		Side	Poor-92			3.3%	6.1%	3.4%
Mazda CX-5	9	Front	Very Good-155	7.6%	8.6%			
		Side	Good-64			2.3%	3.3%	7.1%
Mitsubishi Outlander Sport	4	Front	Average-203	10.0%	11.3%			
		Side	Poor-97			2.8%	6.3%	6.8%
Subaru Forester	6	Front	Poor-205	9.0%	12.7%			
		Side	Very Good-56			3.1%	2.6%	2.9%
Subaru XV Crosstrek	5	Front	Average-200	10.4%	10.7%			
		Side	Poor-82			3.8%	2.8%	12.8%
Toyota RAV4	4	Front	Very Poor-245	11.2%	15.0%			
		Side	Good-63			2.6%	1.6%	13.7%
Volkswagen Tiguan	2	Front	Very Poor-287	13.2%	17.9%			
		Side	Poor-86			3.3%	4.2%	10.0%
Mid-Size SUV								
Acura MDX	8	Front	Very Good-168	8.3%	9.2%			
		Side	Average-68			2.5%	4.2%	3.6%
BMW X3	6	Front	Good-188	8.8%	11.0%			
		Side	Average-75			4.9%	3.5%	0.9%
BMW X5	8	Front	Good-177	8.9%	9.7%			
		Side	Good-62			2.4%	3.1%	6.7%
Chevrolet Equinox	2	Front	Poor-216	9.5%	13.4%			
		Side	Very Poor-120			11.7%	2.0%	4.5%

[5] During the side impact test, the left rear passenger door unlatched and opened. A door opening during a side impact crash test increases the likelihood of occupant ejection.

Crash Test Performance (10=Best, 1=Worst)	Combined Car Book Crash Test Rating	Test Type	Car Book Crash Test Rating-Index (Lower numbers are better)	Likelihood of Life Threatening Injury				
				Front Fixed Barrier		Side Moving Barrier		Side Pole
				Front Driver	Front Pass.	Side Driver	Side Pass.	Pole Driver
Mid-Size SUV (cont.)								
Ford Explorer	7	Front	Good-183	10.4%	8.8%			
		Side	Good-63			4.2%	1.6%	7.1%
GMC Terrain	2	Front	Poor-216	9.5%	13.4%			
		Side	Very Poor-120			11.7%	2.0%	4.5%
Honda Pilot	2	Front	Poor-221	9.4%	14.1%			
		Side	Very Poor-185			6.4%	12.3%	9.8%
Hyundai Santa Fe Sport	6	Front	Good-184	9.2%	10.1%			
		Side	Average-71			3.6%	3.2%	6.3%
Jeep Grand Cherokee	6	Front	Good-178	9.4%	9.3%			
		Side	Poor-93			8.3%	2.3%	2.4%
Kia Sorento	8	Front	Very Good-154	8.2%	7.9%			
		Side	Poor-80			4.3%	3.0%	8.9%
Lexus RX	5	Front	Very Poor-230	12.4%	12.0%			
		Side	Very Good-34			2.5%	0.6%	4.5%
Lincoln MKX	2	Front	Very Poor-313	16.1%	18.1%			
		Side	Poor-81			5.3%	2.3%	8.3%
Mazda CX-9	1	Front	Very Poor-302	16.6%	16.2%			
		Side	Very Poor-100			4.0%	5.7%	6.8%
Mercedes-Benz M-Class	10	Front	Very Good-168	8.1%	9.5%			
		Side	Very Good-41			3.3%	1.1%	2.3%
Mitsubishi Outlander	5	Front	Average-195	12.4%	8.0%			
		Side	Poor-91			3.8%	4.7%	7.8%
Nissan Rogue	1	Front	Very Poor-240	10.5%	15.0%			
		Side	Very Poor-116			6.5%	4.6%	10.4%
Toyota Venza	6	Front	Average-196	9.4%	11.2%			
		Side	Average-65			3.9%	1.7%	9.0%
Volvo XC60	9	Front	Very Good-165	8.2%	9.0%			
		Side	Good-60			4.0%	2.1%	4.0%
Large SUV								
Buick Enclave	9	Front	Good-181	9.6%	9.3%			
		Side	Good-57			2.1%	3.4%	3.8%
Cadillac Escalade		Front	No Index-					
		Side	Very Good-45			3.0%	0.4%	8.6%
Cadillac Escalade ESV		Front	No Index-					
		Side	Average-69			4.5%	1.0%	12.2%
Chevrolet Suburban	6	Front	Average-195	10.4%	10.2%			
		Side	Average-69			4.5%	1.0%	12.2%
Chevrolet Tahoe	8	Front	Good-185	9.7%	9.7%			
		Side	Very Good-45			3.0%	0.4%	8.6%

Crash Test Performance (10=Best, 1=Worst)	Combined Car Book Crash Test Rating	Test Type	Car Book Crash Test Rating-Index (Lower numbers are better)	Front Fixed Barrier		Side Moving Barrier		Side Pole
				Front Driver	Front Pass.	Side Driver	Side Pass.	Pole Driver
Large SUV (cont.)								
Chevrolet Traverse	9	Front	Good-181	9.6%	9.3%			
		Side	Good-57			2.1%	3.4%	3.8%
Dodge Durango	5	Front	Poor-226	14.1%	9.9%			
		Side	Good-63			6.4%	0.6%	2.9%
Ford Expedition	10	Front	Very Good-167	9.1%	8.4%			
		Side	Very Good-37			2.5%	0.5%	6.5%
GMC Acadia	9	Front	Good-181	9.6%	9.3%			
		Side	Good-57			2.1%	3.4%	3.8%
GMC Yukon	8	Front	Good-185	9.7%	9.7%			
		Side	Very Good-45			3.0%	0.4%	8.6%
GMC Yukon XL	6	Front	Average-195	10.4%	10.2%			
		Side	Average-69			4.5%	1.0%	12.2%
Lincoln Navigator	10	Front	Very Good-167	9.1%	8.4%			
		Side	Very Good-37			2.5%	0.5%	6.5%
Toyota 4Runner	2	Front	Very Poor-255	11.9%	15.5%			
		Side	Poor-88			7.1%	0.9%	11.7%
Toyota Highlander	9	Front	Good-192	11.2%	9.0%			
		Side	Very Good-45			2.4%	1.1%	7.3%
Compact Pickup								
Toyota Tacoma	1	Front	Very Poor-239	11.5%	14.1%			
		Side	Very Poor-238			14.7%	9.7%	18.9%
Toyota Tacoma Crew Cab	1	Front	Very Poor-283	14.9%	15.8%			
		Side	Very Poor-104			7.4%	2.3%	11.8%
Standard Pickup								
Chevrolet Silverado Extended and Reg. Cab*	9	Front	Very Good-156	8.1%	8.1%			
		Side	Average-80			2.7%	3.7%	11.7%
Chevrolet Silverado Crew Cab	10	Front	Very Good-172	9.4%	8.7%			
		Side	Very Good-54			2.4%	1.6%	9.8%
GMC Sierra Extended and Reg. Cab	9	Front	Very Good-156	8.1%	8.1%			
		Side	Average-80			2.7%	3.7%	11.7%
GMC Sierra Crew Cab	10	Front	Very Good-172	9.4%	8.7%			
		Side	Very Good-54			2.4%	1.6%	9.8%
Ram 1500 Quad and Reg. Cab*	6	Front	Poor-214	10.8%	11.9%			
		Side	Good-59			5.2%	0.3%	7.3%
Ram 1500 Crew Cab	3	Front	Poor-228	12.6%	11.7%			
		Side	Poor-85			7.2%	0.6%	10.7%
Toyota Tundra Crew Cab	5	Front	Very Poor-267	16.7%	12.1%			
		Side	Very Good-37			2.5%	0.6%	5.3%

*Side passenger rating does not apply to Regular Cab as it does not have a back seat.

AUTOMATIC SAFETY PROTECTION

The concept of automatic safety protection is not new. Automatic fire sprinklers in public buildings, oxygen masks in airplanes, purification of drinking water, and pasteurization of milk are all commonly accepted forms of automatic safety protection. Airbags provide automatic crash protection in cars.

Automatic crash protection protects people from what is called the "second collision," when the occupant collides with the interior of the vehicle. Because the "second collision" occurs within milliseconds, providing automatic rather than manual protection dramatically improves the chances of escaping injury.

Automatic crash protection comes in two basic forms, airbags and automatic control of safety features.

Since airbags were introduced over 30 years ago, they have been so successful in saving lives that car makers now include a variety of types which deploy from 4 to 10 different points.

The automatic control of safety features was first introduced with anti-lock brakes. Today, Electronic Stability Control (ESC) and other automatic functions such as Collision Avoidance Braking and Lane Departure are improving the safety of new cars.

Electronic Stability Control (ESC) takes advantage of anti-lock brake technology and helps minimize the loss of control. Each car maker will have its own name for this feature, but they all work in a similar fashion.

For ESC, anti-lock brakes work by using speed sensors on each wheel to determine if one or more of the wheels is locking up or skidding. ESC then uses these speed sensors and a unit that determines the steering angle to monitor what's happening with the vehicle. A special control device measures the steering and rotation of the tires in order to detect when a vehicle is about to go in a direction different from the one indicated by the steering wheel–or out of control! This will typically occur during a hard turn or on slippery surfaces. The control unit will sense whether the car is over-steering (turning sharper than you intended resulting in the back wheels slipping sideways) or under-steering (continuing to move forward despite your intended turn). When either of these events occur, the control unit will automatically apply the brakes to the appropriate wheels to correct the situation and, in some cases, automatically slow down the engine.

ESC will not keep the vehicle under control in severely out of control situations nor does it work as well on curvey roads as on straight roads. Nevertheless, according to the IIHS, ESC can reduce the chance of a single vehicle crash by over 50%. Its benefit is that it will prevent more typical losses of control from escalating into a crash.

TELEMATICS

Telematic systems are subscription-based services ($100-$300 per year) that use a combination of cellular technology and global positioning systems to provide a variety of safety and convenience features. The main safety feature is automatic crash notification (ACN) which connects the vehicle's occupants to a private call center that directs emergency medical teams to the car. This system can be activated by pressing a button on the dash or rear view mirror or it is automatically activated if the airbag deploys. Once the system is activated, the call center receives the exact location of your vehicle and notifies the local emergency response team. This can potentially reduce the time it takes for an emergency team to reach your vehicle. Other safety features can include roadside assistance, remote door unlocking, stolen vehicle tracking, and driving directions.

Caution! Some manufacturers are adding cell phone capability to the ACN system which increases the risk of a crash 4-fold when talking on the ACN cell phone. This is about the same effect as drinking and driving. Don't drink and drive or phone and drive!

CHILD SAFETY

Seat Belts for Kids: How long should children use car seats? For school-age children, a car seat is twice as effective in preventing injury as an adult lap and shoulder harness—use a booster as long as possible. Most children can start using seat belts at 4'9" and when tall enough for the shoulder belt to cross the chest, not the neck. The lap section of the belt should be snug and as low on the hips as possible. If the shoulder belt does cross the face or neck, use a booster seat.

Never:

☒ Use the same belt on two children.

☒ Move a shoulder belt behind a child's back or under an arm.

☒ Buckle in a pet or any large toys with the child.

☒ Recline a seat with a belted child.

☒ Use a twisted seat belt. The belt must be straight and flat.

☒ Use pillows or cushions to boost your child.

☒ Place a belt around you with a child in your lap. In an accident or sudden stop, your child would absorb most of the crash force.

Incorrect Installation: Surveys show up to 85 percent of parents do not install their child seats properly. Incorrect installation of a child safety seat can deny the child lifesaving protection and may even contribute to further injuring the child. Read the installation instructions carefully. If you have any questions about the correct installation in your particular car, contact the National Highway Traffic Safety Administration's website at www.nhtsa.gov. They can direct you to the nearest child seat inspection station that will check to see if you have installed your child seat correctly and instruct you on the proper way to install the seat if you have any questions. There is no charge for this service.

Following are some common mistakes parents make when installing a child safety seat.

☒ Infant is in safety seat facing forward, rather than to the rear.

☒ Child safety seat in front with an airbag.

☒ Child is not secured by safety seat harness and is sitting loose in safety seat.

☒ Booster seat used without a shield or a shoulder belt.

☒ Safety belt is fastened to or around wrong part of safety seat.

☒ Tether strap is not used, missing, or at wrong angle of attachment, when required.

☒ Use of incompatible safety belts.

☒ Safety belt is not used to secure safety seat in vehicle. The safety seat is loose on vehicle seat.

☒ Harness strap adjustment slides are not securely locked, permitting straps to release in a crash.

Warning: After an accident, rescue experts suggest that the entire seat be removed from the car, rather than unbuckling the child first.

CHILD SAFETY SEAT RECALLS

Manufacturers are required to put address cards in child seat packages. Mail the registration card as soon as you open the box! This is the only way you will receive notification of a seat recall. Keep a copy of the manufacturer's address and contact the manufacturer if you move. To find out if the seat you are using has ever been recalled go to www-odi.nhtsa.dot.gov/owners/SearchSafety Issues. You can also contact the Auto Safety Hotline at 800-424-9393.

ROLLOVER

The risk of rollover is a significant safety issue, especially with sport utility vehicles. Because of their relatively high center of gravity, they don't hug the road like smaller, lower automobiles and trucks. As a result, they are more likely to turn over on sharp turns or when tripped by a curb. Not only does a rollover increase the likelihood of injuries, but it also increases the risk of the occupant being thrown from the vehicle. In fact, the danger of rollover with sport utilities is so severe that manufacturers are required to place a sticker where it can be seen by the driver every time the vehicle is used. Each year, approximately 10,000 people die in rollover-related accidents.

To understand the concept behind these vehicles' propensity to roll over, consider this: place a section of 2x4 lumber on its 2-inch side. It is easily tipped over by a force pushing against the side. But if you place it on its 4-inch side, the same force will cause it to slide rather than tip over. Similarly, in a moving vehicle, the forces generated by a turn can cause a narrow, tall vehicle to roll over. This is why SUVs are more susceptible to rolling over.

In the safety checklist we include a feature called roll-sensing side airbags. Roll-sensing side airbags are a special side airbag system which keeps the side airbags inflated longer in the event of a rollover. This feature is found in many SUVs and can reduce the likelihood of injury when a vehicle flips. See the car pages (81-270) for which 2015 models have this feature.

Congress required the U.S. Department of Transportation to develop a dynamic (moving) rating system to accompany the static (stationary) rating system. To date, this complex test has resulted in a simple "tip" or "no-tip" rating. Consumers are never told the speed of the tip and certain vehicles are not tested, just listed as "no tip."

Following are rollover ratings for many 2015 vehicles. We published these ratings for years before the National Highway Traffic Safety Administration adopted this rating system.

The rollover rating is based on the Static Stability Factor (SSF) and consists of a formula that uses the track width of the vehicle (tire to tire) and height to determine which vehicles are more or less likely to roll over when compared to each other. You can't use this information to exactly predict rollovers. However, all things being equal, if two vehicles are in the same situation where a rollover could occur, the one with a high SSF is less likely to roll over than one with a lower SSF. Because this formula doesn't consider such things as driver behavior and the weight of the vehicle, among other factors, some experts do not believe it tells the whole story. We agree, and urged the government to provide an even better rollover rating system.

In the meantime, knowing how the vehicles rate using the SSF can be a key consideration in your evaluation of the vehicle.

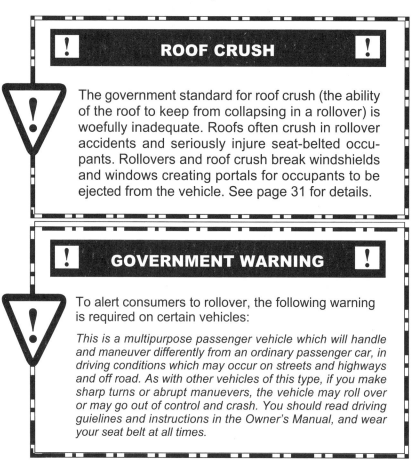

ROOF CRUSH

The government standard for roof crush (the ability of the roof to keep from collapsing in a rollover) is woefully inadequate. Roofs often crush in rollover accidents and seriously injure seat-belted occupants. Rollovers and roof crush break windshields and windows creating portals for occupants to be ejected from the vehicle. See page 31 for details.

GOVERNMENT WARNING

To alert consumers to rollover, the following warning is required on certain vehicles:

This is a multipurpose passenger vehicle which will handle and maneuver differently from an ordinary passenger car, in driving conditions which may occur on streets and highways and off road. As with other vehicles of this type, if you make sharp turns or abrupt manuevers, the vehicle may roll over or may go out of control and crash. You should read driving guielines and instructions in the Owner's Manual, and wear your seat belt at all times.

ROOF CRUSH

Since 1970, the auto industry has fought efforts by the National Highway Traffic Safety Administration to issue a dynamic roof crush standard to protect occupants in rollover crashes. From 1971 to 2005 when NHTSA finally proposed to upgrade the 1971 standard, the number of deaths to occupants in rollover crashes climbed from 1,400 to 10,870 while annual occupant fatalities declined from 43,000 to 31,549. NHTSA stuck with the outdated, static roof crush standard issued in 1971 even though it was to have been phased out by 1977 for a dynamic standard. Yet NHTSA issued effective dynamic front and side crash test standards that have significantly reduced death and serious injury.

The 1971 standard called for roofs to withstand 1.5 times the weight of the vehicle, applied to one side of the roof, for vehicles up to 6,000 pounds. Vehicles weighing more need not meet any standard. The new standard will be phased in for 2013 to 2016 models which will double the roof strength requirement for vehicles weighing up to 6,000 pounds. Both the driver and passenger sides of the roof will have to withstand a force equal to three times the weight of the vehicle. Vehicles over 6,000 pounds have until 2017 to meet a two sided standard at 1.5 times the weight of the vehicle. While a significant improvement, the new standard falls short of requiring a dynamic crash test that better replicates what happens in real world crashes.

Today, some vehicles have strong roofs but all too many have weak roofs. In a rollover crash, the first side of a vehicle that hits the ground generally does not crush but the second, or trailing side, that hits the ground often does crush.

This failure will either break the windows and allow the occupants to eject or crush the occupants that stay in the vehicle. To identify vehicles which have strong roofs, the Center for Auto Safety (CAS) had the Center for Injury Research (CfIR) conduct dynamic rollover roof crush tests using the Jordan Rollover System (JRS). Funded by the Santos Family Foundation, the CAS testing played a major role in NHTSA going to two-sided testing in its new standard.

The table below shows the results of the CAS testing. The cumulative crush is how much the roof will crush inward after two full rolls. More than 5 inches of roof crush is unacceptable because an occupant's head is likely to be hit. The Strength to Weight Ratio (SWR) is how much weight the roof on one side will support before crushing inward 5 inches when tested in a static fashion as the government does.

The dynamic rollover test shows that good roof design can result in a vehicle with a lower static SWR outperforming a vehicle with a higher static SWR in limiting roof intrusion in a roll-over, demonstrating the problem with the static government test. CAS has developed a comparative rating for the roof strength that ranges from Very Good to Very Poor.

Dynamic tests, such as the JRS, show how vehicle geometry effects safety. Vehicles with the very square roofs such as the Tahoe are more vulnerable to roof crush. A vehicle with a more rounded roof, such as the XC90, will roll more like a barrel with less force on the corners of the roof.

The design of the roof in unison with the body of the vehicle is critical to its ability to protect occupants. If any of the critical roof structural elements buckles the roof will collapse and injure belted occupants who are seated underneath.

Good design will also keep windows in place to prevent occupants from being ejected in rollovers. Only a dynamic test can demonstrate whether seat belts, pre-tensioners and side curtains function together to protect occupants from ejection and injury in rollovers.

Center for Auto Safety Roof Crush Test Results

Vehicle*	Cumulative Crush (in.)	Dynamic SWR	Static SWR	Rating
Kia Soul 2010-12	1.6	5.2	4.3	Very Good
Volvo XC90 2005-09	1.8	5.2	4.6	Very Good
Toyota Highlander Hybrid 2008-12	2.3	4.9	4.7	Very Good
VW Tiguan 2009-11	2.4	4.9	4.4	Very Good
VW Jetta 2007-09	3.4	4.4	5.1	Good
Honda CR-V 2007-10	3.6	4.3	2.6	Good
Toyota Camry Hybrid 2007-10	4.3	4.2	3.9	Good
Toyota Prius 2010	3.8	4.2	4.2	Good
Toyota Camry 2007-09	4.3	4	4.3	Good
Nissan Versa 2009-10	4.4	4	3.7	Good
Subaru Forester 2003-08	4.6	3.9	4.3	Moderate
Hyundai Sonata 2006-09	4.6	3.9	3.2	Moderate
Chevrolet Malibu 2009-10	5	3.7	4.4	Moderate
Pontiac G6 2006-09	7	2.8	2.3	Poor
Ford F-150 Supercab 2010-12	7.2	2.7	4.7	Poor
Chrysler 300 2006-09	7.4	2.6	2.5	Poor
Jeep Gr. Cherokee 2007-10	9.1	1.8	2.2	Very Poor
Scion xB 2008-10	10.4	1.2	6.8	Very Poor
Chevy Tahoe 2007-09	10.9	1	2.1	Very Poor
Honda Ridgeline 2006-09	10.9	1	2.4	Very Poor

*Year tested is first model year listed with later models having similar roof strength and design.

This work was funded by the Santos Family Foundation on sixteen vehicles donated by the State Farm Insurance Company.

STATIC STABILITY FACTOR

Vehicle	SSF (High=Better)/ Chance of Rollover		Vehicle	SSF (High=Better)/ Chance of Rollover		Vehicle	SSF (High=Better)/ Chance of Rollover	
Acura ILX	1.42	Low	Ford Fusion	1.41	Low	Mercedes-Benz CLA-Class	1.43*	Low
Acura MDX	1.26	High	Ford Mustang	1.56*	Very Low	Mercedes-Benz E-Class	1.46	Low
Acura RDX	1.26	High	Ford Taurus	1.39	Moderate	Mercedes-Benz GLA-Class	1.33*	Moderate
Acura RLX	1.48*	Low	GMC Acadia	1.23	High	Mercedes-Benz GL-Class	1.16*	Very High
Acura TLX	1.47*	Low	GMC Canyon	1.15*	Very High	Mercedes-Benz GLK-Class	1.21*	High
Audi A3	1.41	Low	GMC Sierra	1.22	High	Mercedes-Benz M-Class	1.21	High
Audi A4	1.46	Low	GMC Terrain	1.19	Very High	Mercedes-Benz S-Class	1.46*	Low
Audi A5	1.54*	Very Low	GMC Yukon	1.15	Very High	Mini Cooper	1.41*	Low
Audi A6	1.51	Very Low	GMC Yukon XL	1.17	Very High	Mini Countryman	1.31*	Moderate
Audi A7	1.54*	Very Low	Honda Accord	1.46	Low	Mitsubishi Lancer	1.36	Moderate
Audi Q3	1.32*	Moderate	Honda Civic	1.37	Moderate	Mitsubishi Mirage	1.24	High
Audi Q5	1.27*	High	Honda Crosstour	1.37*	Moderate	Mitsubishi Outlander	1.24	High
Audi Q7	1.24	High	Honda CR-V	1.22	High	Mitsubishi Outlander FWD	1.2	High
BMW 3 Series	1.48	Low	Honda Fit	1.28	High	Mitsubishi Outlander Sport	1.19	Very High
BMW 4 Series	1.52*	Very Low	Honda Odyssey	1.34	Moderate	Nissan 370Z	1.59*	Very Low
BMW 5 Series	1.49	Low	Honda Pilot	1.24	High	Nissan Altima	1.44	Low
BMW 6 Series	1.59*	Very Low	Hyundai Accent	1.35	Moderate	Nissan Armada	1.14*	Very High
BMW 7 Series	1.48*	Low	Hyundai Elantra	1.41	Low	Nissan Frontier	1.15*	Very High
BMW X1	1.31*	Moderate	Hyundai Genesis	1.48	Low	Nissan Juke	1.25*	High
BMW X3	1.24	High	Hyundai Santa Fe	1.26*	High	Nissan Leaf	1.41	Low
BMW X3 RWD	1.23	High	Hyundai Santa Fe Sport	1.29	High	Nissan Maxima	1.45	Low
BMW X5	1.21	High	Hyundai Sonata	1.43	Low	Nissan Murano	1.26*	High
Buick Enclave	1.23	High	Hyundai Sonata Hybrid	1.47	Low	Nissan Pathfinder	1.23*	High
Buick Encore	1.21	High	Hyundai Tucson	1.21	High	Nissan Quest	1.24*	High
Buick Encore FWD	1.18	High	Hyundai Veloster	1.43	Low	Nissan Rogue	1.24	High
Buick LaCrosse	1.37	Moderate	Infiniti Q50	1.44*	Low	Nissan Sentra	1.36*	Moderate
Buick Regal	1.41	Low	Infiniti Q60	1.49*	Low	Nissan Titan	1.16*	Very High
Buick Verano	1.26	High	Infiniti Q70	1.33*	Moderate	Nissan Versa	1.29	High
Cadillac ATS	1.45	Low	Infiniti QX60	1.27*	High	Nissan Versa Note	1.28	High
Cadillac CTS	1.45	Low	Infiniti QX70	1.29*	High	Nissan Xterra	1.07*	Very High
Cadillac Escalade	1.15	Very High	Infiniti QX80	1.16*	Very High	Porsche Cayenne	1.26*	High
Cadillac Escalade ESV	1.17	Very High	Jeep Cherokee	1.23	High	Porsche Macan	1.33*	Moderate
Cadillac SRX	1.21	High	Jeep Compass	1.19*	Very High	Ram 1500	1.15	Very High
Cadillac XTS	1.37	Moderate	Jeep Grand Cherokee	1.23	High	Scion FR-S	1.66	Very Low
Chevrolet Camaro	1.53	Very Low	Jeep Grand Cherokee 2WD	1.17	Very High	Scion tC	1.41	Low
Chevrolet Colorado	1.15*	Very High	Jeep Patriot	1.16*	Very High	Scion xB	1.26*	High
Chevrolet Corvette	1.71*	Very Low	Jeep Renegade	1.18*	Very High	Smart ForTwo	1.26*	High
Chevrolet Cruze	1.41	Low	Jeep Wrangler	1.13*	Very High	Subaru BRZ	1.66	Very Low
Chevrolet Equinox	1.19	Very High	Kia Cadenza	1.45*	Low	Subaru Forester	1.23	High
Chevrolet Impala	1.36	Moderate	Kia Forte	1.44	Low	Subaru Impreza	1.46	Low
Chevrolet Impala Limited	1.39	Moderate	Kia Optima	1.48	Low	Subaru Legacy	1.45	Low
Chevrolet Malibu	1.4	Low	Kia Rio	1.38	Moderate	Subaru Outback	1.22	High
Chevrolet Silverado	1.22	High	Kia Sedona	1.3*	Moderate	Subaru XV Crosstrek	1.27	High
Chevrolet Sonic	1.34	Moderate	Kia Sorento	1.24	High	Tesla Model S	1.83	Very Low
Chevrolet Spark	1.21	High	Kia Soul	1.28	High	Toyota 4Runner	1.12	Very High
Chevrolet Suburban	1.17	Very High	Kia Sportage	1.22	High	Toyota Avalon	1.42	Low
Chevrolet Tahoe	1.15	Very High	Kia Sportage AWD	1.26	High	Toyota Camry	1.4	Low
Chevrolet Traverse	1.23	High	Land Rover Range Rover	1.19*	Very High	Toyota Corolla	1.37	Moderate
Chevrolet Trax	1.19*	Very High	Land Rover Rng Rvr Evoque	1.29*	High	Toyota Highlander	1.23	High
Chevrolet Trax FWD	1.18	High	Land Rover Rng Rvr Sport	1.23*	High	Toyota Prius	1.36	Moderate
Chevrolet Volt	1.49	Low	Lexus CT	1.39*	Moderate	Toyota Prius C	1.37*	Moderate
Chrysler 200	1.42	Low	Lexus ES	1.4	Low	Toyota Prius V	1.31	Moderate
Chrysler 300	1.45*	Low	Lexus GS	1.45*	Low	Toyota RAV4	1.22	High
Chrysler Town and Country	1.24	High	Lexus GX	1.09*	Very High	Toyota Sequoia	1.19*	Very High
Dodge Challenger	1.4	Low	Lexus IS	1.48	Low	Toyota Sienna	1.3	Moderate
Dodge Charger	1.45*	Low	Lexus NX	1.25*	High	Toyota Tacoma	1.19	Very High
Dodge Dart	1.42	Low	Lexus RX	1.24	High	Toyota Tundra	1.18	Very High
Dodge Durango	1.16	Very High	Lexus RX FWD	1.21	High	Toyota Venza	1.26	High
Dodge Durango 2WD	1.18	Very High	Lincoln MKC	1.23	High	Toyota Yaris	1.31	Moderate
Dodge Journey	1.21*	High	Lincoln MKS	1.39	Moderate	Volkswagen Beetle	1.43	Low
Fiat 500	1.29	High	Lincoln MKX	1.3	Moderate	Volkswagen CC	1.46*	Low
Fiat 500L	1.2*	High	Lincoln MKZ	1.41	Low	Volkswagen Golf	1.41*	Low
Ford C-MAX	1.29	High	Lincoln Navigator	1.18	Very High	Volkswagen Jetta	1.4	Low
Ford Edge	1.23*	High	Lincoln Navigator 2WD	1.16	Very High	Volkswagen Passat	1.42	Low
Ford Escape	1.19	Very High	Mazda CX-5	1.22	High	Volkswagen Tiguan	1.2	High
Ford Expedition	1.18	Very High	Mazda CX-9	1.29	High	Volkswagen Touareg	1.25*	High
Ford Expedition 2WD	1.16	Very High	Mazda CX-9 FWD	1.27	High	Volvo S60	1.45	Low
Ford Explorer	1.22	High	Mazda Mazda3	1.43	Low	Volvo V60	1.42*	Low
Ford F-150	1.14*	Very High	Mazda Mazda5	1.23*	High	Volvo XC60	1.22	High
Ford Fiesta	1.29	High	Mazda Mazda6	1.44	Low			
Ford Flex	1.23*	High	Mazda MX-5 Miata	1.6*	Very Low			
Ford Focus	1.4*	Low	Mercedes-Benz C-Class	1.47*	Low	*Calculated		

FUEL ECONOMY

As gas prices bounce up and down, regular driving still takes a big bite out of our pocketbooks. The good news is that higher fuel efficiency standards are forcing car companies to provide more fuel efficient vehicles. Buying right and practicing more fuel efficient driving will make a huge difference in your vehicle's operating costs.

Using the EPA ratings is the best way to incorporate fuel efficiency in selecting a new car. By comparing these ratings, even among cars of the same size, you'll find that fuel efficiency varies greatly. One compact car might get 36 miles per gallon (mpg) while another compact gets only 22 mpg. If you drive 15,000 miles a year and you pay $2.60 per gallon for fuel, the 36 mpg car will save you $690 *a year* over the "gas guzzler."

In 2008, the EPA changed the way it estimates miles per gallon to better represent today's driving conditions. Their new method adjusts for aggressive driving (high speeds and faster acceleration), air conditioning use, and cold temperature operation.

Octane Ratings: Once you've purchased your car, you'll be faced with choosing the right gasoline. Oil companies spend millions of dollars trying to get you to buy so-called higher performance or high octane fuels. Using high octane fuel can add considerably to your gas bill, and the vast majority of vehicles do not need it. Check your owner's manual and only use what's recommended, which is usually 87. Very few vehicles require "premium" gasoline.

The octane rating of a gasoline is not a measure of power or quality. It is simply a measure of the gas' resistance to engine knock, which is the pinging sound you hear when the air and fuel mixture in your engine ignites prematurely during acceleration.

Your engine may knock when accelerating a heavily loaded car uphill or when the humidity is low. This is normal and does not call for a higher-octane gasoline.

FIVE FACTORS AFFECTING FUEL ECONOMY

1. Engine Size: The smaller the engine the better your fuel efficiency. A 10% increase in the size of your engine can increase your fuel consumption rate by 6%. Smaller engines can be cheaper to maintain as well.

2. Transmission: If used properly, manual transmissions are generally more fuel-efficient than automatics. In fact, a 5-speed manual can add up to 6.5 mpg over a 4-speed automatic transmission. Getting an automatic with an overdrive gear can improve your fuel economy by up to 9 percent.

3. Cruise Control: Using cruise control can save fuel because driving at a constant speed uses less fuel than changing speeds frequently.

4. Trim Packages and Power Options: Upgrading a car's trim level and adding options such as navigation systems or a sunroof can increase the weight of your car. Every 200 pounds of weight shaves off about 1 mile per gallon off your mileage. The weight of the average car in 1981 was 3,202 pounds, today it's around 4,000 pounds.

5. Hybrids: Most manufacturers offer hybrid vehicles that have both gasoline and electric engines. Hybrids can offer 30% better fuel economy and lower emissions.

TWELVE WAYS TO SAVE MONEY AT THE PUMP

Here are a few simple things you can do that will save you a lot of money. Note: Savings are based on gas at $2.60.

1. Make Sure Your Tires are Inflated Properly: 27% of vehicles have tires that are under-inflated. Properly inflated tires can improve mileage by 3%, which is like getting 8 cents off a gallon of gas. Check the label on your door or glove box to find out what the pressure range should be for your tires. Don't use the "max pressure" written on your tire. Electronic gauges are fast, easy to use and accurate. Don't rely on the numbers on the air pump.

2. Check Your Air Filter: A dirty air filter by itself can rob a car by as much as 10% percent of its mileage. If an engine doesn't get enough air, it will burn too much gasoline. Replacing a dirty filter can knock 26 cents off a gallon of gas.

3. Get Your Alignment Checked: Not only does poor alignment cause your tires to wear out faster and cause poor handling, but it can cause your engine to work harder and reduce your fuel efficiency by 10%.

4. Don't Use High Octane Gasoline: Check your owner's manual. Very, very few cars actually need high-octane gas. Using 87-octane gas will save you over 10 cents per gallon over mid-grade and 20 cents over premium.

5. Get a Tune Up: A properly tuned engine is a fuel saver. Have a trusted mechanic tune your engine to exact factory specifications and you could save up to 10 cents a gallon.

6. Check Your Gas Cap: It is estimated that nearly 15 % of the cars on the road have broken or missing gasoline caps. This hurts your mileage and can harm the environment by allowing your gasoline to evaporate. Many Ford products have a capless gas filler, which is a great convenience.

7. Don't Speed: A car moving at 55 mph gets better fuel economy than the same car at 65 mph. For every 5 mph you reduce your highway speed, you can reduce fuel consumption by 7%, which is like getting 18 cents off a gallon of gas.

8. Avoid Excess Idling: An idling car gets 0 mpg. Cars with larger engines typically waste more gas at idle than cars with smaller engines.

9. Drive Smoother: The smoother your accelerations and decelerations, the better your mileage. A smooth foot can save 43 cents a gallon.

10. Combine Trips: Short trips can be expensive because they usually involve a "cold" vehicle. For the first mile or two before the engine gets warmed up, a cold vehicle only gets 30 to 40% of the mileage it gets at full efficiency.

11. Empty your Roof Rack and Trunk: 50% of engine power, traveling at highway speed, is used in overcoming aerodynamic drag or wind resistance. Any protrusion on a vehicle's roof can reduce gas mileage, typical roof racks reduce fuel economy by about 6 mpg. 100 lbs. of extra weight will reduce your mileage by .5 mpg.

12. Choose Your Gas Miser: If you own more than one vehicle, choosing to drive the one with better gas mileage will save you money. If you drive 15,000 miles per year, half in a vehicle with 20 mpg and half with a 30 mpg vehicle and switch to driving 75% of your trips in the 30 mpg vehicle, you will save $162.50 annually with gas at $2.63.

FUEL ECONOMY

TIP

Get up-to-date information about fuel economy at www.fueleconomy.gov, a joint website created by the U.S. Department of Energy and the EPA. There you'll find the EPA's Fuel Economy Guide, allowing you to compare fuel economy estimates for 2015 models back to 1985 models. You'll also find out about the latest technological advances pertaining to fuel efficiency. The site is extremely useful and easy to navigate. We've added fuel economy ratings and a Fuel Factor section to the At-a-glance box on our car rating pages.

FUEL ECONOMY MISERS AND GUZZLERS

Because the success of the EPA program depends on consumers' ability to compare the fuel economy ratings easily, we have included key mileage figures on our ratings pages. Listed below are the best and worst of this year's ratings according to annual fuel cost. The complete EPA fuel economy guide is available at www.fueleconomy.gov.

Vehicle	Specifications	MPG (city/hwy)	Annual Fuel Cost
FUEL ECONOMY MISERS AND GUZZLERS			
THE BEST			
Plug In Hybrid Electric Vehicles (PHEVs)*			
Chevrolet Volt	1.4L, 4 cyl., Continuously Variable, FWD	35/40	$900
Toyota Prius Plug-in Hybrid	1.8L, 4 cyl., Continuously Variable, FWD	51/49	$950
Ford C-MAX Energi	2.0L, 4 cyl., Continuously Variable, FWD	40/36	$1,050
Ford Fusion Energi Plug-in Hybrid	2.0L, 4 cyl., Continuously Variable, FWD	40/36	$1,050
Gas			
Toyota Prius c	1.5L, 4 cyl., Continuously Variable, FWD	53/46	$794
Toyota Prius	1.8L, 4 cyl., Continuously Variable, FWD	51/48	$798
Honda Accord	2.0L, 4 cyl., Continuously Variable, FWD	50/45	$829
Honda Civic Hybrid	1.5L, 4 cyl., Continuously Variable, FWD	44/47	$873
Volkswagen Jetta Hybrid	1.4L, 4 cyl., 7-sp. Automated Manual, FWD	42/48	$886
Ford Fusion Hybrid	2.0L, 4 cyl., Continuously Variable, FWD	44/41	$928
Toyota Prius v	1.8L, 4 cyl., Continuously Variable, FWD	44/40	$938
Lexus CT 200h	1.8L, 4 cyl., Continuously Variable, FWD	43/40	$951
Toyota Camry Hybrid LE	2.5L, 4 cyl., Continuously Variable, FWD	43/39	$961
Mitsubishi Mirage	1.2L, 3 cyl., Continuously Variable, FWD	37/44	$986
Lincoln MKZ Hybrid	2.0L, 4 cyl., Continuously Variable, FWD	41/39	$988
Ford C-MAX Hybrid	2.0L, 4 cyl., Continuously Variable, FWD	42/37	$996
Lexus ES 300h	2.5L, 4 cyl., Selectable Continuously Variable, FWD	40/39	$1,001
Toyota Avalon Hybrid	2.5L, 4 cyl., Continuously Variable, FWD	40/39	$1,001
Toyota Camry Hybrid XLE/SE	2.5L, 4 cyl., Continuously Variable, FWD	40/38	$1,001
Honda CR-Z	1.5L, 4 cyl., Selectable Continuously Variable, FWD	39/39	$1,001
Hyundai Sonata Hybrid	2.4L, 4 cyl., 6-sp. Automated Manual, FWD	36/40	$1,048
Kia Optima Hybrid	2.4L, 4 cyl., 6-sp. Automated Manual, FWD	36/40	$1,048
Hyundai Sonata Hybrid Limited	2.4L, 4 cyl., 6-sp. Automated Manual, FWD	36/40	$1,048
Mitsubishi Mirage	1.2L, 3 cyl., 5-sp. Manual, FWD	34/42	$1,053
Kia Optima Hybrid EX	2.4L, 4 cyl., 6-sp. Automated Manual, FWD	35/39	$1,076
Honda Fit	1.5L, 3 cyl., Continuously Variable, FWD	33/41	$1,082
Scion iQ	1.3L, 4 cyl., Continuously Variable, FWD	36/37	$1,086
Audi A3	2.0L, 4 cyl., 6-sp. Automated Manual, FWD	31/43	$1,088
Ford Fiesta SFE	1.0L, 3 cyl., 5-sp. Manual, FWD	31/43	$1,088
THE WORST**			
Mercedes-Benz G 63 AMG	5.5L, 8 cyl., 7-sp. Automatic, 4WD	12/14	$3,512#
Mercedes-Benz G 550	5.5L, 8 cyl., 7-sp. Automatic, 4WD	12/15	$3,393#
Lexus LX 570	5.7L, 8 cyl., 6-sp. Automatic, AWD	12/17	$3,179#
Audi R8-spyder	5.2L, 10 cyl., 6-sp. Manual, AWD	12/18	$3,082#
Cadillac CTS	6.2L, 8 cyl., 6-sp. Semi-Automatic, RWD	12/18	$3,082#
Chevrolet/GMC Camaro	6.2L, 8 cyl., 6-sp. Semi-Automatic, RWD	12/18	$3,082#
Toyota Sequoia	5.7L, 8 cyl., 6-sp. Semi-Automatic, 4WD	13/17	$3,061#
Mercedes-Benz ML 63 AMG	5.5L, 8 cyl., 7-sp. Automatic, 4WD	13/17	$3,061#
Audi R8	5.2L, 8 cyl., 6-sp. Manual, AWD	12/19	$2,990#
Mercedes-Benz GL 550 4MATIC	4.7L, 8 cyl., 7-sp. Automatic, 4WD	13/18	$2,970#
Chevrolet Camaro	7.0L, 8 cyl., 6-sp. Manual, RWD	13/19	$2,885#
Jeep Grand Cherokee SRT8	6.4L, 8 cyl., 8-sp. Automatic, AWD	13/19	$2,885#
Mercedes-Benz C 63 AMG Coupe	6.2L, 8 cyl., 7-sp. Automatic, RWD	13/19	$2,885#
Mercedes-Benz SLS AMG GT	6.2L, 8 cyl., 7-sp. Automated Manual, RWD	13/19	$2,885#
Dodge Viper SRT	8.4L, 10 cyl., 6-sp. Manual, RWD	12/21	$2,822#
BMW 760Li	6.0L, 12 cyl., 8-sp. Automatic, RWD	13/20	$2,805#
Mercedes-Benz S 65 AMG	6.0L, 12 cyl., 7-sp. Automatic, RWD	13/20	$2,805#
Mercedes-Benz S 600	6.0L, 12 cyl., 7-sp. Automatic, RWD	13/21	$2,729#
Nissan Armada 4WD	5.6L, 8 cyl., 5-sp. Automatic, AWD	12/18	$2,694
Mercedes-Benz GL 63 AMG	5.5L, 8 cyl., 7-sp. Automatic, AWD	13/17	$2,676
Toyota Sequoia 2WD	5.7L, 8 cyl., 6-sp. Automatic, 2WD	13/17	$2,676
Toyota Land Cruiser 4WD	5.7L, 8 cyl., 6-sp. Automatic, 4WD	13/18	$2,597
Nissan Armada 2WD	5.6L, 8 cyl., 5-sp. Automatic, RWD	13/19	$2,522
Ram1500 4WD	5.7L, 8 cyl., 7-sp. Automated Manual, 4WD	13/19	$2,522

Note: 2015 annual fuel cost based on driving 15,000 miles and a projected regular gas price of $2.64; #=Premium Required; *=Fuel Economy rating based on hybrid function only; annual cost based on epa estimate for gas and electric use; **=Low volume exotic vehicles (over $120,000) and cargo vans were excluded.

COMPARING WARRANTIES

After buying your car, maintenance will be a significant portion of your operating costs. The strength of your warranty and the cost of repairs after the warranty expires will determine these costs. Comparing warranties and repair costs, before you buy, can save you thousands of dollars down the road.

Along with your new car comes a warranty which is a promise from the manufacturer that the car will perform as it should. Most of us never read the warranty until it is too late. In fact, because warranties are often difficult to read and understand, most of us don't really know what our warranty offers.

To keep your warranty in effect, you must operate and maintain your car according to the instructions in your owner's manual. It is important to keep a record of all maintenance performed on your car.

Do not confuse a warranty with a service contract. A service contract must be purchased separately while a warranty is yours at no extra cost when you buy the car.

Warranties are difficult to compare because they contain fine print and confusing language. The following table will help you compare this year's warranties. Because the table does not contain all the details about each warranty, review the actual warranty to understand its fine points. You have the right to inspect a warranty before you buy—it's the law.

The table provides information on five critical items in a warranty:

The **Basic Warranty** covers most parts against manufacturer's defects. Tires, batteries, and items you add to the car are covered under separate warranties. The table describes coverage in terms of months and miles. For example, 48/50 means the warranty is good for 48 months or 50,000 miles, whichever comes first. This is the most important part of your warranty because it covers the items most likely to fail. We give the basic warranty the most weight.

The **Power Train Warranty** often lasts longer than the basic warranty. Because each manufacturer's definition of the power train is different, it is important to find out exactly what your warranty will cover. Power train coverage should include the engine, transmission, and drive train. Some luxury cars will cover additional systems such as steering, suspension, and electrical systems. We give the powertrain warranty less weight than the basic because it doesn't cover as much as the basic warranty. Even with less weight in our rating, it can have a lot of influence in the overall index if it is very long.

The **Corrosion Warranty** usually applies only to actual holes due to rust. Read this section carefully because many corrosion warranties do not apply to what the manufacturer may describe as cosmetic rust or bad paint.

The **Roadside Assistance** column indicates whether or not the manufacturer offers a program for helping with breakdowns, lockouts, jump starts, flat tires, running out of gas, and towing. Some have special limitations or added features. Because each one is different, check yours carefully.

The **Scheduled Maint. (Free)** column indicates whether or not free scheduled maintenance is included and for how long. These programs cover parts scheduled to be replaced such as filters. If there is an asterisk next to the coverage, that means the manufacturer also covers the cost of any parts that need to be replaced because of wear. Covering the cost of "wear" parts is a terrific feature and offered by very few manufacturers.

The last column, the **Warranty Rating Index**, provides an overall assessment of this year's warranties. **The higher the Index number, the better the warranty.** We give the most weight to the basic and power train components of the warranties. Roadside assistance was weighted somewhat less, and the corrosion warranty received the least weight.

Finally, we also considered special features such as extra coverage on batteries or wheel alignment. These benefits added to the overall ratings, whereas certain limitations (shortened transferability) took away.

The best ratings are in ***BOLD***.

WARRANTY COMPARISON

Manufacturer	Basic Warranty	Power Train Warranty	Corrosion Warranty	Roadside Assistance	Scheduled Maint. (Free)	Index	Warranty Rating
Acura[1]	48/50	72/70	60/Unlimited	48/50		1106	Poor
Audi	48/50	48/50	144/Unlimited	48/Unlimited	12/5	1221	Average
BMW	**48/50**	**48/50**	**144/Unlimited**	**48/Unlimited**	**48/50[2]**	**1306**	**Very Good**
Buick	48/50	72/70	72/100	72/70	24/24	1229	Good
Cadillac[3]	**48/50**	**72/70**	**72/Unlimited[4]**	**72/70**	**48/50**	**1320**	**Very Good**
Chevrolet	36/36	60/100	72/100[5]	60/100	24/24	1242	Good
Chrysler[6]	36/36	60/100	60/Unlimited[7]	60/100		1190	Average
Dodge[8]	36/36	60/100	60/Unlimited[9]	60/100		1190	Average
Fiat[10]	48/50	48/50	60/Unlimited[11]	48/Unlimited		1066	Poor
Ford[12]	36/36	60/60	60/Unlimited	60/60		974	Poor
GMC	36/36	60/100	72/100	60/100	24/24	1206	Average
Honda[13]	36/36	60/60	60/Unlimited	36/36		897	Very Poor
Hyundai[14]	**60/60**	**120/100[15]**	**84/Unlimited**	**60/Unlimited**		**1470**	**Very Good**
Infiniti[16]	48/60	72/70	84/Unlimited	48/Unlimited		1251	Good
Jeep[17]	36/36	60/100	60/Unlimited[18]	60/100		1190	Average
Kia[19]	**60/60**	**120/100[20]**	**60/100**	**60/60**		**1341**	**Very Good**
Land Rover	48/50	48/50	72/Unlimited	48/50	12/15	1015	Poor
Lexus[21]	48/50	72/70	72/Unlimited	48/Unlimited	12/10	1200	Average
Lincoln[22]	48/50	72/70	60/Unlimited	72/70[23]	24/24	1256	Good
Mazda	36/36	60/60	60/Unlimited	36/36		891	Very Poor
Mercedes-Benz[24]	48/50	48/50	48/50	48/50		937	Poor
Mini	**48/50**	**48/50**	**144/Unlimited**	**48/Unlimited**	**36/36[25]**	**1316**	**Very Good**
Mitsubishi[26]	**60/60**	**120/100**	**84/100[27]**	**60/Unlimited**		**1452**	**Very Good**
Nissan[28]	36/36	60/60	60/Unlimited			789	Very Poor
Porsche	48/50	48/50	144/Unlimited	48/50		1157	Average
Ram	36/36	60/100	60/100[29]	60/100		1184	Average
Scion[30]	36/36	60/60	60/Unlimited	24/Unlimited	24/25	925	Very Poor
Smart[31]	48/50	48/50	48/50	48/50		937	Poor
Subaru[32]	36/36	60/60	60/Unlimited	36/36		918	Very Poor
Tesla	48/50	96/125[33]	48/50	48/50		1300	Good
Toyota[34]	36/36	60/60	60/Unlimited	24/Unlimited	24/25	925	Very Poor
Volkswagen	36/36	60/60	144/Unlimited	36/36	12/10	1096	Poor
Volvo	48/50	48/50	144/Unlimited	48/Unlimited	36/36	1262	Good

[1] Wheel Alignment and Balancing 12/12
[2] Free Scheduled Maintenance includes wear parts but is not transferable
[3] Wheel Alignment and Balancing 12/7.5
[4] All Corrosion 48/50
[5] All Corrosion 36/36
[6] Wheel Alignment and Balancing 12/12
[7] All Corrosion 36/Unlimited
[8] Wheel Alignment and Balancing 12/12
[9] All Corrosion 36/Unlimited
[10] Wheel Alignment and Balancing 12/12

[11] All Corrosion 36/Unlimited
[12] Wheel Alignment and Balancing 12/12; brake Pads 12/18
[13] Wheel Alignment and Balancing 12/12
[14] Wheel Alignment and Balancing 12/12; Wear Items 12/12
[15] Only transferable up to 60/60
[16] Wheel Alignment and Balancing 12/12
[17] Wheel Alignment and Balancing 12/12
[18] All Corrosion 36/Unlimited
[19] Wheel Alignment and Balancing 12/12

[20] Transferable only to 60/60
[21] Wheel Alignement and Balancing 12/12
[22] Wheel Alignment and Balancing 12/12; Brake Pads 12/18
[23] Lifetime for original owner
[24] Wheel Alignment and Balancing 12/12
[25] Maintenance includes wear parts
[26] Lancer only has 36/36 New and 60/60 powertrain
[27] Transferable only up to 60/60

[28] Wheel Alignment and Balancing 12/12
[29] All Corrosion 36/Unlimited
[30] Wheel Alignment and Balancing 12/12
[31] Wheel Alignment and Balancing 12/12
[32] Wear Items 36/36
[33] 96/Unlimited for 85 kWh battery
[34] Wheel Alignment and Balancing 12/12

SECRET WARRANTIES

If dealers report a number of complaints about a certain part and the manufacturer determines that the problem is due to faulty design or assembly, the manufacturer may permit dealers to repair the problem at no charge to the customer even though the warranty is expired. In the past, this practice was often reserved for customers who made a big fuss. The availability of the free repair was never publicized, which is why we call these "secret warranties."

Manufacturers deny the existence of secret warranties. They call these free repairs "policy adjustments" or "goodwill service." Whatever they are called, most consumers never hear about them.

Many secret warranties are disclosed in service bulletins that the manufacturers send to dealers. These bulletins outline free repair or reimbursement programs, as well as other problems and their possible causes and solutions.

Service bulletins from many manufacturers may be on file at the National Highway Traffic Safety Administration. You can visit www.nhtsa.gov to access NHTSA's Service Bulletin database.

If you find that a secret warranty is in effect and repairs are being made at no charge after the warranty has expired, contact the Center for Auto Safety, 1825 Connecticut Ave. NW, #330, Washington, DC 20009. They will publish the information so others can benefit.

Disclosure Laws: Spurred by the proliferation of secret warranties and the failure of the FTC to take action, California, Connecticut, Virginia, Wisconsin, and Maryland have passed legislation that requires consumers to be notified of secret warranties on their cars. Several other states have introduced similar warranty bills.

Typically, the laws require the following: direct notice to consumers within a specified time after the adoption of a warranty adjustment policy; notice of the disclosure law to new car buyers; reimbursement within a number of years after payment to owners who paid for covered repairs before they learned of the extended warranty service; and dealers must inform consumers who complain about a covered defect that it is eligible for repair under warranty.

If you live in a state with a secret warranty law already in effect, write your state attorney general's office (in care of your state capital) for information. To encourage passage of such a bill, contact your state representative (in care of your state capital).

Some state lemon laws require dealers and manufacturers to give you copies of Technical Service Bulletins on problems affecting your vehicle. These bulletins may alert you to a secret warranty on your vehicle or help you make the case for a free repair if there isn't a secret warranty. See page 59 for an overview of your state's lemon law. If you would like to see the complete law, go to www.autosafety.org to view your state's lemon laws.

LITTLE SECRETS OF THE AUTO INDUSTRY

Every auto company makes mistakes building cars. When they do, they often issue technical service bulletins telling dealers how to fix the problem. Rarely do they publicize these fixes, many of which are offered for free, called secret warranties. The Center for Auto Safety has published a book called *Little Secrets of the Auto Industry*, a consumer guide to secret warranties. This book explains how to find out about secret warranties, offers tips for going to small claims court and getting federal and state assistance, and lists information on state secret warranty laws. To order a copy, send $17.50 to: Center for Auto Safety, Pub. Dept. CB, 1825 Connecticut Ave. NW, Suite 330, Washington, DC 20009.

KEEPING IT GOING

Comparing maintenance costs before you buy can help decide which car to purchase. These costs include preventive maintenance servicing—such as changing the oil and filters—as well as the cost of repairs after your warranty expires. Below we enable you to compare the costs of preventive maintenance and nine likely repairs for the 2015 models.

Preventive Maintenance: The first column in the table is the periodic servicing, specified by the manufacturer, that keeps your car running properly. For example, regularly changing the oil and oil filter. Every owner's manual specifies a schedule of recommended servicing for at least the first 60,000 miles and many now go to 100,000 miles. The tables on the following pages estimate the labor cost of following this preventive maintenance schedule for 60,000 miles, the length of a typical warranty. Service parts are not included in this total.

Repairs Costs: The tables also list the costs for nine repairs that typically occur during the first 100,000 miles. There is no precise way to predict exactly when a repair will be needed. But if you keep a car for 75,000 to 100,000 miles, it is likely that you will experience most of these repairs at least once. The last column provides a relative indication of how expensive these nine repairs are for many cars. Repair cost is rated as Very Good if the total for nine repairs is in the lowest fifth of all the cars rated, and Very Poor if the total is in the highest fifth.

Most repair shops use "flat-rate manuals" to estimate repair costs. These manuals list the approximate time required for repairing many items. Each automobile manufacturer publishes its own manual and there are several independent manuals as well. For many repairs, the time varies from one manual to another. Some repair shops even use different manuals for different repairs. To determine a repair bill, a shop multiplies the time listed in its manual by its hourly labor rate and then adds the cost of parts.

Some dealers and repair shops create their own maintenance schedules which call for more frequent (and thus more expensive) servicing than the manufacturer's recommendations. If the service recommended by your dealer or repair shop doesn't match what the manufacturer recommends, make sure you understand and agree to the extra items. Our cost estimates are based on published repair times multiplied by a nationwide average labor rate of $90 per hour and include the cost of replaced parts and related adjustments.

Prices in the following tables may not predict the exact costs of these repairs. For example, labor rates for your area may be more or less than the national average. However, the prices will provide you with a relative comparison of costs for various automobiles.

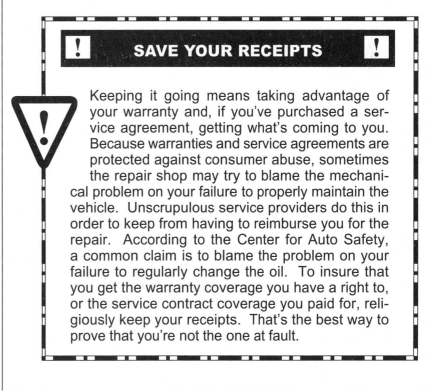

! SAVE YOUR RECEIPTS !

Keeping it going means taking advantage of your warranty and, if you've purchased a service agreement, getting what's coming to you. Because warranties and service agreements are protected against consumer abuse, sometimes the repair shop may try to blame the mechanical problem on your failure to properly maintain the vehicle. Unscrupulous service providers do this in order to keep from having to reimburse you for the repair. According to the Center for Auto Safety, a common claim is to blame the problem on your failure to regularly change the oil. To insure that you get the warranty coverage you have a right to, or the service contract coverage you paid for, religiously keep your receipts. That's the best way to prove that you're not the one at fault.

	PM Costs to 60,000 Miles	REPAIR COSTS									
		Front Brake Pads	Starter	Fuel Injector	Fuel Pump	Struts/ Shocks	Timing Belt/Chain	Water Pump	Muffler	Headlamps	Relative Repair Cost*
Subcompact											
Chevrolet Sonic	576	198	375	81	386	168	277	328	622	789	Vry. Gd.
Chevrolet Spark	342	198	313	138	443	160	458	299	432	898	Vry. Gd.
Fiat 500	657	170	308	394	558	89	370	453	284	760	Vry. Gd.
Ford Fiesta	1044	130	454	104	514	160	380	321	476	642	Vry. Gd.
Honda Fit	945	146	631	217	495	380	579	290	258	881	Good
Hyundai Accent	792	122	430	173	464	175	390	316	359	284	Vry. Gd.
Hyundai Veloster	882	163	351	138	431	320	538	350	406	702	Vry. Gd.
Kia Rio	774	129	421	203	360	224	378	309	395	642	Vry. Gd.
Kia Soul	954	129	425	212	313	266	355	309	435	1026	Vry. Gd.
Mazda MX-5 Miata	864	191	341	219	480	362	474	261	628	1572	Good
Mini Cooper	297	206	550	198	628	358	1032	448	503	1502	Poor
Mini Countryman	360	221	462	198	425	365	1032	423	637	851	Average
Mitsubishi Mirage											
Nissan 370Z	1368	175	502	358	525	566	763	677	597	1971	Poor
Nissan Versa	594	191	401	275	522	189	437	209	323	673	Vry. Gd.
Scion xB	702	169	467	292	425	227	829	411	278	661	Good
Smart ForTwo	1017	175	463	198	438	510	1436	470	971	766	Poor
Toyota Prius C	432	138	0	263	467	212	503	626	249	863	Vry. Gd.
Toyota Yaris	297	139	393	223	460	286	504	240	258	686	Vry. Gd.
Volkswagen Beetle	819	185	552	298	430	327	986	477	891	1107	Average
Compact											
Acura ILX	882	137	582	155	497	451	551	386	173	1095	Good
Audi A3	1377	190	459	294	459	676	727	648	632	847	Average
Audi A4	882	222	787	507	694	710	528	784	646	982	Poor
BMW 3 Series	477	242	585	419	473	349	1323	750	666	1199	Poor
BMW 4 Series	531	240	655	216	500	389	990	762	871	1363	Poor
Buick Verano	576	293	351	420	514	208	589	624	287	1016	Good
Cadillac ATS	126	201	578	421	406	450	493	420	1143	1071	Average
Chevrolet Cruze	864	198	259	230	524	180	840	432	632	602	Good
Chevrolet Volt	72	174	0	119	380	139	1250	453	578	1005	Good
Dodge Dart	864	177	228	391	573	235	607	316	507	1516	Average
Fiat 500L	873	170	308	394	558	89	370	453	284	760	Vry. Gd.
Ford C-MAX	594	181	297	136	342	249	630	180	260	941	Vry. Gd.
Ford Focus	918	148	420	288	479	122	695	242	317	668	Vry. Gd.
Honda Civic	702	142	555	218	443	209	641	257	204	747	Vry. Gd.
Hyundai Elantra	981	149	358	173	285	208	421	262	368	768	Vry. Gd.
Infiniti Q60	594	252	465	389	449	556	1346	448	600	2062	Vry. Pr.
Kia Forte	585	165	236	194	332	210	544	291	331	535	Vry. Gd.
Lexus CT	486	143	0	445	455	244	1707	702	598	2262	Vry. Pr.
Lexus IS	684	156	940	634	414	490	2562	535	865	1346	Vry. Pr.
Mazda Mazda3	855	177	333	305	580	204	452	297	441	712	Vry. Gd.
Mercedes-Benz C-Class	1107	183	719	328	1061	487	409	731	931	1144	Poor
Mercedes-Benz CLA-Class	1260	193	1025	375	579	669	1199	699	973	1212	Vry. Pr.
Mitsubishi Lancer	504	187	870	353	628	334	616	569	422	1300	Average
Nissan Leaf	666	151	0	0	0	224	0	3564	0	1422	Poor
Nissan Sentra	702	155	344	356	562	175	592	238	407	649	Vry. Gd.
Scion FR-S	774	185	637	575	692	355	648	389	627	984	Average
Scion tC	315	169	661	373	452	320	1379	308	270	682	Average
Subaru BRZ	972	181	585	456	438	311	585	361	587	545	Good
Subaru Impreza	1008	154	504	230	453	620	393	455	429	824	Good
AVERAGE OF ALL VEHICLES	**$805**	**$196**	**$472**	**$309**	**$538**	**$392**	**$964**	**$490**	**$637**	**$1152**	

	PM Costs to 60,000 Miles	REPAIR COSTS									
		Front Brake Pads	Starter	Fuel Injector	Fuel Pump	Struts/ Shocks	Timing Belt/Chain	Water Pump	Muffler	Headlamps	Relative Repair Cost*
Toyota Corolla	360	152	467	309	427	333	640	259	392	533	Vry. Gd.
Toyota Prius	360	138	0	445	429	351	1666	693	285	861	Average
Volkswagen Golf	819	180	684	206	365	415	551	457	465	606	Good
Volkswagen Jetta	864	161	670	413	535	420	600	665	721	770	Average
Intermediate											
Acura RLX	1008	303	1216	196	445	485	413	522	537	2422	Vry. Pr.
Acura TLX	1008	142	603	137	441	299	452	221	712	1521	Good
Audi A5	621	208	779	420	476	482	525	775	1496	1935	Vry. Pr.
Audi A6	846	231	931	531	685	548	2864	501	746	1127	Vry. Pr.
BMW 5 Series	225	146	619	297	663	684	1648	731	974	1650	Vry. Pr.
BMW 6 Series	351	129	716	572	483	651	1111	731	781	4168	Vry. Pr.
Buick Regal	747	278	351	337	359	744	544	624	1069	1058	Poor
Cadillac CTS	252	271	333	239	920	422	754	417	1270	1021	Poor
Chevrolet Camaro	891	323	288	372	631	350	659	435	634	509	Good
Chevrolet Corvette	747	548	590	348	3010	203	875	455	847	2356	Vry. Pr.
Chevrolet Malibu	864	273	351	445	529	384	634	624	488	503	Good
Chrysler 200	774	126	244	109	422	203	567	223	598	1080	Vry. Gd.
Ford Fusion	1134	163	192	125	301	123	596	206	402	1020	Vry. Gd.
Ford Mustang	1341	152	175	191	399	155	890	273	260	748	Vry. Gd.
Honda Accord	720	150	506	466	476	262	494	227	457	1079	Good
Hyundai Sonata	1251	149	285	187	327	280	639	376	645	749	Vry. Gd.
Infiniti Q50	594	168	456	408	494	556	1346	686	631	2035	Vry. Pr.
Infiniti Q70	702	248	442	367	458	846	1346	686	698	2611	Vry. Pr.
Kia Cadenza	585										
Kia Optima	864	170	236	194	332	210	526	291	331	535	Vry. Gd.
Lexus GS	585	165	715	544	468	415	2686	373	844	2283	Vry. Pr.
Lincoln MKZ	873	167	435	173	338	788	1448	1331	427	3687	Vry. Pr.
Mazda Mazda6	1161	184	240	224	535	232	542	226	360	744	Vry. Gd.
Nissan Altima	594	148	372	335	449	311	652	280	408	695	Good
Nissan Maxima	828	151	407	412	472	238	984	410	664	881	Average
Subaru Legacy	1323	163	557	203	417	537	318	420	384	889	Good
Subaru Outback	1323	163	557	203	417	537	288	420	384	889	Good
Toyota Camry	558	138	489	328	434	560	2117	313	404	901	Poor
Toyota Prius V	360	166	0	443	467	351	1696	456	271	864	Average
Volkswagen CC	927	176	635	474	486	328	713	831	557	855	Average
Volkswagen Passat	819	171	706	251	480	382	1714	469	706	680	Poor
Volvo S60	513	196	449	311	801	263	569	452	678	502	Good
Large											
Audi A7	846	231	958	531	685	2070	2401	465	759	1177	Vry. Pr.
BMW 7 Series	225	145	646	536	528	2395	1283	731	751	3304	Vry. Pr.
Buick LaCrosse	864	273	424	390	490	770	1168	426	616	1102	Poor
Cadillac XTS	252	302	415	390	548	279	781	426	838	2489	Vry. Pr.
Chevrolet Impala	891	263	415	309	733	283	1105	404	622	613	Average
Chrysler 300	774	222	245	179	365	140	737	359	971	1791	Average
Dodge Challenger	900	222	219	179	242	135	735	168	964	682	Vry. Gd.
Dodge Charger	900	231	219	179	235	137	730	253	1071	674	Good
Ford Taurus	909	157	399	213	342	171	1092	981	693	1358	Poor
Hyundai Genesis	1044	228	451	215	431	341	1843	372	575	1050	Poor
Lexus ES	738	134	489	427	434	865	1842	453	469	3346	Vry. Pr.
Lincoln MKS	612	169	408	164	482	179	1029	1092	634	2311	Vry. Pr.
Mercedes-Benz E-Class	1305	187	800	583	489	493	1127	765	1137	1303	Vry. Pr.
AVERAGE OF ALL VEHICLES	**$805**	**$196**	**$472**	**$309**	**$538**	**$392**	**$964**	**$490**	**$637**	**$1152**	

	PM Costs to 60,000 Miles	REPAIR COSTS									Relative Repair Cost*
		Front Brake Pads	Starter	Fuel Injector	Fuel Pump	Struts/ Shocks	Timing Belt/ Chain	Water Pump	Muffler	Headlamps	
Mercedes-Benz S-Class	1287	298	740	442	518	2959	375	952	1468	1933	Vry. Pr.
Tesla Model S											
Toyota Avalon	558	138	476	355	466	533	1939	370	377	901	Poor
Minivan											
Chrysler Town and Country	639	230	409	393	538	156	910	271	568	536	Good
Honda Odyssey	810	158	490	101	415	191	379	423	657	717	Vry. Gd.
Kia Sedona	1071	161	248	344	372	335	1278	374	543	329	Good
Mazda Mazda5	918	164	329	116	429	208	542	283	460	1241	Good
Nissan Quest	1350	155	510	301	521	375	1018	279	608	774	Average
Toyota Sienna	747	149	503	402	1051	296	1780	353	402	1033	Poor
Small SUV											
Acura RDX	567	163	507	232	486	292	298	447	364	1724	Good
Audi Q3											
Audi Q5	855	213	757	321	684	482	561	775	652	1185	Poor
BMW X1	252	238	585	437	581	520	1298	714	748	1115	Poor
Buick Encore	576	311	268	102	415	207	723	360	607	664	Good
Cadillac SRX	252	207	379	417	434	188	754	399	935	1163	Average
Chevrolet Trax											
Ford Escape	855	148	228	94	369	172	717	215	319	959	Vry. Gd.
Honda Crosstour	999	142	699	146	453	213	506	203	547	729	Vry. Gd.
Honda CR-V	738	142	591	155	341	405	560	221	398	761	Vry. Gd.
Hyundai Tucson	972	131	367	143	336	216	525	430	578	580	Vry. Gd.
Jeep Cherokee	918	225	336	254	726	192	855	244	844	791	Good
Jeep Compass	1314	155	395	110	351	233	554	259	568	1006	Vry. Gd.
Jeep Patriot	1350	117	284	110	342	240	513	259	618	435	Vry. Gd.
Jeep Renegade											
Jeep Wrangler	1359	212	248	260	530	114	855	369	374	374	Vry. Gd.
Kia Sportage	927	156	236	223	349	268	558	403	629	2119	Average
Land Rover Range Rover Evoque	351	280	575	511	688	704	533	298	715	532	Average
Lexus NX											
Lincoln MKC	252										
Mazda CX-5	792	165	383	350	331	224	396	240	463	733	Vry. Gd.
Mercedes-Benz GLA-Class											
Mercedes-Benz GLK-Class	1575	191	980	424	436	627	1307	677	1219	1265	Vry. Pr.
Mitsubishi Outlander Sport	792	277	906	360	780	483	623	529	468	1477	Poor
Nissan Juke	657	151	515	343	501	287	1432	311	496	612	Average
Porsche Macan											
Subaru Forester	1062	154	549	239	417	537	666	457	357	840	Good
Subaru XV Crosstrek	1008	163	549	266	468	490	738	429	404	824	Good
Toyota RAV4	612	178	468	319	693	246	2004	254	905	690	Poor
Volkswagen Tiguan	927	140	670	459	414	414	910	799	431	934	Average
Mid-Size SUV											
Acura MDX	837	160	545	183	448	256	388	483	656	1823	Average
Audi Q7	1017	279	859	499	530	2001	2221	383	1219	2367	Vry. Pr.
BMW X3	252	242	585	266	608	588	895	651	950	1210	Poor
BMW X5	351	295	619	528	518	561	935	591	1367	3691	Vry. Pr.
Chevrolet Equinox	891	295	369	283	870	194	544	624	634	927	Average
Dodge Journey	846	216	413	188	702	349	1054	271	1420	656	Average
Ford Edge	756	184	408	191	447	243	1097	1101	612	924	Average
Ford Explorer	909	157	403	307	686	292	1092	1031	907	1364	Poor
GMC Terrain	891	295	369	283	870	194	544	624	634	927	Average
Honda Pilot	864	158	513	209	495	209	379	513	655	846	Good
Hyundai Santa Fe	972	174	258	138	455	260	511	329	572	1100	Good
AVERAGE OF ALL VEHICLES	**$805**	**$196**	**$472**	**$309**	**$538**	**$392**	**$964**	**$490**	**$637**	**$1152**	

	PM Costs to 60,000 Miles	REPAIR COSTS									
		Front Brake Pads	Starter	Fuel Injector	Fuel Pump	Struts/ Shocks	Timing Belt/ Chain	Water Pump	Muffler	Headlamps	Relative Repair Cost*
Hyundai Santa Fe Sport	972	174	258	138	455	260	511	329	572	1100	Good
Infiniti QX60	702	155	419	390	458	673	1661	686	678	3638	Vry. Pr.
Infiniti QX70	702	176	419	390	458	632	1661	686	678	3638	Vry. Pr.
Jeep Grand Cherokee	918	225	336	254	726	192	855	244	844	791	Good
Kia Sorento	936	146	253	312	473	269	1854	462	674	919	Poor
Land Rover Range Rover Sport	864	242	660	642	631	791	2262	381	570	2703	Vry. Pr.
Lexus RX	774	144	753	378	476	240	1860	1191	1207	1171	Vry. Pr.
Lincoln MKX	504	184	408	191	447	243	1097	1101	612	924	Average
Mazda CX-9	774	190	308	227	568	308	1101	1096	593	870	Average
Mercedes-Benz M-Class	1710	285	920	690	528	1641	1544	636	845	1449	Vry. Pr.
Mitsubishi Outlander	981	187	317	266	759	233	623	524	413	783	Good
Nissan Murano	2403	194	455	385	526	264	1099	458	518	836	Average
Nissan Pathfinder	702	173	458	408	508	189	1097	487	612	968	Average
Nissan Rogue	702	155	376	363	747	198	1123	338	623	1610	Poor
Nissan Xterra	1080	155	398	363	406	130	931	316	522	748	Good
Porsche Cayenne	1080	380	594	410	543	1405	1309	501	1439	1016	Vry. Pr.
Toyota Venza	774	135	474	291	475	517	1892	292	588	931	Poor
Volkswagen Touareg	1008	231	724	873	462	869	1410	751	912	1328	Vry. Pr.
Volvo XC60	513	270	441	244	731	234	630	397	602	542	Good
Large SUV											
Buick Enclave	810	284	379	322	647	176	1424	462	643	1748	Poor
Cadillac Escalade	252	283	318	292	920	223	866	524	1125	2025	Vry. Pr.
Cadillac Escalade ESV	252	283	524	292	679	193	866	524	1099	2025	Vry. Pr.
Chevrolet Suburban	891	283	318	292	679	193	866	524	1099	630	Average
Chevrolet Tahoe	891	283	318	292	920	223	866	524	1125	630	Average
Chevrolet Traverse	819	284	379	322	559	213	1348	462	621	1031	Average
Dodge Durango	918	215	584	134	679	160	883	244	566	626	Good
Ford Expedition	972	176	300	172	579	259	925	275	627	607	Good
Ford Flex	801	148	399	191	430	199	1097	1047	734	1458	Poor
GMC Acadia	819	284	379	322	559	176	1348	462	621	1748	Poor
GMC Yukon	891	283	318	292	920	223	866	524	1125	630	Average
GMC Yukon XL	891	283	318	292	679	193	866	524	1099	560	Average
Infiniti QX80	1080	173	523	300	523	513	1427	291	378	1669	Poor
Land Rover Range Rover	864	242	660	642	631	791	2262	381	570	2703	Vry. Pr.
Lexus GX	711	155	889	445	623	154	1288	593	535	1054	Poor
Lincoln Navigator	648	176	300	172	579	259	925	275	627	607	Good
Mercedes-Benz GL-Class	1341	320	755	619	551	599	369	869	830	1390	Vry. Pr.
Nissan Armada	1080	164	496	300	530	374	1716	296	628	917	Poor
Toyota 4Runner	486	151	537	350	632	239	1869	447	509	842	Poor
Toyota Highlander	486	144	499	398	986	643	1894	559	1189	681	Vry. Pr.
Toyota Sequoia	522	303	864	373	757	390	1230	517	435	835	Poor
Compact Pickup											
Chevrolet Colorado											
GMC Canyon											
Nissan Frontier	1080	164	439	363	558	200	856	308	406	725	Good
Toyota Tacoma	450	148	522	345	816	171	1432	249	466	767	Average
Standard Pickup											
Chevrolet Silverado	864	283	381	292	650	209	866	497	900	706	Average
Ford F-150	1296	184	459	518	621	126	811	269	473	585	Good
GMC Sierra	891	283	381	292	690	209	872	497	995	736	Average
Nissan Titan	1080	164	577	300	563	199	1815	307	606	753	Average
Ram 1500	900	152	294	140	406	162	520	399	413	455	Vry. Gd.
Toyota Tundra	522	168	826	317	859	219	1907	447	508	835	Poor
AVERAGE OF ALL VEHICLES	$805	$196	$472	$309	$538	$392	$964	$490	$637	$1152	

43

SERVICE CONTRACTS

Service contracts are one of the most expensive options you can buy. In fact, service contracts are a major profit source for many dealers.

A service contract is not a warranty. It is more like an insurance plan that, in theory, covers repairs that are not covered by your warranty or that occur after the warranty runs out. They are often inaccurately referred to as "extended warranties."

Service contracts are generally a poor value. The companies who sell contracts are very sure that, on average, your repairs will cost considerably less than what you pay for the contract—if not, they wouldn't be in business.

Here are some important questions to ask before buying a service contract:

How reputable is the company responsible for the contract? If the company offering the contract goes out of business, you will be out of luck. The company may be required to be insured, but find out if they actually are and by whom. Check with your Better Business Bureau or office of consumer affairs if you are not sure of a company's reputation. Service contracts from car and insurance companies are more likely to remain in effect than those from independent companies.

Exactly what does the contract cover and for how long? Service contracts vary considerably—different items are covered and different time limits are offered. This is true even among service contracts offered by the same company. For example, one company has plans that range from 4 years/36,000 miles maximum coverage to 6 years/100,000 miles maximum coverage, with other options for only power train coverage. Make sure you know what components are covered because if a breakdown occurs on a part that is not covered, you are responsible for the repairs.

If you plan to resell your car in a few years, you won't want to purchase a long-running service contract. Some service contracts automatically cancel when you resell the car, while others require a hefty transfer fee before extending privileges to the new owner.

Some automakers offer a "menu" format, which lets you pick the items you want covered in your service contract. Find out if the contract pays for preventive maintenance, towing, and rental car expenses. If not written into the contract, assume they are not covered.

Make sure the contract clearly specifies how you can reach the company. Knowing this before you purchase a service contract can save you time and aggravation in the future.

How will the repair bills be paid? It is best to have the service contractor pay bills directly. Some contracts require you to pay the repair bill, and reimburse you later.

Where can the car be serviced? Can you take the car to any mechanic if you have trouble on the road? What if you move?

What other costs can be expected? Most service contracts will have a deductible expense. Compare deductibles on various plans. Also, some companies charge the deductible for each individual repair while other companies pay per visit, regardless of the number of repairs being made.

What are your responsibilities? Make sure you know what you have to do to uphold the contract. For example if you have to follow the manufacturer's recommended maintenance, keep detailed records or the contract could be voided. You will find your specific responsibilities in the contact. Be sure to have the seller point them out.

SERVICE CONTRACTS VS. SAVINGS ACCOUNT

One alternative to buying a service contract is to deposit the cost of the contract into a savings account. If the car needs a major repair not covered by your warranty, the money in your account will cover the cost. Most likely, you'll be building up a down payment for your next car!

TIPS FOR DEALING WITH A MECHANIC

Call around. Don't choose a shop simply because it's nearby. Calling a few shops may turn up estimates cheaper by half.

Don't necessarily go for the lowest price. A good rule is to eliminate the highest and lowest estimates; the mechanic with the highest estimate is probably charging too much, and the lowest may be cutting too many corners.

Check the shop's reputation. Call your local consumer affairs agency and the Better Business Bureau. They don't have records on every shop, but unfavorable reports on a shop should disqualify it.

Look for certification. Mechanics can be certified by the National Institute for Automotive Service Excellence, an industry-wide yardstick for competence. Certification is offered in eight areas of repair and shops with certified mechanics are allowed to advertise this fact. However, make sure the mechanic working on your car is certified for the repair you need.

Take a look around. A well-kept shop reflects pride in workmanship. A skilled and efficient mechanic would probably not work in a messy shop.

Don't sign a blank check. The service order you sign should have specific instructions or describe your vehicle's symptoms. Avoid signing a vague work order. Be sure you are called for final approval before the shop does extra work. Many states require a written estimate signed by you and require that the shop get your permission for repairs that exceed the estimate by 10%.

Show interest. Ask about the repair. But don't act like an expert if you don't really understand what's wrong. Express your satisfaction. If you're happy with the work, compliment the mechanic and ask for him or her the next time you come in. You will get to know each other and the mechanic will get to know your vehicle.

Take a test-drive. Before you pay for a major repair, you should take the car for a test-drive. The few extra minutes you spend checking out the repair could save you a trip back to the mechanic. If you find that the problem still exists, there will be no question that the repair wasn't properly completed.

REPAIR PROTECTION BY CREDIT CARD

Paying your auto repair bills by credit card can provide a much needed recourse if you are having problems with an auto mechanic. According to federal law, you have the right to withhold payment for sloppy or incorrect repairs. Of course, you may withhold no more than the amount of the repair in dispute.

In order to use this right, you must first try to work out the problem with the mechanic. Also, unless the credit card company owns the repair shop (this might be the case with gasoline credit cards used at gas stations), two other conditions must be met. First, the repair shop must be in your home state (or within 100 miles of your current address), and second, the cost of repairs must be over $50. Until the problem is settled or resolved in court, the credit card company cannot charge you interest or penalties on the amount in dispute.

If you decide to take action, send a letter to the credit card company and a copy to the repair shop, explaining the details of the problem and what you want as settlement. Send the letter by certified mail with a return receipt requested.

Sometimes the credit card company or repair shop will attempt to put a "bad mark" on your credit record if you use this tactic. Legally, you can't be reported as delinquent if you've given the credit card company notice of your dispute, but a creditor can report that you are disputing your bill, which goes in your record. However, you have the right to challenge any incorrect information and add your side of the story to your file.

For more information, write to the Federal Trade Commission, Credit Practices Division, 601 Pennsylvania Avenue, NW, Washington, DC 20580.

TIRE RATINGS

Buying tires has become an infrequent task because today's radial tires last much longer than the tires of the past. Surprisingly, a tire has to perform more functions simultaneously than any other part of the car (steering, bearing the load, cushioning the ride, and stopping).

Because comparing tires is difficult, many consumers mistakenly use price and brand name to determine quality. Because there are hundreds of tire lines to choose from, and only a few tire manufacturers, the difference in many tires may only be the brand name.

But there is help. The U.S. government requires tires to be rated according to their safety and expected mileage.

Treadwear, traction, and heat resistance grades are printed on the sidewall and are attached to the tire on a paper label. Ask the dealer for the grades of the tires they sell. Using this rating system, a sampling of top rated tires follows on page 48.

Treadwear: The treadwear grade gives you an idea of the mileage you can expect from a tire. It is shown in numbers–720, 700, 680, 660, and so forth. Higher numbers mean longer tire life. A tire with a grade of 600 should give you twice as much mileage as one rated 300. Use the treadwear grade as a relative basis of comparison.

Traction: Traction grades of AA, A, B, and C describe the tire's ability to stop on wet surfaces. Tires graded AA will stop on a wet road in a shorter distance than tires graded B or C. Tires rated C have poor traction.

Heat Resistance: Heat resistance is graded A, B, and C. An A rating means the tire will run cooler than one rated B or C and be less likely to fail if driven over long distances at highway speeds. Tires that run cooler tend to be more fuel-efficient. Hot-running tires can result in blow-outs or tread separation.

TIRE CARE

Pump 'em Up: An estimated one-third of us are driving on underinflated tires. Because even good tires lose air, it is important to check your tire pressure monthly. Underinflated tires can be dangerous, use more fuel and cause premature tire failure. When checking your tires, be sure to use an accurate gauge and inflate to the pressure indicated in your owner's manual, not the maximum pressure printed on your tire.

When to Replace: If any part of Lincoln's head is visible when you insert the top of a penny into a tread groove, it's time to replace the tire. While this old rule of thumb is still valid, today's tires also have a built-in wear indicator. A series of horizontal bars appear across the surface when the tread depth reaches the danger zone.

GETTING THE BEST PRICE

The price of the same tire can vary depending on where you shop so shopping around is vital to finding a good buy. Most tire ads appear in the sports section of your Wednesday and Saturday daily newspaper. You are most likely to find the best prices at independent tire dealers who carry a variety of tire brands.

The price of a tire is based on its size, and tires come in as many as nine sizes. For example, the list price of the same tire can range from $74.20 to $134.35, depending on its size.

To get the best buy:

1. Check to see which manufacturer makes the least expensive "off brand." Only a few manufacturers produce the over 1,800 types of tires sold in the U.S.

2. Don't forget to compare balancing and mounting costs. These extra charges can add up to more than $25 or be offered at no cost.

3. Never pay list price for a tire. A good rule of thumb is to pay at least 30-40 percent off the suggested list price.

4. Use the treadwear grade the same way you would the "unit price" in a supermarket. The tire with the lowest cost per grade point is the best value. For example, if tire A costs $100 and has a treadwear grade of 600, and tire B costs $80 and has a tread-wear grade of 300, tire A is the better buy, even though its initial cost is more.

Tire A: $100÷600=$0.17 per point
Tire B: $80÷300=$0.27 per point

Where you live is a key factor in how long your tires will last. In addition to construction and design, tire wear is affected by the level of abrasive material in the road surface. Generally, the road surfaces of the West Coast, Great Lakes region, and northern New England are easiest on tires. The Appalachian and Rocky Mountain areas are usually hardest on tires.

HOW TO READ A TIRE

Tire Type and Size: The most important information on a tire are the letters and the numbers indicating its type and size.

1. Tire Type: The P at the beginning of the tire size indicates that the tire is a passenger vehicle tire. LT indicates light truck tire, and T indicates a temporary or spare tire.

2. Tire Width is the first part of the number and is measured in millimeters, from sidewall to sidewall.

3. Tire Height is the next number and tells you the height of the tire from the bead to the tread. This is described as a percentage of the tire width. In our example, the tire's height is 65 percent of its width. The smaller the aspect ratio, the wider the tire in relation to its height.

4. Tire Construction designates how the tire was made. R indicates radial construction which is the most common type. Older tires were made using diagonal bias D or bias belted B construction, but these tire types are no longer used on passenger vehicles.

5. Wheel Diameter identifies the wheel rim diameter (in inches-15) needed for this tire.

6. Load Index: The load rating indicates the maximum load for that tire. A higher number indicates a higher load capacity. The rating 95, for example, corresponds to a load capacity of 1521 pounds. Larger vehicles, SUVs and pickups need tires with a higher load capacity.

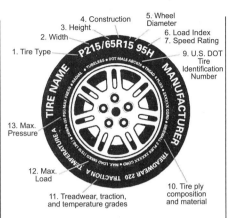

4. Construction
3. Height
2. Width
5. Wheel Diameter
6. Load Index
7. Speed Rating
1. Tire Type
9. U.S. DOT Tire Identification Number
13. Max. Pressure
12. Max. Load
11. Treadwear, traction, and temperature grades
10. Tire ply composition and material

7. Speed Rating indicates the maximum speed that the tire can sustain a ten minute endurance test without being in danger. All passenger car tires are rated at least S and pass the test at speeds up to 112 mph. Other ratings are as follows: T up to 118 mph, H up to 130 mph, V up to 149 mph and Z 150 mph or higher. Other types of tires, temporary spares and snow tires are lower on the rating scale.

8. Severe Conditions: M+S indicates the tire meets the Rubber Manu. Association's definition of a mud and snow tire. There are no performance tests for this standard. If the tire has an M+S and a "mountain and snowflake" symbol then the traction is at least 10% better than the regular version of the tire. These symbols are not in the above example.

9. Tire Identification Number
Example: DOT NJ HR 2AF 5212
The letters DOT certify compliance with all applicable safety standards established by the U.S. Department of Transportation. The next four characters is a code where the first two characters indicate the manufacturer and the second two characters indicate the plant where the tire was made.

Next you may see an optional string of three to four characters. Most manufacturers use these to record company specific information they use to identify their products or that can be used to identify tires in the market for recall purposes.

The last four digits determine the week and year the tire was made. The digits 5212 would signify that the tire was made during the 52nd week of 2012. Don't buy tires more than two years old. Tires naturally degrade with age, so you want the newest possible tires for the longest life (and safe operation.)

10. Tire Ply Composition and Material indicates the type of cord (polyester or steel) and number of plies in the tire, 4-ply, 6-ply, 8-ply, for both the tread and the sidewall.

11. Treadwear, Traction and Temperature Grades are three performance grades assigned to the tire and are the best way to truly evaluate the tires expected performance in these three critical areas. See page 46 for more information.

12. Max Load Limit tells you the cold inflation load limit in lbs. (pounds) and in kg (kilograms). The number corresponds to the load index.

13. Max Pressure is the maximum recommended pressure in psi (pounds per square inch) and in kPa (kilopascals). However, this is not the tire pressure for your car. You must check your owner's manual for the proper tire pressure for the tires on your car.

A Sampling of Top Rated Tires

Brand Name	Model	Description	Traction	Heat	Treadwear
Bridgestone	DUELER H/L ALENZA PLUS "H" & "V" Spd Rtd	All Sizes	A	A	800
Toyo	TOYO ULTRA Z900 (H-rated)	All sizes	A	A	800
Mastercraft	Avenger Touring LSR (TR)	15"-18"	A	A	780
Big O	EURO TOUR (T RATED)	All sizes	A	A	740
Bridgestone	TURANZA SERENITY "H" Spd Rtd	All sizes	A	A	740
Maxxis	MA-T1 Escapade	All sizes	A	A	720
Michelin	LTX M/S2	All sizes	A	A	720
Nokian	Nokian eNTYRE	All sizes	A	A	700
Cordovan	TOUR PLUS LST (T rated)	All sizes	A	A	680
Eldorado	LEGEND TOUR (T rated)	All sizes	A	A	680
Jetzon	GENESIS LST (T rated)	All sizes	A	A	680
Multi-Mile	GRAND TOUR LS (T rated)	All sizes	A	A	680
Sigma	REGENT TOURING LS (T rated)	All sizes	A	A	680
Telstar	ECHELON ULTRA LST (T rated)	All sizes	A	A	680
Vanderbilt	TOURING LSE (T rated)	All sizes	A	A	680
Hankook	VENTUS S1 noble2 (OE)	245/50R20	A	A	660
Big O	BIG FOOT S/T (H & V rated)	All sizes	A	A	640
Cooper	CS4 (TR)	14"	A	A	640
Goodyear	ASSURANCE TRIPLETRED (V)	All sizes	A	A	640
Hankook	Dynapro HP2	All	A	A	640
Mastercraft	Avenger Touring LSR (TR)	14"	A	A	640
Neutral	Mirada Cross Tour SLX (H & V rated)	All sizes	A	A	640
Nitto	NT421Q (H & V rated)	All sizes	A	A	640
Toyo	TOYO ULTRA Z900 (V-rated)	All sizes	A	A	640
Toyo	OPEN COUNTRY H/T	P-METRIC/METRIC H & V	A	A	640
Cooper	CS5 Ultra Touring (H)	All sizes	A	A	620
Cooper	Discoverer CTS (H-rated)	All sizes	A	A	620
Goodyear	FORTERA SILENTARMOR (H)	All sizes	A	A	620
Hankook	Mileage Plus GT	All sizes	A	A	620
Michelin	PRIMACY MXV4	All sizes except	A	A	620
Nitto	CROSSTEK (H-rated)	All sizes	A	A	620
Primewell	PT700	All	A	A	620
Runway	ENDURO-716	Speed rated H	A	A	620
Bridgestone	DUELER H/L ALENZA "H" and "V" Spd Rtd	All sizes except	A	A	600
Bridgestone	TURANZA SERENITY PLUS, "H" & "V" Spd Rtd	All Sizes	A	A	600
Bridgestone	ECOPIA EP422 PLUS	P205/60R16	A	A	600
Continental	Altimax RT	All except	A	A	600
Continental	ContiProContact	All Sizes	A	A	600
Cooper	CS5 Ultra Touring	185/65R15	A	A	600
Falken	AZENIS PT722	All Sizes	A	A	600
Falken	WILDPEAK H/T HT01 (H)	All sizes	A	A	600
Falken	ZE950 (H,V)	All sizes	A	A	600
General	Altimax RT	> 195	A	A	600
Hankook	SF Optimo	All sizes	A	A	600
Hankook	Optimo H725 (OE)	P235/55R19	A	A	600
Hankook	Optimo 4S	55/60/65/70 Series	A	A	600
Nitto	Dura Grappler	P-METRIC/METRIC	A	A	600
Provato	PR208	All	A	A	600
Sumitomo	TOUR PLUS LXV	All sizes	A	A	600
Sumitomo	Enhance L/X (H & V-Rated)	All sizes except	A	A	600
Sumitomo	TOUR PLUS LXH	All sizes	A	A	600
Sumitomo	Enhance C/X (H & V-Rated)	All sizes	A	A	600
Sumitomo	TOUR PLUS LSV	All sizes except	A	A	600
Sumitomo	TOURING LSH	All sizes	A	A	600
Sumitomo	HTR ENHANCE C/X "H,V"	All sizes	A	A	600
Sumitomo	HTR ENHANCE L/X "H, V" (standard load)	All sizes	A	A	600
Toyo	OPEN COUNTRY AT II	ALL SPEED H	A	A	600

For a complete listing of all the tires on the market, you can call the Auto Safety Hot Line toll free, at 888-327-4236 or 800-424-9153(TTY). Or, go to www.safercar.gov

WARNING

As tires age, they naturally dry out and can become potentially dangerous. Some experts recommend getting rid of a six-year-old tire no matter what condition it is in. Recently, a national news organization went undercover and found 12 year old tires for sale, so be sure to check your tire date before purchasing. Ask for tires that are less than one year old.

INSURANCE

Insurance is a big part of ownership expenses, yet it's often forgotten in the showroom. As you shop, remember that the car's design and accident history may affect your insurance rates. Some cars cost less to insure because experience has shown that they are damaged less, less expensive to fix after a collision, or stolen less.

Shop Around: You can save hundreds of dollars by shopping around for insurance.

There are a number of factors that determine what coverage will cost you. A car's design can affect both the chances and severity of an accident. For example, a well-designed bumper may escape damage in a low-speed crash. Some cars are easier to repair than others or may have less expensive parts. Cars with four doors tend to be damaged less than cars with two doors.

Other factors that effect your insurance costs include:

Your Annual Mileage: The more you drive, the more your vehicle will be "exposed" to a potential accident. Driving less than 7,500 miles per year often gets a discount. Ask your insurer if they offer this option.

Where You Drive: If you regularly drive and park in the city, you will most likely pay more than if you drive in rural areas.

Youthful Drivers: Usually the highest premiums are paid by male drivers under the age of 25. Whether or not the under-25-year-old male is married also affects insurance rates. (Married males pay less.) As the driver gets older, rates are lowered.

Insurance discounts and surcharges depend upon the way a vehicle is traditionally driven. Sports cars, for example, are usually surcharged due, in part, to the typical driving habits of their owners. Four-door sedans and station wagons generally merit discounts.

Not all companies offer discounts or surcharges, and many cars receive neither. Some companies offer a discount or impose a surcharge on collision premiums only. Others apply discounts and surcharges on both collision and comprehensive coverage. Discounts and surcharges usually range from 10–30 percent. Remember that one company may offer a discount on a particular car while another may not.

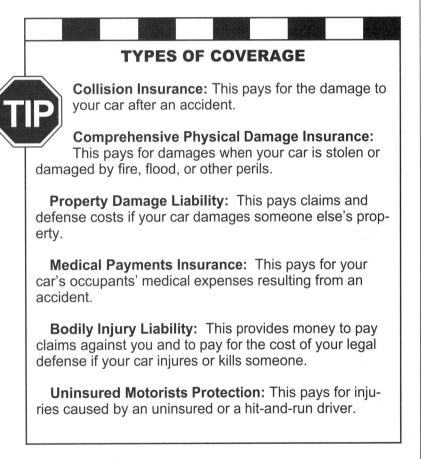

TYPES OF COVERAGE

TIP

Collision Insurance: This pays for the damage to your car after an accident.

Comprehensive Physical Damage Insurance: This pays for damages when your car is stolen or damaged by fire, flood, or other perils.

Property Damage Liability: This pays claims and defense costs if your car damages someone else's property.

Medical Payments Insurance: This pays for your car's occupants' medical expenses resulting from an accident.

Bodily Injury Liability: This provides money to pay claims against you and to pay for the cost of your legal defense if your car injures or kills someone.

Uninsured Motorists Protection: This pays for injuries caused by an uninsured or a hit-and-run driver.

REDUCING INSURANCE COSTS

Get Your Discounts: After you have shopped around and found the best deal by comparing the costs of different coverages, be sure you get all the discounts you are entitled to.

Most insurance companies offer discounts of 5-30 percent on various parts of your insurance bill. Ask your insurance company for a complete list of the discounts that it offers. These can vary by company and from state to state.

Here are some of the most common insurance discounts:

Driver Education/Defensive Driving Courses: Discounts for completing a state-approved driver education course can mean a $40 reduction in the cost of coverage. Discounts of 5–15 percent are available in some states to those who complete a defensive driving course.

Good Student Discounts of up to 25 percent for full-time high school or college students who are in the upper 20 percent of their class, on the dean's list, or have a B or better grade point average.

Good Driver Discounts are available to drivers with an accident and violation-free record, (or no incidents in 3 years).

Mature Driver Credit: Drivers ages 50 and older may qualify for up to a 10 percent discount or a lower price bracket.

Sole Female Driver: Some companies offer discounts of 10 percent for females, ages 30 to 64, who are the only driver in a household.

Non-Drinkers and Non-Smokers: A limited number of companies offer incentives ranging from 10–25 percent to those who abstain.

Farmer Discounts: Many companies offer farmers either a discount of 10–30 percent or a lower price bracket.

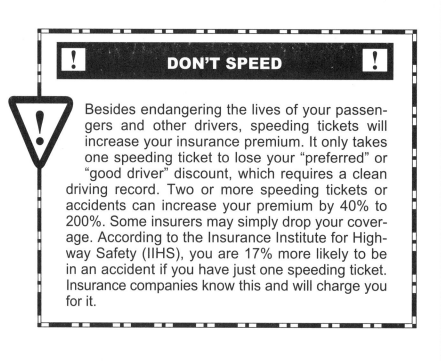

! DON'T SPEED !

Besides endangering the lives of your passengers and other drivers, speeding tickets will increase your insurance premium. It only takes one speeding ticket to lose your "preferred" or "good driver" discount, which requires a clean driving record. Two or more speeding tickets or accidents can increase your premium by 40% to 200%. Some insurers may simply drop your coverage. According to the Insurance Institute for Highway Safety (IIHS), you are 17% more likely to be in an accident if you have just one speeding ticket. Insurance companies know this and will charge you for it.

YOUNG DRIVERS

TIP

Each year, teenagers account for about 15 percent of highway deaths. According to the Insurance Institute for Highway Safety (IIHS), the highest driver death rate per 100,000 people is among 18-year-olds. Parents need to make sure their children are fully prepared to be competent, safe drivers before letting them out on the road. All states issue learner's permits. However, only 35 states and the District of Columbia require permits before getting a driver's license. It isn't difficult for teenagers to get a license and only 14 states prohibit teenagers from driving during night and early morning. Call your state's MVA for young driver laws.

Car Pooling: Commuters sharing driving may qualify for discounts of 5–25 percent or a lower price bracket.

Children away at school don't drive the family car very often, so if they're on your policy and they're at school, let your company know. If you insure them separately, discounts of 10–40 percent or a lower price bracket are available.

Desirable Cars: Premiums are usually much higher for cars with high collision rates or that are the favorite target of thieves.

Anti-Theft Device Credits: Discounts of 5-15 percent are offered in some states for cars equipped with a hood lock and an alarm or a disabling device (active or passive) that prevents the car from being started.

Multipolicy and Multicar Policy Discount: Some companies offer discounts of up to 10–20 percent for insuring your home and auto with the same company, or more than one car.

First Accident Allowance: Some insurers offer a "first accident allowance," which guarantees that if a customer achieves five accident-free years, his or her rates won't go up after the first at-fault accident.

Deductibles: Opting for the largest reasonable deductible is the obvious first step in reducing premiums. Increasing your deductible to $500 from $200 could cut your collision premium about 20 percent. Raising the deductible to $1,000 from

$200 could lower your premium about 45 percent. The discounts may vary by company.

Collision Coverage: The older the car, the less the need for collision insurance. Consider dropping collision insurance entirely on an older car. Regardless of how much coverage you carry, the insurance company will only pay up to the car's "book value." For example, if your car requires $1,000 in

repairs, but its "book value" is only $500, the insurance company is required to pay only $500.

Organizations: If you are a member of AARP, AAA, the military, a union, a professional group, an alumni association, or similar organization, you may be able to get a discount. Often insurance companies will enter joint ventures with organizations.

AUTO THEFT

The Highway Loss Data Institute (HLDI) regularly compiles statistics on motor vehicle thefts. Using the frequency of theft claims per 1,000 insured vehicles, the HLDI lists the following as the most and least stolen vehicles among the 2010-2012 models.

Most Stolen	Claim Frequency*
Ford F-250 crew 4WD	7.0
Chevrolet Silverado 1500 crew	6.7
Chevrolet Avalanche 1500	6.1
GMC Sierra 1500 crew	6.0
Ford F-350 crew 4WD	5.6
Cadillac Escalade 4WD	5.5
Chevrolet Suburban 1500	5.4
GMC Sierra 1500 extended cab	4.7
GMC Yukon	4.5
Chevrolet Tahoe	4.4

Least Stolen	Claim Frequency*
Dodge Journey 4WD	0.4
Volkswagen Tiguan 4WD	0.4
Audi A4 4-door	0.4
Acura RDX	0.4
Toyota Matrix	0.4
Lexus HS 250 hybrid 4-door	0.4
Honda CR-V	0.4
Hyundai Tucson 4WD	0.4
Toyota Sienna 4WD	0.5
Jeep Compass 4WD	0.5
Average All Passenger Vehicles	**1.2**

*Claim Frequency means the number of vehicles stolen per 1000 insured vehicles, for example about 7 Ford F-250s are stolen or broken into for every 1,000 insured. Source: Highway Loss Data Institute (www.iihs.org)

BUMPERS

The main purpose of the bumper is to protect your car in low-speed collisions. Despite this intention, many of us have been victims of a $500-$3500 repair bill resulting from a seemingly minor impact. The federal government used to require that automakers equip cars with bumpers capable of withstanding up to 5 mph crashes with no damage. Unfortunately, in the early eighties, under pressure from car companies, the government rolled back this requirement. Now, the federal law only requires car companies to build bumpers that protect cars in 2.5 mph collisions-about the speed at which we walk. This rollback enables the car companies to sell lots of expensive parts, and has cost consumers millions of dollars in increased insurance premiums and repair costs.

The state of California requires that companies disclose which bumpers meet the old 5 mph standard. Unfortunately, few, if any, California cars contain this disclosure.

In order to see how well bumpers actually protect our vehicles, the Insurance Institute for Highway Safety conducts a variety of bumper tests. In their low speed (6 mph) tests, it's shocking how poorly bumpers protect vehicles. In these tests, it can easily cost $2-$3,700 after a low speed fender bender.

Unfortunately, we can't simply look at a bumper and determine how good it will be at doing its job-protecting a car from inevitable bumps. The solution to this problem is quite simple— require carmakers to tell the consumer the highest speed at which their car could be crashed with no damage.

Federal standards *do* require that car bumpers be designed to match up to each other in a collision. This is an attempt to enable the bumpers to hit each other and absorb the energy of the crash rather than other parts of the car. Unfortunately there is a big hole in this federal requirement because SUVs, pickups, and minivans don't have to meet the same bumper height rules as cars. With such a high percentage of SUVs, pickups and minivans on the road, huge bumper mismatches in crashes are quite common. Mismatching between cars and SUVs results in excessive damage and pricey repairs.

In order to see how well bumpers actually function in car and SUV collisions, the Insurance Institute for Highway Safety conducted two types of tests at 10 mph; one with an SUV hitting the rear of a car and one with a car traveling at 10 mph and crashing into the rear of an SUV. For more results, visit the Insurance Institute for Highway Safety at www.iihs.org. The table below shows how much this bumper mismatch problem can cost you.

DAMAGE REPAIR COSTS IN 10 MPH FRONT-INTO-

Source: Insurance Institute for Highway Safety

REAR CRASH TESTS

SUV INTO CAR	SUV Damage	Car Damage	Total Damage
Honda CR-V into Honda Civic	$1,721	$1,274	$2,995
Toyota RAV4 into Toyota Corolla	$1,434	$2,327	$3,761
Hyundai Tucson into Kia Forte	$850	$3,223	$4,073
Volkswagen Tiguan into Volkswagen Golf	$2,329	$2,058	$4,387
Jeep Patriot into Dodge Caliber	$1,415	$3,095	$4,510
Ford Escape into Ford Focus	$1,470	$3,386	$4,856
Nissan Rogue into Nissan Sentra	$2,884	$4,560	$7,444

CAR INTO SUV	Car Damage	SUV Damage	Total Damage
Kia Forte into Hyundai Tucson	$1,510	$2,091	$3,601
Dodge Caliber into Jeep Patriot	$2,559	$1,338	$3,897
Honda Civic into Honda CR-V	$4,921	$1,053	$5,974
Volkswagen Golf into Volkswagen Tiguan	$4,555	$1,872	$6,427
Nissan Sentra into Nissan Rogue	$5,114	$1,428	$6,542
Ford Focus into Ford Escape	$5,203	$2,208	$7,411
Corolla into Toyota RAV4	$3,852	$6,015	$9,867

See www.IIHS.org

COMPLAINTS

Americans spend billions of dollars on vehicle repairs every year. While many of those repairs are satisfactory, there are times when getting your vehicle fixed can be a very difficult process. In fact, vehicle defects and repairs are the number one cause of consumer complaints, according to the Federal Trade Commission. This chapter is designed to help you resolve your complaint, whether it's for a new vehicle still under warranty or for one you've had for years. In addition, we offer a guide to arbitration, the names and addresses of consumer groups, federal agencies, and the manufacturers themselves. Finally, we tell you how to take the important step of registering your complaint with the U.S. Department of Transportation.

No matter what your complaint, keep accurate records. Copies of the following items are indispensable in helping to resolve your problems:

☑ your service invoices

☑ bills you have paid

☑ letters you have written to the manufacturer or the repair facility owner

☑ written repair estimates from your independent mechanic.

☑ notes on discussion with company representatives including names and dates.

RESOLVING COMPLAINTS

Here are some basic steps to help you resolve your problem:

1 First, return your vehicle to the repair facility that did the work. Bring a written list of the problems and make sure that you keep a copy of the list. Give the repair facility a reasonable opportunity to examine your vehicle and attempt to fix it. Speak directly to the service manager (not to the service writer who wrote up your repair order), and ask him or her to test drive the vehicle with you so that you can point out the problem.

2 If that doesn't resolve the problem, take the vehicle to a diagnostic center for an independent examination. This may cost $45 to $60. Get a written statement defining the problem and outlining how it may be fixed. Give your repair shop a copy. If your vehicle is under warranty, do not allow any warranty repair by an independent mechanic; you may not be reimbursed by the manufacturer.

3 If your repair shop does not respond to the independent assessment, present your problem to a mediation panel. These panels hear both sides of the story and try to come to a resolution.

If the problem is with a new vehicle dealer, or if you feel that the manufacturer is responsible, you may be able to use one of the manufacturer's mediation programs.

If the problem is solely with an independent dealer, a local Better Business Bureau (BBB) may be able to mediate your complaint. It may also offer an arbitration hearing. In any case, the BBB should enter your complaint into its files on that establishment.

When contacting any mediation program, determine how long the process takes, who makes the final decision, whether you are bound by that decision, and whether the program handles all problems or only warranty complaints.

4 If there are no mediation programs in your area, contact private consumer groups, local government agencies, or your local "action line" newspaper columnist, newspaper editor, or radio/TV broadcaster. A phone call or letter from them may persuade a repair facility to take action. Send a copy of your letter to the repair shop.

5 One of your last resorts is to bring a lawsuit against the dealer, manufacturer, or repair facility in small claims court. The fee for filing such an action is usually small, and you generally act as your own attorney, saving attorney's fees. There is a monetary limit on the amount you can claim, which varies from state to state. Your local consumer affairs office, state attorney general's office, or the clerk of the court can tell you how to file such a suit.

6 Finally, talk with an attorney. It's best to select an attorney who is familiar with handling automotive problems. Call the lawyer referral service listed in the telephone directory and ask for the names of attorneys who deal with automobile problems. If you can't afford an attorney, contact the Legal Aid Society.

WARRANTY COMPLAINTS
If your vehicle is under warranty or you are having problems with a factory-authorized dealership, here are some special guidelines:

1 Have the warranty available to show the dealer. Make sure you call the problem to the dealer's attention before the end of the warranty period.

2 If you are still dissatisfied after giving the dealer a reasonable opportunity to fix your vehicle, contact the manufacturer's representative (also called the zone representative) in your area. This person can authorize the dealer to make repairs or take other steps to resolve the dispute. Your dealer will have your zone representative's name and telephone number. Explain the problem and ask for a meeting and a personal inspection of your vehicle.

3 If you can't get satisfaction from the zone representative, call or write the manufacturer's owner relations department. Your owner's manual contains this phone number and address. In each case, as you move up the chain, indicate the steps you have already taken and keep careful records of your efforts.

4 Your next option is to present your problem to a complaint handling panel or to the arbitration program in which the manufacturer of your vehicle participates.

If you complain of a problem during the warranty period, you have a right to have the problem fixed even after the warranty runs out. If your warranty has not been honored, you may be able to "revoke acceptance," which means that you return the vehicle to the dealer. If you are successful, you may be entitled to a replacement vehicle or to a full refund of the purchase price and reimbursement of legal fees under the Magnuson-Moss Warranty Act. Or, if you are covered by one of the state lemon laws, you may be able to return the vehicle and receive a refund or replacement from the manufacturer.

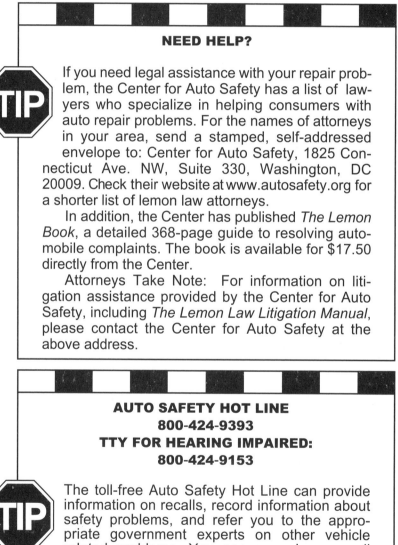

NEED HELP?

If you need legal assistance with your repair problem, the Center for Auto Safety has a list of lawyers who specialize in helping consumers with auto repair problems. For the names of attorneys in your area, send a stamped, self-addressed envelope to: Center for Auto Safety, 1825 Connecticut Ave. NW, Suite 330, Washington, DC 20009. Check their website at www.autosafety.org for a shorter list of lemon law attorneys.

In addition, the Center has published *The Lemon Book*, a detailed 368-page guide to resolving automobile complaints. The book is available for $17.50 directly from the Center.

Attorneys Take Note: For information on litigation assistance provided by the Center for Auto Safety, including *The Lemon Law Litigation Manual*, please contact the Center for Auto Safety at the above address.

AUTO SAFETY HOT LINE
800-424-9393
TTY FOR HEARING IMPAIRED:
800-424-9153

The toll-free Auto Safety Hot Line can provide information on recalls, record information about safety problems, and refer you to the appropriate government experts on other vehicle related problems. You can even have recall information mailed to you within 24 hours of your call at no charge. Most importantly, you can call the hot line to report safety problems which will become part of the National Highway Traffic Safety Administration's complaint database.

COMPLAINT INDEX

Thanks to the efforts of the Center for Auto Safety, we are able to provide you with the vehicle complaints on file with the National Highway Traffic Safety Administration (NHTSA). Each year, thousands of Americans file online or call the government in order to register complaints about their vehicles.

The complaint index is the result of our analysis of these complaints. It is based on a ratio of the number of complaints for each vehicle to the sales of that vehicle. In order to predict the expected complaint performance of the 2015 models, we have examined the complaint history of that car's series. The term series refers to the fact that when a manufacturer introduces a new model, that vehicle remains essentially unchanged, on average, for four to six years. For example, the Cadillac Escalade was redesigned in 2002 and remains essentially the same car for 2015. As such, we have compiled the complaint experience for that series in order to give you some information to use in deciding which car to buy. For vehicles introduced or significantly changed in 2015, we do not yet have enough data to develop a complaint index.

The following table presents the projected best and worst complaint ratings for the 2015 models for which we can develop ratings. Higher index numbers mean the vehicle generated a greater number of complaints. Lower numbers indicate fewer complaints.

2015 PROJECTED COMPLAINT INDEX

THE BEST	INDEX*
Mitsubishi Outlander Sport	85
Infiniti Q60	87
Land Rover Range Rover Sport	578
Scion tC	578
Toyota Yaris	824
Infiniti QX80	858
Mercedes Benz M-Class	862
Toyota Highlander	909
Infiniti QX70	957
Lincoln Navigator	978
Lexus RX	1,110
Acura ILX	1,221
Toyota 4Runner	1,288
Toyota Prius C	1,291
Mini Countryman	1,303
Audi A5	1,308
BMW 6 Series	1,318
Toyota Tundra	1,348
Honda Civic	1,351
Mercedes Benz E-Class	1,356
Lexus GS	1,386

THE WORST	INDEX*
Acura RLX	>20,000
Fiat 500L	>20,000
Mercedes Benz CLA-Class	>20,000
Jeep Cherokee	18,813
Nissan Pathfinder	16,663
Jeep Grand Cherokee	10,221
Ford Focus	13,174
Infiniti QX60	12,355
Mitsubishi Outlander	12,251
Hyundai Santa Fe	11,975
Ford Fiesta	11,215
Kia Forte	11,166
Chevrolet Volt	10,910
Jeep Wrangler	10,745
Acura MDX	9,970
Dodge Durango	9,908
Ford C-MAX	9,908
Chevrolet Spark	9,381
Infiniti Q70	8,812

*IMPORTANT NOTE: The numbers represent relative index scores, not the number of complaints received. The complaint index score considers sales volume and years on the road. Lower index numbers are better. We capped the complaint index at 20,000 for excessively high complaint indices.

CENTER FOR AUTO SAFETY

Every year automobile manufacturers spend millions of dollars making their voices heard in government decision making. For example, General Motors and Ford have large staffs in Detroit and Washington that work solely to influence government activity. But who looks out for the consumer?

For over 40 years, the nonprofit Center for Auto Safety (CAS) has told the consumer's story to government agencies, to Congress, and to the courts. Along with countless recalls, CAS got airbags in every car and lemon laws in every state.

CAS was established in 1970 by Ralph Nader and Consumers Union. As consumer concerns about auto safety issues expanded, so did the work of CAS. CAS' activities include:

Initiating Safety Recalls: CAS analyzes over 20,000 consumer complaints each year. CAS requests government investigations and recalls of defective vehicles. CAS was responsible for the Ford Pinto faulty gas tank recall, the Firestone 500 steel-belted radial tire recall, the record recall of over three million Evenflo One Step child seats, and Jeep Grand Cherokees with Pinto like fuel systems. Other CAS influenced recalls include Fords with transmissions that jump out of park, Toyota unintended acceleration, exploding Honda airbags, Ford cruise control switch fires and many others.

Representing the Consumer in Washington: CAS follows the activities of federal agencies and Congress to ensure that they carry out their responsibilities to the American taxpayer. CAS brings a consumer's point of view to vehicle safety policies and rule-making. Since 1970, CAS has submitted more than 500 petitions and comments on federal safety standards.

One major effort on safety standards has been the successful fight to get airbags in every car. After opposing airbags for decades, the auto industry now can't get enough lifesaving airbags in cars with some models having ten airbags. With airbags to protect consumers in front and side crashes, CAS worked to strengthen weak roofs that crush in rollovers. Beginning in 2013, vehicles will have roofs more than twice as strong as before. Between stronger roofs and Electronic Stability Control deaths and serious injuries in rollovers have already decreased by more than 30% from 27,000 in 2005.

In the 1990's, CAS uncovered a fire defect that dwarfed the highly publicized flammability of the Ford Pinto. Side saddle gas tanks on full size 1973–87 GM pickups and 1988–90 crew cabs can explode on impact. Over 2,000 people have been killed in fire crashes involving these trucks. After mounting a national campaign to warn consumers to steer clear of these GM fire hazards, the Department of Transportation granted CAS' petition and conducted one of its biggest defect investigations in history. The result—GM was asked to recall its pickups. GM, sadly, denied this request and was left off with a $50 million slap on the wrist.

Exposing Secret Warranties: CAS played a prominent role in the disclosure of secret warranties, "policy adjustments," as they are called by manufacturers. These occur when an automaker agrees to pay for repair of certain defects beyond the warranty period but refuses to notify consumers. Thanks to years of CAS prodding, DOT will soon be publishing every auto company Service Bulletin on its website with a index to guide consumes to secret warranties.

Lemon Laws: CAS' work on Lemon Laws aided in the enactment of state laws which make it easier to return a defective new automobile and get money back.

Tire Ratings: Consumers have reliable treadwear ratings to help them get the most miles for their dollar thanks to a CAS' lawsuit overturning DOT's revocation of this valuable tire information program.

Legal Action: When CAS has exhausted other means of obtaining relief for consumer problems, it initiates legal action. For example, in 1978 when the Department of Energy attempted to raise the price of unleaded gasoline four cents per gallon without notice or comment, CAS succeeded in stopping this illegal move through a lawsuit, thus

TIP

CENTER FOR AUTO SAFETY ONLINE

The Center for Auto Safety has a website at www.autosafety.org to provide information to consumers and to organize consumer campaigns against auto companies on safety defects. Detailed information and advice on defects in specific makes and models are on CAS' website. Consumers with lemons can file online complaints with CAS and get referred to lemon lawyers.

www.autosafety.org

saving consumers $2 billion over 3-years.

A 1985 Center for Auto Safety lawsuit against the Environmental Protection Agency (EPA) forced the EPA to recall polluting cars, rather than let companies promise to make cleaner cars in the future. As part of the settlement, GM (which was responsible for the polluting cars) funded a $7 million methanol bus demonstration program in New York City.

In 2003, a CAS lawsuit forced the Department of Transportation to require auto companies to use more accurate tire pressure monitors on the vehicle dash that identified which tire had low pressure versus an indirect system that only told consumers they had low tire pressure on some tire.

CAS also challenges class actions settlements that don't deliver for consumers. We have knocked off coupon settlement after coupon settlement in which consumers got useless coupons to buy a new car while trial lawyers got cold cash. In 2010 we challenged a Honda Civic Hybrid gas mileage settlement that gave consumers a DVD on how to drive better. In 2009, we challenged a Ford Explorer rollover settlement that gave consumers a restricted $300-500 coupon toward a new $30,000 Ford that only 148 out of 1,000,000 class members redeemed while attorneys got $25 million in fees and costs.

CAS is your safety and lemon insurance. CAS depends on public support to do all its good work. Annual membership is $25. All contributions are tax-deductible. To contribute by credit card, go to the CAS website at: www.autosafety.org/make-donation-cas.

To contribute by mail, send a check to: Center for Auto Safety, 1825 Connecticut Ave., NW #330, Washington, DC 20009-5708.

Consumer Groups and Government

Below are the names of additional consumer groups you may find helpful:

Advocates for Highway and Auto Safety
750 First St., NE, Suite 901
Washington, DC 20002
(202) 408-1711/408-1699 fax
www.saferoads.org
An alliance of consumer, health and safety groups and insurance companies.

Consumer Action
221 Main St., Suite 480
San Francisco, CA 94105
(415) 777-9635
www.consumer-action.org
Complaint handling and advocacy related to consumer rights.

Consumers for Auto Reliability and Safety
1303 J St., Suite 270
Sacramento, CA 95814
(530) 759-9440
www.carconsumers.org
Auto safety, airbags, and lemon laws.

KIDS AND CARS
(816) 216-7085
www.kidsandcars.org
email@kidsandcars.org
Safety and advocacy related to protecting children in and around motor vehicles.

Public Health Advocacy Institute
Motor Vehicle Hazard Archives Project
www.AutoHazardInfo.org
mvhap_phai@yahoo.com
The Project's mission is to preserve and broaden access to historical and current information about motor vehicle hazards and injury control. The website offers free information about vehicle safety and motor vehicle hazard control.

SafetyBelt Safe, U.S.A.
P.O. Box 553
Altadena, CA 91003
(800) 745-SAFE
www.carseat.org
stombrella@carseat.org
Excellent information and training on child safety seats and safety belt usage.

Several federal agencies conduct automobile- related programs. Following is each agency with a description of the type of work it performs and how to contact them.

National Highway Traffic Safety Administration
1200 New Jersey Ave., SE, West Bldg.
Washington, DC 20590
(888) 327-4236/www.nhtsa.gov
www.safercar.gov
NHTSA issues safety and fuel economy standards for new motor vehicles; investigates safety defects and enforces recall of defective vehicles and equipment; conducts research and demonstration programs on vehicle safety, fuel economy, driver safety, and automobile inspection and repair; provides grants for state highway safety programs in areas such as police traffic services, driver education and licensing, emergency medical services, pedestrian safety, and alcohol abuse.

Environmental Protection Agency
1200 Pennsylvania Ave., NW
Washington, DC 20460
(202) 272-0167/www.epa.gov
www.fueleconomy.gov
EPA's responsibilities include setting and enforcing air and noise emission standards for motor vehicles and measuring fuel economy in new vehicles (EPA Fuel Economy Guide).

Federal Trade Commission
600 Pennsylvania Ave., NW
Washington, DC 20580
(202) 326-2222/www.ftc.gov
The FTC regulates advertising, credit practices, marketing abuses, and professional services and ensures that products are properly labeled (as in fuel economy ratings). The commission covers unfair or deceptive trade practices in motor vehicle sales and repairs, as well as non-safety defects.

U.S. Department of Justice
Civil Division
950 Pennsylvania Ave., NW
Washington, DC 20530
(202) 307-0066
www.justice.gov/civil
feedback@doj.gov
The DOJ enforces federal law that requires manufacturers to label new automobiles and forbids removal or alteration of labels before delivery to consumers. Labels must contain make, model, vehicle identification number, dealer's name, suggested base price, manufacturer option costs, and manufacturer's suggested retail price.

AUTOMOBILE MANUFACTURERS

Acura (Division of Honda)
Michael Accavitti, Vice President-General
Manager
See Honda for address
Customer Relations: 800-382-2238

Audi (Division of Volkswagen)
Scott Keogh, President
See Volkswagen for address
Customer Relations: 800-822-2834

BMW
Ludwig Willisch, President
300 Chestnut Ridge Road
Woodcliff Lake, NJ 07677-7731
Customer Relations: 800-831-1117

Buick (Division of General Motors)
P.O. Box 33136
Detroit, MI 48232-5136
Customer Relations: 800-521-7300

Cadillac (Division of General Motors)
P.O. Box 33169
Detroit, MI 48232-5169
Customer Relations: 800-458-8006

Chevrolet (Division of General Motors)
P.O. Box 33136
Detroit, MI 48323-5136
Customer Relations: 800-222-1020

Chrysler (Chrysler, Dodge, Jeep, Ram, Fiat)
Sergio Marchionne, CEO
1000 Chrysler Drive
Auburn Hills, MI 48326
Customer Relations: 800-247-9753

Dodge (Division of Chrysler)
P.O. Box 21-8004
Auburn Hills, MI 48321-8004
Customer Relations: 800-423-6343

Fiat (Division of Chrysler)
P.O. Box 21-8004
Auburn Hills, MI 48321-8004
Customer Relations: 888-242-6342

Ford (Ford, Lincoln)
Mark Fields, President and CEO
P.O. Box 6248
Dearborn, MI 48126
Customer Relations 800-392-3673

General Motors (Buick, Cadillac, Chevrolet, GMC)
Mary Barra, CEO
300 Renaisance Center
Detorit, MI 48265

GMC (Division of General Motors)
P.O. Box 33172
Detroit, MI 48232
Customer Relations: 800-462-8782

Honda (Honda, Acura)
Takuji Yamada, President and CEO
1919 Torrance Blvd.
Torrance, CA 90501
Customer Relations: 800-999-1009

Hyundai
David Zuchowski, President and CEO
P.O. Box 20850
Fountain Valley, CA 92728-0850
Customer Relations: 800-633-5151
Email: consumeraffairs@hmausa.com

Infiniti (Division of Nissan)
Roland Krueger, President
See Nissan for address
Customer Relations: 800-662-6200

Jaguar, Land Rover
Joachim Eberhardt, President
555 MacArthur Blvd.
Mahwah, NJ 07430
Jaguar Customer Relations: 800-452-4827
Land Rover Cust. Relations: 800-637-6837

Jeep (Division of Chrysler)
P.O. Box 21-8004
Auburn Hills, MI 48321-8004
Customer Relations: 877-426-5337

Kia
Byung Mo Ahn, CEO
P.O. Box 52410
Irvine, CA 92619-2410
Customer Relations: 800-333-4542

Lexus (Division of Toyota)
Jeff Bracken, Vice President and General
Manager
P.O. Box 2991-Mail Drop L201
Torrance, CA 90509-2991
Customer Relations: 800-255-3987

Lincoln (Division of Ford)
Kumar Galhotra, President
See Ford for address
Customer Relations: 800-521-4140

Mazda
Jim O' Sullivan, President and CEO
P.O. Box 19734
Irvine, CA 92623-9734
Customer Relations: 800-222-5500

Mercedes-Benz
Stephen Cannon, President and CEO
1 Mercedes Drive
Montvale, NJ 07645
Customer Relations 800-367-6372

Mini (Division of BMW)
David Duncan, Vice President
See BMW for address
Customer Relations: 866-275-6464

Mitsubishi
Ryujiro Kobashi, President and CEO
P.O. Box 6400
Cypress, CA 90630-9998
Customer Reloations: 800-648-7820

Nissan
Carlos Ghosn, President and CEO
P.O. Box 685003
Franklin, TN 37068-5003
Customer Relations: 800-647-7261

Porsche
Detlev von Platen, President and CEO
980 Hammond Dr., Suite 1000
Atlanta, GA 30328
Customer Relations: 800-767-7243

Ram (Division of Chrysler)
P.O. Box 21-8007
Auburn Hills, MI 48321-8004
Customer Relations: 866-726-4636

Scion (Division of Toyota)
Doug Murtha, Vice President
D102 P.O. Box 2742
Torrance, CA 90509-2742
Customer Relations: 800-707-2466

Smart (Division of Mercedes-Benz)
Mark Webster, General Manager
See Mercedes-Benz for address
Customer Relations: 800-762-7887

Subaru
Tomomi Nakamura, Chairman and CEO
P.O. Box 6000
Cherry Hill, NJ 08034-6000
Customer Relations: 800-782-2783

Telsa
Elon Musk, Chairman and CEO
3500 Deer Creek
Palo Alto, CA 94304
Customer Relations: 877-798-3752

Toyota (Toyota, Lexus, Scion)
Jim Lentz, President and CEO
19001 South Western Ave. Dept. WC11
Torrance, CA 90501
Customer Relations: 800-331-4331

Volkswagen
Michael Horn, President and CEO
2200 Ferdinand Porsche Dr.
Herndon, VA 20171
Customer Relations: 800-822-8987

Volvo
Tony Nicolosi, President and CEO
One Volvo Drive
P.O. Box 914
Rockleigh, NJ 07647
Customer Relations: 800-458-1552

LEMON LAWS

Sometimes, despite our best efforts, we buy a vehicle that just doesn't work right. There may be little problem after little problem, or perhaps one big problem that never seems to be fixed. Because of the "sour" taste that such vehicles leave in the mouths of consumers who buy them, these vehicles are known as "lemons."

In the past, it's been difficult to obtain a refund or replacement if a vehicle was a lemon. The burden of proof was left to the consumer. Because it is hard to define exactly what constitutes a lemon, many lemon owners were unable to win a case against a manufacturer. And when they won, consumers had to pay for their attorneys giving them less than if they had traded in their lemon.

Thanks to "Lemon Laws" passed by all states, lemon-aide is available when consumers get stuck with a lemon. Although there are some important state-to-state variations, all of the laws have similarities: They establish a period of coverage, usually two years from delivery or the written warranty period, whichever is shorter; they may require some form of noncourt arbitration; and most importantly they define a lemon. In most states a new car, truck, or van is "presumed" to be a lemon when it has been taken back to the shop 3 to 4 times for the same problem or is out of service for a total of 30 days during the covered period. This time does not mean consecutive days and can be for different problems. 15 states have safety lemon provisions which presume a vehicle is a lemon after only 1 to 2 repairs of a defect likely to cause death or serious injury. Be sure to keep careful records of your repairs since some states now require only one of the repairs to be within the specified time period. Thirty-three states provide for the award of attorney fees with the other 17 relying on the Federal lemon law for fees.

A vehicle may be covered by the lemon law even though it doesn't meet the "presumption."

Specific information about your state's law can be obtained from your state attorney general's office or at the Center for Auto Safety's website. The following table offers a general description of the Lemon Law in your state and what you need to do to set it in motion (Notification/Trigger). We indicate where state-run arbitration programs are available. State-run programs are the best type of arbitration. Be aware, a few state lemon laws are so bad consumers should only rely on the Federal lemon law and state contract law. We have marked these bad laws with a ☒ while the best laws have a ☑.

☑ **The Best Lemon Laws**
☒ **The Worst Lemon Laws**

Alabama	Qualification: 3 unsuccessful repairs or 30 calendar days within shorter of 24 months or 24,000 miles, provided 1 repair attempt or 1 day out of service is within shorter of 1 year or 12,000 miles. Notice/Trigger: Certified mail to manufacturer + opportunity for final repair attempt within 14 calendar days.
Alaska	Qualification: 3 unsuccessful repairs or 30 business days out of service within shorter of 1 year or warranty. Notice/Trigger: Certified mail to manufacturer + dealer (or repair agent) that problem has not been corrected in reasonable number of attempts + refund or replacement demanded within 60 days. Manufacturer has 30 calendar days for final repair attempt.
Arizona	Qualification: 4 unsuccessful repairs or 30 calendar days out of service within warranty period or shorter of 2 years or 24,000 miles. Notice/Trigger: Written notice + opportunity to repair to manufacturer.
Arkansas ☑ BEST	Qualification: 3 unsuccessful repairs, 5 total repairs of any nonconformity, or 1 unsuccessful repair of problem likely to cause death or serious bodily injury within longer of 24 months or 24,000 miles. Notice/Trigger: Certified or registered mail to manufacturer who has 10 days to notify consumer of repair facility. Facility has 10 days to repair.

L—Law specifically applies to leased vehicles; S-C—State has certified guidelines for arbitration; S-R—State-run arbitration mechanism available

California ☑ BEST	Qualification: 4 repair attempts or 30 calendar days out of service or 2 repair attempts for defect likely to cause death or serious bodily injury within shorter of 18 months or 18,000 miles, or "reasonable" number of attempts during entire express warranty period. Notice/Trigger: Direct written notice to manufacturer at address clearly specified in owner's manual. Covers small businesses with up to 5 vehicles under 10,000 pounds GVWR.
Colorado ☒ WORST	Qualification: 4 unsuccessful repairs or 30 business days out of service within shorter of 1 year or warranty. Notice/Trigger: Prior certified mail notice + opportunity to repair for manufacturer.
Connecticut	Qualification: 4 unsuccessful repairs or 30 calendar days out of service within shorter of 2 years or 24,000 miles, or 2 unsuccessful repairs of problem likely to cause death or serious bodily injury within warranty period or 1 year. Notice/Trigger: Report to manufacturer, agent, or dealer. Written notice to manufacturer only if required in owner's manual or warranty. S-R
Delaware	Qualification: 4 unsuccessful repairs or 30 calendar days out of service within shorter of 1 year or warranty. Notice/Trigger: Written notice + opportunity to repair to manufacturer.
D.C.	Qualification: 4 unsuccessful repairs or 30 calendar days out of service or 1 unsuccessful repair of safety-related defect, within shorter of 2 years or 18,000 miles. Notice/Trigger: Report to manufacturer, agent, or dealer.
Florida	Qualification: 3 unsuccessful repairs or 15 calendar days within 24 months from delivery. Notice/Trigger: Certified or express mail notice to manufacturer who has 10 days to notify consumer of repair facility plus 10 more calendar days for final repair attempt after delivery to designated dealer. S-R
Georgia	Qualification: 1 unsuccessful repair of serious safety defect or 3 unsuccessful repair attempts or 30 calendar days out of service within shorter of 24,000 miles or 24 months. Notification/Trigger: Overnight or certified mail notice return receipt requested. Manufacturer has 7 days to notify consumer of repair facility & consumer has 14 days from manufacturer receipt of original notice to deliver vehicle to repair facility. Facility has 28 calendar days from manufacturer receipt of original notice to repair. State-run arbitration mechanism available. Law specifically applies to leased vehicles.
Hawaii	Qualification: 3 unsuccessful repair attempts, or 1 unsuccessful repair attempt of defect likely to cause death or serious bodily injury, or out of service for total of 30 days within shorter of 2 years or 24,000 miles. Notice/Trigger: Written notice + opportunity to repair to manufacturer. S-R
Idaho	Qualification: 4 repair attempts or 30 business days out of service within shorter of 2 years or 24,000 miles, or 1 repair of complete failure of braking or steering likely to cause death or serious bodily injury. Notice/Trigger: Written notice to manufacturer or dealer + one opportunity to repair to manufacturer. S-R.
Illinois	Qualification: 4 unsuccessful repairs or 30 business days out of service within shorter of 1 year or 12,000 miles. Notice/Trigger: Written notice + opportunity to repair to manufacturer.
Indiana ☒ WORST	Qualification: 4 unsuccessful repairs or 30 business days out of service within shorter of 18 months or 18,000 miles. Notice/Trigger: Written notice to manufacturer only if required in the warranty.

L—Law specifically applies to leased vehicles; S-C—State has certified guidelines for arbitration; S-R—State-run arbitration mechanism available

Iowa	Qualification: 3 unsuccessful repairs, or 1 unsuccessful repair of nonconformity likely to cause death or serious bodily injury, or 30 calendar days out of service within shorter of 2 years or 24,000 miles. Notice/Trigger: Certified registered mail + final opportunity to repair within 10 calendar days of receipt of notice to manufacturer.
Kansas	Qualification: 4 unsuccessful repairs or 30 calendar days out of service or 10 total repairs within shorter of 1 year or warranty. Notice/Trigger: Actual notice to manufacturer.
Kentucky	Qualification: 4 unsuccessful repairs or 30 calendar days out of service within shorter of 1 year or 12,000 miles. Notice/Trigger: Written notice to manufacturer.
Louisiana	Qualification: 4 unsuccessful repairs or 90 calendar days out of service within shorter of 1 year or warranty. Notice/Trigger: Report to manufacturer or dealer.
Maine	Qualification: 3 unsuccessful repairs (or 1 unsuccessful repair of serious failure of brakes or steering) or 15 business days out of service within shorter of warranty or 3 years or 18,000 miles. Applies to vehicles within first 18,000 miles or 3 years regardless of whether claimant is original owner. Notice/Trigger: Written notice to manufacturer or dealer. Manufacturer has 7 business days after receipt for final repair attempt. S-R
Maryland	Qualification: 4 unsuccessful repairs, 30 calendar days out of service or 1 unsuccessful repair of braking or steering system within shorter of 15 months or 15,000 miles. Notice/Trigger: Certified mail return receipt requested + opportunity to repair within 30 calendar days of receipt of notice to manufacturer or factory branch.
Massachusetts	Qualification: 3 unsuccessful repairs or 10 business days out of service within shorter of 1 year or 15,000 miles. Notice/Trigger: Notice to manufacturer or dealer who has 7 business days to attempt final repair. S-R
Michigan	Qualification: 4 unsuccessful repairs within 2 years from date of first unsuccessful repair or 30 calendar days within shorter of 1 year or warranty. Notice/Trigger: Certified mail return receipt requested to manufacturer who has 5 business days to repair after delivery. Consumer may notify manufacturer after third repair attempt.
Minnesota	Qualification: 4 unsuccessful repairs or 30 business days or 1 unsuccessful repair of total braking or steering loss likely to cause death or serious bodily injury within shorter of 2 years or warranty. Notice/Trigger: Written notice + opportunity to repair to manufacturer, agent, or dealer.
Mississippi	Qualification: 3 unsuccessful repairs or 15 business days out of service within shorter of 1 year or warranty. Notice/Trigger: Written notice to manufacturer who has 10 business days to repair after delivery to designated dealer.
Missouri	Qualification: 4 unsuccessful repairs or 30 business days out of service within shorter of 1 year or warranty. Notice/Trigger: Written notice to manufacturer who has 10 calendar days to repair after delivery to designated dealer.
Montana	Qualification: 4 unsuccessful repairs or 30 business days out of service after notice within shorter of 2 years or 18,000 miles. Notice/Trigger: Written notice + opportunity to repair to manufacturer. S-R
Nebraska	Qualification: 4 unsuccessful repairs or 40 calendar days out of service within shorter of 1 year or warranty. Notice/Trigger: Certified mail + opportunity to repair to manufacturer.

L—Law specifically applies to leased vehicles; S-C—State has certified guidelines for arbitration; S-R—State-run arbitration mechanism available

Nevada	Qualification: 4 unsuccessful repairs or 30 calendar days out of service within shorter of 1 year or warranty. Notice/Trigger: Written notice to manufacturer.
New Hampshire	Qualification: 3 unsuccessful repairs by same dealer or 30 business days out of service within warranty. Notice/Trigger: Report to manufacturer, distributor, agent, or dealer (on forms provided by manufacturer) + final opportunity to repair before arbitration. S-R
New Jersey ☑ BEST	Qualification: 3 Unsuccessful repairs or 20 calendar days out of service within shorter of 2 years or 24,000 miles; or 1 unsuccessful repair of a serious safety defect likely to cause death or serious bodily injury. Notice/Trigger: Certified mail notice, return receipt requested to manufacturer who has 10 days to repair. Consumer may notify manufacturer at any time after the second repair attempt, or after the first repair attempt in the case of a serious safety defect.
New Mexico ☒ WORST	Qualification: 4 unsuccessful repairs or 30 business days out of service within shorter of 1 year or warranty. Notice/Trigger: Written notice + opportunity to repair to manufacturer, agent, or dealer.
New York	Qualification: 4 unsuccessful repairs or 30 calendar days out of service within shorter of 2 years or 18,000 miles. Notice/Trigger: Notice to manufacturer, agent, or dealer.
North Carolina	Qualification: 4 unsuccessful repairs within shorter of 24 months, 24,000 miles or warranty or 20 business days out of service during any 12 month period of warranty. Notice/Trigger: Written notice to manufacturer + opportunity to repair within 15 calendar days of receipt only if required in warranty or owner's manual.
North Dakota ☒ WORST	Qualification: 3 unsuccessful repairs or 30 business days out of service within shorter of 1 year or warranty. Notice/Trigger: Direct written notice + opportunity to repair to manufacturer. (Manufacturer's informal arbitration process serves as prerequisite to consumer refund or replacement.)
Ohio ☑ BEST	Qualification: 3 unsuccessful repairs of same nonconformity, 30 calendar days out of service, 8 total repairs of any nonconformity, or 1 unsuccessful repair of problem likely to cause death or serious bodily injury within shorter of 1 year or 18,000 miles. Notice/Trigger: Report to manufacturer, its agent, or dealer.
Oklahoma	Qualification: 4 unsuccessful repairs or 30 calendar days out of service within shorter of 1 year or warranty. Notice/Trigger: Written notice + opportunity to repair to manufacturer.
Oregon	Qualification: 4 unsuccessful repairs or 30 business days within shorter of 1 year or 12,000 miles. Notice/Trigger: Direct written notice + opportunity to repair to manufacturer.
Pennsylvania	Qualification: 3 unsuccessful repairs or 30 calendar days within shorter of 1 year, 12,000 miles, or warranty. Notice/Trigger: Delivery to authorized service + repair facility. If delivery impossible, written notice to manufacturer or its repair facility obligates them to pay for delivery.
Rhode Island	Qualification: 4 unsuccessful repairs or 30 calendar days out of service within shorter of 1 year or 15,000 miles. Notice/Trigger: Report to dealer or manufacturer who has 7 days for final repair opportunity.

L—Law specifically applies to leased vehicles; S-C—State has certified guidelines for arbitration; S-R—State-run arbitration mechanism available

South Carolina	Qualification: 3 unsuccessful repairs or 30 calendar days out of service within shorter of 1 year or 12,000 miles. Notice/Trigger: Certified mail + opportunity to repair (not more than 10 business days) to manufacturer only if manufacturer informed consumer of such at time of sale.
South Dakota	Qualification: 4 unsuccessful repairs, 1 of which occurred during shorter of 1 year or 12,000 miles, or 30 calendar days out of service during shorter of 24 months or 24,000 miles. Notice/Trigger: Certified mail to manufacturer + final opportunity to repair + 7 calendar days to notify consumer of repair facility.
Tennessee	Qualification: 4 unsuccessful repairs or 30 calendar days out of service within shorter of 1 year or warranty. Notice/Trigger: Certified mail notice to manufacturer + final opportunity to repair within 10 calendar days.
Texas	Qualification: 4 unsuccessful repairs when 2 occurred within shorter of 1 year or 12,000 miles, + other 2 occur within shorter of 1 year or 12,000 miles immediately following second repair attempt; or 2 unsuccessful repairs of serious safety defect when 1 occurred within shorter of 1 year or 12,000 miles + other occurred within shorter of 1 year or 12,000 miles immediately following first repair; or 30 calendar days out of service within shorter of 2 years or 24,000 miles + at least 2 attempts were made within shorter of 1 year or 12,000 miles. Notice/Trigger: Written notice to manufacturer. S-R
Utah	Qualification: 4 unsuccessful repairs or 30 business days out of service within shorter of 1 year or warranty. Notice/Trigger: Report to manufacturer, agent, or dealer. S-R
Vermont	Qualification: 3 unsuccessful repairs when at least first repair was within warranty, or 30 calendar days out of service within warranty. Notice/Trigger: Written notice to manufacturer (on provided forms) after third repair attempt, or 30 days. Arbitration must be held within 45 days after notice, during which time manufacturer has 1 final repair. S-R Note: Repairs must been done by same authorized agent or dealer, unless consumer shows good cause for taking vehicle to different agent or dealer.
Virginia	Qualification: 3 unsuccessful repairs, or 1 repair attempt of serious safety defect, or 30 calendar days out of service within 18 months. Notice/Trigger: Written notice to manufacturer. If 3 unsuccessful repairs or 30 days already exhausted before notice, manufacturer has 1 more repair attempt not to exceed 15 days.
Washington	Qualification: 4 unsuccessful repairs, 30 calendar days out of service (15 during warranty period), or 2 repairs of serious safety defect, first reported within shorter of warranty or 24 months or 24,000 miles. One repair attempt + 15 of 30 days must fall within manufacturer's express warranty of at least 1 year of 12,000 miles. Notice/Trigger: Written notice to manufacturer. S-R Note: Consumer should receive replacement or refund within 40 calendar days of request.
West Virginia ☑ BEST	Qualification: 3 unsuccessful repairs or 30 calendar days out of service or 1 unsuccessful repair of problem likely to cause death or serious bodily injury within shorter of 1 year or warranty. Notice/Trigger: Written notice + opportunity to repair to manufacturer.
Wisconsin	Qualification: 4 unsuccessful repairs or 30 calendar days out of service within shorter of 1 year or warranty. Notice/Trigger: Report to manufacturer or dealer. Note: Consumer should receive replacement or refund within 30 calendar days after offer to return title.
Wyoming	Qualification: 3 unsuccessful repairs or 30 business days out of service within 1 year. Notice/Trigger: Direct written notice + opportunity to repair to manufacturer. S-R

L—Law specifically applies to leased vehicles; S-C—State has certified guidelines for arbitration; S-R—State-run arbitration mechanism available

5 BASIC STEPS TO CAR BUYING

Buying a car means matching wits with a seasoned professional. But if you know what to expect, you'll have a much better chance of getting a really good deal!

There's no question that buying a car can be an intimidating experience. But it doesn't have to be. First of all, you have in your hands all of the information you need to make an informed choice. Secondly, if you approach the purchase logically, you'll always maintain control of the decision. Start with the following basic steps:

1 Narrow your choice down to a particular class of car—sports, station wagon, minivan, sedan, large luxury, SUV, truck, or economy car. These are general classifications and some cars may fit into more than one category. In most cases, *The Car Book* presents the vehicles by size class.

2 Determine what features are really important to you. Most buyers consider safety on the top of their list, which is why the "Safety" chapter is right up front in *The Car Book*. Airbags, power options, ABS, and the number of passengers, as well as "hidden" elements such as maintenance and insurance costs, should be considered at this stage in your selection process.

3 Find three or four cars that meet the needs you outlined above and your pocketbook. It's important not to narrow your choice down to one car because then you lose all your bargaining power in the showroom. (Why? Because you might lose the psychological ability to walk away from a bad deal!) In fact, because cars today are more similar than dissimilar, it's not hard to keep three or four choices in mind. In the car rating pages in the back of the book, we suggest some competitive choices for your consideration. For example, if you are interested in the Honda Accord, you should also consider the Toyota Camry and Ford Fusion.

4 Make sure you take a good, long test drive. The biggest car buying mistake most of us make is to overlook those nagging problems that seem to surface only after we've brought the car home. Spend at least an hour driving the car without a salesperson preferably. If a dealership won't allow you to testdrive a car without a salesperson, go somewhere else. The test-drive should include time on the highway, parking, taking the car in and out of your driveway or garage, sitting in the back seat, and using the trunk or storage area.

TIP: Whatever you do, don't talk price until you're ready to buy!

5 This is the stage most of us dread—negotiating the price. While price negotiation is a car buying tradition, a few dealers are trying to break tradition by offering so-called "no-haggle pricing." Since they're still in the minority and because it's very hard for an individual to establish true competition between dealers, we recommend avoiding negotiating altogether by using the non-profit CarBargains pricing service described on page 68.

THE 180-DEGREE TURN

TIP

When buying a car, remember that you have the most important weapon in the bargaining process: the 180-degree turn. Be prepared to walk away from a deal, even at the risk of losing the "very best deal" your salesperson has ever offered, and you will be in the best position to get a real "best deal." Remember: Dealerships need you, the buyer, to survive.

IN THE SHOWROOM

Being prepared is the best way to turn a potentially intimidating showroom experience into a profitable one. Here's some advice on handling what you'll find in the showroom.

Beware of silence. Silence is often used to intimidate, so be prepared for long periods of time when the salesperson is "talking with the manager." This tactic is designed to make you want to "just get the negotiation over with." Instead of becoming a victim, do something that indicates you are serious about looking elsewhere. Bring the classified section of the newspaper and begin circling other cars or review brochures from other manufacturers. By sending the message that you have other options, you increase your bargaining power and speed up the process.

Don't fall in love with a car. Never look too interested in any particular car. Advise family members who go with you against being too enthusiastic about any one car. Tip: Beat the dealers at their own game—bring along a friend who tells you that the price is "too much compared to the other deal," or "I really liked that other car much better," or "wasn't that other car much cheaper?"

Keep your wallet in your pocket. Don't leave a deposit, even if it's refundable. You'll feel pressure to rush your shopping, and you'll have to return and face the salesperson again before you are ready.

Shop at the end of the month. Salespeople anxious to meet sales goals are more willing to negotiate a lower price at this time.

Buy last year's model. The majority of new cars are the same as the previous year, with minor cosmetic changes. You can save considerably by buying in early fall when dealers are clearing space for "new" models. The important trade-off you make using this technique is that the carmaker may have added a new safety feature to an otherwise unchanged vehicle.

Buying from stock. You can often get a better deal on a car that the dealer has on the lot. However, these cars often have expensive options you may not want or need. Do not hesitate to ask the dealer to remove an option (and its accompanying charge) or sell you the car without charging for the option. The longer the car sits there, the more interest the dealer pays on the car, which increases the dealer's incentive to sell.

Ordering a car. Cars can be ordered from the manufacturer with exactly the options you want. Simply offering a fixed amount over invoice may be attractive because it's a sure sale and the dealership has not invested in the car. All the salesperson has to do is take your order.

If you do order a car, make sure when it arrives that it includes only the options you requested. Don't fall for the trick where the dealer offers you unordered options at a "special price," because it was their mistake. If you didn't order an option, don't pay for it.

BEWARE OF MANDATORY ARBITRATION AGREEMENTS

More and more dealers are adding mandatory binding arbitration agreements, which they often call "dispute resolution mechanisms," to your purchase contract. What this means is that you waive the right to sue or appeal any problem you have with the vehicle. Before you start negotiating the price, ask if the dealer requires Mandatory Binding Arbitration. If so, and they won't remove that requirement, you should buy elsewhere. Many dealers do not have this requirement.

GETTING THE BEST PRICE

One of the most difficult aspects of buying a new car is getting the best price. Most of us are at a disadvantage negotiating because we don't know how much the car actually cost the dealer. The difference between what the dealer paid and the sticker price represents the negotiable amount.

Beware, now that most savvy consumers know to check the so-called "dealer invoice," the industry has camouflaged this number. Special incentives, rebates, and kickbacks can account for $500 to $2,000 worth of extra profit to a dealer selling a car at "dealer invoice." The non-profit Center for the Study of Services recently discovered that in 37 percent of cases when dealers are forced to bid against each other for the sale, they offered the buyer a price below the "dealer invoice"—an unlikely event if the dealer was actually losing money. The bottom line is that "dealer invoice" doesn't really mean dealer cost.

You can't really negotiate with only one dealer, you need to get two or three bidding against each other. Introducing competition is the best way to get the lowest price on a new car. To do this you have to convince two or three dealers that you are, in fact, prepared to buy a car; that you have decided on the make, model, and features; and that your decision now rests solely on which dealer will give you the best price. You can try to do this by phone, but often dealers will not give you the best price, or will quote you a price over the phone that they will not honor later. Instead, you should try to do this in person. As anyone knows who

has ventured into an auto showroom simply to get the best price, the process can be lengthy as well as terribly arduous. Nevertheless, if you can convince the dealer that you are serious and are willing to take the time to go to a number of dealers, it will pay off. Other-wise, we suggest you use the CarBargains service described on page 68.

Here are some other showroom strategies:

Shop away from home. If you find a big savings at a dealership far from your home or on the Internet, call a local dealer with the price. They may very well match it. If not, pick up the car from the distant dealer, knowing your trip has saved you hundreds of dollars. You can still bring it to your local dealer for warranty work and repairs.

Beware of misleading advertising. New car ads are meant to get you into the showroom. They usually promise low prices, big rebates, high trade-in, and spotless integrity—don't be deceived. Advertised prices are rarely the true selling price. They usually exclude transportation charges, service fees, or document fees. And always look out for the asterisk, both in advertisements and on invoices. It can be a signal that the advertiser has something to hide.

Don't talk price until you're ready to buy. On your first few trips to the showroom, simply look over the cars, decide what options you want, and do your test-driving.

Shop the corporate twins. Page 75 contains a list of corporate twins—nearly identical cars that carry different name plates. Check the price and options of the twins of the car you like. A higher-priced twin may have more options, so it may be a better deal than the lower-priced car without the options you want.

Watch out for dealer preparation overcharges. Before paying the dealer to clean your car, make sure that preparation is not included in the basic price. The price sticker will state: "Manufacturer's suggested retail price of this model includes dealer preparation."

If you must negotiate . . . negotiate up from the "invoice" price rather than down from the sticker price. Simply make an offer close to or at the "invoice" price. If the salesperson says that your offer is too low to make a profit, ask to see the factory invoice.

Don't trade in. Although it is more work, you can usually do better by selling your old car yourself than by trading it in. To determine what you'll gain by selling the car yourself, check the NADA Official Used Car Guide at your credit union or library. On the web, the Kelly Blue Book website at kbb.com is a good source for invoice pricing. The difference between the trade-in price (what the dealer will give you) and the retail price (what you typically can sell it for) is your extra payment for selling the car yourself.

If you do decide to trade your car in at the dealership, keep the buying and selling separate. First, negotiate the best price for your new car, then find out how much the dealer will give you for your old car. Keeping the two deals separate ensures that you know what you're paying for your new car and simplifies the entire transaction.

Question everything the dealer writes down. Nothing is etched in stone. Because things are written down, we tend not to question them. This is wrong—always assume that anything written down is negotiable.

BUYING FOR SAFETY

So how do you buy for safety? Many consumers mistakenly believe that handling and performance are the key elements in the safety of a car. While an extremely unresponsive car could cause an accident, most new cars meet basic handling requirements. In fact, many people actually feel uncomfortable driving high performance cars because the highly responsive steering, acceleration, and suspension systems can be difficult to get used to. But the main reason handling is overrated as a safety measure is that automobile collisions are, by nature, accidents. Once they've begun, they are beyond human capacity to prevent, no matter how well your car handles. So the key to protecting yourself is to purchase a car that offers a high degree of crash protection.

AVOIDING LEMONS

One way to avoid the sour taste of a lemon after you've bought your car is to protect yourself before you sign on the dotted line. These tips will help you avoid problems down the road.

1 Avoid new models. Any new car in its very first year of production often turns out to have a lot of defects. Sometimes the manufacturer isn't able to remedy the defects until the second, third, or even fourth year of production. If the manufacturer has not worked out problems by the third model year, the car will likely be a lemon forever.

2 Avoid the first cars off the line. Most companies close down their assembly lines every year to make annual changes. In addition to adding hundreds of dollars to the price of a new car, these changes can introduce new defects. It can take a few months to iron out these bugs. Ask the dealer when the vehicle you are interested in was manufactured, or look on the metal tag found on the inside of the driver-side door frame to find the date of manufacture.

3 Avoid delicate options. Delicate options have the highest frequency-of-repair records. Power seats, power windows, and special roofs are nice conveniences—until they break down. Of all the items on the vehicles, they tend to be the most expensive to repair.

4 Inspect the dealer's checklist. Request a copy of the dealer's pre-delivery service and adjustment checklist (also called a "make-ready list") at the time your new vehicle is delivered. Write the request directly on the new vehicle order. This request informs the dealer that you are aware of the dealer's responsibility to check your new car for defects.

5 Examine the car on delivery. Most of us are very excited to take the vehicle home. A few minutes of careful inspection can save hours of misery later. Look over the body for any damage; check for the spare tire and jack equipment; make sure all electrical items work, and all the hubcaps and body molding are on. You may want to take a short test-drive. Finally, make sure you have the owner's manual, warranty forms, and all the legal documents.

CARBARGAINS' BEST PRICE SERVICE

Even with the information that we provide you in this chapter of *The Car Book*, many of us still will not be comfortable negotiating for a fair price. In fact, as we indicated on the previous page, we believe it's really very difficult to negotiate the best price with a single dealer. The key to getting the best price is to get dealers to compete with each other.

CarBargains is a service of the non-profit Consumers' CHECK-BOOK, a consumer group that provides comparative price and quality information for many products and services.

CarBargains will "shop" the dealerships in your area and obtain at least five price quotes for the make and model of the car that you want to buy. The dealers who submit quotes know that they are competing with other area dealerships and have agreed to honor the prices that they submit. It is important to note that CarBargains is not an auto broker or "car buying" service; they have no affiliation with dealers.

Here's how the service works:

1. You provide CarBargains with the make, model, and style of car you wish to buy (Toyota Camry XLE, for example) by phone or mail.

2. Within two weeks, CarBargains will send you dealer quote sheets from at least five local dealers who have bid against one another to sell you that car. Each dealer's offer is actually a commitment to a dollar amount above (or below) "factory invoice cost" for that model. You get the name and phone number of the manager responsible for handling the quote.

You will also receive a print-out that enables you to figure the exact cost for each available option you might want on the vehicle.

3. Determine which dealer offers the best price using the dealer quote sheets. Add up the cost including the specific options you want. Contact the sales manager of that dealership and arrange to purchase the car.

If a car with the options you want is not available on the dealer's lot, you can, in many cases, have the dealer order the car from the factory or from another dealer at the agreed price.

When you receive your quotes, you will also get some suggestions on low-cost sources of financing and a valuation of your used car (trade-in).

The price for this service ($250) may seem expensive, but when you consider the savings that will result by having dealers bid against each other, as well as the time and effort of trying to get these bids yourself, we believe it's a great value. The dealers know they have a bona fide buyer (you've paid for the service); they know they are bidding against five to seven of their competitors; and, you have Car-Bargains' experts on your side.

To obtain CarBargains' competitive price quotes, call them at 800-475-7283 or visit their website at www.carbargains.org. Or, you can send a check for $250 to CarBargains, 1625 K St., NW, 8th Floor, Washington, DC 20006. Be sure to include your complete mailing address, phone number, and e-mail address (in case of questions), and the exact make, model, style, and year of the car you want to buy. You should receive your report within two weeks.

! AUTO BROKERS !

While CarBargains is a non-profit organization created to help you find the best price for the car you want to purchase, auto brokers are typically in the business to make money. As such, the price you end up paying for the car will include additional profit for the broker. There have been cases where the auto broker makes certain promises, takes your money, and you never hear from him again. While many brokers are legitimately trying to get their customers the best price, others have developed special relationships with certain dealers and may not do much shopping for you. As a consumer, it is difficult to tell which are which. This is why we recommend CarBargains. If CarBargains is not for you, then we suggest you consider using a buying service associated with your credit union or auto club. They can arrange for the purchase of a car at some fixed price over "dealer invoice."

FINANCING

You've done your test-drive, researched prices, studied crash tests, determined the options you want, and haggled to get the best price. Now you have to decide how to pay for the car.

If you have the cash, pay for the car right away. You avoid finance charges, you won't have a large debt haunting you, and the full value of the car is yours. You can then make the monthly payments to yourself to save up for your next car.

However, most of us cannot afford to pay cash for a car, which leaves two options: financing or leasing. While leasing may seem more affordable, financing will actually cost you less. When you finance a car, you own it after you finish your payments. At the end of a lease, you have nothing. We don't recommend leasing, but if you want more information, see page 71.

Shop around for interest rates. Most banks and credit unions will knock off at least a quarter of a percent for their customers. Have these quotes handy when you talk financing with the dealer.

The higher your down payment, the less you'll have to finance. This will not only reduce your overall interest charges, but often qualifies you for a lower interest rate.

Avoid long car loans. The monthly payments are lower, but you'll pay far more in overall interest charges. For example, a two-year, $25,000 loan at 4 percent will cost you $1,055 in interest; the same amount at five years will cost you $2,625—well over twice as much!

Beware of manufacturer promotional rates—the 0 to 1 percent rates you see advertised. These low rates are usually only valid on two or three-year loans and only for the most credit-worthy customers.

Read everything you are asked to sign and ask questions about anything you don't fully understand.

Make sure that an extended warranty has not been added to the purchase price. Dealers will sometimes do this without telling you. Extended warranties are generally a bad value. See the "Warranties" chapter for more information.

Credit Unions vs. Banks: Credit unions generally charge fewer and lower fees and offer better rates than banks. In addition, credit unions offer counseling services where consumers can find pricing information on cars or compare monthly payments for financing. You can join a credit union either through your employer, an organization or club, or if you have a relative who is part of a credit union.

DON'T BE TONGUE-TIED

TIP

Beware of high-pressure phrases like "I've talked to the manager and this is really the best we can do. As it is, we're losing money on this deal." Rarely is this true. Dealers are in the business to make money and most do very well. Don't tolerate a take-it-or-leave-it attitude. Simply repeat that you will only buy when you see the deal you want and that you don't appreciate the dealer pressuring you. Threaten to leave if the dealer continues to pressure you to buy today.

Don't let the dealer answer your questions with a question. If you ask, "Can I get air conditioning with this car?" and the salesperson answers, "If I get you air conditioning in this car, will you buy today?" this response tries to force you to decide to buy before you are ready. Ask the dealer to just answer your question and say that you'll buy when you're ready. It's the dealer's job to answer questions, not yours.

If you are having a difficult time getting what you want, ask the dealer: "Why won't you let me buy a car today?" Most salespeople will be thrown off by this phrase as they are often too busy trying to use it on you. If they respond in frustration, "OK, what do you want?" then you can make straightforward answers to simple questions.

Get a price; don't settle for: "If you're shopping price, go to the other dealers first and then come back." This technique ensures that they don't have to truly negotiate. Your best response is: "I only plan to come back if your price is the lowest, so that's what I need today, your lowest price."

TYPICAL OPERATING COSTS

Here are the annual operating costs for some popular vehicles. These costs include operating expenses (fuel, oil, maintenance, and tires) and ownership expenses (insurance, financing, taxes, depreciation, and licensing) and are based on keeping the vehicle for 3 years and driving 20,000 miles per year. This information is from Runzheimer International. Runzheimer evaluated thirty 2015 model cars, vans, SUVs, and light trucks and determined the most and least expensive to operate among those vehicles. (Source: Runzheimer International, www.runzheimer.com)

Projected Ownership and Operating Costs for Selected 2015 Cars

Most Expensive

Hyundai Equus Signature 8-cyl. 5.0L	$24,802
Mercedes-Benz E350 6-cyl. 3.5L	$21,243
Cadillac CTS Luxury 6-cyl. 3.6L	$20,640
Buick Lacrosse Leather 6-cyl. 3.6L	$17,061
Ford Taurus Limited AWD 6-cyl. 3.5L	$16,685

Least Expensive

Ford Fusion SE 4-cyl. 2.5L	$11,793
Nissan Altima S 4-cyl. 2.5L	$11,390
Mazda Mazda3 I Touring 4-cyl. 2.0L	$10,344
Chevrolet Sonic LT 4-cyl. 1.8L	$10,055
Toyota Corolla LE 4-cyl. 1.8L	$9,751

Projected Ownership and Operating Costs for Selected 2015 Light Trucks, Vans, and SUVs

Most Expensive

Chevrolet Tahoe LS 4WD 8-cyl. 5.3L	$18,396
GMC Sierra 2500 Work 8-cyl. 6.0L	$17,578
Dodge Grand Caravan R/T 6-cyl. 3.6L	$14,866
Jeep Grand Cherokee Laredo 6-cyl. 3.6L	$14,088
Chevrolet Silverado 1500 LS 6-cyl. 4.3L	$13,569

Least Expensive

Chevrolet Equinox 2LT FWD 4-cyl. 2.4L	$13,042
Chevrolet Silverado 1500 Work 2WD 6-cyl. 4.3L	$12,749
Ford Escape SE ECO 4-cyl. 2L	$12,508
Dodge Grand Caravan AVP 6-cyl. 3.6L	$12,412
Toyota Tacoma Prerunner 4-cyl. 2.7L	$10,217

LEASING VS. BUYING

Because the unpredictibility of the value of a vehicle at the end of a lease, more and more companies are getting out of the leasing business. That's good news because, in general, leasing costs more than buying outright or financing. When you pay cash or finance a car, you own an asset; leasing leaves you with nothing except all the headaches and responsibilities of ownership with none of the benefits. When you lease you pay a monthly fee for a predetermined time in exchange for the use of a car. However, you also pay for maintenance, insurance, and repairs as if you owned the car. Finally, when it comes time to turn in the car, it has to be in top shape—otherwise, you'll have to pay for repairs or body work.

If you are considering a lease, here are some leasing terms you need to know and some tips to get you through the process:

Capitalized Cost is the price of the car on which the lease is based. Negotiate this as if you were buying the car. Capitalized Cost Reduction is your down payment.

Know the make and model of the vehicle you want. Tell the agent exactly how you want the car equipped. You don't have to pay for options you don't request. Decide in advance how long you will keep the car.

Find out the price of the options on which the lease is based. Typically, they will be full retail price. Their cost can be negotiated (albeit with some difficulty) before you settle on the monthly payment.

Make sure options like a sunroof or stereo are added to the Capitalized Cost. When you purchase dealer-added options, be sure they add the full cost of the option to the Capitalized Cost so that you only pay for the depreciated value of the option, not the full cost.

Find out how much you are required to pay at delivery. Most leases require at least the first month's payment. Others have a security deposit, registration fees, or other "hidden costs." When shopping around, make sure price quotes include security deposit and taxes—sales tax, monthly use tax, or gross receipt tax. Ask how the length of the lease affects your monthly cost.

Find out how the lease price was determined. Lease prices are generally based on the manufacturer's suggested retail price, less the predetermined residual value. The best values are cars with a high expected residual value. To protect themselves, leasers tend to underestimate residual value, but you can do little about this estimate.

Find out the annual mileage limit. Don't accept a contract with a lower limit than you need. Most standard contracts allow 15,000 to 18,000 miles per year. If you go under the allowance one year, you can go over it the next. Watch out for Excess Mileage fees. If you go over, you'll get charged per mile.

Avoid "capitalized cost reduction" or "equity leases." Here the leaser offers to lower the monthly payment by asking you for more money up front—in other words, a down payment.

Ask about early termination. Between 30 and 40 percent of two-year leases are terminated early and 40–60 percent of four-year leases terminate early—this means expensive early termination fees. If you terminate the lease before it is up, what are the financial penalties? Typically, they are very high so watch out. Ask the dealer exactly what you would owe at the end of each year if you wanted out of the lease. Remember, if your car is stolen, the lease will typically be terminated. While your insurance should cover the value of

---

LEASEWISE

If you must lease, why haggle when you can let someone else do it for you? LeaseWise, a service from the non-profit Center for the Study of Services, makes dealers bid for your lease. First, they get leasing bids from dealers on the vehicles you're interested in. Next, you'll receive a detailed report with all the bids, the dealer and invoice cost of the vehicle, and a complete explanation of the various bids. Then, you can lease from the lowest bidder or use the report as leverage with another dealer. The service costs $350. For more information, call 800-475-7283, or visit www.checkbook.org/auto/leasew.cfm

the car, you still may owe additional amounts per your lease contract.

Avoid maintenance contracts. Getting work done privately is cheaper in the long run. And don't forget, this is a new car with a standard warranty.

Arrange for your own insurance. By shopping around, you can generally find less expensive insurance than what's offered by the leaser.

Ask how quickly you can expect delivery. If your agent can't deliver in a reasonable time, maybe he or she can't meet the price quoted.

Retain your option to buy the car at the end of the lease at a predetermined price. The price should equal the residual value; if it is more then the leaser is trying to make an additional profit. Regardless of how the end-of-lease value is determined, if you want the car, make an offer based on the current "Blue Book" value of the car at the end of the lease.

Residual Value is the value of your car at the end of the lease.

Here's what Automotive Lease Guide estimates the residual value after five years will be for a few 2015 vehicles:

Acura MDX	42%
Subaru Forester	41%
Hyundai Elantra	40%
Jeep Patriot	34%
Nissan Titan	32%

LEASING VS. BUYING

The following table compares the costs of leasing vs. buying the same car over three and six years. Your actual costs may vary, but you can use this format to compare the cars you are considering. Our example assumes the residual value to be 68 percent after three years and 43 percent after six years.

3 Years	Lease 36 month Year Lease	Finance 5 Year Loan 4.5% Sell in 3 years
MSRP	$29,000.00	$29,000.00
Lease Value/Purchase Cost of Car[1]	$26,100.00	$26,100.00
Initial Payment/Down Payment[2]	$2,365.00	$2,610.00
Loan Amount		$23,490.00
Monthly Payments2	$248.00	$438.00
Total Payments (first 3 years of loan)[3]	$8,928.00	$15,768.00
Amount Left on Loan		$9,633.00
Less Value of Vehicle .68 residual		$19,720.00
Excess miles and disposition fees[4]	$825.00	
Overall Cost, first 3 years	**$12,118.00**	**$8,291.00**
Savings over Leasing 3 Years		$3,827.00

6 Years[56]	Lease 2-3 Year Lease	Finance 5 Yr Loan 4.5%- Keep Car 6 years
MSRP-2nd Car 5% increase in cost	$30,450.00	$29,000.00
Lease Value/Purchase Cost of Car	$27,405.00	$26,100.00
Initial Payment/Down Payment[2]	$2,740.50	$2,610.00
Loan Amount		$23,490.00
Monthly Payment[2]	$248.00	$438.00
Total Payments	$8,928.00	$26,280.00
Amount Left on Loan		$-
Less Value of Vehicle .43 residual 6 yrs[7]		$12,470.00
Excess miles and disposition fees[4]	$825.00	
Overall Cost, 6 years[8]	**$21,871.00**	**$16,420.00**
Savings Over Leasing 6 Years		$5,451.00

[1]Purchase Cost of car reflects fact that very few buyer's pay MSRP for a new car and is representative of 90% of MSRP
[2]Initial lease and monthly payments based on lease deals for January 2012 offered by major manufactures on US News and World Report; Monthly loan payments and amount left on loan were calculated using bankrate.com Car Payment Calculator and Amortization Table
[3]First 3 years of 5 year loan with 4.5 percent annaul percentage rate.
[4]Total average excess miles fee of $475 based on 12000 miles limit and 25% of consumers driving over the mile limit unexpectedly for 1500 miles with charges of $0.17/mile, 50% pre-paying for expected mile overages of 1500 miles at $0.12/mile, and 25% not exceeding the mileage limit. Disposition fee based on average of $350.
[5]Second 3-year lease costs assume a 5% increase for a similar vehicle
[6]Five-year loan with 4.5 percent annual percentage rate, no monthly payment in the sixth year
[7]Three-year residual value 68 percent based on average actual 36-month residual value for the top 100 selling vehicles for model year 2006, 07 and 08. Six-year residual value 43 percent based on average actual 36-month residual value for the top 100 selling vehicles for model year 2003, 04 and 05.
[8]Six-year overall cost for lease is total of first 3-year lease and second 3-year lease

USING THE INTERNET

The Internet is changing the way car buyers research and shop for cars. But the Internet should be used with caution. Anyone—and we mean *anyone*—can publish a website with no guarantee concerning the accuracy of the information on it. We advise that you only visit websites that have a familiar non-web counterpart. A good example is the Center for Auto Safety's website at www.autosafety.org where you can find information on auto safety, including publications and newsletters which are typically mailed out to subscribers.

Use the Internet as an information resource. Unfortunately, most automaker websites are nothing more than sophisticated ads with little comparative information.

Good information, like pricing and features, *can* be found online. We've listed some useful websites on this page.

There are also several online car shopping services that have launched. We view most of them with skepticism. Many online car shopping services are tied to a limited, often non-competitive, group of dealers. They may claim the lowest price, but you'll most likely have a dealer calling you with a price that is not much better than what you'd get if you went into a dealership to haggle.

Auto insurance and financing sites are sometimes no better. Don't rely solely on these online services; getting quotes from other sources is the only way to make sure you truly have the best deal.

Finally, clicking a mouse is no substitute for going out and test-driving a car. If you are shopping for a used car, you must check out the actual car before signing on the dotted line. Do not rely on online photos. In fact, online classifieds for cars are no more reliable than looking in a newspaper.

If you do use an online car shopping service, be sure to shop around on your own. Visit dealerships, get quotes from several car shopping services, and research the value of your used car (see www.nadaguides.com). Beware that if you give anyone online your phone number, or email address, you are opening yourself up to unwanted email, junk mail, and even sales calls.

ON THE WEB

autosafety.org
The Center for Auto Safety (CAS) provides consumers with a voice for auto safety and quality in Washington and to help lemon owners fight back across the country.

carfax.com
Used car buyers will want to visit Carfax. Carfax collects information from numerous sources to provide a vehicle history on a specific vehicle, based on the Vehicle Identification Number (VIN). Carfax can help uncover costly and potentially dangerous hidden problems or confirm the clean history of a vehicle.

checkbook.org
The Center for the Study of Services (CSS) is an independent, nonprofit consumer organization and the creator of Consumers' CHECKBOOK. One of the few car buying services worth using, CHECKBOOK's CarBargains service pits dealers against each other, keeping you from haggling, and using the power of competitive bidding to get you a great price.

nhtsa.gov
The National Highway Traffic Safety Administration (NHTSA) website contains useful information on safety standards, crash tests, recalls, technical service bulletins, child seats, and safety advisories.

fueleconomy.gov
This joint effort by the Department of Energy and the Environmental Protection Agency contains EPA fuel economy ratings for passenger cars and trucks from 1985 to the present, gas saving tips, greenhouse gas and air pollution ratings, energy impact scores, a downloadable Fuel Economy Guide, and a variety of other useful information in a very user-friendly format.

DEPRECIATION

Over the past 20 years, new vehicle depreciation costs have steadily increased. A study conducted by Runzheimer International shows that depreciation and interest now account for just over 50 percent of the costs of owning and operating a vehicle. Recently, however, the increasing cost of depreciation has slowed down. This is due to the relatively stable prices of new vehicles and to the stabilization in finance rates. Gasoline consumes an unpredicatable per-centage of the automotive dollar. While early 2015 saw some low gas prices–they always spike higher after a low point. Other costs, including insurance, maintenance, and tires, have remained at relatively steady shares of the automotive dollar.

While there is no foolproof method for predicting retained vehicle value, your best bet is to purchase a popular vehicle model. Chances are it will also be a popular used vehicle model, meaning that the retained value may be higher when you go to sell it.

Most new cars are traded in within four years and are then available on the used car market. The priciest used cars may not be the highest quality. Supply and demand, as well as appearance, are important factors in determining used car prices.

The following table indicates which of the top-selling 2011 cars held their value the best and which did not.

2011 VEHICLES WITH THE BEST AND WORST RESALE VALUE

THE BEST				THE WORST			
Model	2011 Price	2014 Price	Retain. Value	Model	2011 Price	2014 Price	Retain. Value
Toyota Tacoma	$27,025	$26,750	99.0%	Chevrolet Impala	$24,390	$12,275	50.3%
Jeep Wrangler	$22,045	$20,325	92.2%	Buick Regal	$26,245	$13,500	51.4%
Toyota 4Runner	$31,415	$28,200	89.8%	Dodge Grand Caravan	$24,995	$13,650	54.6%
Toyota Tundra	$30,715	$26,050	84.8%	Cadillac CTS	$35,165	$19,375	55.1%
Nissan Frontier	$25,510	$20,950	82.1%	Buick LaCrosse	$26,495	$14,650	55.3%
Jeep Patriot	$17,695	$14,475	81.8%	Chrys. Town & Country	$30,160	$16,700	55.4%
Toyota Highlander	$27,390	$22,175	81.0%	Ford Expedition	$42,015	$23,325	55.5%
Subaru Forester	$21,695	$17,425	80.3%	Chevrolet Malibu	$21,975	$12,275	55.9%
Honda Fit	$15,900	$12,550	78.9%	Merc.-Benz E-class	$49,400	$28,100	56.9%
Toyota Prius	$21,650	$17,075	78.9%	Chevrolet HHR	$18,720	$10,850	58.0%
Ford Ranger	$17,935	$13,725	76.5%	Buick Enclave	$37,615	$21,850	58.1%
Dodge Challenger	$24,670	$18,675	75.7%	Nissan Maxima	$30,810	$17,975	58.3%
Ram 1500	$29,075	$22,000	75.7%	Mazda Mazda6	$20,990	$12,275	58.5%
Chevrolet Camaro	$22,680	$16,925	74.6%	Chevrolet Express	$28,700	$16,825	58.6%
Ford F-150	$29,385	$21,800	74.2%	Chevrolet Traverse	$31,224	$18,350	58.8%
Nissan Versa	$12,240	$9,075	74.1%	Ford Focus	$16,640	$9,850	59.2%
Toyota Corolla	$16,400	$12,150	74.1%	Dodge Caliber	$16,880	$10,100	59.8%
Subaru Impreza	$18,495	$13,650	73.8%	Nissan Murano	$30,100	$18,150	60.3%
Nissan Juke	$18,960	$13,975	73.7%	GMC Acadia	$33,840	$20,450	60.4%
Kia Soul	$16,495	$12,100	73.4%	Volkswagen Golf	$19,065	$11,575	60.7%
Lexus RX	$39,375	$28,825	73.2%	Merc.-Benz M-class	$46,490	$28,375	61.0%
Kia Sportage	$21,795	$15,775	72.4%	Chrysler 200	$19,245	$11,800	61.3%
Toyota RAV4	$23,325	$16,775	71.9%	Dodge Avenger	$19,245	$11,825	61.4%
Jeep Grand Cherokee	$32,215	$23,150	71.9%	Dodge Journey	$22,245	$13,750	61.8%
Mini Cooper S	$23,000	$16,475	71.6%	Audi A4	$31,950	$19,825	62.1%

CORPORATE TWINS

"Corporate twins" refers to vehicles that have different names but share the same mechanics, drivetrain, and chassis. In many cases the vehicles are identical. Sometimes the difference is in body style, price, or options as with the Chevrolet Tahoe and the Cadillac Escalade. Traditionally, corporate twins have been limited mainly to domestic car companies. However, several Asian and European car companies have started the practice.

CORPORATE TWINS

Chrysler Corp.
Chrysler 300
Dodge Charger

Ford Motor Co.
Ford Escape
Lincoln MKC

Ford Expedition
Lincoln Navigator

Ford Fusion
Lincoln MKZ

General Motors
Buick Encore
Chevrolet Trax

Buick LaCrosse
Cadillac XTS
Chevrolet Impala

Buick Regal
Chevrolet Malibu

Buick Verano
Chevrolet Cruze

Cadillac Escalade
Chevrolet Tahoe
GMC Yukon

General Motors (cont.)
Cadillac Escalade ESV
Chevrolet Suburban
GMC Yukon XL

Chevrolet Colorado
GMC Canyon

Chevrolet Equinox
GMC Terrain

Chevrolet Silverado
GMC Sierra

Chevrolet Traverse
GMC Acadia

Honda
Acura ILX
Honda Civic

Acura TLX
Honda Accord

Hyundai-Kia
Hyundai Accent
Kia Rio

Hyundai Azera
Kia Cadenza

Hyundai Elantra
Kia Forte

Hyundai-Kia (cont.)
Hyundai Santa Fe Sport
Kia Sorento

Hyundai Tucson
Kia Sportage

Nissan
Nissan Pathfinder
Infiniti QX60

Toyota
Lexus ES
Toyota Avalon

Lexus NX
Toyota RAV4

Lexus GX
Toyota 4Runner

Scion FR-S
Subaru BRZ

Volkswagen-Audi-Porsche
Audi A3
Volkswagen Golf

Audi Q3
Volkswagen Tiguan

Porsche Cayenne
Volkswagen Touareg

Cadillac Escalade

Chevrolet Tahoe

GMC Yukon

T his section provides an overview of the most important features of this year's new models. Nearly all the information you'll need to make a smart choice is concisely presented on one page. (The data are collected for the model expected to be the most popular.) Here's what you'll find and how to interpret the data we've provided:

The Ratings

These are the ratings in nine important categories, as well as an overall comparative rating. We have adopted the Olympic rating system with "10" being the best.

Overall Rating: This is the "bottom line." Using a combination of all of the key ratings, this tells how this vehicle stacks up against the others on a scale of 1 to 10. Due to the importance of safety, the combined crash test rating is 20 percent of the overall rating while the other eight ratings are 10 percent each. Vehicles with no front or side crash test results, as of our publication date, cannot be given an overall rating. In other categories, if information is unavailable, an "average" is included in order to develop an overall rating.

Overall Crash Test: This rating represents a combination of the front and side crash test ratings and provides a relative comparison of how this year's models did against each other. We give the best performers a 10 and the worst a 1. Remember to compare crash test results relative to other cars in the same size class. For details, see page 19.

Safety Features: This is an evaluation of how much extra safety is built into the car. We give credit for torso and pelvis side airbags, roll-sensing side airbags, knee bolster bag, crash imminent braking, daytime running lamps, adjustable upper seat belt anchorages, lane keeping assist, pedestrian crash avoidance, automatic crash notification, lane departure warning, dynamic brake support, and frontal collision warning. We also include dynamic head restraint, backup cameras and blind spot detection among other important safety features. See the "Safety Checklist" box on each page for more details.

Rollover: Many consumers are aware that vehicles with higher centers of gravity could be more likely to roll over. Comparing the tendency of a vehicle to roll over is very difficult, as there is no agreed upon comparative rating system. The U.S. government adopted the rating system that we have been using called the static stability formula (SSF). The government provides the SSF rating for some vehicles. For those vehicles not on the government list, we use the SSF formula to provide a rating. The details behind the SSF appear on page 32.

Preventive Maintenance: Each manufacturer suggests a preventive maintenance schedule designed to keep the car in good shape and to protect your rights under the warranty. Those with the lowest estimated PM costs get a 10 and the highest a 1. See pages 39-43 for the estimated costs and more information.

Repair Costs: It is virtually impossible to predict exactly what any new car will cost you in repairs. As such, we take nine typical repairs that you are likely to experience after your warranty expires and compare those costs among this year's models. Those with the lowest cost get a 10 and the highest a 1. See pages 39-43 for specific part repair cost and more information.

Warranty: This is an overall assessment of the manufacturer's basic, powertrain, corrosion, and roadside assistance warranties compared to all other manufacturer warranties. We also give credit for perks like free scheduled maintenance. We give the highest-rated warranties a 10 and the lowest a 1. For details, see page 36.

Fuel Economy: Here we compare the EPA mileage ratings of each car. The misers get a 10 and the guzzlers get a 1. For the purposes of the overall rating we pick the fuel economy rating of what is expected to be the most popular engine and drive train configuration. See page 33 for more information.

Complaints: This is where you'll find how each vehicle stacks up against hundreds of others on the road, based on the U.S. government complaint data for that vehicle. If the car has not been around long enough to have developed a complaint history, it is given a 5 (average).

The least complained about cars get a 10 and the most problematic a 1. See page 55 for details.

Insurance Costs: Insurance companies rate vehicles to determine how much they plan to charge for insurance. While each insurer may have slightly different methods of rating, vehicles typically get a discount (max and min), a surcharge (max and min) or neither (average or typical). We looked at data from the insurance rating program of the largest insurer in America. This rating can predict the cost of insuring that vehicle, however, your location, age, driving record, and other factors also play a significant role in your cost of insurance. (See The Insurance Section page 49.) Vehicles with a low rating (1 or 3) are more expensive to insure than other vehicles in that class or category. On the other hand, vehicles with a high rating (8 or 10) would be less expensive to insure in that particular class of vehicles. Because insurance companies may rate vehicles differently, it's important to compare prices between companies before you buy the car.

At-a-Glance

Status: Here we tell you if a vehicle is all-new, unchanged, or has received appearance change. All-new vehicles (the minority) are brand new from the ground up. Unchanged vehicles are essentially the same, but could have some different color or feature options. Vehicles with an appearance change are those whose internal workings stayed essentially the same, but have updated body panels.

Year Series Started: We generally recommend against buying a car during its first model year of production. Each year the model is made, the production usually improves and as a result there are fewer defects. Therefore, the longer a car has been made, the less likely you are to be plagued with manufacturing and design defects. On the other hand, the newer a car is, the more likely it is to have the latest in features and safety.

Twins: These are cars with different make and model names but share the same mechanics, drive train, and chassis. In some cases the vehicles are identical, in other cases the body style, pricing or options are different.

Body Styles: This is a listing of the various body styles available such as coupe, sedan, wagon, etc. SUVs and minivans are only offered in one body style. Data on the page are for the first style listed.

Seating: This is the number of seating positions in the most popular model. When more than one number is listed (for example, 5/6) it means that different seat configurations are available.

Anti-theft Device: This lists the anti-theft devices standard for the vehicle. An immobilizer is an electronic device fitted to an automobile which prevents the engine from running unless the correct key (or other token) is present. This prevents the car from being "hot-wired" and driven away. A car alarm is an electronic device that emits high-volume sound and can sometimes flash the vehicles headlights in an attempt to discourage theft of the vehicle itself, its contents, or both. Passive devices automatically enter an armed state after the ignition is turned off and doors are closed. Active devices require the user to perform some action like pressing a button to arm and disarm the system.

Parking Index Rating: Using the car's length, wheelbase, and turning circle, we have calculated how easy it will be to maneuver this car in tight spots. This rating of "very easy" to "very hard" is an indicator of how much difficulty you may have parking.

Where Made: Here we tell you where the car was assembled. You'll find that traditional domestic companies often build their vehicles in other countries. Also, many foreign companies build their cars in the U.S.

Fuel Factor

MPG Rating (city/hwy): This is the EPA-rated fuel economy for city and highway driving measured in miles per gallon. Most models have a variety of fuel economy ratings because of different engine and transmission options. We've selected the combination expected to be most popular.

Driving Range: Given the car's expected fuel economy and gas tank size, this value gives you an idea of the number of miles you can expect to go on one tank of gas.

Fuel: The type of fuel specified by the manufacturer: regular, premium, E85.

Annual Fuel Cost: This is an estimate based on driving 15,000 miles per year at $2.80/gallon for regular and $3.20/gallon for premium. If the vehicle takes E85 (85% ethanol and 15% gasoline) or gasoline we calculated the annual cost using gasoline.

Gas Guzzler Tax: Auto companies are required to pay a gas guzzler tax on the sale of cars with exceptionally low fuel economy. This tax does not apply to light trucks.

Greenhouse Gas Emissions: This shows the amount (in tons) of greenhouse gases (carbon dioxide, nitrous oxide, and methane) that a vehicle emits per year along with the CO_2 emitted in producing and distributing the fuel.

Barrels of Oil Used Per Year: This is the number of barrels of petroleum the vehicle will likely use each year. One barrel, once refined, makes about 19.5 gallons of gas.

Competition

Here we tell you how the car stacks up with some of its key competitors. Use this information to broaden your choice of new car possibilities. This list is only a guideline, not an all-inclusive list of every possible alternative.

Price Range

This box contains information on the MSRP. When available, we offer a variety of prices between the base and the most luxurious version of the car. The difference is often substantial. Usually the more expensive versions have fancy trim, larger engines, and lots of automatic

equipment. The least expensive versions usually have manual transmissions and few extra features. In addition to the price range, we provide the estimated dealer markup. Be prepared for higher retail prices when you get to the showroom. Manufacturers like to load their cars with factory options, and dealers like to add their own items such as fabric protection and paint sealant. Remember, prices and dealer costs can change during the year. Use these figures for general reference and comparisons, not as a precise indication of exactly how much the car you are interested in will cost.

See page 68 for a buying service designed to ensure that you get the very best price.

Safety Checklist

Crash Tests

Frontal and Side Crash Test Ratings: Here's where we tell you if the front or side crash test index was very good, good, average, poor or very poor when compared to 2015 cars tested to date. To provide this rating we use the crash test for the vehicles with the best available safety equipment among the models

TYPES OF AIRBAGS

Airbags were introduced over 30 years ago and have been so successful in saving lives that car makers now include a variety of types. Here's a rundown of the basic types of airbags available. Manufacturers have varying marketing names for these airbags.

Front: These deploy toward the front occupants and are now standard in all vehicles.

Side: These deploy from the side of the seat or door and protect both the front and rear passengers in a side impact. Bags mounted in seats offer protection in a wider range of seating positions.

Head: These deploy from above the doors and are often called curtain airbags. They can reduce head injuries, shield from spraying glass, and provide protection in rollovers.

Rollover Protection: These head curtain airbags remain inflated for five seconds to protect in a sustained rollover.

Knee Bolster: These fill space between the front occupant's knees and instrument panel protecting the knees and legs.

when multiple models were tested. Unfortunately, not all of the 2015 models have been crash tested. If the car has been previously tested and the 2015 model is unchanged, we can carry those results forward. For details about the crash test programs, see page 19.

Airbags

All vehicles have dual front airbags and nearly all have head airbags. We've identified four additional types of airbags that the vehicle may have. The first two we list, Torso and Pelvis, have historically been seperate bag systems. Recently, most manufaturers have been combining torso and pelvis protection into one bag. When the two are combined, we list *Front Pelvis/Torso from Seat* after each airbag type. Otherwise we identify specific bag type (or not) that comes with the vehicle.

Torso Side Airbag: This type of side airbag protects the chest from serious injury in a side impact crash.

Pelvis Side Airbag: Provides extra protection around the pelvis and hip area, as this portion of the body is usually closest to the vehicles interior.

Rollover Sensing Airbags: Some companies offer a special side airbag system which keeps the side airbags inflated longer in the event of a rollover. This can reduce the likelihood of injury when a vehicle flips.

Knee Bolster Airbag: The airbag is inflated to fill space between the knees of the front occupant and the instrument panel.

Crash Avoidance

Collision Avoidance: Great new technology is available that is designed to react faster than you can in the event of a frontal collision. These systems are designed to be most effective in lower speed collisions. There are three basic technologies available and are combined in this safety feature rating: Crash Imminent Braking (CIB), Dynamic Brake Support (DBS), and Frontal Collision Warning (FCW). All of these systems use radar or laser sensors to either alert the driver (FCW) or actively intervene to apply the brakes prior to a crash. Crash Imminent Braking will actually apply the brakes if you are about to experience a frontal crash. Dynamic Brake Support will increase your braking force if the sensors determine that you are not applying enough force to stop the car in time. Frontal Collision Warning will merely sound an alarm in the event of an imminent frontal collision. We believe that Crash Imminent Braking and Dynamic Brake Support are more useful than Frontal Collision Warning (and thus rated higher), however Frontal Collision Warning is still a useful safety feature.

Blind Spot Detection: This is a blind spot monitor that uses radar or other technologies to detect objects in the driver's blind spot. When switching lanes a visible and/or audible alert warns if a vehicle has entered your blind spot.

Lane Keeping Assist: Going one step beyond a Lane Departure Warning, cars with this technology will actually apply pressure to the brakes

or adjust the steering when it senses that a car is drifting out of its lane. Lane Departure Warning will simply alert the driver. We have combined the two since the technology for Lane Departure Warning is required for Lane Keeping Assist, which we believe to be a better technology.

Backup Camera: This camera placed on the rear of the car and allows the driver to see what is behind them on a dashboard screen. It will also alert you to an object that is in the way of your car. This is a critically important safety feature if you have children or drive near or around children.

Pedestrian Crash Avoidance: These systems utilize a variety of technologies (infrared, camera, radar) to detect pedestrians and adjust the car's course to avoid a collision.

General

Automatic Crash Notification: Using cellular technology and global positioning systems, some vehicles have the ability to send a call for help in the event of airbag deployment or accident. Often free initially, you'll have to pay extra for this feature. There are several different types of ACN system. Some simply dial 911 in the event of a crash while others connect your car to a call center which can determine the severity of the crash and dispatch emergency services. Some systems even send information about the crash to the call center.

Daytime Running Lights: Some cars offer daytime running lights that can reduce your chances of being in a crash by up to 40 percent by increasing the visibility of your vehicle. We indicate whether daytime running lights are standard, optional, or not available.

Safety Belts/Restraints

Dynamic Head Restraints: Many people position their seat and head restraint according to their own body and comfort requirements. This may not be the best position to protect you in a crash. These adjustors, sensing a crash, will automatically move the seat and headrest to the optimal position to help reduce injury during a rear-end crash.

Adjustable Belts: Proper positioning of the safety belt across your chest is critical to obtaining the benefits of buckling up. Some systems allow you to adjust the height of the belt so it crosses your chest properly.

Specifications

Drive: This indicates the type of drive the manufacturer offers. This could be two wheel drive in the front (FWD) or rear (RWD) or all or four wheel drive (AWD/4WD).

Engine: This is the engine size (liters) and type that is expected to be the most popular. The engine types specify V6 or V8 for six or eight cylinders and I4 for four in-line.

Transmission: This is the type of transmission expected to be the most popular. Most drivers today prefer automatic transmissions. The number listed with the transmission (5-sp.) is the number of gears or speeds.

Then we list whether it's automatic or manual and if the transmission is a continuously variable transmission (CVT). CVT changes smoothly and efficiently between gears. This can provide better fuel economy than other transmissions by enabling the engine to run at its most efficient speed.

Tow Rating: Ratings of very low, low, average, high, and very high indicate the vehicle's relative ability to tow trailers or other loads. Some manufacturers do not provide a tow rating.

Head/Leg Room: This tells how roomy the front seat is. The values are given in inches and rated in comparison to all other vehicles.

Interior Space: This tells how roomy the car's passenger area should feel. This value is given in cubic feet and rated in comparison to all other vehicles. Many SUVs do not provide interior space specifications.

Cargo Space: This gives you the cubic feet available for cargo. For minivans, the volume is behind the last row of seats. In cars, it's the trunk space. We rate the roominess of the cargo space compared to all trucks, SUVs, and cars.

Wheelbase/Length: The wheelbase is the distance between the centers of the front and rear wheels and the length is the distance from front bumper to rear bumper. Wheelbase can affect the ride and length affects how big the car "feels."

DESTINATION CHARGES

Destination charges are a non-negotiable part of buying a new car, no matter where you purchase it. They are an important factor when comparing prices. You'll find the destination charges on the price sticker attached to the vehicle. According to automakers, destination charges are the cost of shipping a vehicle from its "final assembly point" to the dealership. But, the following table illustrates that there is little correlation between destination charges and where the cars are assembled:

Vehicle	Destination Charge*	Assembly Country
Chevrolet Silverado	$1195	U.S.A.
Jeep Patriot	$995	U.S.A.
BMW 5 Series	$950	Germany
Kia Forte	$800	South Korea

*Data based on 2015 model year cars.

Acura ILX   Compact

Ratings—10 Best, 1 Worst

Combo Crash Tests	5
Safety Features	2
Rollover	7
Preventive Maintenance	5
Repair Costs	8
Warranty	4
Fuel Economy	7
Complaints	10
Insurance Costs	8
OVERALL RATING	**7**

Acura ILX

Acura ILX

At-a-Glance

Status/Year Series Started	Unchanged/2013
Twins	Honda Civic
Body Styles	Sedan
Seating	5
Anti-Theft Device	Std. Pass. Immobil. & Alarm
Parking Index Rating	Easy
Where Made	Greensburg, IN
Fuel Factor	
MPG Rating (city/hwy)	Good-24/35
Driving Range (mi.)	Very Short-369.0
Fuel Type	Premium
Annual Fuel Cost	Average-$1,717
Gas Guzzler Tax	No
Greenhouse Gas Emissions (tons/yr.)	Low-6.4
Barrels of Oil Used per year	Average-11.8

How the Competition Rates

Competitors	Rating	Pg.
Audi A4	6	87
Cadillac ATS	9	107
Mercedes-Benz CLA-Class	–	204

Price Range

	Retail	Markup
Base 2.0L	$27,050	8%
Base 2.4L w/Prem. Package	$29,350	8%
Base 2.0L w/ Prem. Package	$29,350	8%
Base 2.0L w/Tech. Package	$31,750	8%

Safety Checklist

Crash Tests:
Frontal . . . . Average
Side . . . . Poor

Airbags:
Torso . . . . Front Torso from Seat
Pelvis . . . . None
Roll Sensing . . . . No
Knee Bolster . . . . None

Crash Avoidance:
Collision Avoidance . . . . None
Blind Spot Detection . . . . None
Lane Keeping Assist . . . . None
Backup Camera . . . . Standard
Pedestrian Crash Avoidance . . . . None

General:
Auto. Crash Notification . . . Operator Assist.-Fee
Day Running Lamps . . . . Standard

Safety Belt/Restraint:
Dynamic Head Restraints . . . . None
Adjustable Belt . . . . Standard Front

Acura ILX

Specifications

Drive	FWD
Engine	2.0-liter I4
Transmission	5-sp. Automatic
Tow Rating (lbs.)	–
Head/Leg Room (in.)	Cramped-38/42.3
Interior Space (cu. ft.)	Very Cramped-89.3
Cargo Space (cu. ft.)	Very Cramped-12.3
Wheelbase/Length (in.)	105.1/179.1

Ratings—10 Best, 1 Worst

Combo Crash Tests	8
Safety Features	9
Rollover	4
Preventive Maintenance	6
Repair Costs	5
Warranty	4
Fuel Economy	3
Complaints	1
Insurance Costs	10
OVERALL RATING	**6**

Acura MDX

Acura MDX

At-a-Glance

Status/Year Series Started Unchanged/2014
Twins . . . . –
Body Styles . . . . SUV
Seating 7
Anti-Theft Device . . . . . . Std. Pass. Immobil. & Alarm
Parking Index Rating . . . . Hard
Where Made . . . . Lincoln, AL
Fuel Factor . . . .
  MPG Rating (city/hwy) Poor-18/27
  Driving Range (mi.) Average-412.9
  Fuel Type . . . . Premium
  Annual Fuel Cost . . . . High-$2,266
  Gas Guzzler Tax . . . . .No
  Greenhouse Gas Emissions (tons/yr.) High-8.6
  Barrels of Oil Used per year High-15.7

How the Competition Rates

Competitors	Rating	Pg.
BMW X5	6	101
Infiniti QX70	–	167
Volvo XC60	9	270

Price Range

	Retail	Markup
Base	$42,565	9%
SH-AWD w/Tech. Package	$48,840	9%
Advance w/RES	$54,780	9%
SH-AWD Advance w/RES	$56,780	9%

Safety Checklist

Crash Tests:
  Frontal . . . . Very Good
  Side . . . . Average

Airbags:
  Torso . . . . .Front Pelvis/Torso from Seat
  Pelvis . . . . .Front Pelvis/Torso from Seat
  Roll Sensing . . . . .Yes
  Knee Bolster . . . . Standard Driver

Crash Avoidance:
  Collision Avoidance . . . . . . Optional CIB & DBS
  Blind Spot Detection . . . . Optional
  Lane Keeping Assist . . . . Optional
  Backup Camera . . . . Standard
  Pedestrian Crash Avoidance . . . . None

General:
  Auto. Crash Notification . . . Operator Assist.-Fee
  Day Running Lamps . . . . Standard

Safety Belt/Restraint:
  Dynamic Head Restraints . . . . . .Standard Front
  Adjustable Belt . . . . .Standard Front

Acura MDX

Specifications

Drive . . . . AWD
Engine 3.5-liter V6
Transmission . . . . .6-sp. Automatic
Tow Rating (lbs.) Low-3500
Head/Leg Room (in.) . . . . .Very Cramped-38.1/41.4
Interior Space (cu. ft.) . . . . Very Roomy-132.3
Cargo Space (cu. ft.) Cramped-14.8
Wheelbase/Length (in.) 111/193.6

Ratings—10 Best, 1 Worst

Combo Crash Tests	9
Safety Features	5
Rollover	4
Preventive Maintenance	8
Repair Costs	7
Warranty	4
Fuel Economy	4
Complaints	6
Insurance Costs	10
OVERALL RATING	**8**

Acura RDX

Acura RDX

At-a-Glance

Status/Year Series Started........ Unchanged/2013
Twins . . . .–
Body Styles . . . . SUV
Seating 5
Anti-Theft Device . . . . . . Std. Pass. Immobil. & Alarm
Parking Index Rating . . . . Hard
Where Made. . . . . .East Liberty, OH
Fuel Factor . . . .
  MPG Rating (city/hwy) Poor-19/27
  Driving Range (mi.) . . . . . . Very Short-350.8
  Fuel Type . . . . .Premium
  Annual Fuel Cost . . . . High-$2,189
  Gas Guzzler Tax . . . . .No
  Greenhouse Gas Emissions (tons/yr.). High-8.2
  Barrels of Oil Used per year High-15.0

How the Competition Rates

Competitors	Rating	Pg.
BMW X3	8	100
Buick Encore	10	103
Lexus RX	6	192

Price Range

Price Range	Retail	Markup
FWD	$34,895	8%
AWD	$36,295	8%
FWD w/Tech. Package	$38,595	8%
AWD w/Tech. Package	$39,995	8%

Safety Checklist

Crash Tests:
  Frontal. . . . . Very Good
  Side. . . . . Average
Airbags:
  Torso . . . . .Front Pelvis/Torso from Seat
  Pelvis . . . . .Front Pelvis/Torso from Seat
  Roll Sensing. . . . . .Yes
  Knee Bolster . . . . None
Crash Avoidance:
  Collision Avoidance . . . . None
  Blind Spot Detection . . . . None
  Lane Keeping Assist . . . . None
  Backup Camera. . . . . Standard
  Pedestrian Crash Avoidance . . . . None
General:
  Auto. Crash Notification . . . Operator Assist.-Fee
  Day Running Lamps . . . . Standard
Safety Belt/Restraint:
  Dynamic Head Restraints . . . . None
  Adjustable Belt . . . . .Standard Front

Acura RDX

Specifications

Drive. . . . . AWD
Engine 3.5-liter V6
Transmission . . . . .6-sp. Automatic
Tow Rating (lbs.) . . . . Very Low-1500
Head/Leg Room (in.) Cramped-38.7/42
Interior Space (cu. ft.). Average-103.5
Cargo Space (cu. ft.). Roomy-26.1
Wheelbase/Length (in.) 105.7/183.5

Acura RLX

Ratings—10 Best, 1 Worst

Combo Crash Tests	–
Safety Features	9
Rollover	8
Preventive Maintenance	4
Repair Costs	2
Warranty	4
Fuel Economy	5
Complaints	1
Insurance Costs	5
OVERALL RATING	**–**

Acura RLX

At-a-Glance

Status/Year Series Started. Unchanged/2014
Twins . . . . –
Body Styles . . . . .Sedan
Seating 5
Anti-Theft Device . . . . . . Std. Pass. Immobil. & Alarm
Parking Index Rating . . . . .Very Hard
Where Made. . . . . Saitama, Japan
Fuel Factor. . . . .
  MPG Rating (city/hwy) Average-20/31
  Driving Range (mi.) Long-440.3
  Fuel Type. . . . . .Premium
  Annual Fuel Cost . . . . High-$2,016
  Gas Guzzler Tax . . . . .No
  Greenhouse Gas Emissions (tons/yr.). . Average-7.5
  Barrels of Oil Used per year High-13.7

How the Competition Rates

Competitors	Rating	Pg.
Audi A6	7	89
Cadillac CTS	10	108
Lexus GS	–	188

Price Range	Retail	Markup
Base	$48,450	8%
Technology Package	$54,450	8%
Audio Package	$56,950	8%
Advance Package	$60,450	8%

Safety Checklist

Crash Tests:
  Frontal. . . . .–
  Side. . . . .–
Airbags:
  Torso . . . . .Front Pelvis/Torso from Seat
  Pelvis . . . . .Front Pelvis/Torso from Seat
  Roll Sensing. . . . . .Yes
  Knee Bolster . . . . Standard Driver
Crash Avoidance:
  Collision Avoidance . . . . . . Optional CIB & DBS
  Blind Spot Detection . . . . Optional
  Lane Keeping Assist . . . . Optional
  Backup Camera. . . . . Standard
  Pedestrian Crash Avoidance . . . . None
General:
  Auto. Crash Notification. . . Operator Assist.-Fee
  Day Running Lamps . . . . Standard
Safety Belt/Restraint:
  Dynamic Head Restraints . . . . None
  Adjustable Belt. . . . . .Standard Front

Acura RLX

Specifications

Drive. . . . . AWD
Engine 3.5-liter V6
Transmission . . . . .6-sp. Automatic
Tow Rating (lbs.) . . . . –
Head/Leg Room (in.) Cramped-37.6/42.3
Interior Space (cu. ft.). Average-102.1
Cargo Space (cu. ft.) Cramped-14.9
Wheelbase/Length (in.) 112.2/196.1

Acura TLX

Intermediate

Ratings—10 Best, 1 Worst	
Combo Crash Tests	–
Safety Features	6
Rollover	8
Preventive Maintenance	4
Repair Costs	7
Warranty	4
Fuel Economy	7
Complaints	–
Insurance Costs	5
OVERALL RATING	**–**

Acura TLX

Acura TLX

At-a-Glance

Status/Year Series Started	All New/2015
Twins	Honda Accord
Body Styles	Sedan
Seating	5
Anti-Theft Device	Std. Pass. Immobil. & Alarm
Parking Index Rating	Hard
Where Made	Marysville, OH
Fuel Factor	
MPG Rating (city/hwy)	Good-24/35
Driving Range (mi.)	Very Long-480.8
Fuel Type	Premium
Annual Fuel Cost	Average-$1,717
Gas Guzzler Tax	No
Greenhouse Gas Emissions (tons/yr.)	Low-6.4
Barrels of Oil Used per year	Average-11.8

How the Competition Rates

Competitors	Rating	Pg.
Cadillac CTS	10	108
Infiniti Q70	–	165
Lexus ES	7	187

Price Range	Retail	Markup
Base 2.4L	$30,995	8%
Base 3.5L	$35,220	8%
3.5L w/Tech. Package	$39,250	8%
SH-AWD w/Advance Package	$44,700	8%

Safety Checklist

Crash Tests:
Frontal . . . . –
Side . . . . –
Airbags:
Torso . . . . Front Pelvis/Torso from Seat
Pelvis . . . . Front Pelvis/Torso from Seat
Roll Sensing. . . . . No
Knee Bolster . . . . None

Crash Avoidance:
Collision Avoidance . . . . . . Optional CIB & DBS
Blind Spot Detection . . . . Optional
Lane Keeping Assist . . . . Optional
Backup Camera . . . . Standard
Pedestrian Crash Avoidance . . . . None

General:
Auto. Crash Notification . . . Operator Assist.-Fee
Day Running Lamps . . . . Standard

Safety Belt/Restraint:
Dynamic Head Restraints . . . . None
Adjustable Belt. . . . . Standard Front

Acura TLX

Specifications

Drive	FWD
Engine	2.4-liter I4
Transmission	8-sp. Automatic
Tow Rating (lbs.)	–
Head/Leg Room (in.)	Cramped-37.2/42.6
Interior Space (cu. ft.)	Cramped-93.3
Cargo Space (cu. ft.)	Cramped-13.2
Wheelbase/Length (in.)	109.3/190.3

Audi A3   Compact

Ratings—10 Best, 1 Worst	
Combo Crash Tests	7
Safety Features	8
Rollover	7
Preventive Maintenance	1
Repair Costs	5
Warranty	6
Fuel Economy	7
Complaints	–
Insurance Costs	3
OVERALL RATING	**5**

Audi A3

Audi A3

At-a-Glance

Status/Year Series Started	All New/2015
Twins	Volkswagen Golf
Body Styles	Sedan, Wagon
Seating	5
Anti-Theft Device	Std. Pass. Immobil. & Alarm
Parking Index Rating	Easy
Where Made	Gyor, Hungary
Fuel Factor	
MPG Rating (city/hwy)	Good-24/33
Driving Range (mi.)	Short-396.7
Fuel Type	Premium
Annual Fuel Cost	Average-$1,754
Gas Guzzler Tax	No
Greenhouse Gas Emissions (tons/yr.)	Average-6.6
Barrels of Oil Used per year	Average-12.2

How the Competition Rates

Competitors	Rating	Pg.
Acura ILX	7	81
Buick Verano	9	106
Mercedes-Benz CLA-Class	–	204

Price Range	Retail	Markup
1.8T Premium Sedan	$29,900	8%
2.0 TDI Premium Sedan	$32,600	8%
2.0T Premium Plus Sedan Quattro	$35,450	8%
2.0T Prestige Cabriolet Quattro	$47,050	8%

Safety Checklist

Crash Tests:
Frontal . . . . Average
Side . . . . Good

Airbags:
Torso Std. Fr. & Opt. Rr. Pelvis/Torso from Seat
Pelvis Std. Fr. & Opt. Rr. Pelvis/Torso from Seat
Roll Sensing . . . . Yes
Knee Bolster . . . . Standard Front

Crash Avoidance:
Collision Avoidance . . . . . . Optional CIB & DBS
Blind Spot Detection . . . . Optional
Lane Keeping Assist . . . . Optional
Backup Camera . . . . Optional
Pedestrian Crash Avoidance . . . . None

General:
Auto. Crash Notification . . . . None
Day Running Lamps . . . . Standard

Safety Belt/Restraint:
Dynamic Head Restraints . . . . None
Adjustable Belt . . . . Standard Front

Audi A3

Specifications

Drive	AWD
Engine	2.0-liter I4
Transmission	6-sp. Automatic
Tow Rating (lbs.)	–
Head/Leg Room (in.)	Very Cramped-36.5/41.2
Interior Space (cu. ft.)	Very Cramped-86
Cargo Space (cu. ft.)	Very Cramped-10.03
Wheelbase/Length (in.)	103.8/175.4

Ratings—10 Best, 1 Worst

Combo Crash Tests	6
Safety Features	3
Rollover	8
Preventive Maintenance	5
Repair Costs	3
Warranty	6
Fuel Economy	6
Complaints	8
Insurance Costs	8
OVERALL RATING	**6**

Audi A4

Audi A4

At-a-Glance

Status/Year Series Started	Unchanged/2009
Twins	–
Body Styles	Sedan
Seating	5
Anti-Theft Device	Std. Pass. Immobil. & Alarm
Parking Index Rating	Average
Where Made	Ingolstadt, Germany
Fuel Factor	
MPG Rating (city/hwy)	Average-22/31
Driving Range (mi.)	Average-407.4
Fuel Type	Premium
Annual Fuel Cost	Average-$1,896
Gas Guzzler Tax	No
Greenhouse Gas Emissions (tons/yr.)	Average-7.2
Barrels of Oil Used per year	High-13.2

How the Competition Rates

Competitors	Rating	Pg.
BMW 3 Series	9	94
Cadillac ATS	9	107
Mercedes-Benz C-Class	–	203

Price Range

	Retail	Markup
2.0T Premium Sedan	$35,500	8%
2.0T Premium Sedan Quattro	$37,600	8%
2.0T Premium Plus Sedan Quattro	$39,700	8%
2.0T Prestige Sedan Quattro	$45,000	8%

Safety Checklist

Crash Tests:
Frontal . . . . Good
Side . . . . Poor

Airbags:
Torso Std. Fr. & Opt. Rr. Pelvis/Torso from Seat
Pelvis Std. Fr. & Opt. Rr. Pelvis/Torso from Seat
Roll Sensing . . . . No
Knee Bolster . . . . None

Crash Avoidance:
Collision Avoidance . . . . Optional CIB
Blind Spot Detection . . . . Optional
Lane Keeping Assist . . . . None
Backup Camera . . . . Optional
Pedestrian Crash Avoidance . . . . None

General:
Auto. Crash Notification . . . . None
Day Running Lamps . . . . Standard

Safety Belt/Restraint:
Dynamic Head Restraints . . . . None
Adjustable Belt . . . . Standard Front

Audi A4

Specifications

Drive	AWD
Engine	2.0-liter I4
Transmission	8-sp. Automatic
Tow Rating (lbs.)	–
Head/Leg Room (in.)	Very Cramped-36.9/41.3
Interior Space (cu. ft.)	Very Cramped-91
Cargo Space (cu. ft.)	Very Cramped-12.4
Wheelbase/Length (in.)	110.6/185.1

Ratings—10 Best, 1 Worst

Combo Crash Tests	–
Safety Features	3
Rollover	9
Preventive Maintenance	8
Repair Costs	2
Warranty	6
Fuel Economy	6
Complaints	10
Insurance Costs	5
OVERALL RATING	**–**

Audi A5

At-a-Glance

Status/Year Series Started. Unchanged/2008
Twins . . . . –
Body Styles . . . . Coupe, Convertible
Seating 4
Anti-Theft Device . . . . . . Std. Pass. Immobil. & Alarm
Parking Index Rating . . . . Average
Where Made. . . . . .Ingolstadt, Germany
Fuel Factor. . . . .
  MPG Rating (city/hwy) Average-22/31
  Driving Range (mi.) Average-407.4
  Fuel Type. . . . . .Premium
  Annual Fuel Cost . . . . Average-$1,896
  Gas Guzzler Tax . . . . .No
  Greenhouse Gas Emissions (tons/yr.). . Average-7.2
  Barrels of Oil Used per year High-13.2

How the Competition Rates

Competitors	Rating	Pg.
BMW 4 Series	–	95
Infiniti Q60	–	164
Lexus IS	5	190

Price Range	Retail	Markup
2.0T Premium Coupe Quattro	$40,000	8%
2.0T Premium Plus Coupe Quattro AT	$43,500	8%
2.0T Premium Cabriolet Quattro	$47,600	8%
2.0T Prestige Cabrio Tip Quattro	$56,000	8%

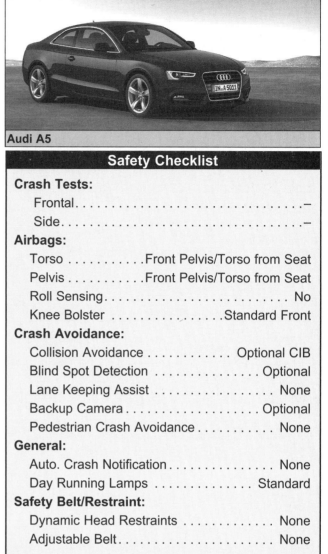

Audi A5

Safety Checklist

Crash Tests:
  Frontal. . . . .–
  Side. . . . .–
Airbags:
  Torso . . . . .Front Pelvis/Torso from Seat
  Pelvis . . . . .Front Pelvis/Torso from Seat
  Roll Sensing. . . . . No
  Knee Bolster . . . . .Standard Front
Crash Avoidance:
  Collision Avoidance . . . . Optional CIB
  Blind Spot Detection . . . . Optional
  Lane Keeping Assist . . . . None
  Backup Camera. . . . . Optional
  Pedestrian Crash Avoidance . . . . None
General:
  Auto. Crash Notification . . . . None
  Day Running Lamps . . . . Standard
Safety Belt/Restraint:
  Dynamic Head Restraints . . . . None
  Adjustable Belt. None

Audi A5

Specifications

Drive. . . . . AWD
Engine 2.0-liter I4
Transmission . . . . .8-sp. Automatic
Tow Rating (lbs.) . . . . –
Head/Leg Room (in.) . . . . .Very Cramped-37.6/41.3
Interior Space (cu. ft.). . . . . Very Cramped-84
Cargo Space (cu. ft.) . . . . .Very Cramped-12.2
Wheelbase/Length (in.) 108.3/182.1

Ratings—10 Best, 1 Worst	
Combo Crash Tests	8
Safety Features	8
Rollover	9
Preventive Maintenance	5
Repair Costs	1
Warranty	6
Fuel Economy	3
Complaints	7
Insurance Costs	5
OVERALL RATING	**7**

Audi A6

Audi A6

At-a-Glance

Status/Year Series Started. Unchanged/2012
Twins . . . . –
Body Styles . . . . Sedan, Wagon
Seating 5
Anti-Theft Device . . . . . . Std. Pass. Immobil. & Alarm
Parking Index Rating . . . . Hard
Where Made. . . . . Neckarsulm, Germany
Fuel Factor . . . .
  MPG Rating (city/hwy) Poor-18/27
  Driving Range (mi.) Average-419.3
  Fuel Type . . . . Premium
  Annual Fuel Cost . . . . High-$2,266
  Gas Guzzler Tax . . . . No
  Greenhouse Gas Emissions (tons/yr.) High-8.2
  Barrels of Oil Used per year High-15.0

How the Competition Rates

Competitors	Rating	Pg.
BMW 5 Series	8	96
Mercedes-Benz E-Class	4	205
Volvo S60	10	268

Price Range	Retail	Markup
2.0T Premium	$44,800	8%
2.0T Premium Plus Quattro	$50,450	8%
3.0 Prestige Quattro	$60,100	8%
3.0 Prestige TDI	$62,500	8%

Safety Checklist

Crash Tests:
  Frontal . . . . Very Good
  Side . . . . Average
Airbags:
  Torso Std. Fr. & Opt. Rr. Pelvis/Torso from Seat
  Pelvis Std. Fr. & Opt. Rr. Pelvis/Torso from Seat
  Roll Sensing . . . . Yes
  Knee Bolster . . . . Standard Front
Crash Avoidance:
  Collision Avoidance . . . . . . Optional CIB & DBS
  Blind Spot Detection . . . . Optional
  Lane Keeping Assist . . . . Optional
  Backup Camera . . . . Optional
  Pedestrian Crash Avoidance . . . . None
General:
  Auto. Crash Notification . . . . None
  Day Running Lamps . . . . Standard
Safety Belt/Restraint:
  Dynamic Head Restraints . . . . None
  Adjustable Belt . . . . Standard Front

Audi A6

Specifications

Drive . . . . AWD
Engine 3.0-liter V6
Transmission . . . . 8-sp. Automatic
Tow Rating (lbs.) . . . . –
Head/Leg Room (in.) . . . . . Very Cramped-37.2/41.3
Interior Space (cu. ft.) Average-98
Cargo Space (cu. ft.) Cramped-14.1
Wheelbase/Length (in.) 114.7/193.9

Audi A7 Large

Ratings—10 Best, 1 Worst	
Combo Crash Tests	–
Safety Features	9
Rollover	9
Preventive Maintenance	5
Repair Costs	1
Warranty	6
Fuel Economy	3
Complaints	5
Insurance Costs	3
OVERALL RATING	**–**

Audi A7

Audi A7

At-a-Glance

Status/Year Series Started	Unchanged/2012
Twins	–
Body Styles	Hatchback
Seating	5
Anti-Theft Device	Std. Pass. Immobil. & Alarm
Parking Index Rating	Hard
Where Made	Neckarsulm, Germany
Fuel Factor	
MPG Rating (city/hwy)	Poor-18/28
Driving Range (mi.)	Long-424.6
Fuel Type	Premium
Annual Fuel Cost	High-$2,238
Gas Guzzler Tax	No
Greenhouse Gas Emissions (tons/yr.)	High-8.6
Barrels of Oil Used per year	High-15.7

How the Competition Rates

Competitors	Rating	Pg.
BMW 6 Series	–	97
Cadillac XTS	9	110
Mercedes-Benz S-Class	–	210

Price Range

	Retail	Markup
3.0T Premium Plus	$65,900	8%
3.0 Premium Plus TDI	$68,300	8%
3.0T Prestige	$69,750	8%
3.0 Prestige TDI	$72,150	8%

Safety Checklist

Crash Tests:
Frontal . . . . –
Side . . . . –

Airbags:
Torso Std. Fr. & Opt. Rr. Pelvis/Torso from Seat
Pelvis Std. Fr. & Opt. Rr. Pelvis/Torso from Seat
Roll Sensing . . . . Yes
Knee Bolster . . . . Standard Front

Crash Avoidance:
Collision Avoidance . . . . . . Optional CIB & DBS
Blind Spot Detection . . . . Standard
Lane Keeping Assist . . . . Optional
Backup Camera . . . . Standard
Pedestrian Crash Avoidance . . . . None

General:
Auto. Crash Notification . . . . None
Day Running Lamps . . . . Standard

Safety Belt/Restraint:
Dynamic Head Restraints . . . . None
Adjustable Belt . . . . Standard Front

Audi A7

Specifications

Drive	AWD
Engine	3.0-liter V6
Transmission	8-sp. Automatic
Tow Rating (lbs.)	–
Head/Leg Room (in.)	Very Cramped-36.9/41.3
Interior Space (cu. ft.)	Cramped-94
Cargo Space (cu. ft.)	Roomy-24.5
Wheelbase/Length (in.)	114.7/195.6

Audi Q3

Audi Q3

Ratings—10 Best, 1 Worst

Combo Crash Tests	–
Safety Features	4
Rollover	5
Preventive Maintenance	–
Repair Costs	–
Warranty	6
Fuel Economy	4
Complaints	–
Insurance Costs	5
OVERALL RATING	**–**

Audi Q3

At-a-Glance

Status/Year Series Started	All New/2015
Twins	Volkswagen Tiguan
Body Styles	SUV
Seating	5
Anti-Theft Device	Std. Pass. Immobil & Alarm
Parking Index Rating	Average
Where Made	Martorell, Spain
Fuel Factor	
MPG Rating (city/hwy)	Poor-20/28
Driving Range (mi.)	Short-387.9
Fuel Type	Premium
Annual Fuel Cost	High-$2,091
Gas Guzzler Tax	No
Greenhouse Gas Emissions (tons/yr.)	High-7.8
Barrels of Oil Used per year	High-14.3

How the Competition Rates

Competitors	Rating	Pg.
BMW X1	–	99
Lexus NX	–	191
Mercedes-Benz GLA-Class	–	206

Price Range

	Retail	Markup
2.0T Premium Plus	$32,500	8%
2.0T Premium Plus Quattro	$34,600	8%
2.0T Prestige	$36,400	8%
2.0T Prestige Quattro	$38,500	8%

Safety Checklist

Crash Tests:
Frontal	–
Side	–

Airbags:
Torso	Front Pelvis/Torso from Seat
Pelvis	Front Pelvis/Torso from Seat
Roll Sensing	Yes
Knee Bolster	None

Crash Avoidance:
Collision Avoidance	None
Blind Spot Detection	Optional
Lane Keeping Assist	None
Backup Camera	Optional
Pedestrian Crash Avoidance	None

General:
Auto. Crash Notification	None
Day Running Lamps	Standard

Safety Belt/Restraint:
Dynamic Head Restraints	None
Adjustable Belt	Standard Front

Audi Q3

Specifications

Drive	AWD
Engine	2.0-liter I4
Transmission	6-sp. Automatic
Tow Rating (lbs.)	–
Head/Leg Room (in.)	Very Cramped-37/40
Interior Space (cu. ft.)	Very Cramped-84
Cargo Space (cu. ft.)	Average-16.7
Wheelbase/Length (in.)	102.5/172.6

Audi Q5

Ratings—10 Best, 1 Worst

Combo Crash Tests	3
Safety Features	5
Rollover	4
Preventive Maintenance	5
Repair Costs	4
Warranty	6
Fuel Economy	4
Complaints	9
Insurance Costs	8
OVERALL RATING	**4**

Audi Q5

At-a-Glance

Status/Year Series Started	Unchanged/2009
Twins	—
Body Styles	SUV
Seating	5
Anti-Theft Device	Std. Pass. Immobil. & Alarm
Parking Index Rating	Average
Where Made	Ingolstadt, Germany
Fuel Factor	
MPG Rating (city/hwy)	Poor-20/28
Driving Range (mi.)	Long-454.4
Fuel Type	Premium
Annual Fuel Cost	High-$2,091
Gas Guzzler Tax	No
Greenhouse Gas Emissions (tons/yr.)	High-7.8
Barrels of Oil Used per year	High-14.3

How the Competition Rates

Competitors	Rating	Pg.
BMW X3	8	100
Lexus RX	6	192
Mercedes-Benz M-Class	5	209

Price Range

Price Range	Retail	Markup
2.0T Premium	$38,900	8%
3.0T Premium Plus	$44,900	8%
Prestige Hybird	$51,900	8%
3.0 Prestige TDI	$54,500	8%

Safety Checklist

Crash Tests:
Frontal . . . . Very Poor
Side . . . . Average
Airbags:
Torso Std. Fr. & Opt. Rr. Pelvis/Torso from Seat
Pelvis Std. Fr. & Opt. Rr. Pelvis/Torso from Seat
Roll Sensing . . . . Yes
Knee Bolster . . . . None
Crash Avoidance:
Collision Avoidance . . . . . . Optional CIB & DBS
Blind Spot Detection . . . . Optional
Lane Keeping Assist . . . . None
Backup Camera . . . . Optional
Pedestrian Crash Avoidance . . . . None
General:
Auto. Crash Notification . . . . None
Day Running Lamps . . . . Standard
Safety Belt/Restraint:
Dynamic Head Restraints . . . . None
Adjustable Belt . . . . Standard Front

Audi Q5

Specifications

Drive	AWD
Engine	2.0-liter I4
Transmission	8-sp. Automatic
Tow Rating (lbs.)	Low-4400
Head/Leg Room (in.)	Very Cramped-38.1/41
Interior Space (cu. ft.)	Average-101.5
Cargo Space (cu. ft.)	Roomy-29.1
Wheelbase/Length (in.)	110.5/182.6

Ratings—10 Best, 1 Worst

Combo Crash Tests	–
Safety Features	3
Rollover	3
Preventive Maintenance	3
Repair Costs	1
Warranty	6
Fuel Economy	2
Complaints	8
Insurance Costs	8
OVERALL RATING	**–**

Audi Q7

At-a-Glance

Status/Year Series Started. Unchanged/2007
Twins . . . .–
Body Styles . . . . SUV
Seating 7
Anti-Theft Device . . . . . . Std. Pass. Immobil. & Alarm
Parking Index Rating . . . . .Very Hard
Where Made. . . . . Bratislava, Slovakia
Fuel Factor . . . .
　MPG Rating (city/hwy). . . . .Very Poor-16/22
　Driving Range (mi.) . . . . .Very Long-481.5
　Fuel Type . . . . .Premium
　Annual Fuel Cost . . . . .Very High-$2,631
　Gas Guzzler Tax . . . . .No
　Greenhouse Gas Emissions (tons/yr.)Very High-10.0
　Barrels of Oil Used per year . . . . . . .Very High-18.3

How the Competition Rates

Competitors	Rating	Pg.
BMW X5	6	101
Infiniti QX60	–	166
Mercedes-Benz GL-Class	–	207

Price Range	Retail	Markup
3.0 Premium	$47,700	8%
3.0 Premium Plus	$54,200	8%
3.0 Prestige S-Line	$61,400	8%
3.0 Prestige TDI	$64,900	8%

Audi Q7

Safety Checklist

Crash Tests:
　Frontal. . . . .–
　Side. . . . .–
Airbags:
　Torso　Std. Fr. & Opt. Rr. Pelvis/Torso from Seat
　Pelvis　Std. Fr. & Opt. Rr. Pelvis/Torso from Seat
　Roll Sensing. . . . . .Yes
　Knee Bolster . . . . None
Crash Avoidance:
　Collision Avoidance . . . . None
　Blind Spot Detection . . . . Optional
　Lane Keeping Assist . . . . None
　Backup Camera. . . . . Optional
　Pedestrian Crash Avoidance . . . . None
General:
　Auto. Crash Notification. . . . . None
　Day Running Lamps . . . . Standard
Safety Belt/Restraint:
　Dynamic Head Restraints . . . . None
　Adjustable Belt. . . . . . . .Standard Front and Rear

Audi Q7

Specifications

Drive. . . . . AWD
Engine 3.0-liter V6
Transmission . . . . .8-sp. Automatic
Tow Rating (lbs.) Average-6600
Head/Leg Room (in.) Cramped-39.5/41.3
Interior Space (cu. ft.). . . . . Very Roomy-133.2
Cargo Space (cu. ft.) . . . . .Very Cramped-10.9
Wheelbase/Length (in.) 118.2/200.3

Ratings—10 Best, 1 Worst

Combo Crash Tests	7
Safety Features	9
Rollover	8
Preventive Maintenance	9
Repair Costs	3
Warranty	9
Fuel Economy	6
Complaints	5
Insurance Costs	8
OVERALL RATING	**9**

BMW 3 Series

At-a-Glance

Status/Year Series Started........ Unchanged/2013
Twins . . . . –
Body Styles . . . . .Sedan, Wagon, Convertible
Seating 5
Anti-Theft Device . . . . Std. Passive Alarm Only
Parking Index Rating . . . . Average
Where Made. . . . . .Munich, Germany
Fuel Factor . . . .
  MPG Rating (city/hwy) Average-23/35
  Driving Range (mi.) Long-429.7
  Fuel Type . . . . .Premium
  Annual Fuel Cost . . . . Average-$1,764
  Gas Guzzler Tax . . . . .No
  Greenhouse Gas Emissions (tons/yr.). . Average-6.7
  Barrels of Oil Used per year Average-12.2

How the Competition Rates

Competitors	Rating	Pg.
Audi A4	6	87
Lexus IS	5	190
Mercedes-Benz C-Class	–	203

Price Range

Price Range	Retail	Markup
320i	$32,750	9%
328d	$38,900	9%
335xi	$45,500	9%
335i Hybrid	$49,900	9%

BMW 3 Series

Safety Checklist

Crash Tests:
  Frontal . . . . Average
  Side . . . . Good
Airbags:
  Torso . . . . Front Torso from Seat
  Pelvis . . . . None
  Roll Sensing. . . . . .Yes
  Knee Bolster . . . . .Standard Front
Crash Avoidance:
  Collision Avoidance . . . . . . Optional CIB & DBS
  Blind Spot Detection . . . . Optional
  Lane Keeping Assist . . . .Warning Only Optional
  Backup Camera. . . . . Standard
  Pedestrian Crash Avoidance . . . . Optional
General:
  Auto. Crash Notif. . . . Oper. Assist. & Crash Info-Free
  Day Running Lamps . . . . Standard
Safety Belt/Restraint:
  Dynamic Head Restraints . . . . None
  Adjustable Belt. . . . . None

BMW 3 Series

Specifications

Drive. . . . . .RWD
Engine 2.0-liter I4
Transmission . . . . .8-sp. Automatic
Tow Rating (lbs.) . . . . –
Head/Leg Room (in.) Average-40.3/42
Interior Space (cu. ft.). Cramped-96
Cargo Space (cu. ft.) Average-17
Wheelbase/Length (in.) 110.6/182.2

Ratings—10 Best, 1 Worst

Combo Crash Tests	–
Safety Features	8
Rollover	9
Preventive Maintenance	9
Repair Costs	3
Warranty	9
Fuel Economy	6
Complaints	8
Insurance Costs	5
OVERALL RATING	**–**

BMW 4 Series

BMW 4 Series

At-a-Glance

Status/Year Series Started	Unchanged/2014
Twins	–
Body Styles	Coupe, Convertible
Seating	4
Anti-Theft Device	Std. Passive Alarm Only
Parking Index Rating	Average
Where Made	Munich, Germany
Fuel Factor	
MPG Rating (city/hwy)	Average-23/35
Driving Range (mi.)	Long-429.7
Fuel Type	Premium
Annual Fuel Cost	Average-$1,764
Gas Guzzler Tax	No
Greenhouse Gas Emissions (tons/yr.)	Average-6.7
Barrels of Oil Used per year	Average-12.2

How the Competition Rates

Competitors	Rating	Pg.
Audi A5	–	88
Infiniti Q60	–	164
Mercedes-Benz C-Class	–	203

Price Range	Retail	Markup
428i Coupe	$40,600	9%
435i Gran Coupe	$45,800	9%
435i Convertible	$54,900	9%
435xi Convertible	$56,900	9%

Safety Checklist

Crash Tests:
Frontal . . . . –
Side . . . . –

Airbags:
Torso . . . . Front Torso from Seat
Pelvis . . . . None
Roll Sensing . . . . Yes
Knee Bolster . . . . Standard Front

Crash Avoidance:
Collision Avoidance . . . . . . Optional CIB & DBS
Blind Spot Detection . . . . None
Lane Keeping Assist . . . . Warning Only Optional
Backup Camera . . . . Standard
Pedestrian Crash Avoidance . . . . Optional

General:
Auto. Crash Notif. . . . . . Oper. Assist. & Crash Info-Free
Day Running Lamps . . . . Standard

Safety Belt/Restraint:
Dynamic Head Restraints . . . . None
Adjustable Belt . . . . None

BMW 4 Series

Specifications

Drive	RWD
Engine	2.0-liter I4
Transmission	8-sp. Automatic
Tow Rating (lbs.)	–
Head/Leg Room (in.)	Average-39.8/42.2
Interior Space (cu. ft.)	Very Cramped-90
Cargo Space (cu. ft.)	Cramped-15.7
Wheelbase/Length (in.)	110.6/182.6

Ratings—10 Best, 1 Worst

Combo Crash Tests	5
Safety Features	10
Rollover	8
Preventive Maintenance	10
Repair Costs	2
Warranty	9
Fuel Economy	6
Complaints	4
Insurance Costs	8
OVERALL RATING	**8**

BMW 5 Series

At-a-Glance

Status/Year Series Started........ Unchanged/2011
Twins . . . . –
Body Styles . . . . Sedan, Wagon
Seating 5
Anti-Theft Device . . . . Std. Passive Alarm Only
Parking Index Rating . . . . Hard
Where Made. . . . . Dingolfing, Germany
Fuel Factor . . . .
  MPG Rating (city/hwy) Average-23/34
  Driving Range (mi.) . . . . .Very Long-498.0
  Fuel Type. . . . . .Premium
  Annual Fuel Cost . . . . Average-$1,783
  Gas Guzzler Tax . . . . .No
  Greenhouse Gas Emissions (tons/yr.). . Average-6.6
  Barrels of Oil Used per year Average-12.2

How the Competition Rates

Competitors	Rating	Pg.
Audi A6	7	89
Infiniti Q70	–	165
Mercedes-Benz E-Class	4	205

Price Range	Retail	Markup
528i	$49,750	9%
535i	$55,350	9%
535i Hybrid	$61,650	9%
550xi	$66,850	9%

BMW 5 Series

Safety Checklist

Crash Tests:
  Frontal. . . . . .Very Poor
  Side. . . . . Very Good
Airbags:
  Torso . . . . Front Torso from Seat
  Pelvis . . . . None
  Roll Sensing. . . . . .Yes
  Knee Bolster . . . . .Standard Front
Crash Avoidance:
  Collision Avoidance . . . . . . Optional CIB & DBS
  Blind Spot Detection . . . . Optional
  Lane Keeping Assist . . . .Warning Only Optional
  Backup Camera . . . . Standard
  Pedestrian Crash Avoidance . . . . Optional
General:
  Auto. Crash Notif. . . .Oper. Assist. & Crash Info-Free
  Day Running Lamps . . . . Standard
Safety Belt/Restraint:
  Dynamic Head Restraints . . . . . .Standard Front
  Adjustable Belt. . . . . None

Specifications

Drive. . . . . RWD
Engine 2.0-liter I4
Transmission . . . . .8-sp. Automatic
Tow Rating (lbs.) . . . . –
Head/Leg Room (in.) Average-40.5/41.4
Interior Space (cu. ft.). Average-102
Cargo Space (cu. ft.) Average-18.4
Wheelbase/Length (in.) 116.9/193.4

Ratings—10 Best, 1 Worst

Combo Crash Tests	–
Safety Features	8
Rollover	10
Preventive Maintenance	10
Repair Costs	1
Warranty	9
Fuel Economy	2
Complaints	10
Insurance Costs	1

OVERALL RATING   –

BMW 6 Series

BMW 6 Series

At-a-Glance

Status/Year Series Started. Unchanged/2012
Twins . . . . –
Body Styles . . . . Coupe, Convertible
Seating 4
Anti-Theft Device . . . . Std. Passive Alarm Only
Parking Index Rating . . . . Hard
Where Made. . . . . Dingolfing, Germany
Fuel Factor . . . .
  MPG Rating (city/hwy). . . . . Very Poor-17/25
  Driving Range (mi.) . . . . Very Short-367.4
  Fuel Type. . . . . .Premium
  Annual Fuel Cost . . . . Very High-$2,416
  Gas Guzzler Tax . . . . .No
  Greenhouse Gas Emissions (tons/yr.). High-9.0
  Barrels of Oil Used per year High-16.5

How the Competition Rates

Competitors	Rating	Pg.
Audi A7	–	90
Cadillac CTS	10	108
Mercedes-Benz E-Class	4	205

Price Range	Retail	Markup
640i Coupe	$76,100	9%
640xi Convertible	$86,600	9%
650xi Gran Coupe	$92,600	9%
650xi Convertible	$97,900	9%

Safety Checklist

Crash Tests:
  Frontal. . . . . –
  Side. . . . . –
Airbags:
  Torso . . . . Front Head/Torso from Seat
  Pelvis . . . . None
  Roll Sensing. . . . . No
  Knee Bolster . . . . .Standard Front
Crash Avoidance:
  Collision Avoidance . . . . . . Optional CIB & DBS
  Blind Spot Detection . . . . Optional
  Lane Keeping Assist . . . .Warning Only Optional
  Backup Camera. . . . . Standard
  Pedestrian Crash Avoidance . . . . Optional
General:
  Auto. Crash Notif. . . .Oper. Assist. & Crash Info-Free
  Day Running Lamps . . . . Standard
Safety Belt/Restraint:
  Dynamic Head Restraints . . . . . .Standard Front
  Adjustable Belt. . . . . None

BMW 6 Series

Specifications

Drive. . . . . RWD
Engine 4.4-liter V8
Transmission . . . . .8-sp. Automatic
Tow Rating (lbs.) . . . . –
Head/Leg Room (in.) Average-40.3/42.1
Interior Space (cu. ft.). . . . . Very Cramped-88
Cargo Space (cu. ft.) . . . . .Very Cramped-12.4
Wheelbase/Length (in.) 112.4/192.8

Ratings—10 Best, 1 Worst

Combo Crash Tests	–
Safety Features	10
Rollover	8
Preventive Maintenance	10
Repair Costs	1
Warranty	9
Fuel Economy	2
Complaints	8
Insurance Costs	3
OVERALL RATING	**–**

BMW 7 Series

BMW 7 Series

At-a-Glance

Status/Year Series Started. Unchanged/2011
Twins . . . . –
Body Styles . . . . .Sedan
Seating 5
Anti-Theft Device . . . . Std. Passive Alarm Only
Parking Index Rating . . . . .Very Hard
Where Made. . . . . Dingolfing, Germany
Fuel Factor. . . . .
  MPG Rating (city/hwy) . . . . .Very Poor-17/25
  Driving Range (mi.) Average-419.0
  Fuel Type. . . . . .Premium
  Annual Fuel Cost . . . . .Very High-$2,416
  Gas Guzzler Tax . . . . .No
  Greenhouse Gas Emissions (tons/yr.). High-9.0
  Barrels of Oil Used per year High-16.5

How the Competition Rates

Competitors	Rating	Pg.
Acura RLX	–	84
Cadillac XTS	9	110
Mercedes-Benz S-Class	–	210

Price Range

	Retail	Markup
740i	$74,000	9%
750i	$87,300	9%
750i xDrive	$90,300	9%
760Li	$141,200	9%

Safety Checklist

Crash Tests:
  Frontal . . . . –
  Side . . . . –
Airbags:
  Torso . . . . Front Torso from Seat
  Pelvis . . . . None
  Roll Sensing. . . . . .Yes
  Knee Bolster . . . . .Standard Front
Crash Avoidance:
  Collision Avoidance . . . . . . Optional CIB & DBS
  Blind Spot Detection . . . . Optional
  Lane Keeping Assist . . . .Warning Only Optional
  Backup Camera . . . . Standard
  Pedestrian Crash Avoidance . . . . Optional
General:
  Auto. Crash Notif. . . .Oper. Assist. & Crash Info-Free
  Day Running Lamps . . . . Standard
Safety Belt/Restraint:
  Dynamic Head Restraints . . . . . .Standard Front
  Adjustable Belt . . . . None

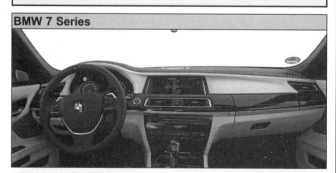

BMW 7 Series

Specifications

Drive. . . . . RWD
Engine 4.4-liter V8
Transmission . . . . .8-sp. Automatic
Tow Rating (lbs.) . . . . –
Head/Leg Room (in.) Average-40.6/41.3
Interior Space (cu. ft.). Roomy-107
Cargo Space (cu. ft.) Average-18
Wheelbase/Length (in.) 120.9/200

BMW X1

Ratings—10 Best, 1 Worst

Combo Crash Tests	–
Safety Features	5
Rollover	5
Preventive Maintenance	10
Repair Costs	3
Warranty	9
Fuel Economy	6
Complaints	7
Insurance Costs	5
OVERALL RATING	**–**

BMW X1

At-a-Glance

Status/Year Series Started. Unchanged/2013
Twins . . . .–
Body Styles . . . . SUV
Seating 5
Anti-Theft Device . . . . Std. Passive Alarm Only
Parking Index Rating . . . . Easy
Where Made. . . . . .Leipzig, Germany
Fuel Factor . . . .
   MPG Rating (city/hwy) Average-22/32
   Driving Range (mi.) Long-425.0
   Fuel Type . . . . .Premium
   Annual Fuel Cost . . . . Average-$1,875
   Gas Guzzler Tax . . . . .No
   Greenhouse Gas Emissions (tons/yr.). . Average-6.9
   Barrels of Oil Used per year Average-12.7

How the Competition Rates

Competitors	Rating	Pg.
Lexus NX	–	191
Mercedes-Benz GLA-Class	–	206
Porsche Macan	–	233

Price Range	Retail	Markup
sDrive28i	$30,900	9%
XDrive28i	$32,700	9%
XDrive35i	$38,800	9%

Safety Checklist

Crash Tests:
   Frontal. . . . .–
   Side. . . . .–
Airbags:
   Torso . . . . Front Torso from Seat
   Pelvis . . . . None
   Roll Sensing. . . . . .Yes
   Knee Bolster . . . . Standard Driver
Crash Avoidance:
   Collision Avoidance . . . . None
   Blind Spot Detection . . . . None
   Lane Keeping Assist . . . . None
   Backup Camera . . . . Standard
   Pedestrian Crash Avoidance . . . . None
General:
   Auto. Crash Notif. . . . . .Oper. Assist. & Crash Info-Free
   Day Running Lamps . . . . Standard
Safety Belt/Restraint:
   Dynamic Head Restraints . . . . None
   Adjustable Belt . . . . None

BMW X1

Specifications

Drive . . . . AWD
Engine 2.0-liter I4
Transmission . . . . 8-sp. Automatic
Tow Rating (lbs.) . . . .–
Head/Leg Room (in.) Roomy-41.3/41.4
Interior Space (cu. ft.). Average-98
Cargo Space (cu. ft.) Roomy-25
Wheelbase/Length (in.) 108.7/176.5

Ratings—10 Best, 1 Worst	
Combo Crash Tests	6
Safety Features	9
Rollover	3
Preventive Maintenance	10
Repair Costs	3
Warranty	9
Fuel Economy	5
Complaints	8
Insurance Costs	8
OVERALL RATING	**8**

BMW X3

BMW X3

At-a-Glance

Status/Year Series Started	Unchanged/2011
Twins	–
Body Styles	SUV
Seating	5
Anti-Theft Device	Std. Passive Alarm Only
Parking Index Rating	Hard
Where Made	Spartanburg, SC
Fuel Factor	
MPG Rating (city/hwy)	Average-21/28
Driving Range (mi.)	Average-418.8
Fuel Type	Premium
Annual Fuel Cost	High-$2,028
Gas Guzzler Tax	No
Greenhouse Gas Emissions (tons/yr.)	Average-7.5
Barrels of Oil Used per year	High-13.7

How the Competition Rates

Competitors	Rating	Pg.
Audi Q5	4	92
Mercedes-Benz M-Class	5	209
Volvo XC60	9	270

Price Range	Retail	Markup
sDrive28i	$38,400	9%
XDrive28i	$40,400	9%
XDrive28d	$41,900	9%
XDrive35i	$45,100	9%

Safety Checklist

Crash Tests:
Frontal	Good
Side	Average

Airbags:
Torso	Front Torso from Seat
Pelvis	None
Roll Sensing	Yes
Knee Bolster	Standard Driver

Crash Avoidance:
Collision Avoidance	Optional CIB & DBS
Blind Spot Detection	Optional
Lane Keeping Assist	Warning Only Optional
Backup Camera	Standard
Pedestrian Crash Avoidance	Optional

General:
Auto. Crash Notif.	Oper. Assist. & Crash Info-Free
Day Running Lamps	Standard

Safety Belt/Restraint:
Dynamic Head Restraints	Standard Front
Adjustable Belt	None

BMW X3

Specifications

Drive	AWD
Engine	3.0-liter I6
Transmission	8-sp. Automatic
Tow Rating (lbs.)	–
Head/Leg Room (in.)	Cramped-40.7/39.9
Interior Space (cu. ft.)	Very Cramped-90.1
Cargo Space (cu. ft.)	Roomy-27.6
Wheelbase/Length (in.)	110.6/183.8

Ratings—10 Best, 1 Worst	
Combo Crash Tests	8
Safety Features	10
Rollover	3
Preventive Maintenance	10
Repair Costs	1
Warranty	9
Fuel Economy	3
Complaints	4
Insurance Costs	3
OVERALL RATING	6

BMW X5

BMW X5

At-a-Glance

Status/Year Series Started	Unchanged/2014
Twins	–
Body Styles	SUV
Seating	5
Anti-Theft Device	Std. Passive Alarm Only
Parking Index Rating	Very Hard
Where Made	Spartanburg, SC
Fuel Factor	
MPG Rating (city/hwy)	Poor-18/27
Driving Range (mi.)	Very Long-474.4
Fuel Type	Premium
Annual Fuel Cost	High-$2,266
Gas Guzzler Tax	No
Greenhouse Gas Emissions (tons/yr.)	High-8.5
Barrels of Oil Used per year	High-15.7

How the Competition Rates

Competitors	Rating	Pg.
Cadillac SRX	8	109
Infiniti QX70	–	167
Lexus RX	6	192

Price Range	Retail	Markup
sDrive35i	$53,200	9%
XDrive35i	$55,500	9%
XDrive35d	$57,000	9%
XDrive50i	$69,100	9%

Safety Checklist

Crash Tests:
Frontal	Good
Side	Good

Airbags:
Torso	Front Torso from Seat
Pelvis	None
Roll Sensing	Yes
Knee Bolster	Standard Front

Crash Avoidance:
Collision Avoidance	Optional CIB & DBS
Blind Spot Detection	Optional
Lane Keeping Assist	Warning Only Optional
Backup Camera	Standard
Pedestrian Crash Avoidance	Optional

General:
Auto. Crash Notif.	Oper. Assist. & Crash Info-Free
Day Running Lamps	Standard

Safety Belt/Restraint:
Dynamic Head Restraints	Standard Front
Adjustable Belt	None

BMW X5

Specifications

Drive	AWD
Engine	3.0-liter I6
Transmission	8-sp. Automatic
Tow Rating (lbs.)	–
Head/Leg Room (in.)	Cramped-40.5/40.4
Interior Space (cu. ft.)	–
Cargo Space (cu. ft.)	Roomy-23
Wheelbase/Length (in.)	115.5/193.2

Ratings—10 Best, 1 Worst

Combo Crash Tests	9
Safety Features	7
Rollover	3
Preventive Maintenance	6
Repair Costs	3
Warranty	7
Fuel Economy	2
Complaints	4
Insurance Costs	10
OVERALL RATING	**7**

Buick Enclave

Buick Enclave

Safety Checklist

Crash Tests:
Frontal . . . . Good
Side . . . . Good

Airbags:
Torso . . . . Front Pelvis/Torso from Seat
Pelvis . . . . Front Pelvis/Torso from Seat
Roll Sensing . . . . Yes
Knee Bolster . . . . None

Crash Avoidance:
Collision Avoidance . . . . . Warning Only Optional
Blind Spot Detection . . . . Optional
Lane Keeping Assist . . . . Warning Only Optional
Backup Camera . . . . Standard
Pedestrian Crash Avoidance . . . . None

General:
Auto. Crash Notif. . . . Oper. Assist. & Crash Info-Fee
Day Running Lamps . . . . Standard

Safety Belt/Restraint:
Dynamic Head Restraints . . . . None
Adjustable Belt . . . . Standard Front

At-a-Glance

Status/Year Series Started Unchanged/2008
Twins . . . . –
Body Styles . . . . SUV
Seating 7/8
Anti-Theft Device . . . . . . Std. Pass. Immobil. & Alarm
Parking Index Rating . . . . Very Hard
Where Made . . . . Lansing, MI
Fuel Factor . . . .
  MPG Rating (city/hwy) . . . . Very Poor-17/24
  Driving Range (mi.) Long-430.5
  Fuel Type . . . . Regular
  Annual Fuel Cost . . . . High-$2,146
  Gas Guzzler Tax . . . . No
  Greenhouse Gas Emissions (tons/yr.) Very High-9.5
  Barrels of Oil Used per year . . . . Very High-17.3

How the Competition Rates

Competitors	Rating	Pg.
Audi Q7	–	93
Infiniti QX60	–	166
Lexus GX	–	189

Price Range	Retail	Markup
Convenience FWD	$38,950	5%
Leather FWD	$43,215	5%
Leather AWD	$45,215	5%
Premium AWD	$49,070	5%

Buick Enclave

Specifications

Drive . . . . FWD
Engine 3.6-liter V6
Transmission . . . . 6-sp. Automatic
Tow Rating (lbs.) Low-4500
Head/Leg Room (in.) Average-40.4/41.3
Interior Space (cu. ft.) . . . . Very Roomy-151.1
Cargo Space (cu. ft.) Roomy-23.3
Wheelbase/Length (in.) 119/201.9

Ratings—10 Best, 1 Worst

Combo Crash Tests	8
Safety Features	10
Rollover	3
Preventive Maintenance	8
Repair Costs	8
Warranty	7
Fuel Economy	6
Complaints	7
Insurance Costs	8
OVERALL RATING	**10**

Buick Encore

Buick Encore

Buick Encore

At-a-Glance

Status/Year Series Started	Unchanged/2013
Twins	Chevrolet Trax
Body Styles	SUV
Seating	5
Anti-Theft Device	Std. Pass. Immobil. & Alarm
Parking Index Rating	Easy
Where Made	Bupyong, South Korea
Fuel Factor	
MPG Rating (city/hwy)	Average-23/30
Driving Range (mi.)	Very Short-359.8
Fuel Type	Regular
Annual Fuel Cost	Low-$1,634
Gas Guzzler Tax	No
Greenhouse Gas Emissions (tons/yr.)	Average-6.9
Barrels of Oil Used per year	Average-12.7

How the Competition Rates

Competitors	Rating	Pg.
BMW X1	—	99
Ford Escape	5	138
Lincoln MKC	5	193

Price Range

	Retail	Markup
Base FWD	$24,065	4%
Convenience FWD	$26,155	4%
Leather AWD	$29,450	4%
Premium AWD	$30,935	4%

Safety Checklist

Crash Tests:
Frontal . . . . Very Good
Side . . . . Average

Airbags:
Torso . . . . Fr. & Rr. Pelvis/Torso from Seat
Pelvis . . . . Fr. & Rr. Pelvis/Torso from Seat
Roll Sensing . . . . Yes
Knee Bolster . . . . Standard Front

Crash Avoidance:
Collision Avoidance . . . . . Warning Only Optional
Blind Spot Detection . . . . Optional
Lane Keeping Assist . . . . Warning Only Optional
Backup Camera . . . . Standard
Pedestrian Crash Avoidance . . . . None

General:
Auto. Crash Notif. . . . Oper. Assist. & Crash Info-Fee
Day Running Lamps . . . . Standard

Safety Belt/Restraint:
Dynamic Head Restraints . . . . None
Adjustable Belt . . . . Standard Front

Buick Encore

Specifications

Drive	AWD
Engine	1.4-liter I4
Transmission	6-sp. Automatic
Tow Rating (lbs.)	—
Head/Leg Room (in.)	Cramped-39.6/40.8
Interior Space (cu. ft.)	Cramped-92.8
Cargo Space (cu. ft.)	Average-18.8
Wheelbase/Length (in.)	100.6/168.4

Ratings—10 Best, 1 Worst

Combo Crash Tests	9
Safety Features	9
Rollover	6
Preventive Maintenance	5
Repair Costs	4
Warranty	7
Fuel Economy	3
Complaints	7
Insurance Costs	5
OVERALL RATING	**8**

Buick LaCrosse

Buick LaCrosse

At-a-Glance

Status/Year Series Started........ Unchanged/2010
Twins ....Cadillac XTS, Chevrolet Impala
Body Styles ....Sedan
Seating....................................5
Anti-Theft Device ...... Std. Pass. Immobil. & Alarm
Parking Index Rating .... Hard
Where Made......................... Fairfax, KS
Fuel Factor.................................
  MPG Rating (city/hwy)..............Poor-18/28
  Driving Range (mi.) Average-396.8
  Fuel Type..........................Regular
  Annual Fuel Cost .... High-$1,958
  Gas Guzzler Tax ....No
  Greenhouse Gas Emissions (tons/yr.)..... High-8.6
  Barrels of Oil Used per year High-15.7

How the Competition Rates

Competitors	Rating	Pg.
Cadillac XTS	9	110
Chevrolet Impala	6	116
Toyota Avalon	7	247

Price Range

Price Range	Retail	Markup
Base FWD	$33,635	4%
Leather FWD	$35,510	4%
Premium II FWD	$39,755	4%
Premium I AWD	$40,285	4%

Safety Checklist

Crash Tests:
  Frontal......................... Very Good
  Side................................. Good
Airbags:
  Torso .... Fr. & Rr. Pelvis/Torso from Seat
  Pelvis .... Fr. & Rr. Pelvis/Torso from Seat
  Roll Sensing..........................Yes
  Knee Bolster .... None
Crash Avoidance:
  Collision Avoidance .... Optional CIB
  Blind Spot Detection .... Optional
  Lane Keeping Assist .... None
  Backup Camera................... Standard
  Pedestrian Crash Avoidance .... None
General:
  Auto. Crash Notif. ... Oper. Assist. & Crash Info-Fee
  Day Running Lamps .... Standard
Safety Belt/Restraint:
  Dynamic Head Restraints .... None
  Adjustable Belt...............Standard Front

Buick LaCrosse

Specifications

Drive.................................. FWD
Engine 3.6-liter V6
Transmission .... 6-sp. Automatic
Tow Rating (lbs.) .... Very Low-1000
Head/Leg Room (in.) Cramped-38/41.7
Interior Space (cu. ft.)............ Average-99
Cargo Space (cu. ft.) Cramped-13.3
Wheelbase/Length (in.) 111.7/197

Ratings—10 Best, 1 Worst	
Combo Crash Tests	6
Safety Features	6
Rollover	7
Preventive Maintenance	7
Repair Costs	4
Warranty	7
Fuel Economy	4
Complaints	9
Insurance Costs	3
OVERALL RATING	**6**

Buick Regal

Buick Regal

At-a-Glance

Status/Year Series Started	Unchanged/2011
Twins	Chevrolet Malibu
Body Styles	Sedan
Seating	5
Anti-Theft Device	Std. Pass. Immobil. & Alarm
Parking Index Rating	Average
Where Made	Oshawa, Ontario
Fuel Factor	
MPG Rating (city/hwy)	Poor-19/31
Driving Range (mi.)	Very Short-363.5
Fuel Type	Regular
Annual Fuel Cost	Average-$1,825
Gas Guzzler Tax	No
Greenhouse Gas Emissions (tons/yr.)	High-7.9
Barrels of Oil Used per year	High-14.3

How the Competition Rates

Competitors	Rating	Pg.
Acura TLX	–	85
Cadillac CTS	10	108
Lincoln MKZ	4	196

Price Range	Retail	Markup
Base FWD	$29,840	4%
Premium I FWD	$31,750	4%
Premium II AWD	$36,375	4%
GS AWD	$39,660	4%

Safety Checklist

Crash Tests:
Frontal . . . . Average
Side . . . . Average

Airbags:
Torso . . . . Front Pelvis/Torso from Seat
Pelvis . . . . Opt. Rear Pelvis/Torso
Roll Sensing . . . . Yes
Knee Bolster . . . . None

Crash Avoidance:
Collision Avoidance . . . . Optional CIB
Blind Spot Detection . . . . Optional
Lane Keeping Assist . . . . Warning Only Optional
Backup Camera . . . . Standard
Pedestrian Crash Avoidance . . . . None

General:
Auto. Crash Notif. . . . Oper. Assist. & Crash Info-Fee
Day Running Lamps . . . . Standard

Safety Belt/Restraint:
Dynamic Head Restraints . . . . None
Adjustable Belt . . . . Standard Front

Buick Regal

Specifications

Drive	FWD
Engine	2.4-liter I4
Transmission	6-sp. Automatic
Tow Rating (lbs.)	–
Head/Leg Room (in.)	Cramped-38.8/42.1
Interior Space (cu. ft.)	Cramped-96.8
Cargo Space (cu. ft.)	Very Cramped-11.1
Wheelbase/Length (in.)	107.8/190.2

Ratings—10 Best, 1 Worst

Combo Crash Tests	8
Safety Features	10
Rollover	4
Preventive Maintenance	8
Repair Costs	7
Warranty	7
Fuel Economy	5
Complaints	6
Insurance Costs	5
OVERALL RATING	**9**

Buick Verano

Buick Verano

At-a-Glance

Status/Year Series Started. Unchanged/2012
Twins . . . . Chevrolet Cruze
Body Styles . . . . Sedan
Seating 5
Anti-Theft Device . . . . . . Std. Pass. Immobil. & Alarm
Parking Index Rating . . . . Easy
Where Made. . . . . Orion Township, MI
Fuel Factor. . . . .
  MPG Rating (city/hwy) Average-21/32
  Driving Range (mi.) Short-387.5
  Fuel Type. . . . . Regular
  Annual Fuel Cost . . . . Average-$1,690
  Gas Guzzler Tax . . . . No
  Greenhouse Gas Emissions (tons/yr.) . . Average-7.2
  Barrels of Oil Used per year High-13.2

How the Competition Rates

Competitors	Rating	Pg.
Acura ILX	7	81
Dodge Dart	5	131
Lexus IS	5	190

Price Range	Retail	Markup
Base	$23,230	4%
Convenience	$24,870	4%
Leather	$26,900	4%
Turbo	$29,065	4%

Safety Checklist

Crash Tests:
  Frontal. . . . . Average
  Side. . . . . Very Good

Airbags:
  Torso . . . . Fr. & Rr. Pelvis/Torso from Seat
  Pelvis . . . . Fr. & Rr. Pelvis/Torso from Seat
  Roll Sensing. . . . . .Yes
  Knee Bolster . . . . .Standard Front

Crash Avoidance:
  Collision Avoidance . . . . .Warning Only Optional
  Blind Spot Detection . . . . Optional
  Lane Keeping Assist . . . .Warning Only Optional
  Backup Camera. . . . . Standard
  Pedestrian Crash Avoidance . . . . None

General:
  Auto. Crash Notif. . . . Oper. Assist. & Crash Info-Fee
  Day Running Lamps . . . . Standard

Safety Belt/Restraint:
  Dynamic Head Restraints . . . . None
  Adjustable Belt . . . . .Standard Front

Buick Verano

Specifications

Drive. . . . . FWD
Engine 2.4-liter I4
Transmission . . . . 6-sp. Automatic
Tow Rating (lbs.) . . . . Very Low-1000
Head/Leg Room (in.) Cramped-38.3/42
Interior Space (cu. ft.). Cramped-95
Cargo Space (cu. ft.) Cramped-14.3
Wheelbase/Length (in.) 105.7/183.9

Ratings—10 Best, 1 Worst	
Combo Crash Tests	8
Safety Features	8
Rollover	8
Preventive Maintenance	10
Repair Costs	5
Warranty	9
Fuel Economy	5
Complaints	2
Insurance Costs	8
OVERALL RATING	**9**

Cadillac ATS

Cadillac ATS

At-a-Glance

Status/Year Series Started Appearance Change/2013	
Twins	–
Body Styles	Sedan, Coupe
Seating	5
Anti-Theft Device	Std. Pass. Immobil. & Alarm
Parking Index Rating	Easy
Where Made	Lansing, MI
Fuel Factor	
MPG Rating (city/hwy)	Average-21/33
Driving Range (mi.)	Average-401.7
Fuel Type	Regular
Annual Fuel Cost	Average-$1,672
Gas Guzzler Tax	No
Greenhouse Gas Emissions (tons/yr.)	Average-7.2
Barrels of Oil Used per year	High-13.2

How the Competition Rates

Competitors	Rating	Pg.
Acura ILX	7	81
Infiniti Q50	–	163
Mercedes-Benz C-Class	–	203

Price Range	Retail	Markup
Base 2.5L Sedan	$33,215	6%
Luxury 2.0T Sedan AWD	$41,340	6%
Performance 3.6L Sedan	$44,660	7%
Premium 3.6L Coupe AWD	$51,435	7%

Safety Checklist

Crash Tests:
Frontal . . . . Very Good
Side . . . . Poor

Airbags:
Torso . . . . Front Pelvis/Torso from Seat
Pelvis . . . . Opt. Rear Pelvis/Torso
Roll Sensing . . . . Yes
Knee Bolster . . . . Standard Front

Crash Avoidance:
Collision Avoidance . . . . . . Optional CIB & DBS
Blind Spot Detection . . . . Optional
Lane Keeping Assist . . . . Optional
Backup Camera . . . . Optional
Pedestrian Crash Avoidance . . . . None

General:
Auto. Crash Notif. . . . Oper. Assist. & Crash Info-Fee
Day Running Lamps . . . . Standard

Safety Belt/Restraint:
Dynamic Head Restraints . . . . None
Adjustable Belt . . . . Optional Rear

Cadillac ATS

Specifications

Drive	RWD
Engine	2.5-liter I4
Transmission	6-sp. Automatic
Tow Rating (lbs.)	–
Head/Leg Room (in.)	Average-38.6/42.5
Interior Space (cu. ft.)	Very Cramped-90.9
Cargo Space (cu. ft.)	Very Cramped-10.4
Wheelbase/Length (in.)	109.3/182.8

Cadillac CTS   Intermediate

Ratings—10 Best, 1 Worst

Combo Crash Tests	8
Safety Features	8
Rollover	8
Preventive Maintenance	10
Repair Costs	4
Warranty	9
Fuel Economy	3
Complaints	6
Insurance Costs	10
OVERALL RATING	**10**

Cadillac CTS

Cadillac CTS

At-a-Glance

Status/Year Series Started	Unchanged/2014
Twins	–
Body Styles	Sedan, Coupe, Wagon
Seating	5
Anti-Theft Device	Std. Pass. Immobil. & Alarm
Parking Index Rating	Average
Where Made	Lansing, MI
Fuel Factor	
MPG Rating (city/hwy)	Poor-18/29
Driving Range (mi.)	Average-412.4
Fuel Type	Regular
Annual Fuel Cost	Average-$1,935
Gas Guzzler Tax	No
Greenhouse Gas Emissions (tons/yr.)	High-8.2
Barrels of Oil Used per year	High-15.0

How the Competition Rates

Competitors	Rating	Pg.
Acura TLX	–	85
Lexus ES	7	187
Mercedes-Benz E-Class	4	205

Price Range

Price Range	Retail	Markup
2.0T Base RWD	$45,345	6%
3.6L Luxury AWD	$55,970	6%
3.6L Premium AWD	$66,770	7%
Vsport Premium RWD	$69,340	7%

Safety Checklist

Crash Tests:
Frontal .... Good
Side .... Good

Airbags:
Torso .... Front Pelvis/Torso from Seat
Pelvis .... Opt. Rear Pelvis/Torso
Roll Sensing .... Yes
Knee Bolster .... Standard Front

Crash Avoidance:
Collision Avoidance ...... Optional CIB & DBS
Blind Spot Detection .... Optional
Lane Keeping Assist .... Optional
Backup Camera .... Optional
Pedestrian Crash Avoidance .... None

General:
Auto. Crash Notif. ... Oper. Assist. & Crash Info-Fee
Day Running Lamps .... Standard

Safety Belt/Restraint:
Dynamic Head Restraints .... None
Adjustable Belt .... Standard Front and Rear

Cadillac CTS

Specifications

Drive	RWD
Engine	3.6-liter V6
Transmission	6-sp. Automatic
Tow Rating (lbs.)	Very Low-1000
Head/Leg Room (in.)	Average-42.6/39.2
Interior Space (cu. ft.)	Cramped-97
Cargo Space (cu. ft.)	Cramped-13.7
Wheelbase/Length (in.)	114.6/195.5

Ratings—10 Best, 1 Worst

Combo Crash Tests	7
Safety Features	7
Rollover	3
Preventive Maintenance	10
Repair Costs	6
Warranty	9
Fuel Economy	2
Complaints	6
Insurance Costs	8
OVERALL RATING	**8**

Cadillac SRX

Cadillac SRX

At-a-Glance

Status/Year Series Started	Unchanged/2010
Twins	–
Body Styles	SUV
Seating	5
Anti-Theft Device	Std. Pass. Immobil. & Alarm
Parking Index Rating	Very Hard
Where Made	Ramos Arizpe, Mexico
Fuel Factor	
MPG Rating (city/hwy)	Very Poor-17/24
Driving Range (mi.)	Average-410.9
Fuel Type	Regular
Annual Fuel Cost	High-$2,146
Gas Guzzler Tax	No
Greenhouse Gas Emissions (tons/yr.)	High-9.4
Barrels of Oil Used per year	Very High-17.3

How the Competition Rates

Competitors	Rating	Pg.
Acura RDX	8	83
Lexus RX	6	192
Volvo XC60	9	270

Price Range	Retail	Markup
Base FWD	$37,605	6%
Luxury FWD	$43,640	6%
Performance AWD	$48,840	7%
Premium AWD	$51,730	7%

Safety Checklist

Crash Tests:
Frontal . . . . Good
Side . . . . Average

Airbags:
Torso . . . . Front Pelvis/Torso from Seat
Pelvis . . . . .Front Pelvis/Torso from Seat
Roll Sensing . . . . .Yes
Knee Bolster . . . . None

Crash Avoidance:
Collision Avoidance . . . . Optional CIB
Blind Spot Detection . . . . Optional
Lane Keeping Assist . . . .Warning Only Optional
Backup Camera . . . . Standard
Pedestrian Crash Avoidance . . . . None

General:
Auto. Crash Notif. . . . Oper. Assist. & Crash Info-Fee
Day Running Lamps . . . . Standard

Safety Belt/Restraint:
Dynamic Head Restraints . . . . None
Adjustable Belt . . . . . . .Standard Front and Rear

Cadillac SRX

Specifications

Drive	FWD
Engine	3.6-liter V6
Transmission	6-sp. Automatic
Tow Rating (lbs.)	Low-3500
Head/Leg Room (in.)	Cramped-39.7/41.2
Interior Space (cu. ft.)	Average-100.6
Cargo Space (cu. ft.)	Roomy-29.9
Wheelbase/Length (in.)	110.5/190.3

Cadillac XTS | Large

Ratings—10 Best, 1 Worst

Combo Crash Tests	10
Safety Features	8
Rollover	6
Preventive Maintenance	10
Repair Costs	2
Warranty	9
Fuel Economy	3
Complaints	5
Insurance Costs	8
OVERALL RATING	**9**

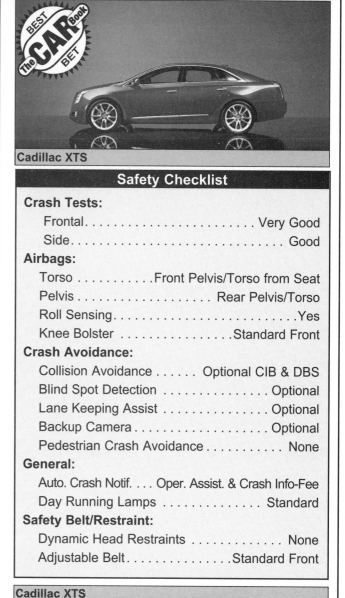

Cadillac XTS

Cadillac XTS

At-a-Glance

Status/Year Series Started	Unchanged/2013
Twins	Buick LaCrosse, Chevrolet Impala
Body Styles	Sedan
Seating	5
Anti-Theft Device	Std. Pass. Immobil. & Active Alarm
Parking Index Rating	Hard
Where Made	Oshawa, Ontario
Fuel Factor	
MPG Rating (city/hwy)	Poor-18/28
Driving Range (mi.)	Average-407.5
Fuel Type	Regular
Annual Fuel Cost	High-$1,958
Gas Guzzler Tax	No
Greenhouse Gas Emissions (tons/yr.)	High-8.6
Barrels of Oil Used per year	High-15.7

How the Competition Rates

Competitors	Rating	Pg.
BMW 7 Series	–	98
Chrysler 300	–	127
Lincoln MKS	5	194

Price Range

	Retail	Markup
Base	$44,600	6%
Luxury AWD	$51,000	6%
Platinum	$62,015	7%
Platinum Vsport AWD	$69,785	7%

Safety Checklist

Crash Tests:
Frontal.........................Very Good
Side.................................Good
Airbags:
Torso ....Front Pelvis/Torso from Seat
Pelvis ....Rear Pelvis/Torso
Roll Sensing............................Yes
Knee Bolster ....Standard Front
Crash Avoidance:
Collision Avoidance ...... Optional CIB & DBS
Blind Spot Detection ....Optional
Lane Keeping Assist ....Optional
Backup Camera...................Optional
Pedestrian Crash Avoidance .... None
General:
Auto. Crash Notif. .... Oper. Assist. & Crash Info-Fee
Day Running Lamps .... Standard
Safety Belt/Restraint:
Dynamic Head Restraints .... None
Adjustable Belt...............Standard Front

Cadillac XTS

Specifications

Drive	FWD
Engine	3.6-liter V6
Transmission	6-sp. Automatic
Tow Rating (lbs.)	Very Low-1000
Head/Leg Room (in.)	Very Roomy-39/45.8
Interior Space (cu. ft.)	Roomy-104.2
Cargo Space (cu. ft.)	Average-18
Wheelbase/Length (in.)	111.7/202

Ratings—10 Best, 1 Worst	
Combo Crash Tests	10
Safety Features	5
Rollover	9
Preventive Maintenance	5
Repair Costs	7
Warranty	7
Fuel Economy	3
Complaints	5
Insurance Costs	1
OVERALL RATING	**7**

Chevrolet Camaro

Chevrolet Camaro

At-a-Glance

Status/Year Series Started	Unchanged/2010
Twins	–
Body Styles	Coupe, Convertible
Seating	4
Anti-Theft Device	Std. Pass. Immobil. & Alarm
Parking Index Rating	Average
Where Made	Oshawa, Ontario
Fuel Factor	
MPG Rating (city/hwy)	Poor-18/27
Driving Range (mi.)	Average-402.4
Fuel Type	Regular
Annual Fuel Cost	High-$1,983
Gas Guzzler Tax	No
Greenhouse Gas Emissions (tons/yr.)	High-8.6
Barrels of Oil Used per year	High-15.7

How the Competition Rates

Competitors	Rating	Pg.
Dodge Challenger	5	129
Ford Mustang	–	146
Nissan 370Z	–	217

Price Range	Retail	Markup
1LS Coupe	$23,555	4%
2LT Convertible	$34,955	4%
ZL1 Coupe	$55,355	4%
Z28 Coupe	$72,305	4%

Safety Checklist

Crash Tests:
Frontal . . . . Very Good
Side . . . . Very Good

Airbags:
Torso . . . . Front Pelvis/Torso from Seat
Pelvis . . . . Front Pelvis/Torso from Seat
Roll Sensing . . . . Yes
Knee Bolster . . . . None

Crash Avoidance:
Collision Avoidance . . . . None
Blind Spot Detection . . . . None
Lane Keeping Assist . . . . None
Backup Camera . . . . Optional
Pedestrian Crash Avoidance . . . . None

General:
Auto. Crash Notif. . . . Oper. Assist. & Crash Info-Fee
Day Running Lamps . . . . Standard

Safety Belt/Restraint:
Dynamic Head Restraints . . . . None
Adjustable Belt . . . . Optional Rear

Chevrolet Camaro

Specifications

Drive	RWD
Engine	3.6-liter V6
Transmission	6-sp. Automatic
Tow Rating (lbs.)	–
Head/Leg Room (in.)	Cramped-37.4/42.4
Interior Space (cu. ft.)	Cramped-93
Cargo Space (cu. ft.)	Very Cramped-11.3
Wheelbase/Length (in.)	112.3/190.6

Ratings—10 Best, 1 Worst

	Colorado	Canyon
Combo Crash Tests	–	–
Safety Features	6	5
Rollover	2	1
Preventive Maintenance	–	–
Repair Costs	–	–
Warranty	7	6
Fuel Economy	4	2
Complaints	–	–
Insurance Costs	10	8
OVERALL RATING	–	–

GMC Canyon

At-a-Glance

Status/Year Series Started	All New/2015
Twins	GMC Canyon
Body Styles	Pickup
Seating	5
Anti-Theft Device	Std. Pass. Immob. & Opt. Pass. Alarm
Parking Index Rating	Very Hard
Where Made	Wentzville, MO
Fuel Factor	
MPG Rating (city/hwy)	Poor-20/27
Driving Range (mi.)	Very Long-475.5
Fuel Type	Regular
Annual Fuel Cost	Average-$1,855
Gas Guzzler Tax	No
Greenhouse Gas Emissions (tons/yr.)	High-8.2
Barrels of Oil Used per year	High-15.0

How the Competition Rates

Competitors	Rating	Pg.
Nissan Frontier	–	220
Toyota Tacoma	1	257

Price Range

	Retail	Markup
Base Ext. Cab 2WD	$20,120	1%
W/T Crew Cab 4WD	$29,705	5%
LT Crew Cab 4WD	$32,385	5%
Z71 Crew Cab 4WD	$34,415	5%

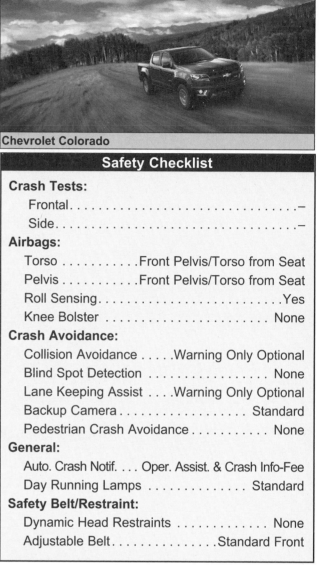
Chevrolet Colorado

Safety Checklist

Crash Tests:
Frontal .... –
Side .... –

Airbags:
Torso .... Front Pelvis/Torso from Seat
Pelvis .... Front Pelvis/Torso from Seat
Roll Sensing .... Yes
Knee Bolster .... None

Crash Avoidance:
Collision Avoidance ..... Warning Only Optional
Blind Spot Detection .... None
Lane Keeping Assist .... Warning Only Optional
Backup Camera .... Standard
Pedestrian Crash Avoidance .... None

General:
Auto. Crash Notif. .... Oper. Assist. & Crash Info-Fee
Day Running Lamps .... Standard

Safety Belt/Restraint:
Dynamic Head Restraints .... None
Adjustable Belt .... Standard Front

Chevrolet Colorado

Specifications

Drive	RWD
Engine	2.5-liter I4
Transmission	6-sp. Automatic
Tow Rating (lbs.)	Low-3500
Head/Leg Room (in.)	Very Roomy-41.4/45
Interior Space (cu. ft.)	–
Cargo Space (cu. ft.)	Very Roomy-49.9
Wheelbase/Length (in.)	128.3/212.7

Chevrolet Corvette Intermediate

Ratings—10 Best, 1 Worst

Combo Crash Tests	–
Safety Features	2
Rollover	10
Preventive Maintenance	7
Repair Costs	1
Warranty	7
Fuel Economy	3
Complaints	4
Insurance Costs	10
OVERALL RATING	**–**

Chevrolet Corvette

Chevrolet Corvette

At-a-Glance

Status/Year Series Started	Unchanged/2014
Twins	–
Body Styles	Coupe, Convertible
Seating	2
Anti-Theft Device	Std. Pass. Immobil. & Alarm
Parking Index Rating	Average
Where Made	Bowling Green, KY
Fuel Factor	
MPG Rating (city/hwy)	Poor-16/29
Driving Range (mi.)	Short-370.8
Fuel Type	Premium
Annual Fuel Cost	Very High-$2,394
Gas Guzzler Tax	No
Greenhouse Gas Emissions (tons/yr.)	High-9.0
Barrels of Oil Used per year	High-16.5

How the Competition Rates

Competitors	Rating	Pg.
Dodge Challenger	5	129
Ford Mustang	–	146
Nissan 370Z	–	217

Price Range

	Retail	Markup
Base Coupe	$53,000	10%
Z51 Coupe	$58,000	10%
Base Convertible	$58,000	10%
Z51 Convertible	$63,000	10%

Safety Checklist

Crash Tests:
Frontal . . . . –
Side . . . . –

Airbags:
Torso . . . . Front Head/Torso from Seat
Pelvis . . . . None
Roll Sensing . . . . No
Knee Bolster . . . . None

Crash Avoidance:
Collision Avoidance . . . . None
Blind Spot Detection . . . . None
Lane Keeping Assist . . . . None
Backup Camera . . . . Standard
Pedestrian Crash Avoidance . . . . None

General:
Auto. Crash Notif. . . . . Oper. Assist. & Crash Info-Fee
Day Running Lamps . . . . Standard

Safety Belt/Restraint:
Dynamic Head Restraints . . . . None
Adjustable Belt . . . . None

Chevrolet Corvette

Specifications

Drive	RWD
Engine	6.2-liter V8
Transmission	8-sp. Automatic
Tow Rating (lbs.)	–
Head/Leg Room (in.)	Cramped-38/43
Interior Space (cu. ft.)	Very Cramped-52
Cargo Space (cu. ft.)	Cramped-15
Wheelbase/Length (in.)	106.7/176.9

Ratings—10 Best, 1 Worst

Combo Crash Tests	8
Safety Features	9
Rollover	7
Preventive Maintenance	5
Repair Costs	8
Warranty	7
Fuel Economy	8
Complaints	5
Insurance Costs	1
OVERALL RATING	**8**

Chevrolet Cruze

Chevrolet Cruze

At-a-Glance

Status/Year Series Started Appearance Change/2010
Twins . . . . Buick Verano
Body Styles . . . . .Sedan
Seating 5
Anti-Theft Device . . . . . . Std. Pass. Immobil. & Alarm
Parking Index Rating . . . . Easy
Where Made . . . . Lordstown, OH
Fuel Factor . . . .
MPG Rating (city/hwy) Good-26/38
Driving Range (mi.) . . . . .Very Long-472.8
Fuel Type . . . . .Regular
Annual Fuel Cost . . . . Very Low-$1,385
Gas Guzzler Tax . . . . .No
Greenhouse Gas Emissions (tons/yr.) Low-6.0
Barrels of Oil Used per year Average-11.0

How the Competition Rates

Competitors	Rating	Pg.
Ford Focus	–	144
Honda Civic	6	149
Toyota Corolla	8	249

Price Range

Price Range	Retail	Markup
LS MT	$17,745	4%
1LT AT	$20,095	4%
Eco AT	$21,370	4%
Diesel	$25,660	4%

Safety Checklist

Crash Tests:
Frontal . . . . Good
Side . . . . Average
Airbags:
Torso . . . . Fr. & Rr. Pelvis/Torso from Seat
Pelvis . . . . Fr. & Rr. Pelvis/Torso from Seat
Roll Sensing . . . . .Yes
Knee Bolster . . . . .Standard Front
Crash Avoidance:
Collision Avoidance . . . . None
Blind Spot Detection . . . . Optional
Lane Keeping Assist . . . . None
Backup Camera . . . . Optional
Pedestrian Crash Avoidance . . . . None
General:
Auto. Crash Notif. . . . Oper. Assist. & Crash Info-Fee
Day Running Lamps . . . . Standard
Safety Belt/Restraint:
Dynamic Head Restraints . . . . None
Adjustable Belt . . . . . . .Standard Front and Rear

Chevrolet Cruze

Specifications

Drive . . . . FWD
Engine 1.4-liter I4
Transmission . . . . .6-sp. Automatic
Tow Rating (lbs.) . . . . Very Low-1000
Head/Leg Room (in.) Average-39.3/42.3
Interior Space (cu. ft.) Cramped-95
Cargo Space (cu. ft.) Cramped-15
Wheelbase/Length (in.) 105.7/181

Ratings—10 Best, 1 Worst	Equinox	Terrain
Combo Crash Tests	2	2
Safety Features	6	6
Rollover	2	2
Preventive Maintenance	5	5
Repair Costs	6	6
Warranty	7	6
Fuel Economy	6	6
Complaints	4	7
Insurance Costs	5	–
OVERALL RATING	**2**	**3**

Chevrolet Equinox

GMC Terrain

At-a-Glance

Status/Year Series Started	Unchanged/2005
Twins	GMC Terrain
Body Styles	SUV
Seating	5
Anti-Theft Device	Std. Pass. Immobil. & Alarm
Parking Index Rating	Hard
Where Made	Oshawa, Ontario / Spring Hill, TN
Fuel Factor	
MPG Rating (city/hwy)	Average-22/32
Driving Range (mi.)	Very Long-481.3
Fuel Type	Regular
Annual Fuel Cost	Low-$1,640
Gas Guzzler Tax	No
Greenhouse Gas Emissions (tons/yr.)	Average-6.9
Barrels of Oil Used per year	Average-12.7

How the Competition Rates

Competitors	Rating	Pg.
Dodge Journey	–	133
Ford Explorer	3	140
Honda Pilot	2	154

Price Range	Retail	Markup
LS FWD	$24,370	5%
LT FWD	$26,020	5%
2LT AWD	$29,770	5%
LTZ AWD	$33,520	5%

Safety Checklist

Crash Tests:
Frontal	Poor
Side	Very Poor

Airbags:
Torso	Front Pelvis/Torso from Seat
Pelvis	Front Pelvis/Torso from Seat
Roll Sensing	Yes
Knee Bolster	None

Crash Avoidance:
Collision Avoidance	Warning Only Optional
Blind Spot Detection	None
Lane Keeping Assist	Warning Only Optional
Backup Camera	Optional
Pedestrian Crash Avoidance	None

General:
Auto. Crash Notif.	Oper. Assist. & Crash Info-Fee
Day Running Lamps	Standard

Safety Belt/Restraint:
Dynamic Head Restraints	None
Adjustable Belt	Standard Front and Rear

Chevrolet Equinox

Specifications

Drive	FWD
Engine	2.4-liter I4
Transmission	6-sp. Automatic
Tow Rating (lbs.)	Very Low-1500
Head/Leg Room (in.)	Average-40.9/41.2
Interior Space (cu. ft.)	Average-99.7
Cargo Space (cu. ft.)	Roomy-31.5
Wheelbase/Length (in.)	112.5/187.8

Chevrolet Impala

Ratings—10 Best, 1 Worst

Combo Crash Tests	7*
Safety Features	7
Rollover	6
Preventive Maintenance	5
Repair Costs	6
Warranty	7
Fuel Economy	3
Complaints	2
Insurance Costs	8
OVERALL RATING	**6**

Chevrolet Impala

Chevrolet Impala

At-a-Glance

Status/Year Series Started Unchanged/2014
Twins . . . . .Buick LaCrosse, Cadillac XTS
Body Styles . . . . .Sedan
Seating 5
Anti-Theft Device . . . . . . Std. Pass. Immobil. & Alarm
Parking Index Rating . . . . Hard
Where Made. . . . . Hamtramck, MI / Oshawa, Ontario
Fuel Factor. . . . .
  MPG Rating (city/hwy) Poor-18/28
  Driving Range (mi.) Average-396.8
  Fuel Type. . . . . .Regular
  Annual Fuel Cost . . . . High-$1,958
  Gas Guzzler Tax . . . . .No
  Greenhouse Gas Emissions (tons/yr.) High-8.6
  Barrels of Oil Used per year High-15.7

How the Competition Rates

Competitors	Rating	Pg.
Buick LaCrosse	8	104
Ford Taurus	4	147
Toyota Avalon	7	247

Price Range	Retail	Markup
LS	$26,910	4%
2LT	$30,135	5%
LTZ	$34,315	6%
2LZ	$35,290	6%

Safety Checklist

Crash Tests:
  Frontal. . . . . Good
  Side. . . . . .Poor
Airbags:
  Torso . . . . .Front Pelvis/Torso from Seat
  Pelvis . . . . Rear Pelvis/Torso
  Roll Sensing. . . . . .Yes
  Knee Bolster . . . . .Standard Front
Crash Avoidance:
  Collision Avoidance . . . . Optional CIB
  Blind Spot Detection . . . . Optional
  Lane Keeping Assist . . . .Warning Only Optional
  Backup Camera . . . . Optional
  Pedestrian Crash Avoidance . . . . None
General:
  Auto. Crash Notif. . . . Oper. Assist. & Crash Info-Fee
  Day Running Lamps . . . . Standard
Safety Belt/Restraint:
  Dynamic Head Restraints . . . . None
  Adjustable Belt. . . . . . .Standard Front and Rear

Chevrolet Impala

Specifications

Drive. . . . . FWD
Engine 3.6-liter V6
Transmission . . . . .6-sp. Automatic
Tow Rating (lbs.) . . . . Very Low-1000
Head/Leg Room (in.) . . . . . . Very Roomy-39.9/45.8
Interior Space (cu. ft.). Roomy-105
Cargo Space (cu. ft.) Average-18.8
Wheelbase/Length (in.) 111.7/201.3

*Crash test does not apply to Impala Limited. For Impala Limited results see page 24.

Chevrolet Malibu Intermediate

Ratings—10 Best, 1 Worst

Combo Crash Tests	7
Safety Features	7
Rollover	7
Preventive Maintenance	5
Repair Costs	7
Warranty	7
Fuel Economy	8
Complaints	5
Insurance Costs	1
OVERALL RATING	**7**

Chevrolet Malibu

Chevrolet Malibu

At-a-Glance

Status/Year Series Started. Unchanged/2013
Twins . . . . Buick Regal
Body Styles . . . . .Sedan
Seating 5
Anti-Theft Device . . . . . . Std. Pass. Immobil. & Alarm
Parking Index Rating . . . . Average
Where Made. . . . . Fairfax, KS / Hamtramck, MI
Fuel Factor . . . .
  MPG Rating (city/hwy) Good-25/36
  Driving Range (mi.) . . . . .Very Long-536.2
  Fuel Type . . . . .Regular
  Annual Fuel Cost . . . . Low-$1,449
  Gas Guzzler Tax . . . . .No
  Greenhouse Gas Emissions (tons/yr.). Low-6.2
  Barrels of Oil Used per year Average-11.4

How the Competition Rates

Competitors	Rating	Pg.
Ford Fusion	4	145
Honda Accord	7	148
Toyota Camry	7	248

Price Range

	Retail	Markup
LS	$22,340	4%
2LT	$25,470	5%
LTZ	$28,195	6%
2LZ	$30,355	6%

Safety Checklist

Crash Tests:
  Frontal. . . . . Average
  Side. . . . . Good
Airbags:
  Torso . . . . .Front Pelvis/Torso from Seat
  Pelvis . . . . Rear Pelvis/Torso
  Roll Sensing. . . . . .Yes
  Knee Bolster . . . . .Standard Front
Crash Avoidance:
  Collision Avoidance . . . . .Warning Only Optional
  Blind Spot Detection . . . . Optional
  Lane Keeping Assist . . . .Warning Only Optional
  Backup Camera . . . . Optional
  Pedestrian Crash Avoidance . . . . None
General:
  Auto. Crash Notif. . . . Oper. Assist. & Crash Info-Fee
  Day Running Lamps . . . . Standard
Safety Belt/Restraint:
  Dynamic Head Restraints . . . . None
  Adjustable Belt. . . . . . .Standard Front and Rear

Chevrolet Malibu

Specifications

Drive. . . . . FWD
Engine 2.5-liter I4
Transmission . . . . .6-sp. Automatic
Tow Rating (lbs.) . . . . —
Head/Leg Room (in.) Average-39/42.1
Interior Space (cu. ft.). Average-100.3
Cargo Space (cu. ft.) Cramped-16.3
Wheelbase/Length (in.) 107.8/191.5

117

Ratings—10 Best, 1 Worst	Silverado	Sierra
Combo Crash Tests	9*	9*
Safety Features	6	4
Rollover	3	3
Preventive Maintenance	5	5
Repair Costs	6	5
Warranty	7	6
Fuel Economy	2	2
Complaints	5	4
Insurance Costs	10	10
OVERALL RATING	**7**	**6**

Chevrolet Silverado

At-a-Glance

GMC Sierra

Status/Year Series Started	Unchanged/2014
Twins	GMC Sierra
Body Styles	Pickup
Seating	5/6
Anti-Theft Device	Std. Pass. Immobil. & Opt. Pass. Alarm
Parking Index Rating	Very Hard
Where Made	Fort Wayne, IN
Fuel Factor	
MPG Rating (city/hwy)	Very Poor-16/22
Driving Range (mi.)	Very Long-474.2
Fuel Type	Regular
Annual Fuel Cost	High-$2,302
Gas Guzzler Tax	No
Greenhouse Gas Emissions (tons/yr.)	Very High-10.0
Barrels of Oil Used per year	Very High-18.3

How the Competition Rates

Competitors	Rating	Pg.
Ford F-150	–	141
Ram 1500	3	234
Toyota Tundra	3	258

Price Range

	Retail	Markup
W/T Reg. Cab 2WD	$26,105	4%
LT Dbl. Cab 4WD	$37,730	8%
LTZ Crew Cab 4WD	$45,420	8%
High Country Crew Cab 4WD	$51,150	8%

Safety Checklist

Crash Tests:
Frontal	Very Good
Side	Average

Airbags:
Torso	Front Pelvis/Torso from Seat
Pelvis	Front Pelvis/Torso from Seat
Roll Sensing	Yes
Knee Bolster	None

Crash Avoidance:
Collision Avoidance	Warning Only Optional
Blind Spot Detection	None
Lane Keeping Assist	Warning Only Optional
Backup Camera	Optional
Pedestrian Crash Avoidance	None

General:
Auto. Crash Notif.	Oper. Assist. & Crash Info-Fee
Day Running Lamps	Standard

Safety Belt/Restraint:
Dynamic Head Restraints	None
Adjustable Belt	Standard Front and Rear

Chevrolet Silverado

Specifications

Drive	4WD
Engine	5.3-liter V8
Transmission	6-sp. Automatic
Tow Rating (lbs.)	Very High-9200
Head/Leg Room (in.)	Very Roomy-42.8/45.2
Interior Space (cu. ft.)	–
Cargo Space (cu. ft.)	Very Roomy-61
Wheelbase/Length (in.)	143.5/230

*Crash test is for 1500 Extended and Regular Cab only. For 1500 Crew Cab results see page 27.

Ratings—10 Best, 1 Worst	
Combo Crash Tests	9
Safety Features	9
Rollover	5
Preventive Maintenance	8
Repair Costs	10
Warranty	7
Fuel Economy	8
Complaints	5
Insurance Costs	1
OVERALL RATING	**9**

Chevrolet Sonic

Chevrolet Sonic

Safety Checklist

Crash Tests:
Frontal . . . . Very Good
Side . . . . Good

Airbags:
Torso . . . . Fr. & Rr. Pelvis/Torso from Seat
Pelvis . . . . Fr. & Rr. Pelvis/Torso from Seat
Roll Sensing . . . . .Yes
Knee Bolster . . . . .Standard Front

Crash Avoidance:
Collision Avoidance . . . . .Warning Only Optional
Blind Spot Detection . . . . None
Lane Keeping Assist . . . .Warning Only Optional
Backup Camera . . . . Optional
Pedestrian Crash Avoidance . . . . None

General:
Auto. Crash Notif. . . . Oper. Assist. & Crash Info-Fee
Day Running Lamps . . . . Standard

Safety Belt/Restraint:
Dynamic Head Restraints . . . . None
Adjustable Belt . . . . . . .Standard Front and Rear

At-a-Glance

Status/Year Series Started Unchanged/2012
Twins . . . . –
Body Styles . . . . Sedan, Hatchback
Seating 5
Anti-Theft Device . . . . . . Std. Pass. Immobil. & Alarm
Parking Index Rating . . . . .Very Easy
Where Made . . . . Orion Township, MI
Fuel Factor . . . .
  MPG Rating (city/hwy) Good-25/35
  Driving Range (mi.) . . . . Very Short-350.0
  Fuel Type . . . . .Regular
  Annual Fuel Cost . . . . Low-$1,464
  Gas Guzzler Tax . . . . .No
  Greenhouse Gas Emissions (tons/yr.) Low-6.5
  Barrels of Oil Used per year Average-11.8

How the Competition Rates

Competitors	Rating	Pg.
Ford Fiesta	2	142
Nissan Versa	2	230
Toyota Yaris	5	260

Price Range	Retail	Markup
LS Sedan MT	$14,170	3%
LT Hatchback AT	$17,770	4%
LTZ Sedan AT	$19,605	5%
RS Hatchback AT	$21,870	5%

Chevrolet Sonic

Specifications

Drive . . . . FWD
Engine 1.8-liter I4
Transmission . . . . .6-sp. Automatic
Tow Rating (lbs.) . . . . –
Head/Leg Room (in.) Cramped-38.7/41.8
Interior Space (cu. ft.) . . . . .Very Cramped-90.6
Cargo Space (cu. ft.) Average-19
Wheelbase/Length (in.) 99.4/159

Chevrolet Spark Subcompact

Ratings—10 Best, 1 Worst	
Combo Crash Tests	3
Safety Features	8
Rollover	3
Preventive Maintenance	10
Repair Costs	9
Warranty	7
Fuel Economy	9
Complaints	2
Insurance Costs	1
OVERALL RATING	**5**

Chevrolet Spark

Chevrolet Spark

At-a-Glance

Status/Year Series Started	Unchanged/2014
Twins	–
Body Styles	Hatchback
Seating	4
Anti-Theft Device	Std. Pass. Immobil. & Opt. Pass. Alarm
Parking Index Rating	Very Easy
Where Made	South Korea
Fuel Factor	
MPG Rating (city/hwy)	Very Good-30/39
Driving Range (mi.)	Very Short-308.0
Fuel Type	Regular
Annual Fuel Cost	Very Low-$1,254
Gas Guzzler Tax	No
Greenhouse Gas Emissions (tons/yr.)	Very Low-5.3
Barrels of Oil Used per year	Low-9.7

How the Competition Rates

Competitors	Rating	Pg.
Fiat 500	2	134
Kia Rio	5	178
Smart ForTwo	–	238

Price Range

	Retail	Markup
LS MT	$12,170	3%
1LT AT	$14,995	4%
2LT AT	$16,435	4%
2LT EV	$27,060	4%

Safety Checklist

Crash Tests:
Frontal . . . . Very Poor
Side . . . . Poor

Airbags:
Torso . . . . Fr. & Rr. Pelvis/Torso from Seat
Pelvis . . . . Fr. & Rr. Pelvis/Torso from Seat
Roll Sensing . . . . Yes
Knee Bolster . . . . Standard Front

Crash Avoidance:
Collision Avoidance . . . . None
Blind Spot Detection . . . . None
Lane Keeping Assist . . . . None
Backup Camera . . . . None
Pedestrian Crash Avoidance . . . . None

General:
Auto. Crash Notif. . . . Oper. Assist. & Crash Info-Fee
Day Running Lamps . . . . Standard

Safety Belt/Restraint:
Dynamic Head Restraints . . . . None
Adjustable Belt . . . . Standard Front and Rear

Chevrolet Spark

Specifications

Drive	FWD
Engine	1.2-liter I4
Transmission	CVT
Tow Rating (lbs.)	–
Head/Leg Room (in.)	Average-39.4/42
Interior Space (cu. ft.)	Very Cramped-86.3
Cargo Space (cu. ft.)	Very Cramped-11.4
Wheelbase/Length (in.)	93.5/144.7

Ratings—10 Best, 1 Worst	Suburban	Yukon XL	Escalade ESV
Combo Crash Tests	6	6	–
Safety Features	6	4	7
Rollover	2	2	2
Preventive Maintenance	5	5	10
Repair Costs	6	6	2
Warranty	7	6	9
Fuel Economy	2	1	1
Complaints	–	–	–
Insurance Costs	10	10	–
OVERALL RATING	**5**	**4**	**–**

GMC Yukon XL

At-a-Glance

Status/Year Series Started. . . . . All New/2015
Twins . . . . . .Cadillac Escalade ESV, GMC Yukon XL
Body Styles . . . . SUV
Seating 6/9
Anti-Theft Device . . . . . . Std. Pass. Immobil. & Alarm
Parking Index Rating . . . . .Very Hard
Where Made. Arlington, TX
Fuel Factor . . . .
  MPG Rating (city/hwy) . . . . .Very Poor-15/22
  Driving Range (mi.) . . . . .Very Long-542.7
  Fuel Type . . . . .Regular
  Annual Fuel Cost . . . . .Very High-$2,399
  Gas Guzzler Tax . . . . .No
  Greenhouse Gas Emissions (tons/yr.)Very High-10.0
  Barrels of Oil Used per year . . . . . . .Very High-18.3

How the Competition Rates

Competitors	Rating	Pg.
Ford Expedition	7	139
Nissan Armada	–	219
Toyota Sequoia	–	255

Price Range	Retail	Markup
1500 LS 2WD	$47,300	8%
1500 LT 2WD	$52,700	8%
1500 LT 4WD	$55,700	8%
1500 LTZ 4WD	$64,700	8%

Chevrolet Suburban

Safety Checklist

Crash Tests:
  Frontal. . . . . Average
  Side. . . . . Average
Airbags:
  Torso . . . . .Front Pelvis/Torso from Seat
  Pelvis . . . . .Front Pelvis/Torso from Seat
  Roll Sensing. . . . . .Yes
  Knee Bolster . . . . None
Crash Avoidance:
  Collision Avoidance . . . . Optional CIB
  Blind Spot Detection . . . . Optional
  Lane Keeping Assist . . . .Warning Only Optional
  Backup Camera. . . . . Standard
  Pedestrian Crash Avoidance . . . . None
General:
  Auto. Crash Notif. . . . Oper. Assist. & Crash Info-Fee
  Day Running Lamps . . . . Standard
Safety Belt/Restraint:
  Dynamic Head Restraints . . . . None
  Adjustable Belt. . . . . . .Standard Front and Rear

Cadillac Escalade ESV

Specifications

Drive. 4WD
Engine 5.3-liter V8
Transmission . . . . .6-sp. Automatic
Tow Rating (lbs.) High-8000
Head/Leg Room (in.) . . . . . . Very Roomy-42.8/45.3
Interior Space (cu. ft.). . . . . Very Roomy-122.4
Cargo Space (cu. ft.) . . . . Very Roomy-39.3
Wheelbase/Length (in.) 130/224.4

Ratings—10 Best, 1 Worst

	Tahoe	Yukon	Escalade
Combo Crash Tests	8	8	–
Safety Features	6	6	7
Rollover	2	2	2
Preventive Maintenance	5	5	10
Repair Costs	5	5	2
Warranty	7	6	9
Fuel Economy	2	1	1
Complaints	–	–	–
Insurance Costs	10	10	–
OVERALL RATING	**6**	**5**	**–**

Chevrolet Tahoe

GMC Yukon

At-a-Glance

Status/Year Series Started. . . . . All New/2015
Twins . . . . .Cadillac Escalade, GMC Yukon
Body Styles . . . . SUV
Seating 6/9
Anti-Theft Device . . . . . . Std. Pass. Immobil. & Alarm
Parking Index Rating . . . . .Very Hard
Where Made. Arlington, TX
Fuel Factor . . . .
  MPG Rating (city/hwy) . . . . .Very Poor-16/22
  Driving Range (mi.) . . . . .Very Long-474.2
  Fuel Type. . . . . .Regular
  Annual Fuel Cost . . . . High-$2,302
  Gas Guzzler Tax . . . . .No
  Greenhouse Gas Emissions (tons/yr.)Very High-10.0
  Barrels of Oil Used per year . . . . . . .Very High-18.3

How the Competition Rates

Competitors	Rating	Pg.
Dodge Durango	2	132
Ford Expedition	7	139
Toyota 4Runner	3	246

Price Range

	Retail	Markup
LS FWD	$44,600	8%
LT 2WD	$50,000	8%
LT4WD	$53,000	8%
LTZ 4WD	$62,000	8%

Safety Checklist

Crash Tests:
  Frontal. . . . . Good
  Side. . . . . .Very Good
Airbags:
  Torso . . . . .Front Pelvis/Torso from Seat
  Pelvis . . . . .Front Pelvis/Torso from Seat
  Roll Sensing. . . . . .Yes
  Knee Bolster . . . . None
Crash Avoidance:
  Collision Avoidance . . . . Optional CIB
  Blind Spot Detection . . . . Optional
  Lane Keeping Assist . . . .Warning Only Optional
  Backup Camera . . . . Standard
  Pedestrian Crash Avoidance . . . . None
General:
  Auto. Crash Notif. . . . . Oper. Assist. & Crash Info-Fee
  Day Running Lamps . . . . Standard
Safety Belt/Restraint:
  Dynamic Head Restraints . . . . None
  Adjustable Belt. . . . . . .Standard Front and Rear

Cadillac Escalade

Specifications

Drive. 4WD
Engine 5.3-liter V8
Transmission . . . . .6-sp. Automatic
Tow Rating (lbs.) . . . . .Very High-8400
Head/Leg Room (in.) . . . . . . Very Roomy-42.8/45.3
Interior Space (cu. ft.). Roomy-120.8
Cargo Space (cu. ft.) Cramped-15.3
Wheelbase/Length (in.) 116/204

Ratings—10 Best, 1 Worst	Traverse	Acadia
Combo Crash Tests	9	9
Safety Features	7	6
Rollover	3	3
Preventive Maintenance	6	3
Repair Costs	5	6
Warranty	7	6
Fuel Economy	2	2
Complaints	5	3
Insurance Costs	10	10
OVERALL RATING	**7**	**6**

Chevrolet Traverse

GMC Acadia

At-a-Glance

Status/Year Series Started. Unchanged/2009
Twins . . . . .GMC Acadia
Body Styles . . . . SUV
Seating 7/8
Anti-Theft Device . . . . . . Std. Pass. Immobil. & Alarm
Parking Index Rating . . . . .Very Hard
Where Made. . . . . .Lansing, MI
Fuel Factor . . . .
 MPG Rating (city/hwy) . . . . .Very Poor-17/24
 Driving Range (mi.) Long-430.5
 Fuel Type . . . . .Regular
 Annual Fuel Cost . . . . High-$2,146
 Gas Guzzler Tax . . . . .No
 Greenhouse Gas Emissions (tons/yr.) Very High-9.5
 Barrels of Oil Used per year . . . . . . .Very High-17.3

How the Competition Rates

Competitors	Rating	Pg.
Buick Enclave	7	102
Ford Flex	–	143
Toyota Highlander	7	250

Price Range

Price Range	Retail	Markup
LS FWD	$30,820	4%
LT FWD	$33,620	5%
2LT AWD	$38,120	5%
LTZ AWD	$43,760	6%

Safety Checklist

Crash Tests:
 Frontal. . . . . Good
 Side. . . . . Good
Airbags:
 Torso . . . . .Front Pelvis/Torso from Seat
 Pelvis . . . . .Front Pelvis/Torso from Seat
 Roll Sensing. . . . . .Yes
 Knee Bolster . . . . None
Crash Avoidance:
 Collision Avoidance . . . . .Warning Only Optional
 Blind Spot Detection . . . . Optional
 Lane Keeping Assist . . . .Warning Only Optional
 Backup Camera . . . . Optional
 Pedestrian Crash Avoidance . . . . None
General:
 Auto. Crash Notif. . . . Oper. Assist. & Crash Info-Fee
 Day Running Lamps . . . . Standard
Safety Belt/Restraint:
 Dynamic Head Restraints . . . . None
 Adjustable Belt . . . . . . .Standard Front and Rear

Chevrolet Traverse

Specifications

Drive. . . . . FWD
Engine 3.6-liter V6
Transmission . . . . .6-sp. Automatic
Tow Rating (lbs.) Low-5200
Head/Leg Room (in.) Average-40.4/41.3
Interior Space (cu. ft.). . . . . Very Roomy-150.8
Cargo Space (cu. ft.) Roomy-24.4
Wheelbase/Length (in.) 118.9/203.7

Chevrolet Trax

Ratings—10 Best, 1 Worst

Combo Crash Tests	8
Safety Features	9
Rollover	2
Preventive Maintenance	–
Repair Costs	–
Warranty	7
Fuel Economy	6
Complaints	–
Insurance Costs	5
OVERALL RATING	**7**

Chevrolet Trax

Safety Checklist

Crash Tests:
Frontal......................... Very Good
Side.............................. Average
Airbags:
Torso........ Fr. & Rr. Pelvis/Torso from Seat
Pelvis........ Fr. & Rr. Pelvis/Torso from Seat
Roll Sensing.........................Yes
Knee Bolster ....Standard Front
Crash Avoidance:
Collision Avoidance .... None
Blind Spot Detection .... None
Lane Keeping Assist .... None
Backup Camera................. Standard
Pedestrian Crash Avoidance .... None
General:
Auto. Crash Notif. ... Oper. Assist. & Crash Info-Fee
Day Running Lamps .... Standard
Safety Belt/Restraint:
Dynamic Head Restraints .... None
Adjustable Belt.......Standard Front and Rear

At-a-Glance

Status/Year Series Started.......... All New/2015
Twins .... Buick Encore
Body Styles .... SUV
Seating 5
Anti-Theft Device ...... Std. Pass. Immobil. & Alarm
Parking Index Rating .... Easy
Where Made............San Luis Potosi, Mexico
Fuel Factor.............................
  MPG Rating (city/hwy) Average-24/31
  Driving Range (mi.) Short-374.0
  Fuel Type.........................Regular
  Annual Fuel Cost .... Low-$1,572
  Gas Guzzler Tax ....No
  Greenhouse Gas Emissions (tons/yr.).. Average-6.7
  Barrels of Oil Used per year Average-12.2

Chevrolet Trax

How the Competition Rates

Competitors	Rating	Pg.
Ford Escape	5	138
Honda CR-V	6	151
Jeep Compass	–	170

Specifications

Drive................................. AWD
Engine 1.4-liter I4
Transmission ....6-sp. Automatic
Tow Rating (lbs.) .... –
Head/Leg Room (in.) Cramped-39.6/40.8
Interior Space (cu. ft.)...........Cramped-92.8
Cargo Space (cu. ft.) Average-18.7
Wheelbase/Length (in.) 100.6/168.5

Price Range	Retail	Markup
LS FWD	$20,120	4%
LT FWD	$22,445	4%
LT AWD	$23,945	4%
LTZ AWD	$26,530	4%

Chevrolet Volt

Ratings—10 Best, 1 Worst	
Combo Crash Tests	4
Safety Features	7
Rollover	8
Preventive Maintenance	10
Repair Costs	7
Warranty	7
Fuel Economy	10
Complaints	1
Insurance Costs	8
OVERALL RATING	**8**

Chevrolet Volt

Chevrolet Volt

At-a-Glance

Status/Year Series Started	Unchanged/2011
Twins	—
Body Styles	Sedan
Seating	4
Anti-Theft Device	Std. Pass. Immobil. & Alarm
Parking Index Rating	Easy
Where Made	Hamtramck, MI
Fuel Factor	
MPG Rating (city/hwy)	Very Good-35/40
Driving Range (mi.)	Very Short-380.0
Fuel Type	Premium
Annual Fuel Cost	Very Low-$853
Gas Guzzler Tax	No
Greenhouse Gas Emissions (tons/yr.)	Very Low-4.1
Barrels of Oil Used per year	Very Low-3.1

How the Competition Rates

Competitors	Rating	Pg.
Ford C-MAX	5	136
Nissan Leaf	2	222
Toyota Prius	4	251

Price Range	Retail	Markup
Base	$34,170	4%

Safety Checklist

Crash Tests:
Frontal	Poor
Side	Poor

Airbags:
Torso	Front Pelvis/Torso from Seat
Pelvis	Front Pelvis/Torso from Seat
Roll Sensing	Yes
Knee Bolster	Standard Front

Crash Avoidance:
Collision Avoidance	Warning Only Optional
Blind Spot Detection	None
Lane Keeping Assist	Warning Only Optional
Backup Camera	Optional
Pedestrian Crash Avoidance	None

General:
Auto. Crash Notif.	Oper. Assist. & Crash Info-Fee
Day Running Lamps	Standard

Safety Belt/Restraint:
Dynamic Head Restraints	None
Adjustable Belt	Standard Rear

Chevrolet Volt

Specifications

Drive	FWD
Engine	1.4-liter I4
Transmission	CVT
Tow Rating (lbs.)	—
Head/Leg Room (in.)	Cramped-37.8/42
Interior Space (cu. ft.)	Very Cramped-90
Cargo Space (cu. ft.)	Very Cramped-10.6
Wheelbase/Length (in.)	105.7/177.1

Ratings—10 Best, 1 Worst

Combo Crash Tests	8
Safety Features	6
Rollover	7
Preventive Maintenance	6
Repair Costs	9
Warranty	5
Fuel Economy	7
Complaints	–
Insurance Costs	3
OVERALL RATING	**8**

Chrysler 200

Chrysler 200

At-a-Glance

Status/Year Series Started. . . . . All New/2015
Twins . . . . –
Body Styles . . . . .Sedan
Seating 5
Anti-Theft Device . . . . . . Std. Pass. Immobil. & Alarm
Parking Index Rating . . . . Hard
Where Made. . . . . Sterling Heights, MI
Fuel Factor. . . . .
  MPG Rating (city/hwy) Good-23/36
  Driving Range (mi.) Long-433.9
  Fuel Type. . . . . .Regular
  Annual Fuel Cost . . . . Low-$1,529
  Gas Guzzler Tax . . . . .No
  Greenhouse Gas Emissions (tons/yr.). Low-6.4
  Barrels of Oil Used per year Average-11.8

How the Competition Rates

Competitors	Rating	Pg.
Chevrolet Malibu	7	117
Ford Fusion	4	145
Kia Optima	7	177

Price Range

Price Range	Retail	Markup
LX	$21,700	0%
Limited	$23,255	3%
S AWD	$28,695	4%
C AWD	$30,195	4%

Chrysler 200

Safety Checklist

Crash Tests:
  Frontal. . . . . Good
  Side. . . . . Average
Airbags:
  Torso . . . . .Front Pelvis/Torso from Seat
  Pelvis . . . . .Front Pelvis/Torso from Seat
  Roll Sensing. . . . . .Yes
  Knee Bolster . . . . .Standard Front
Crash Avoidance:
  Collision Avoidance . . . . .Warning Only Optional
  Blind Spot Detection . . . . None
  Lane Keeping Assist . . . .Warning Only Optional
  Backup Camera. . . . . None
  Pedestrian Crash Avoidance . . . . None
General:
  Auto. Crash Notification . . . . None
  Day Running Lamps . . . . None
Safety Belt/Restraint:
  Dynamic Head Restraints . . . . . .Standard Front
  Adjustable Belt. . . . . .Standard Front

Chrysler 200

Specifications

Drive. . . . . FWD
Engine 2.4-liter I4
Transmission . . . . .9-sp. Automatic
Tow Rating (lbs.) . . . . Very Low-0
Head/Leg Room (in.) Cramped-37.7/42.2
Interior Space (cu. ft.). Average-101.4
Cargo Space (cu. ft.) Cramped-16
Wheelbase/Length (in.) 108/192.3

Ratings—10 Best, 1 Worst

Combo Crash Tests	–
Safety Features	6
Rollover	8
Preventive Maintenance	6
Repair Costs	5
Warranty	5
Fuel Economy	4
Complaints	4
Insurance Costs	3
OVERALL RATING	**–**

Chrysler 300

Chrysler 300

At-a-Glance

Status/Year Series Started Appearance Change/2011
Twins . . . . .Dodge Charger
Body Styles . . . . .Sedan
Seating 5
Anti-Theft Device . . . . . . Std. Pass. Immobil. & Alarm
Parking Index Rating . . . . .Very Hard
Where Made. . . . . Brampton, Ontario
Fuel Factor . . . .
  MPG Rating (city/hwy) Poor-19/31
  Driving Range (mi.) Long-425.6
  Fuel Type . . . . .Regular
  Annual Fuel Cost . . . . Average-$1,825
  Gas Guzzler Tax . . . . .No
  Greenhouse Gas Emissions (tons/yr.) High-7.8
  Barrels of Oil Used per year High-14.3

How the Competition Rates

Competitors	Rating	Pg.
Buick LaCrosse	8	104
Cadillac XTS	9	110
Toyota Avalon	7	247

Price Range	Retail	Markup
Base	$30,765	4%
S V8 AWD	$38,565	5%
C V8	$39,115	5%
SRT8	$48,900	4%

Safety Checklist

Crash Tests:
  Frontal . . . .–
  Side. . . . .–
Airbags:
  Torso . . . . .Front Pelvis/Torso from Seat
  Pelvis . . . . .Front Pelvis/Torso from Seat
  Roll Sensing. . . . . No
  Knee Bolster . . . . Standard Driver
Crash Avoidance:
  Collision Avoidance . . . . . . Optional CIB & DBS
  Blind Spot Detection . . . . Optional
  Lane Keeping Assist . . . . Optional
  Backup Camera . . . . Optional
  Pedestrian Crash Avoidance . . . . None
General:
  Auto. Crash Notification . . . . None
  Day Running Lamps . . . . Optional
Safety Belt/Restraint:
  Dynamic Head Restraints . . . . . .Standard Front
  Adjustable Belt . . . . .Standard Front

Chrysler 300

Specifications

Drive. . . . . RWD
Engine 3.6-liter V6
Transmission . . . . .8-sp. Automatic
Tow Rating (lbs.) . . . . –
Head/Leg Room (in.) Cramped-38.6/41.8
Interior Space (cu. ft.). Roomy-106.3
Cargo Space (cu. ft.). Cramped-16.3
Wheelbase/Length (in.) 120.2/198.6

Chrysler Town and Country Minivan

Ratings—10 Best, 1 Worst

Combo Crash Tests	2
Safety Features	7
Rollover	3
Preventive Maintenance	8
Repair Costs	8
Warranty	5
Fuel Economy	2
Complaints	3
Insurance Costs	8
OVERALL RATING	**3**

Chrysler Town and Country

Chrysler Town and Country

At-a-Glance

Status/Year Series Started........ Unchanged/2008
Twins .... –
Body Styles .... Minivan
Seating 7
Anti-Theft Device ...... Std. Pass. Immobil. & Alarm
Parking Index Rating .... Very Hard
Where Made................... Windsor, Ontario
Fuel Factor....................................
 MPG Rating (city/hwy)......Very Poor-17/25
 Driving Range (mi.) Average-397.2
 Fuel Type............................Regular
 Annual Fuel Cost .... High-$2,114
 Gas Guzzler Tax ....No
 Greenhouse Gas Emissions (tons/yr.)..... High-9.0
 Barrels of Oil Used per year High-16.5

How the Competition Rates

Competitors	Rating	Pg.
Honda Odyssey	7	153
Nissan Quest	–	226
Toyota Sienna	3	256

Price Range	Retail	Markup
LX	$29,995	2%
Touring	$30,765	4%
S	$32,995	4%
Limited	$39,995	5%

Safety Checklist

Crash Tests:
 Frontal............................Poor
 Side........................Very Poor
Airbags:
 Torso ....Front Pelvis/Torso from Seat
 Pelvis ....Front Pelvis/Torso from Seat
 Roll Sensing...........................Yes
 Knee Bolster .... Standard Driver
Crash Avoidance:
 Collision Avoidance .... None
 Blind Spot Detection .... Standard
 Lane Keeping Assist .... None
 Backup Camera.................. Standard
 Pedestrian Crash Avoidance .... None
General:
 Auto. Crash Notification.............. None
 Day Running Lamps .... None
Safety Belt/Restraint:
 Dynamic Head Restraints ......Standard Front
 Adjustable Belt.......Standard Front and Rear

Chrysler Town and Country

Specifications

Drive.................................... FWD
Engine 3.6-liter V6
Transmission .... 6-sp. Automatic
Tow Rating (lbs.) Low-3600
Head/Leg Room (in.) Cramped-39.8/40.7
Interior Space (cu. ft.)......... Very Roomy-163.5
Cargo Space (cu. ft.) Roomy-33
Wheelbase/Length (in.) 121.2/202.8

Ratings—10 Best, 1 Worst

Combo Crash Tests	7
Safety Features	6
Rollover	7
Preventive Maintenance	5
Repair Costs	9
Warranty	5
Fuel Economy	4
Complaints	–
Insurance Costs	1
OVERALL RATING	**5**

Dodge Challenger

Dodge Challenger

At-a-Glance

Status/Year Series Started	All New/2015
Twins	–
Body Styles	Coupe
Seating	5
Anti-Theft Device	Std. Pass. Immobil. & Alarm
Parking Index Rating	Hard
Where Made	Brampton, Ontario
Fuel Factor	
MPG Rating (city/hwy)	Poor-19/30
Driving Range (mi.)	Average-421.0
Fuel Type	Regular
Annual Fuel Cost	Average-$1,845
Gas Guzzler Tax	No
Greenhouse Gas Emissions (tons/yr.)	High-7.8
Barrels of Oil Used per year	High-14.3

How the Competition Rates

Competitors	Rating	Pg.
Chevrolet Camaro	7	111
Ford Mustang	–	146
Nissan 370Z	–	217

Price Range	Retail	Markup
SXT	$26,995	3%
R/T Plus	$34,495	4%
SCAT PACK	$37,495	5%
SRT Hellcat	$57,895	6%

Safety Checklist

Crash Tests:
Frontal	Average
Side	Very Good

Airbags:
Torso	Front Pelvis/Torso from Seat
Pelvis	Front Pelvis/Torso from Seat
Roll Sensing	Yes
Knee Bolster	None

Crash Avoidance:
Collision Avoidance	Warning Only Optional
Blind Spot Detection	Standard
Lane Keeping Assist	None
Backup Camera	Standard
Pedestrian Crash Avoidance	None

General:
Auto. Crash Notification	None
Day Running Lamps	None

Safety Belt/Restraint:
Dynamic Head Restraints	Standard Front
Adjustable Belt	None

Dodge Challenger

Specifications

Drive	RWD
Engine	3.6-liter V6
Transmission	8-sp. Automatic
Tow Rating (lbs.)	Very Low-1000
Head/Leg Room (in.)	Average-39.3/42
Interior Space (cu. ft.)	Cramped-93.9
Cargo Space (cu. ft.)	Cramped-16.2
Wheelbase/Length (in.)	116.2/197.9

Dodge Charger

Ratings—10 Best, 1 Worst

Combo Crash Tests	–
Safety Features	4
Rollover	7
Preventive Maintenance	5
Repair Costs	8
Warranty	5
Fuel Economy	4
Complaints	2
Insurance Costs	1
OVERALL RATING	**–**

Dodge Charger

Dodge Charger

At-a-Glance

Status/Year Series Started Appearance Change/2011
Twins . . . . .Chrysler 300
Body Styles . . . . .Sedan
Seating 5
Anti-Theft Device . . . . . . Std. Pass. Immobil. & Alarm
Parking Index Rating . . . . Hard
Where Made. . . . . Brampton, Ontario
Fuel Factor. . . . .
  MPG Rating (city/hwy) Poor-19/31
  Driving Range (mi.) Long-425.6
  Fuel Type. . . . . .Regular
  Annual Fuel Cost . . . . Average-$1,825
  Gas Guzzler Tax . . . . .No
  Greenhouse Gas Emissions (tons/yr.). High-7.8
  Barrels of Oil Used per year High-14.3

How the Competition Rates

Competitors	Rating	Pg.
Acura RLX	–	84
Chevrolet Impala	6	116
Ford Taurus	4	147

Price Range

	Retail	Markup
SE	$26,995	5%
SXT	$29,295	4%
R/T AWD	$32,995	5%
SRT8 Super Bee	$43,385	3%

Safety Checklist

Crash Tests:
  Frontal. . . . .–
  Side. . . . .–
Airbags:
  Torso . . . . .Front Pelvis/Torso from Seat
  Pelvis . . . . .Front Pelvis/Torso from Seat
  Roll Sensing. . . . . No
  Knee Bolster . . . . Standard Driver
Crash Avoidance:
  Collision Avoidance . . . . .Warning Only Optional
  Blind Spot Detection . . . . Optional
  Lane Keeping Assist . . . .Warning Only Optional
  Backup Camera. None
  Pedestrian Crash Avoidance . . . . None
General:
  Auto. Crash Notification. . . . . None
  Day Running Lamps . . . . Optional
Safety Belt/Restraint:
  Dynamic Head Restraints . . . . . .Standard Front
  Adjustable Belt. . . . . .Standard Front

Dodge Charger

Specifications

Drive. . . . . .RWD
Engine 3.6-liter V6
Transmission . . . . .8-sp. Automatic
Tow Rating (lbs.) . . . . Very Low-1000
Head/Leg Room (in.) Cramped-38.6/41.8
Interior Space (cu. ft.). Roomy-104.7
Cargo Space (cu. ft.) Cramped-16.1
Wheelbase/Length (in.) 120.2/198.4

Dodge Dart

Ratings—10 Best, 1 Worst	
Combo Crash Tests	8
Safety Features	3
Rollover	7
Preventive Maintenance	5
Repair Costs	6
Warranty	5
Fuel Economy	7
Complaints	–
Insurance Costs	1
OVERALL RATING	**5**

Dodge Dart

Dodge Dart

At-a-Glance

Status/Year Series Started	Unchanged/2013
Twins	–
Body Styles	Sedan
Seating	5
Anti-Theft Device	Std. Pass. Immobil. & Alarm
Parking Index Rating	Easy
Where Made	Belvedere, IL
Fuel Factor	
MPG Rating (city/hwy)	Good-24/34
Driving Range (mi.)	Short-392.8
Fuel Type	Regular
Annual Fuel Cost	Low-$1,518
Gas Guzzler Tax	No
Greenhouse Gas Emissions (tons/yr.)	Average-6.7
Barrels of Oil Used per year	Average-12.2

How the Competition Rates

Competitors	Rating	Pg.
Acura ILX	7	81
Chevrolet Cruze	8	114
Ford Focus	–	144

Price Range	Retail	Markup
SE	$16,495	0%
SXT	$18,595	2%
GT	$20,995	2%
Limited	$22,995	3%

Safety Checklist

Crash Tests:
- Frontal .... Good
- Side .... Very Good

Airbags:
- Torso .... Front Pelvis/Torso from Seat
- Pelvis .... Rear Pelvis
- Roll Sensing .... No
- Knee Bolster .... Standard Front

Crash Avoidance:
- Collision Avoidance .... None
- Blind Spot Detection .... Standard
- Lane Keeping Assist .... None
- Backup Camera .... Standard
- Pedestrian Crash Avoidance .... None

General:
- Auto. Crash Notification .... None
- Day Running Lamps .... None

Safety Belt/Restraint:
- Dynamic Head Restraints .... None
- Adjustable Belt .... Standard Front

Dodge Dart

Specifications

Drive	FWD
Engine	2.0-liter I4
Transmission	6-sp. Automatic
Tow Rating (lbs.)	Very Low-1000
Head/Leg Room (in.)	Cramped-38.6/42.2
Interior Space (cu. ft.)	Cramped-97.2
Cargo Space (cu. ft.)	Cramped-13.1
Wheelbase/Length (in.)	106.4/183.9

Dodge Durango

Ratings—10 Best, 1 Worst

Combo Crash Tests	5
Safety Features	7
Rollover	2
Preventive Maintenance	5
Repair Costs	7
Warranty	5
Fuel Economy	1
Complaints	1
Insurance Costs	8
OVERALL RATING	**2**

Dodge Durango

At-a-Glance

Status/Year Series Started	Unchanged/2011
Twins	–
Body Styles	SUV
Seating	6/7
Anti-Theft Device	Std. Pass. Immobil. & Alarm
Parking Index Rating	Hard
Where Made	Detroit, MI
Fuel Factor	
MPG Rating (city/hwy)	Very Poor-14/22
Driving Range (mi.)	Average-411.8
Fuel Type	Regular
Annual Fuel Cost	Very High-$2,509
Gas Guzzler Tax	No
Greenhouse Gas Emissions (tons/yr.)	Very High-11.3
Barrels of Oil Used per year	Very High-20.6

How the Competition Rates

Competitors	Rating	Pg.
Chevrolet Tahoe	6	122
Ford Expedition	7	139
Toyota 4Runner	3	246

Price Range	Retail	Markup
SXT	$30,395	2%
Limited	$36,895	5%
R/T AWD	$42,195	5%
Citadel AWD	$43,495	5%

Dodge Durango

Safety Checklist

Crash Tests:
Frontal . . . . Poor
Side . . . . Good
Airbags:
Torso . . . . Front Pelvis/Torso from Seat
Pelvis . . . . Front Pelvis/Torso from Seat
Roll Sensing . . . . Yes
Knee Bolster . . . . Standard Driver
Crash Avoidance:
Collision Avoidance . . . . . . Optional CIB & DBS
Blind Spot Detection . . . . Optional
Lane Keeping Assist . . . . None
Backup Camera . . . . Optional
Pedestrian Crash Avoidance . . . . None
General:
Auto. Crash Notification . . . . None
Day Running Lamps . . . . Optional
Safety Belt/Restraint:
Dynamic Head Restraints . . . . . . Standard Front
Adjustable Belt . . . . Standard Front

Dodge Durango

Specifications

Drive	4WD
Engine	5.7-liter V8
Transmission	6-sp. Automatic
Tow Rating (lbs.)	Average-7200
Head/Leg Room (in.)	Cramped-39.9/40.3
Interior Space (cu. ft.)	Very Roomy-133.9
Cargo Space (cu. ft.)	Average-17.2
Wheelbase/Length (in.)	119.8/201.2

Ratings—10 Best, 1 Worst	
...ombo Crash Tests	4
...afety Features	5
...ollover	4
...reventive Maintenance	8
...epair Costs	10
...arranty	3
...uel Economy	10
...omplaints	1
...nsurance Costs	5
OVERALL RATING	**5**

...rd C-MAX

At-a-Glance

...tatus/Year Series Started	Unchanged/2013
...wins	–
...ody Styles	Hatchback
...eating	5
...nti-Theft Device	Std. Pass. Immobil. & Alarm
...arking Index Rating	Average
...here Made	Wayne, MI
...uel Factor	
...MPG Rating (city/hwy)	Very Good-42/37
...Driving Range (mi.)	Very Long-534.5
...Fuel Type	Regular
...Annual Fuel Cost	Very Low-$1,060
...Gas Guzzler Tax	No
...Greenhouse Gas Emissions (tons/yr.)	Very Low-4.5
...Barrels of Oil Used per year	Very Low-8.2

How the Competition Rates

...Competitors	Rating	Pg.
...hevrolet Volt	8	125
...issan Leaf	2	222
...oyota Prius	4	251

...rice Range	Retail	Markup
...E	$24,170	7%
...EL	$27,170	7%
...EL Energi	$31,635	7%

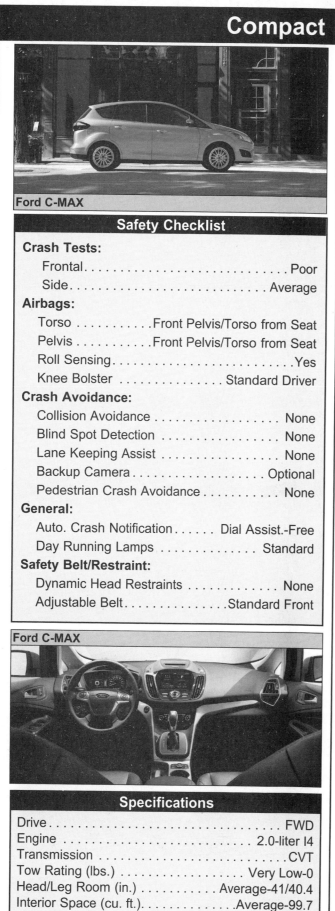
Ford C-MAX

Safety Checklist

Crash Tests:
Frontal .... Poor
Side .... Average

Airbags:
Torso .... Front Pelvis/Torso from Seat
Pelvis .... Front Pelvis/Torso from Seat
Roll Sensing .... Yes
Knee Bolster .... Standard Driver

Crash Avoidance:
Collision Avoidance .... None
Blind Spot Detection .... None
Lane Keeping Assist .... None
Backup Camera.................... Optional
Pedestrian Crash Avoidance .... None

General:
Auto. Crash Notification ...... Dial Assist.-Free
Day Running Lamps .... Standard

Safety Belt/Restraint:
Dynamic Head Restraints .... None
Adjustable Belt..............Standard Front

Ford C-MAX

Specifications

Drive	FWD
Engine	2.0-liter I4
Transmission	CVT
Tow Rating (lbs.)	Very Low-0
Head/Leg Room (in.)	Average-41/40.4
Interior Space (cu. ft.)	Average-99.7
Cargo Space (cu. ft.)	Roomy-24.5
Wheelbase/Length (in.)	104.3/173.6

Ratings—10 Best, 1 Worst	
Combo Crash Tests	–
Safety Features	5
Rollover	3
Preventive Maintenance	5
Repair Costs	5
Warranty	5
Fuel Economy	2
Complaints	2
Insurance Costs	5
OVERALL RATING	**–**

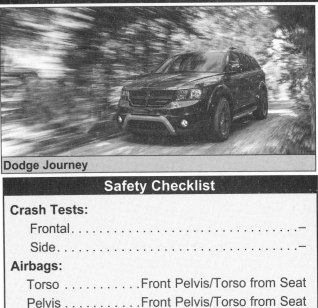
Dodge Journey

Dodge Journey

At-a-Glance

Status/Year Series Started	Unchanged/2009
Twins	–
Body Styles	SUV
Seating	5/7
Anti-Theft Device	Std. Pass. Immobil. & Alarm
Parking Index Rating	Hard
Where Made	Toluca, Mexico
Fuel Factor	
MPG Rating (city/hwy)	Very Poor-17/25
Driving Range (mi.)	Average-407.1
Fuel Type	Regular
Annual Fuel Cost	High-$2,114
Gas Guzzler Tax	No
Greenhouse Gas Emissions (tons/yr.)	High-9.4
Barrels of Oil Used per year	Very High-17.3

How the Competition Rates

Competitors	Rating	Pg.
Chevrolet Equinox	2	115
Ford Edge	–	137
Nissan Murano	–	224

Price Range	Retail	Markup
SE FWD	$19,995	1%
SXT FWD	$23,295	4%
Crossroad AWD	$28,395	5%
R/T AWD	$30,895	5%

Safety Checklist

Crash Tests:
Frontal.......................... –
Side.......................... –

Airbags:
Torso .... Front Pelvis/Torso from Seat
Pelvis .... Front Pelvis/Torso from Seat
Roll Sensing .... Yes
Knee Bolster .... Standard Driver

Crash Avoidance:
Collision Avoidance .... None
Blind Spot Detection .... None
Lane Keeping Assist .... None
Backup Camera .... Standard
Pedestrian Crash Avoidance .... None

General:
Auto. Crash Notification .... None
Day Running Lamps .... None

Safety Belt/Restraint:
Dynamic Head Restraints ...... Standard Front
Adjustable Belt.............. Standard Front

Dodge Journey

Specifications

Drive	FWD
Engine	3.6-liter V6
Transmission	6-sp. Automatic
Tow Rating (lbs.)	Very Low-2500
Head/Leg Room (in.)	Average-40.8/40.8
Interior Space (cu. ft.)	Very Roomy-123.7
Cargo Space (cu. ft.)	Very Cramped-10.7
Wheelbase/Length (in.)	113.8/192.4

Ratings—10 Best, 1 Worst

Combo Crash Tests	1
Safety Features	2
Rollover	4
Preventive Maintenance	7
Repair Costs	9
Warranty	4
Fuel Economy	8
Complaints	2
Insurance Costs	5
OVERALL RATING	**2**

Fiat 500

At-a-Glance

Status/Year Series Started	Unchanged/2012
Twins	–
Body Styles	Hatchback
Seating	4
Anti-Theft Device	Std. Pass. Immobil. & Alarm
Parking Index Rating	Very Easy
Where Made	Toluca, Mexico
Fuel Factor	
MPG Rating (city/hwy)	Good-27/34
Driving Range (mi.)	Very Short-312.4
Fuel Type	Regular
Annual Fuel Cost	Very Low-$1,411
Gas Guzzler Tax	No
Greenhouse Gas Emissions (tons/yr.)	Low-6.0
Barrels of Oil Used per year	Average-11.0

How the Competition Rates

Competitors	Rating	Pg.
Chevrolet Sonic	9	119
Mini Cooper	–	211
Volkswagen Beetle	3	261

Price Range	Retail	Markup
Pop Hatchback	$16,445	2%
Lounge Hatchback	$18,500	2%
Sport Hatchback	$19,500	3%
Abarth Cabriolet	$26,195	3%

Fiat 500

Safety Checklist

Crash Tests:
Frontal	Very Poor
Side	Poor

Airbags:
Torso	Front Pelvis/Torso from Seat
Pelvis	Front Pelvis/Torso from Seat
Roll Sensing	No
Knee Bolster	Standard Driver

Crash Avoidance:
Collision Avoidance	None
Blind Spot Detection	None
Lane Keeping Assist	None
Backup Camera	None
Pedestrian Crash Avoidance	None

General:
Auto. Crash Notification	None
Day Running Lamps	None

Safety Belt/Restraint:
Dynamic Head Restraints	Standard Front
Adjustable Belt	None

Fiat 500

Specifications

Drive	FWD
Engine	1.4-liter I4
Transmission	6-sp. Automatic
Tow Rating (lbs.)	Very Low-0
Head/Leg Room (in.)	Very Cramped-38.9/40.7
Interior Space (cu. ft.)	Very Cramped-75.5
Cargo Space (cu. ft.)	Very Cramped-9.5
Wheelbase/Length (in.)	90.6/139.6

Ratings—10 Best, 1 Worst

Combo Crash Tests	–
Safety Features	4
Rollover	3
Preventive Maintenance	5
Repair Costs	9
Warranty	4
Fuel Economy	5
Complaints	1
Insurance Costs	5
OVERALL RATING	**–**

Fiat 500L

At-a-Glance

Status/Year Series Started	Unchanged/2014
Twins	–
Body Styles	Hatchback
Seating	5
Anti-Theft Device	Std. Pass. Immobil. & Alarm
Parking Index Rating	Very Easy
Where Made	Kragujevac, Serbia
Fuel Factor	
MPG Rating (city/hwy)	Average-22/30
Driving Range (mi.)	Very Short-330.0
Fuel Type	Regular
Annual Fuel Cost	Average-$1,680
Gas Guzzler Tax	No
Greenhouse Gas Emissions (tons/yr.)	Average-7.2
Barrels of Oil Used per year	High-13.2

How the Competition Rates

Competitors	Rating	Pg.
Ford Focus	–	144
Kia Forte	5	176
Volkswagen Golf	–	263

Price Range	Retail	Markup
Pop	$19,195	2%
Lounge	$24,495	3%

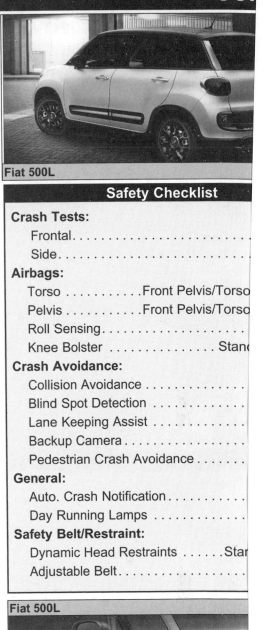
Fiat 500L

Safety Checklist

Crash Tests:
Frontal	
Side	

Airbags:
Torso	Front Pelvis/Torso...
Pelvis	Front Pelvis/Torso...
Roll Sensing	
Knee Bolster	Stand...

Crash Avoidance:
Collision Avoidance	
Blind Spot Detection	
Lane Keeping Assist	
Backup Camera	
Pedestrian Crash Avoidance	

General:
Auto. Crash Notification	
Day Running Lamps	

Safety Belt/Restraint:
Dynamic Head Restraints	Star...
Adjustable Belt	

Fiat 500L

Specifications

Drive	
Engine	
Transmission	6-sp...
Tow Rating (lbs.)	
Head/Leg Room (in.)	Cram...
Interior Space (cu. ft.)	A...
Cargo Space (cu. ft.)	A...
Wheelbase/Length (in.)	

Ratings—10 Best, 1 Worst

Combo Crash Tests	–
Safety Features	8
Rollover	3
Preventive Maintenance	6
Repair Costs	5
Warranty	3
Fuel Economy	–
Complaints	–
Insurance Costs	8
OVERALL RATING	**–**

Ford Edge

Ford Edge

At-a-Glance

Status/Year Series Started	All New/2015
Twins	–
Body Styles	SUV
Seating	5
Anti-Theft Device	Std. Pass. Immobil. & Alarm
Parking Index Rating	–
Where Made	Oakville, Ontario
Fuel Factor	
MPG Rating (city/hwy)	–
Driving Range (mi.)	–
Fuel Type	Regular
Annual Fuel Cost	–
Gas Guzzler Tax	No
Greenhouse Gas Emissions (tons/yr.)	–
Barrels of Oil Used per year	–

How the Competition Rates

Competitors	Rating	Pg.
Chevrolet Equinox	2	115
Dodge Journey	–	133
Nissan Murano	–	224

Price Range

	Retail	Markup
SE FWD	$28,100	6%
SEL FWD	$31,300	7%
Limited AWD	$37,050	7%
Sport AWD	$39,550	7%

Safety Checklist

Crash Tests:
Frontal . . . . –
Side . . . . –

Airbags:
Torso . . . . Front Pelvis/Torso from Seat
Pelvis . . . . Front Pelvis/Torso from Seat
Roll Sensing . . . . Yes
Knee Bolster . . . . Standard Front

Crash Avoidance:
Collision Avoidance . . . . . Warning Only Optional
Blind Spot Detection . . . . Optional
Lane Keeping Assist . . . . Optional
Backup Camera . . . . Optional
Pedestrian Crash Avoidance . . . . None

General:
Auto. Crash Notification . . . . . . Dial Assist.-Free
Day Running Lamps . . . . Standard

Safety Belt/Restraint:
Dynamic Head Restraints . . . . None
Adjustable Belt . . . . Standard Front

Ford Edge

Specifications

Drive	FWD
Engine	3.5-liter V6
Transmission	6-sp. Automatic
Tow Rating (lbs.)	Low-3500
Head/Leg Room (in.)	Roomy-40.2/42.6
Interior Space (cu. ft.)	Roomy-113.9
Cargo Space (cu. ft.)	Very Roomy-39.2
Wheelbase/Length (in.)	112.2/188.1

Ratings—10 Best, 1 Worst

Combo Crash Tests	6
Safety Features	6
Rollover	2
Preventive Maintenance	5
Repair Costs	10
Warranty	3
Fuel Economy	6
Complaints	3
Insurance Costs	8
OVERALL RATING	**5**

Ford Escape

Ford Escape

At-a-Glance

Status/Year Series Started	Unchanged/2013
Twins	Lincoln MKC
Body Styles	SUV
Seating	5
Anti-Theft Device	Std. Pass. Immobil. & Alarm
Parking Index Rating	Average
Where Made	Louisville, KY
Fuel Factor	
MPG Rating (city/hwy)	Average-22/31
Driving Range (mi.)	Short-389.7
Fuel Type	Regular
Annual Fuel Cost	Low-$1,659
Gas Guzzler Tax	No
Greenhouse Gas Emissions (tons/yr.)	Average-7.2
Barrels of Oil Used per year	High-13.2

How the Competition Rates

Competitors	Rating	Pg.
Honda CR-V	6	151
Jeep Cherokee	4	169
Toyota RAV4	4	254

Price Range

	Retail	Markup
S FWD	$23,100	6%
SE FWD	$25,550	7%
SE 4WD	$27,300	7%
Titanium 4WD	$31,260	7%

Safety Checklist

Crash Tests:
Frontal . . . . Average
Side . . . . Good
Airbags:
Torso . . . . Front Pelvis/Torso from Seat
Pelvis . . . . Front Pelvis/Torso from Seat
Roll Sensing . . . . .Yes
Knee Bolster . . . . Standard Driver
Crash Avoidance:
Collision Avoidance . . . . None
Blind Spot Detection . . . . Optional
Lane Keeping Assist . . . . None
Backup Camera . . . . Standard
Pedestrian Crash Avoidance . . . . None
General:
Auto. Crash Notification . . . . . . Dial Assist.-Free
Day Running Lamps . . . . Standard
Safety Belt/Restraint:
Dynamic Head Restraints . . . . None
Adjustable Belt . . . . .Standard Front

Ford Escape

Specifications

Drive	FWD
Engine	2.5-liter I4
Transmission	6-sp. Automatic
Tow Rating (lbs.)	Very Low-1500
Head/Leg Room (in.)	Roomy-39.9/43.1
Interior Space (cu. ft.)	Average-98.1
Cargo Space (cu. ft.)	Very Roomy-34.3
Wheelbase/Length (in.)	105.9/178.1

Ford Expedition/Lincoln Navigator   Large SUV

Ratings—10 Best, 1 Worst	Expedition	Navigator
Combo Crash Tests	10	10
Safety Features	5	5
Rollover	2	2
Preventive Maintenance	4	7
Repair Costs	8	8
Warranty	3	8
Fuel Economy	1	1
Complaints	7	10
Insurance Costs	10	8
OVERALL RATING	7	9

Ford Expedition

Lincoln Navigator

(Lincoln Navigator pictured)

At-a-Glance

Status/Year Series Started Appearance Change/2003
Twins . . . . Lincoln Navigator
Body Styles . . . . SUV
Seating 7/8
Anti-Theft Device . . . . . . Std. Pass. Immobil. & Alarm
Parking Index Rating . . . . Very Hard
Where Made . . . . Louisville, KY
Fuel Factor . . . .
  MPG Rating (city/hwy) . . . . Very Poor-15/20
  Driving Range (mi.) . . . . Very Long-473.2
  Fuel Type . . . . Regular
  Annual Fuel Cost . . . . Very High-$2,485
  Gas Guzzler Tax . . . . No
  Greenhouse Gas Emissions (tons/yr.)Very High-10.6
  Barrels of Oil Used per year . . . . . . Very High-19.4

How the Competition Rates

Competitors	Rating	Pg.
Chevrolet Suburban	5	121
Nissan Armada	–	219
Toyota Sequoia	–	255

Price Range	Retail	Markup
XL 2WD	$38,975	7%
XLT 2WD	$43,390	7%
King Ranch 4WD	$59,910	7%
Platinum 4WD	$60,990	7%

Safety Checklist

Crash Tests:
  Frontal . . . . –
  Side . . . . –
Airbags:
  Torso . . . . Front Torso from Seat
  Pelvis . . . . None
  Roll Sensing . . . . Yes
  Knee Bolster . . . . None
Crash Avoidance:
  Collision Avoidance . . . . None
  Blind Spot Detection . . . . Optional
  Lane Keeping Assist . . . . None
  Backup Camera . . . . Standard
  Pedestrian Crash Avoidance . . . . None
General:
  Auto. Crash Notification . . . . . . Dial Assist.-Free
  Day Running Lamps . . . . None
Safety Belt/Restraint:
  Dynamic Head Restraints . . . . . . Standard Front
  Adjustable Belt . . . . Standard Front

Ford Expedition

Specifications

Drive 4WD
Engine 3.5-liter V6
Transmission . . . . 6-sp. Automatic
Tow Rating (lbs.) . . . . Very High-9200
Head/Leg Room (in.) Roomy-39.63/43
Interior Space (cu. ft.) . . . . Very Roomy-160.3
Cargo Space (cu. ft.) Average-18.6
Wheelbase/Length (in.) 119/206

Ratings—10 Best, 1 Worst

Combo Crash Tests	7
Safety Features	6
Rollover	3
Preventive Maintenance	5
Repair Costs	3
Warranty	3
Fuel Economy	2
Complaints	3
Insurance Costs	8
OVERALL RATING	**3**

Ford Explorer

Ford Explorer

Safety Checklist

Crash Tests:
Frontal. . . . . Good
Side. . . . . Good

Airbags:
Torso Std. Fr. & Opt. Rr. Pelvis/Torso from Seat
Pelvis Std. Fr. & Opt. Rr. Pelvis/Torso from Seat
Roll Sensing. . . . . .Yes
Knee Bolster . . . . Standard Passenger

Crash Avoidance:
Collision Avoidance . . . . .Warning Only Optional
Blind Spot Detection . . . . Optional
Lane Keeping Assist . . . . Optional
Backup Camera . . . . Optional
Pedestrian Crash Avoidance . . . . None

General:
Auto. Crash Notification. . . . . . Dial Assist.-Free
Day Running Lamps . . . . None

Safety Belt/Restraint:
Dynamic Head Restraints . . . . None
Adjustable Belt . . . . .Standard Front

At-a-Glance

Status/Year Series Started. Unchanged/2011
Twins . . . . –
Body Styles . . . . SUV
Seating 6/7
Anti-Theft Device . . . . . . Std. Pass. Immobil. & Alarm
Parking Index Rating . . . . Hard
Where Made. .Chicago, IL
Fuel Factor . . . .
  MPG Rating (city/hwy) . . . . .Very Poor-17/23
  Driving Range (mi.) . . . . Very Short-358.3
  Fuel Type. . . . . .Regular
  Annual Fuel Cost . . . . High-$2,180
  Gas Guzzler Tax . . . . .No
  Greenhouse Gas Emissions (tons/yr.) Very High-9.5
  Barrels of Oil Used per year . . . . Very High-17.3

Ford Explorer

How the Competition Rates

Competitors	Rating	Pg.
Dodge Journey	–	133
Honda Pilot	2	154
Toyota Highlander	7	250

Price Range

Price Range	Retail	Markup
Base FWD	$30,600	6%
XLT FWD	$32,900	7%
Limited 4WD	$40,100	7%
Sport 4WD	$42,670	7%

Specifications

Drive. . . . . AWD
Engine 3.5-liter V6
Transmission . . . . .6-sp. Automatic
Tow Rating (lbs.) Low-5000
Head/Leg Room (in.) Average-41.4/40.6
Interior Space (cu. ft.). . . . . Very Roomy-151.7
Cargo Space (cu. ft.) Average-21
Wheelbase/Length (in.) 112.6/197.1

Ratings—10 Best, 1 Worst

Combo Crash Tests	–
Safety Features	5
Rollover	1
Preventive Maintenance	2
Repair Costs	7
Warranty	3
Fuel Economy	2
Complaints	–
Insurance Costs	8
OVERALL RATING	**–**

Ford F-150

Ford F-150

At-a-Glance

Status/Year Series Started . . . . All New/2015
Twins . . . . –
Body Styles . . . . Pickup
Seating 5/6
Anti-Theft Device . . . . . . Std. Pass. Immobil. & Alarm
Parking Index Rating . . . . Very Hard
Where Made. . . . . Dearborn, MI
Fuel Factor . . . .
  MPG Rating (city/hwy) . . . . .Very Poor-17/23
  Driving Range (mi.) . . . . .Very Long-693.4
  Fuel Type. . . . . .Regular
  Annual Fuel Cost . . . . High-$2,180
  Gas Guzzler Tax . . . . .No
  Greenhouse Gas Emissions (tons/yr.) Very High-9.5
  Barrels of Oil Used per year . . . . Very High-17.3

How the Competition Rates

Competitors	Rating	Pg.
Chevrolet Silverado	7	118
Ram 1500	3	234
Toyota Tundra	3	258

Price Range

Price Range	Retail	Markup
XL Reg. Cab 2WD	$25,420	8%
XLT Supercab 2WD	$33,580	10%
Lariat Supercrew 4WD	$44,465	10%
Platinum Supercrew 4WD	$54,680	10%

Safety Checklist

Crash Tests:
  Frontal. . . . . –
  Side. . . . . –
Airbags:
  Torso . . . . .Front Pelvis/Torso from Seat
  Pelvis . . . . .Front Pelvis/Torso from Seat
  Roll Sensing. . . . . .Yes
  Knee Bolster . . . . None
Crash Avoidance:
  Collision Avoidance . . . . .Warning Only Optional
  Blind Spot Detection . . . . None
  Lane Keeping Assist . . . . Optional
  Backup Camera . . . . Optional
  Pedestrian Crash Avoidance . . . . None
General:
  Auto. Crash Notification . . . . . . Dial Assist.-Free
  Day Running Lamps . . . . None
Safety Belt/Restraint:
  Dynamic Head Restraints . . . . None
  Adjustable Belt. . . . . .Standard Front

Ford F-150

Specifications

Drive. 4WD
Engine 3.5-liter V6
Transmission . . . . .6-sp. Automatic
Tow Rating (lbs.) . . . . .Very High-10700
Head/Leg Room (in.) . . . . . . Very Roomy-40.8/43.9
Interior Space (cu. ft.). Roomy-116
Cargo Space (cu. ft.) . . . . Very Roomy-49.4
Wheelbase/Length (in.) 145/231.9

Ratings—10 Best, 1 Worst

Combo Crash Tests	3
Safety Features	2
Rollover	4
Preventive Maintenance	3
Repair Costs	10
Warranty	3
Fuel Economy	9
Complaints	1
Insurance Costs	3
OVERALL RATING	**2**

Ford Fiesta

Ford Fiesta

At-a-Glance

Status/Year Series Started	Unchanged/2011
Twins	–
Body Styles	Sedan, Hatchback
Seating	5
Anti-Theft Device	Std. Pass. Immobil. & Alarm
Parking Index Rating	Very Easy
Where Made	Cuautitlán, Mexico
Fuel Factor	
MPG Rating (city/hwy)	Very Good-27/37
Driving Range (mi.)	Short-381.2
Fuel Type	Regular
Annual Fuel Cost	Very Low-$1,366
Gas Guzzler Tax	No
Greenhouse Gas Emissions (tons/yr.)	Low-5.8
Barrels of Oil Used per year	Low-10.6

How the Competition Rates

Competitors	Rating	Pg.
Chevrolet Sonic	9	119
Hyundai Accent	5	155
Toyota Yaris	5	260

Price Range

	Retail	Markup
S Sedan	$14,355	4%
SE Hatchback	$16,085	4%
Titanium Sedan	$18,305	4%
ST Hatchback	$21,405	4%

Safety Checklist

Crash Tests:
Frontal	Average
Side	Very Poor*

Airbags:
Torso	Front Pelvis/Torso from Seat
Pelvis	Front Pelvis/Torso from Seat
Roll Sensing	No
Knee Bolster	Standard Driver

Crash Avoidance:
Collision Avoidance	None
Blind Spot Detection	None
Lane Keeping Assist	None
Backup Camera	Optional
Pedestrian Crash Avoidance	None

General:
Auto. Crash Notification	Dial Assist.-Free
Day Running Lamps	None

Safety Belt/Restraint:
Dynamic Head Restraints	None
Adjustable Belt	Standard Front

Ford Fiesta

Specifications

Drive	FWD
Engine	1.6-liter I4
Transmission	6-sp. Automatic
Tow Rating (lbs.)	Very Low-0
Head/Leg Room (in.)	Average-39.1/42.2
Interior Space (cu. ft.)	Very Cramped-85.1
Cargo Space (cu. ft.)	Cramped-14.9
Wheelbase/Length (in.)	98/159.7

*Additional injury potential in side test. See footnote on page 20.

Ratings—10 Best, 1 Worst

Combo Crash Tests	–
Safety Features	4
Rollover	3
Preventive Maintenance	6
Repair Costs	3
Warranty	3
Fuel Economy	3
Complaints	4
Insurance Costs	5
OVERALL RATING	**–**

Ford Flex

Ford Flex

At-a-Glance

Status/Year Series Started	Unchanged/2009
Twins	–
Body Styles	SUV
Seating	6/7
Anti-Theft Device	Std. Pass. Immobil. & Alarm
Parking Index Rating	Very Hard
Where Made	Oakville, Ontario
Fuel Factor	
MPG Rating (city/hwy)	Poor-18/25
Driving Range (mi.)	Short-383.1
Fuel Type	Regular
Annual Fuel Cost	High-$2,039
Gas Guzzler Tax	No
Greenhouse Gas Emissions (tons/yr.)	High-9.0
Barrels of Oil Used per year	High-16.5

How the Competition Rates

Competitors	Rating	Pg.
Chevrolet Traverse	7	123
Dodge Journey	–	133
Honda Pilot	2	154

Price Range

Price Range	Retail	Markup
SE FWD	$31,100	6%
SEL AWD	$35,450	7%
Limited FWD	$39,400	7%
Limited Ecoboost AWD	$44,020	7%

Safety Checklist

Crash Tests:
Frontal . . . . . –
Side . . . . . –

Airbags:
Torso Std. Fr. & Opt. Rr. Pelvis/Torso from Seat
Pelvis Std. Fr. & Opt. Rr. Pelvis/Torso from Seat
Roll Sensing . . . . . Yes
Knee Bolster . . . . . None

Crash Avoidance:
Collision Avoidance . . . . . None
Blind Spot Detection . . . . . Optional
Lane Keeping Assist . . . . Warning Only Optional
Backup Camera . . . . . Optional
Pedestrian Crash Avoidance . . . . . None

General:
Auto. Crash Notification . . . . . Dial Assist.-Free
Day Running Lamps . . . . . None

Safety Belt/Restraint:
Dynamic Head Restraints . . . . . None
Adjustable Belt . . . . . Standard Front

Ford Flex

Specifications

Drive	FWD
Engine	3.5-liter V6
Transmission	6-sp. Automatic
Tow Rating (lbs.)	Low-4500
Head/Leg Room (in.)	Roomy-41.8/40.8
Interior Space (cu. ft.)	Very Roomy-155.8
Cargo Space (cu. ft.)	Average-20
Wheelbase/Length (in.)	117.9/201.8

Ratings—10 Best, 1 Worst

Combo Crash Tests	–
Safety Features	6
Rollover	7
Preventive Maintenance	5
Repair Costs	9
Warranty	3
Fuel Economy	9
Complaints	1
Insurance Costs	3
OVERALL RATING	**–**

Ford Focus

Ford Focus

At-a-Glance

Status/Year Series Started Appearance Change/2012
Twins . . . .–
Body Styles . . . . Sedan, Hatchback
Seating 5
Anti-Theft Device . . . . . . Std. Pass. Immobil. & Alarm
Parking Index Rating . . . . Easy
Where Made. . . . . Wayne, MI
Fuel Factor. . . . .
  MPG Rating (city/hwy) . . . . Very Good-27/40
  Driving Range (mi.) . . . . .Very Short-392
  Fuel Type. . . . . .Regular
  Annual Fuel Cost . . . . Average-$1,328
  Gas Guzzler Tax . . . . .No
  Greenhouse Gas Emissions (tons/yr.). Low-5.8
  Barrels of Oil Used per year Low-10.6

How the Competition Rates

Competitors	Rating	Pg.
Honda Civic	6	149
Kia Forte	5	176
Mazda Mazda3	5	199

Price Range

	Retail	Markup
S Sedan	$16,310	6%
Titanum Sedan	$23,515	7%
ST Hatchback	$24,115	7%
Electric Hatchback	$39,200	7%

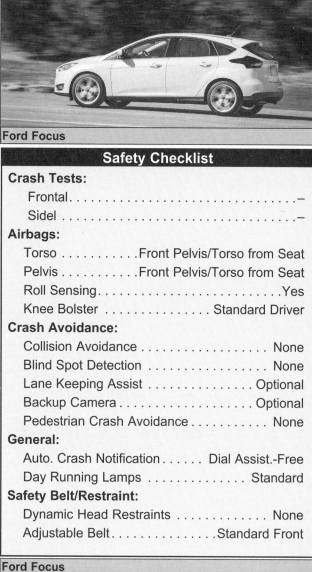

Ford Focus

Safety Checklist

Crash Tests:
  Frontal. . . . .–
  Sidel . . . .–
Airbags:
  Torso . . . . .Front Pelvis/Torso from Seat
  Pelvis . . . . .Front Pelvis/Torso from Seat
  Roll Sensing. . . . . .Yes
  Knee Bolster . . . . Standard Driver
Crash Avoidance:
  Collision Avoidance . . . . None
  Blind Spot Detection . . . . None
  Lane Keeping Assist . . . . Optional
  Backup Camera . . . . Optional
  Pedestrian Crash Avoidance . . . . None
General:
  Auto. Crash Notification . . . . . . Dial Assist.-Free
  Day Running Lamps . . . . Standard
Safety Belt/Restraint:
  Dynamic Head Restraints . . . . None
  Adjustable Belt. . . . . .Standard Front

Ford Focus

Specifications

Drive. . . . . FWD
Engine 2.0-liter I4
Transmission . . . . .6-sp. Automatic
Tow Rating (lbs.) . . . . Very Low-0
Head/Leg Room (in.) Average-38.3/43.7
Interior Space (cu. ft.). . . . .
Cargo Space (cu. ft.) Cramped-13.2
Wheelbase/Length (in.) 104.3/178.5

Ratings—10 Best, 1 Worst

Combo Crash Tests	6*
Safety Features	5
Rollover	7
Preventive Maintenance	3
Repair Costs	10
Warranty	3
Fuel Economy	6
Complaints	3
Insurance Costs	1
OVERALL RATING	**4**

Ford Fusion

Ford Fusion

At-a-Glance

Status/Year Series Started	Unchanged/2013
Twins	Lincoln MKZ
Body Styles	Sedan
Seating	5
Anti-Theft Device	Std. Pass. Immobil. & Alarm
Parking Index Rating	Average
Where Made	Hermosillo, Mexico / Flat Rock, MI
Fuel Factor	
MPG Rating (city/hwy)	Average-22/34
Driving Range (mi.)	Long-431.5
Fuel Type	Regular
Annual Fuel Cost	Low-$1,605
Gas Guzzler Tax	No
Greenhouse Gas Emissions (tons/yr.)	Average-6.9
Barrels of Oil Used per year	Average-12.7

How the Competition Rates

Competitors	Rating	Pg.
Chevrolet Malibu	7	117
Hyundai Sonata	8	160
Toyota Camry	7	248

Price Range	Retail	Markup
S	$22,400	7%
Titanium Hybrid	$32,170	8%
Titanium AWD	$32,600	8%
Titanium Energi	$36,500	8%

Ford Fusion

Safety Checklist

Crash Tests:
Frontal . . . . Good
Side . . . . Very Poor

Airbags:
Torso Std. Fr. & Opt. Rr. Pelvis/Torso from Seat
Pelvis Std. Fr. & Opt. Rr. Pelvis/Torso from Seat
Roll Sensing . . . . No
Knee Bolster . . . . Standard Front

Crash Avoidance:
Collision Avoidance . . . . . Warning Only Optional
Blind Spot Detection . . . . Optional
Lane Keeping Assist . . . . Optional
Backup Camera . . . . Standard
Pedestrian Crash Avoidance . . . . None

General:
Auto. Crash Notification . . . . . . Dial Assist.-Free
Day Running Lamps . . . . Standard

Safety Belt/Restraint:
Dynamic Head Restraints . . . . None
Adjustable Belt . . . . Standard Front

Ford Fusion

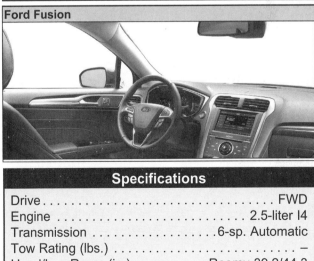

Specifications

Drive	FWD
Engine	2.5-liter I4
Transmission	6-sp. Automatic
Tow Rating (lbs.)	–
Head/Leg Room (in.)	Roomy-39.2/44.3
Interior Space (cu. ft.)	Roomy-118.8
Cargo Space (cu. ft.)	Cramped-16
Wheelbase/Length (in.)	112.2/191.7

*Crash test is for non-Energi models only. For Energi results see page 23.

Ratings—10 Best, 1 Worst

Combo Crash Tests	–
Safety Features	6
Rollover	9
Preventive Maintenance	2
Repair Costs	10
Warranty	3
Fuel Economy	4
Complaints	–
Insurance Costs	5
OVERALL RATING	**–**

Ford Mustang

At-a-Glance

Status/Year Series Started	All New/2015
Twins	–
Body Styles	Coupe, Convertible
Seating	4
Anti-Theft Device	Std. Pass. Immobil. & Alarm
Parking Index Rating	Easy
Where Made	Flat Rock, MI
Fuel Factor	
MPG Rating (city/hwy)	Poor-19/28
Driving Range (mi.)	Very Short-355.4
Fuel Type	Regular
Annual Fuel Cost	Average-$1,890
Gas Guzzler Tax	No
Greenhouse Gas Emissions (tons/yr.)	High-8.1
Barrels of Oil Used per year	High-15.0

How the Competition Rates

Competitors	Rating	Pg.
Chevrolet Camaro	7	111
Chevrolet Corvette	–	113
Dodge Challenger	5	129

Price Range

	Retail	Markup
Base Coupe	$23,600	6%
Eco Premium Coupe	$29,170	8%
GT Premium Convertible	$41,600	8%
GT 50 yr LTD Ed.	$46,170	8%

Ford Mustang

Safety Checklist

Crash Tests:
Frontal . . . . –
Side . . . . –
Airbags:
Torso . . . . Front Pelvis/Torso from Seat
Pelvis . . . . Front Pelvis/Torso from Seat
Roll Sensing . . . . Yes
Knee Bolster . . . . Standard Front
Crash Avoidance:
Collision Avoidance . . . . . Warning Only Optional
Blind Spot Detection . . . . Optional
Lane Keeping Assist . . . . None
Backup Camera . . . . Standard
Pedestrian Crash Avoidance . . . . None
General:
Auto. Crash Notification . . . . . . Dial Assist.-Free
Day Running Lamps . . . . None
Safety Belt/Restraint:
Dynamic Head Restraints . . . . None
Adjustable Belt . . . . None

Ford Mustang

Specifications

Drive	RWD
Engine	3.7-liter V6
Transmission	6-sp. Automatic
Tow Rating (lbs.)	–
Head/Leg Room (in.)	Average-37.6/44.5
Interior Space (cu. ft.)	Very Cramped-84.5
Cargo Space (cu. ft.)	Cramped-13.5
Wheelbase/Length (in.)	107.1/188.3

Ratings—10 Best, 1 Worst

Combo Crash Tests	7
Safety Features	5
Rollover	6
Preventive Maintenance	5
Repair Costs	4
Warranty	3
Fuel Economy	4
Complaints	8
Insurance Costs	1
OVERALL RATING	**4**

Ford Taurus

Ford Taurus

At-a-Glance

Status/Year Series Started. Unchanged/2010
Twins . . . . –
Body Styles . . . . .Sedan
Seating 5
Anti-Theft Device . . . . . . Std. Pass. Immobil. & Alarm
Parking Index Rating . . . . .Very Hard
Where Made. . . . . .Chicago, IL
Fuel Factor . . . .
  MPG Rating (city/hwy) Poor-19/29
  Driving Range (mi.) Long-427.3
  Fuel Type. . . . . .Regular
  Annual Fuel Cost . . . . Average-$1,867
  Gas Guzzler Tax . . . . .No
  Greenhouse Gas Emissions (tons/yr.). High-7.8
  Barrels of Oil Used per year High-14.3

How the Competition Rates

Competitors	Rating	Pg.
Buick LaCrosse	8	104
Chevrolet Impala	6	116
Toyota Avalon	7	247

Price Range	Retail	Markup
SE	$26,790	8%
SEL	$29,370	8%
Limited AWD	$36,140	8%
SHO AWD	$40,105	8%

Safety Checklist

Crash Tests:
  Frontal. . . . . Very Good
  Side. . . . . .Poor
Airbags:
  Torso Std. Fr. & Opt. Rr. Pelvis/Torso from Seat
  Pelvis Std. Fr. & Opt. Rr. Pelvis/Torso from Seat
  Roll Sensing. . . . . .Yes
  Knee Bolster . . . . None
Crash Avoidance:
  Collision Avoidance . . . . .Warning Only Optional
  Blind Spot Detection . . . . Optional
  Lane Keeping Assist . . . . Optional
  Backup Camera . . . . Optional
  Pedestrian Crash Avoidance . . . . None
General:
  Auto. Crash Notification . . . . . . Dial Assist.-Free
  Day Running Lamps . . . . None
Safety Belt/Restraint:
  Dynamic Head Restraints . . . . None
  Adjustable Belt. . . . . .Standard Front

Ford Taurus

Specifications

Drive. . . . . FWD
Engine 3.5-liter V6
Transmission . . . . .6-sp. Automatic
Tow Rating (lbs.) . . . . Very Low-1000
Head/Leg Room (in.) Cramped-39/41.9
Interior Space (cu. ft.). Average-102.2
Cargo Space (cu. ft.) Cramped-13.5
Wheelbase/Length (in.) 112/202.9

Ratings—10 Best, 1 Worst

Combo Crash Tests	7*
Safety Features	5
Rollover	8
Preventive Maintenance	7
Repair Costs	7
Warranty	1
Fuel Economy	9
Complaints	5
Insurance Costs	5
OVERALL RATING	**7**

Honda Accord

At-a-Glance

Status/Year Series Started	Unchanged/2013
Twins	Acura TLX
Body Styles	Sedan, Coupe
Seating	5
Anti-Theft Device	Std. Pass. Immobil. & Alarm
Parking Index Rating	Hard
Where Made	Marysville, OH
Fuel Factor	
MPG Rating (city/hwy)	Very Good-27/36
Driving Range (mi.)	Very Long-523.3
Fuel Type	Regular
Annual Fuel Cost	Very Low-$1,380
Gas Guzzler Tax	No
Greenhouse Gas Emissions (tons/yr.)	Low-5.8
Barrels of Oil Used per year	Low-10.6

How the Competition Rates

Competitors	Rating	Pg.
Ford Fusion	4	145
Nissan Altima	5	218
Toyota Camry	7	248

Price Range

Price Range	Retail	Markup
LX Sedan MT	$22,105	9%
EX Sedan AT	$25,830	9%
EX-L Coupe V6 AT	$30,775	9%
Hybrid Touring Sedan	$35,055	9%

Honda Accord

Safety Checklist

Crash Tests:
Frontal . . . . Average
Side . . . . Very Good

Airbags:
Torso . . . . Front Pelvis/Torso from Seat
Pelvis . . . . Front Pelvis/Torso from Seat
Roll Sensing . . . . Yes
Knee Bolster . . . . None

Crash Avoidance:
Collision Avoidance . . . . None
Blind Spot Detection . . . . None
Lane Keeping Assist . . . .Warning Only Optional
Backup Camera . . . . Standard
Pedestrian Crash Avoidance . . . . None

General:
Auto. Crash Notification . . . . . . Dial Assist.-Free
Day Running Lamps . . . . Standard

Safety Belt/Restraint:
Dynamic Head Restraints . . . . None
Adjustable Belt . . . . .Standard Front

Honda Accord

Specifications

Drive	FWD
Engine	2.4-liter I4
Transmission	CVT
Tow Rating (lbs.)	–
Head/Leg Room (in.)	Average-39.1/42.5
Interior Space (cu. ft.)	Average-103.2
Cargo Space (cu. ft.)	Cramped-15.8
Wheelbase/Length (in.)	109.3/191.4

*Crash test is for sedan only. For coupe results see page 23.

Ratings—10 Best, 1 Worst

Combo Crash Tests	4*
Safety Features	5
Rollover	6
Preventive Maintenance	7
Repair Costs	9
Warranty	1
Fuel Economy	9
Complaints	9
Insurance Costs	3
OVERALL RATING	**6**

Honda Civic

Honda Civic

At-a-Glance

Status/Year Series Started	Unchanged/2012
Twins	Acura ILX
Body Styles	Sedan, Coupe
Seating	5
Anti-Theft Device	Std. Pass. Immobil. & Alarm
Parking Index Rating	Easy
Where Made	Greensburg, IN / Alliston, Ontario
Fuel Factor	
MPG Rating (city/hwy)	Very Good-30/39
Driving Range (mi.)	Long-441.9
Fuel Type	Regular
Annual Fuel Cost	Very Low-$1,254
Gas Guzzler Tax	No
Greenhouse Gas Emissions (tons/yr.)	Low-5.4
Barrels of Oil Used per year	Low-10.0

How the Competition Rates

Competitors	Rating	Pg.
Nissan Sentra	–	228
Subaru Impreza	4	241
Volkswagen Jetta	5	264

Price Range

	Retail	Markup
LX Coupe MT	$18,190	8%
LX Sedan AT	$19,190	8%
EX-L Sedan w/Nav	$24,240	8%
Hybird-L Sedan w/Nav	$27,060	8%

Safety Checklist

Crash Tests:
Frontal.............................Poor
Side..............................Average

Airbags:
Torso ....Front Pelvis/Torso from Seat
Pelvis ....Front Pelvis/Torso from Seat
Roll Sensing...........................Yes
Knee Bolster ....None

Crash Avoidance:
Collision Avoidance .... None
Blind Spot Detection .... None
Lane Keeping Assist .... None
Backup Camera.................. Standard
Pedestrian Crash Avoidance......... None

General:
Auto. Crash Notification...... Dial Assist.-Free
Day Running Lamps .... Standard

Safety Belt/Restraint:
Dynamic Head Restraints .... None
Adjustable Belt...............Standard Front

Honda Civic

Specifications

Drive	FWD
Engine	1.8-liter I4
Transmission	CVT
Tow Rating (lbs.)	–
Head/Leg Room (in.)	Cramped-39/42
Interior Space (cu. ft.)	Cramped-94.6
Cargo Space (cu. ft.)	Very Cramped-12.5
Wheelbase/Length (in.)	105.1/179.4

*Crash test is for sedan only. For coupe results see page 21.

Ratings—10 Best, 1 Worst

Combo Crash Tests	–
Safety Features	6
Rollover	6
Preventive Maintenance	4
Repair Costs	9
Warranty	1
Fuel Economy	4
Complaints	–
Insurance Costs	8

OVERALL RATING   –

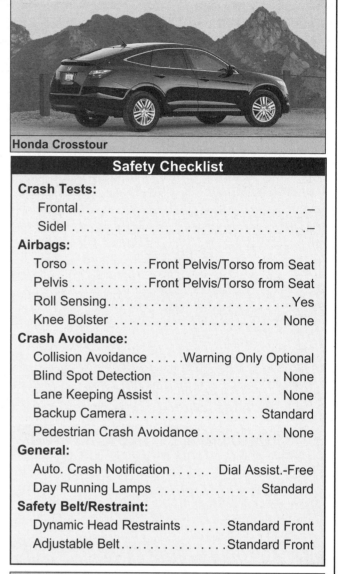

Honda Crosstour

Honda Crosstour

Safety Checklist

Crash Tests:
Frontal . . . . –
Sidel . . . . –
Airbags:
Torso . . . . .Front Pelvis/Torso from Seat
Pelvis . . . . .Front Pelvis/Torso from Seat
Roll Sensing. . . . . .Yes
Knee Bolster . . . . None
Crash Avoidance:
Collision Avoidance . . . . .Warning Only Optional
Blind Spot Detection . . . . None
Lane Keeping Assist . . . . None
Backup Camera . . . . Standard
Pedestrian Crash Avoidance . . . . None
General:
Auto. Crash Notification . . . . . . Dial Assist.-Free
Day Running Lamps . . . . Standard
Safety Belt/Restraint:
Dynamic Head Restraints . . . . . .Standard Front
Adjustable Belt . . . . .Standard Front

At-a-Glance

Status/Year Series Started. Unchanged/2014
Twins . . . . –
Body Styles . . . . SUV
Seating 5
Anti-Theft Device . . . . . . Std. Pass. Immobil. & Alarm
Parking Index Rating . . . . .Very Hard
Where Made. . . . . .East Liberty, OH
Fuel Factor . . . .
  MPG Rating (city/hwy) Poor-19/28
  Driving Range (mi.) Average-410.9
  Fuel Type . . . . .Regular
  Annual Fuel Cost . . . . Average-$1,890
  Gas Guzzler Tax . . . . .No
  Greenhouse Gas Emissions (tons/yr.) High-8.2
  Barrels of Oil Used per year High-15.0

Honda Crosstour

How the Competition Rates

Competitors	Rating	Pg.
Acura RDX	8	83
Subaru Forester	2	240
Toyota Venza	3	259

Specifications

Drive . . . . AWD
Engine 3.5-liter V6
Transmission . . . . .6-sp. Automatic
Tow Rating (lbs.) . . . . Very Low-1500
Head/Leg Room (in.) Average-39.5/42.2
Interior Space (cu. ft.). Average-100.8
Cargo Space (cu. ft.) Roomy-25.7
Wheelbase/Length (in.) 110.1/196.6

Price Range

Price Range	Retail	Markup
EX I4	$27,530	9%
EX V6	$31,190	9%
EX-L V6	$33,840	9%
EX-L V6 4WD w/Nav	$37,390	9%

Honda CR-V

Small SUV

Ratings—10 Best, 1 Worst	
Combo Crash Tests	5
Safety Features	6
Rollover	3
Preventive Maintenance	7
Repair Costs	9
Warranty	1
Fuel Economy	8
Complaints	6
Insurance Costs	8
OVERALL RATING	**6**

Honda CR-V

Honda CR-V

At-a-Glance

```
Status/Year Series Started  Appearance Change/2012
Twins . . . . . . . . . . . . . . . . . . . . . . . . . . . . . . . –
Body Styles . . . . . . . . . . . . . . . . . . . . . . . . SUV
Seating . . . . . . . . . . . . . . . . . . . . . . . . . . . . . . 5
Anti-Theft Device  Std. Pass. Immob. & Opt. Pass. Alarm
Parking Index Rating . . . . . . . . . . . . . . . . . . . Easy
Where Made . . . . . . . . . . . . . . . . .East Liberty, OH
Fuel Factor . . . . . . . . . . . . . . . . . . . . . . . . . . .
  MPG Rating (city/hwy) . . . . . . . . . Good-26/33
  Driving Range (mi.) . . . . . . . . . . .Long-439.8
  Fuel Type . . . . . . . . . . . . . . . . . . . . .Regular
  Annual Fuel Cost . . . . . . . . . . . Low-$1,461
  Gas Guzzler Tax . . . . . . . . . . . . . . . . . . . .No
  Greenhouse Gas Emissions (tons/yr.) . . . . . Low-6.4
  Barrels of Oil Used per year . . . . . . . Average-11.8
```

How the Competition Rates

Competitors	Rating	Pg.
Ford Escape	5	138
Jeep Cherokee	4	169
Toyota RAV4	4	254

Price Range	Retail	Markup
LX 2WD	$22,945	7%
EX 2WD	$25,045	6%
EX AWD	$26,295	7%
EX-L AWD w/RES	$29,645	7%

Safety Checklist

```
Crash Tests:
  Frontal . . . . . . . . . . . . . . . . . . . . . . . . Average
  Sidel . . . . . . . . . . . . . . . . . . . . . . . . . Average
Airbags:
  Torso . . . . . . . . . . . . . . Front Torso from Seat
  Pelvis . . . . . . . . . . . . . . . . . . . . . . . . . . . None
  Roll Sensing . . . . . . . . . . . . . . . . . . . . . . . .Yes
  Knee Bolster . . . . . . . . . . . . . . . . . . . . . None
Crash Avoidance:
  Collision Avoidance . . . . . . Optional CIB & DBS
  Blind Spot Detection . . . . . . . . . . . . . . . None
  Lane Keeping Assist . . . . . . . . . . . . . Optional
  Backup Camera . . . . . . . . . . . . . . . . Standard
  Pedestrian Crash Avoidance . . . . . . . . . None
General:
  Auto. Crash Notification . . . . . . Dial Assist.-Free
  Day Running Lamps . . . . . . . . . . . . . Standard
Safety Belt/Restraint:
  Dynamic Head Restraints . . . . . . . . . . . None
  Adjustable Belt . . . . . . . . . . . . .Standard Front
```

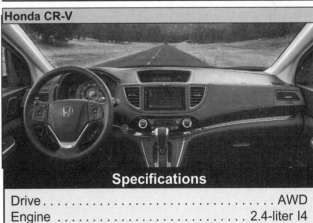

Honda CR-V

Specifications

```
Drive . . . . . . . . . . . . . . . . . . . . . . . . . . . AWD
Engine . . . . . . . . . . . . . . . . . . . . 2.4-liter I4
Transmission . . . . . . . . . . . . . . . . . . . . . .CVT
Tow Rating (lbs.) . . . . . . . . . Very Low-1500
Head/Leg Room (in.) . . . . . . . . Average-39.9/41.3
Interior Space (cu. ft.) . . . . . . . . Roomy-104.1
Cargo Space (cu. ft.) . . . . . . . Very Roomy-35.2
Wheelbase/Length (in.) . . . . . . . . .103.1/179.4
```

Honda Fit

Ratings—10 Best, 1 Worst

Combo Crash Tests	9
Safety Features	5
Rollover	4
Preventive Maintenance	4
Repair Costs	8
Warranty	1
Fuel Economy	10
Complaints	–
Insurance Costs	3
OVERALL RATING	**6**

Honda Fit

At-a-Glance

Status/Year Series Started	All New/2015
Twins	–
Body Styles	Hatchback
Seating	5
Anti-Theft Device	Std. Pass. Immob. & Opt. Pass. Alarm
Parking Index Rating	Very Easy
Where Made	Celaya, Mexico
Fuel Factor	
MPG Rating (city/hwy)	Very Good-33/41
Driving Range (mi.)	Short-383.5
Fuel Type	Regular
Annual Fuel Cost	Very Low-$1,160
Gas Guzzler Tax	No
Greenhouse Gas Emissions (tons/yr.)	Very Low-5.0
Barrels of Oil Used per year	Low-9.1

How the Competition Rates

Competitors	Rating	Pg.
Chevrolet Sonic	9	119
Nissan Versa	2	230
Toyota Yaris	5	260

Price Range

Price Range	Retail	Markup
LX MT	$15,525	3%
EX MT	$17,435	3%
EX AT	$18,235	3%
EX-L AT w/Nav	$20,800	3%

Safety Checklist

Crash Tests:
Frontal	Good
Sidel	Very Good

Airbags:
Torso	Front Pelvis/Torso from Seat
Pelvis	Front Pelvis/Torso from Seat
Roll Sensing	Yes
Knee Bolster	None

Crash Avoidance:
Collision Avoidance	None
Blind Spot Detection	None
Lane Keeping Assist	None
Backup Camera	Standard
Pedestrian Crash Avoidance	None

General:
Auto. Crash Notification	Dial Assist.-Free
Day Running Lamps	Standard

Safety Belt/Restraint:
Dynamic Head Restraints	None
Adjustable Belt	Standard Front

Honda Fit

Specifications

Drive	FWD
Engine	1.5-liter I4
Transmission	CVT
Tow Rating (lbs.)	–
Head/Leg Room (in.)	Cramped-39.5/41.4
Interior Space (cu. ft.)	Cramped-95.7
Cargo Space (cu. ft.)	Average-16.6
Wheelbase/Length (in.)	99.6/160

Ratings—10 Best, 1 Worst

Combo Crash Tests	8
Safety Features	7
Rollover	5
Preventive Maintenance	6
Repair Costs	9
Warranty	1
Fuel Economy	4
Complaints	5
Insurance Costs	10
OVERALL RATING	**7**

Honda Odyssey

Honda Odyssey

At-a-Glance

Status/Year Series Started	Unchanged/2005
Twins	–
Body Styles	Minivan
Seating	7/8
Anti-Theft Device	Standard Pass. Immobil.
Parking Index Rating	Hard
Where Made	Lincoln, AL
Fuel Factor	
MPG Rating (city/hwy)	Poor-19/28
Driving Range (mi.)	Very Long-466.5
Fuel Type	Regular
Annual Fuel Cost	Average-$1,890
Gas Guzzler Tax	No
Greenhouse Gas Emissions (tons/yr.)	Average-7.1
Barrels of Oil Used per year	High-15.0

How the Competition Rates

Competitors	Rating	Pg.
Chrysler Town and Country	3	128
Nissan Quest	–	226
Toyota Sienna	3	256

Price Range	Retail	Markup
LX	$28,975	9%
EX	$32,275	9%
EX-L w/Nav	$37,775	9%
Touring Elite	$44,600	9%

Safety Checklist

Crash Tests:
Frontal . . . . Good
Side . . . . Very Good

Airbags:
Torso . . . . .Front Pelvis/Torso from Seat
Pelvis . . . . .Front Pelvis/Torso from Seat
Roll Sensing . . . . .Yes
Knee Bolster . . . . None

Crash Avoidance:
Collision Avoidance . . . . .Warning Only Optional
Blind Spot Detection . . . . Optional
Lane Keeping Assist . . . . None
Backup Camera . . . . Standard
Pedestrian Crash Avoidance . . . . None

General:
Auto. Crash Notification . . . . . . Dial Assist.-Free
Day Running Lamps . . . . Standard

Safety Belt/Restraint:
Dynamic Head Restraints . . . . . .Standard Front
Adjustable Belt . . . . . . .Standard Front and Rear

Honda Odyssey

Specifications

Drive	FWD
Engine	3.5-liter V6
Transmission	5-sp. Automatic
Tow Rating (lbs.)	Low-3500
Head/Leg Room (in.)	Cramped-39.7/40.9
Interior Space (cu. ft.)	Very Roomy-172.6
Cargo Space (cu. ft.)	Very Roomy-38.4
Wheelbase/Length (in.)	118.1/202.9

Ratings—10 Best, 1 Worst

Combo Crash Tests	2
Safety Features	5
Rollover	3
Preventive Maintenance	5
Repair Costs	8
Warranty	1
Fuel Economy	2
Complaints	7
Insurance Costs	10
OVERALL RATING	**2**

Honda Pilot

Honda Pilot

At-a-Glance

Status/Year Series Started	Unchanged/2009
Twins	–
Body Styles	SUV
Seating	8
Anti-Theft Device	Standard Pass. Immobil.
Parking Index Rating	Average
Where Made	Lincoln, AL
Fuel Factor	
MPG Rating (city/hwy)	Very Poor-17/24
Driving Range (mi.)	Average-410.9
Fuel Type	Regular
Annual Fuel Cost	High-$2,146
Gas Guzzler Tax	No
Greenhouse Gas Emissions (tons/yr.)	High-9.0
Barrels of Oil Used per year	High-16.5

How the Competition Rates

Competitors	Rating	Pg.
Chevrolet Equinox	2	115
Ford Explorer	3	140
Toyota 4Runner	3	246

Price Range	Retail	Markup
LX 2WD	$29,870	9%
SE 2WD	$33,120	9%
EX-L 4WD	$36,970	9%
Touring 4WD	$41,620	9%

Safety Checklist

Crash Tests:
Frontal . . . . Poor
Side . . . . Very Poor
Airbags:
Torso . . . . Front Pelvis/Torso from Seat
Pelvis . . . . Front Pelvis/Torso from Seat
Roll Sensing . . . . Yes
Knee Bolster . . . . None
Crash Avoidance:
Collision Avoidance . . . . None
Blind Spot Detection . . . . None
Lane Keeping Assist . . . . None
Backup Camera . . . . Standard
Pedestrian Crash Avoidance . . . . None
General:
Auto. Crash Notification . . . . None
Day Running Lamps . . . . Standard
Safety Belt/Restraint:
Dynamic Head Restraints . . . . . . Standard Front
Adjustable Belt . . . . Standard Front and Rear

Honda Pilot

Specifications

Drive	AWD
Engine	3.5-liter V6
Transmission	5-sp. Automatic
Tow Rating (lbs.)	Low-4500
Head/Leg Room (in.)	Average-40/41.4
Interior Space (cu. ft.)	Very Roomy-153.7
Cargo Space (cu. ft.)	Average-18
Wheelbase/Length (in.)	109.2/191.4

Hyundai Accent

Ratings—10 Best, 1 Worst

Combo Crash Tests	2
Safety Features	3
Rollover	6
Preventive Maintenance	6
Repair Costs	10
Warranty	10
Fuel Economy	8
Complaints	8
Insurance Costs	1
OVERALL RATING	**5**

Hyundai Accent

At-a-Glance

Status/Year Series Started	Unchanged/2012
Twins	Kia Rio
Body Styles	Sedan, Hatchback
Seating	5
Anti-Theft Device	None
Parking Index Rating	Very Easy
Where Made	Ulsan, South Korea
Fuel Factor	
MPG Rating (city/hwy)	Good-26/37
Driving Range (mi.)	Very Short-342.2
Fuel Type	Regular
Annual Fuel Cost	Very Low-$1,399
Gas Guzzler Tax	No
Greenhouse Gas Emissions (tons/yr.)	Low-6.0
Barrels of Oil Used per year	Average-11.0

How the Competition Rates

Competitors	Rating	Pg.
Ford Fiesta	2	142
Nissan Versa	2	230
Toyota Yaris	5	260

Price Range

	Retail	Markup
GLS Sedan MT	$14,745	3%
GS Hatchback AT	$16,195	3%
Sport Hatchback MT	$16,495	3%
Sport Hatchback AT	$17,495	3%

Safety Checklist

Crash Tests:
Frontal . . . . Poor
Side . . . . Very Poor*

Airbags:
Torso . . . . Front Pelvis/Torso from Seat
Pelvis . . . . Front Pelvis/Torso from Seat
Roll Sensing. . . . . Yes
Knee Bolster . . . . None

Crash Avoidance:
Collision Avoidance . . . . None
Blind Spot Detection . . . . None
Lane Keeping Assist . . . . None
Backup Camera . . . . None
Pedestrian Crash Avoidance . . . . None

General:
Auto. Crash Notification . . . . None
Day Running Lamps . . . . None

Safety Belt/Restraint:
Dynamic Head Restraints . . . . None
Adjustable Belt . . . . Standard Front

Hyundai Accent

Specifications

Drive	FWD
Engine	1.6-liter I4
Transmission	6-sp. Automatic
Tow Rating (lbs.)	–
Head/Leg Room (in.)	Average-39.9/41.8
Interior Space (cu. ft.)	Very Cramped-90.1
Cargo Space (cu. ft.)	Average-21.2
Wheelbase/Length (in.)	101.2/162

*Additional injury potential in side test. See footnote on page 20.

Ratings—10 Best, 1 Worst

Combo Crash Tests	5
Safety Features	2
Rollover	7
Preventive Maintenance	4
Repair Costs	10
Warranty	10
Fuel Economy	9
Complaints	6
Insurance Costs	1
OVERALL RATING	**6**

Hyundai Elantra

At-a-Glance

Status/Year Series Started. Unchanged/2011
Twins . . . . .Kia Forte
Body Styles . . . . .Sedan, Coupe, Hatchback
Seating 5
Anti-Theft Device . Std. Pass. Immobil. & Active Alarm
Parking Index Rating . . . . Easy
Where Made. . . . . .Montgomery, AL
Fuel Factor. . . . .
  MPG Rating (city/hwy) . . . . Very Good-28/38
  Driving Range (mi.) Average-406.5
  Fuel Type. . . . . .Regular
  Annual Fuel Cost . . . . Very Low-$1,322
  Gas Guzzler Tax . . . . .No
  Greenhouse Gas Emissions (tons/yr.) Low-5.6
  Barrels of Oil Used per year Low-10.3

How the Competition Rates

Competitors	Rating	Pg.
Honda Civic	6	149
Nissan Sentra	–	228
Toyota Corolla	8	249

Price Range	Retail	Markup
SE MT	$17,250	3%
Sport MT	$21,600	4%
Limited AT	$21,700	4%
Sport AT	$22,600	5%

Hyundai Elantra

Safety Checklist

Crash Tests:
  Frontal. . . . . Average
  Side. . . . . .Poor
Airbags:
  Torso . . . . .Front Pelvis/Torso from Seat
  Pelvis . . . . .Front Pelvis/Torso from Seat
  Roll Sensing. . . . . No
  Knee Bolster . . . . None
Crash Avoidance:
  Collision Avoidance . . . . None
  Blind Spot Detection . . . . None
  Lane Keeping Assist . . . . None
  Backup Camera . . . . Optional
  Pedestrian Crash Avoidance . . . . None
General:
  Auto. Crash Notification . . . Operator Assist.-Fee
  Day Running Lamps . . . . Standard
Safety Belt/Restraint:
  Dynamic Head Restraints . . . . None
  Adjustable Belt. . . . . .Standard Front

Hyundai Elantra

Specifications

Drive. . . . . FWD
Engine 1.8-liter I4
Transmission . . . . .6-sp. Automatic
Tow Rating (lbs.) . . . . –
Head/Leg Room (in.) Roomy-40/43.6
Interior Space (cu. ft.). Cramped-95.6
Cargo Space (cu. ft.) Cramped-14.8
Wheelbase/Length (in.) 106.3/179.1

Hyundai Genesis
Large

Ratings—10 Best, 1 Worst	
Combo Crash Tests	9
Safety Features	6
Rollover	8
Preventive Maintenance	3
Repair Costs	4
Warranty	10
Fuel Economy	3
Complaints	–
Insurance Costs	3
OVERALL RATING	**7**

Hyundai Genesis

Hyundai Genesis

At-a-Glance

Status/Year Series Started. . . . . All New/2015
Twins . . . . –
Body Styles . . . . .Sedan
Seating 5
Anti-Theft Device . Std. Pass. Immobil. & Active Alarm
Parking Index Rating . . . . Average
Where Made. . . . . Ulsan, South Korea
Fuel Factor. . . . .
  MPG Rating (city/hwy) Poor-18/29
  Driving Range (mi.) Long-440.6
  Fuel Type. .Regular
  Annual Fuel Cost . . . . Average-$1,935
  Gas Guzzler Tax .No
  Greenhouse Gas Emissions (tons/yr.). High-8.2
  Barrels of Oil Used per year High-15.0

How the Competition Rates

Competitors	Rating	Pg.
Acura TLX	–	85
Lexus ES	7	187
Volkswagen CC	–	262

Price Range

Price Range	Retail	Markup
Ultimate 3.8L Coupe	$34,600	7%
3.8L V6 FWD	$38,000	7%
3.8L V6 AWD	$40,500	7%
5.0L V8 FWD	$51,500	8%

Safety Checklist

Crash Tests:
  Frontal. . . . . Very Good
  Side. . . . . Good
Airbags:
  Torso . . . . .Front Pelvis/Torso from Seat
  Pelvis . . . . Rear Pelvis/Torso
  Roll Sensing. . . . . .Yes
  Knee Bolster . . . . Standard Driver
Crash Avoidance:
  Collision Avoidance . . . . . . Optional CIB & DBS
  Blind Spot Detection . . . . Optional
  Lane Keeping Assist . . . . Optional
  Backup Camera. . . . . None
  Pedestrian Crash Avoidance . . . . None
General:
  Auto. Crash Notification. . . . . None
  Day Running Lamps . . . . Standard
Safety Belt/Restraint:
  Dynamic Head Restraints . . . . None
  Adjustable Belt. . . . . .Standard Front

Hyundai Genesis

Specifications

Drive. . . . . .RWD
Engine 3.8-liter V6
Transmission . . . . .8-sp. Automatic
Tow Rating (lbs.) . . . . –
Head/Leg Room (in.) . . . . . . Very Roomy-41.1/45.7
Interior Space (cu. ft.). Roomy-107.7
Cargo Space (cu. ft.) Cramped-15.3
Wheelbase/Length (in.) 118.5/196.5

Ratings—10 Best, 1 Worst

Combo Crash Tests	–
Safety Features	6
Rollover	4
Preventive Maintenance	4
Repair Costs	8
Warranty	10
Fuel Economy	3
Complaints	1
Insurance Costs	8
OVERALL RATING	**–**

Hyundai Santa Fe

Hyundai Santa Fe

Safety Checklist

Crash Tests:
Frontal. . . . .–
Sidel . . . .–

Airbags:
Torso . . . . .Front Pelvis/Torso from Seat
Pelvis . . . . .Front Pelvis/Torso from Seat
Roll Sensing. . . . . .Yes
Knee Bolster . . . . Standard Driver

Crash Avoidance:
Collision Avoidance . . . . None
Blind Spot Detection . . . . Optional
Lane Keeping Assist . . . . None
Backup Camera . . . . Standard
Pedestrian Crash Avoidance . . . . None

General:
Auto. Crash Notification . . . Operator Assist.-Fee
Day Running Lamps . . . . Standard

Safety Belt/Restraint:
Dynamic Head Restraints . . . . . .Standard Front
Adjustable Belt. . . . . .Standard Front

At-a-Glance

Status/Year Series Started. Unchanged/2013
Twins . . . .–
Body Styles . . . . SUV
Seating 6/7
Anti-Theft Device . Std. Pass. Immobil. & Active Alarm
Parking Index Rating . . . . Average
Where Made. . . . . West Point, GA
Fuel Factor. . . . .
 MPG Rating (city/hwy) Poor-18/25
 Driving Range (mi.) Short-387.2
 Fuel Type . . . . .Regular
 Annual Fuel Cost . . . . High-$2,039
 Gas Guzzler Tax . . . . .No
 Greenhouse Gas Emissions (tons/yr.) High-8.5
 Barrels of Oil Used per year High-15.7

How the Competition Rates

Competitors	Rating	Pg.
Acura MDX	6	82
Mitsubishi Outlander	4	215
Nissan Pathfinder	–	225

Price Range	Retail	Markup
GLS FWD	$30,150	4%
GLS AWD	$31,900	5%
Limited FWD	$34,250	5%
Limited AWD	$36,000	6%

Hyundai Santa Fe

Specifications

Drive. . . . . FWD
Engine 3.3-liter V6
Transmission . . . . .6-sp. Automatic
Tow Rating (lbs.) Low-5000
Head/Leg Room (in.) Cramped-39.6/41.3
Interior Space (cu. ft.). . . . . Very Roomy-146.6
Cargo Space (cu. ft.) Cramped-13.5
Wheelbase/Length (in.) 110.2/193.1

Hyundai Santa Fe Sport

Ratings—10 Best, 1 Worst	
Combo Crash Tests	6
Safety Features	5
Rollover	4
Preventive Maintenance	4
Repair Costs	8
Warranty	10
Fuel Economy	4
Complaints	–
Insurance Costs	8
OVERALL RATING	**7**

Hyundai Santa Fe Sport

Hyundai Santa Fe Sport

At-a-Glance

Status/Year Series Started Unchanged/2014
Twins . . . . Kia Sorento
Body Styles . . . . SUV
Seating 5
Anti-Theft Device . Std. Pass. Immobil. & Active Alarm
Parking Index Rating . . . . Easy
Where Made. . . . . West Point, GA
Fuel Factor . . . .
  MPG Rating (city/hwy) Poor-20/27
  Driving Range (mi.) Short-394.0
  Fuel Type . . . . .Regular
  Annual Fuel Cost . . . . Average-$1,855
  Gas Guzzler Tax . . . . .No
  Greenhouse Gas Emissions (tons/yr.) High-7.9
  Barrels of Oil Used per year High-14.3

How the Competition Rates

Competitors	Rating	Pg.
Kia Sorento	4	180
Mitsubishi Outlander Sport	4	216
Toyota Venza	3	259

Price Range	Retail	Markup
2.4L I4 FWD	$24,950	5%
2.4L I4 AWD	$26,700	5%
2.0T I4 Turbo FWD	$31,250	5%
2.0T I4 Turbo AWD	$33,000	5%

Safety Checklist

Crash Tests:
  Frontal. . . . . Good
  Side. . . . . Average
Airbags:
  Torso . . . . .Front Pelvis/Torso from Seat
  Pelvis . . . . .Front Pelvis/Torso from Seat
  Roll Sensing. . . . . .Yes
  Knee Bolster . . . . Standard Driver
Crash Avoidance:
  Collision Avoidance . . . . None
  Blind Spot Detection . . . . Optional
  Lane Keeping Assist . . . . None
  Backup Camera . . . . Optional
  Pedestrian Crash Avoidance . . . . None
General:
  Auto. Crash Notification . . . Operator Assist.-Fee
  Day Running Lamps . . . . Standard
Safety Belt/Restraint:
  Dynamic Head Restraints . . . . None
  Adjustable Belt. . . . . .Standard Front

Hyundai Santa Fe Sport

Specifications

Drive. . . . . FWD
Engine 2.4-liter I4
Transmission . . . . .6-sp. Automatic
Tow Rating (lbs.) . . . . Very Low-2000
Head/Leg Room (in.) Cramped-39.6/41.3
Interior Space (cu. ft.). Roomy-108
Cargo Space (cu. ft.) . . . . Very Roomy-35.4
Wheelbase/Length (in.) 106.3/184.6

Hyundai Sonata Intermediate

Hyundai Sonata

Ratings—10 Best, 1 Worst

Combo Crash Tests	9*
Safety Features	5
Rollover	7
Preventive Maintenance	2
Repair Costs	9
Warranty	10
Fuel Economy	8
Complaints	–
Insurance Costs	3
OVERALL RATING	**8**

Hyundai Sonata

At-a-Glance

Status/Year Series Started	All New/2015
Twins	–
Body Styles	Sedan
Seating	5
Anti-Theft Device	Std. Pass. Immobil. & Active Alarm
Parking Index Rating	Easy
Where Made	Montgomery, AL
Fuel Factor	
MPG Rating (city/hwy)	Good-25/37
Driving Range (mi.)	Very Long-541.5
Fuel Type	Regular
Annual Fuel Cost	Low-$1,434
Gas Guzzler Tax	No
Greenhouse Gas Emissions (tons/yr.)	Low-6.2
Barrels of Oil Used per year	Average-11.4

How the Competition Rates

Competitors	Rating	Pg.
Mazda Mazda6	4	201
Toyota Camry	7	248
Volkswagen Passat	5	265

Price Range

Price Range	Retail	Markup
SE 2.4L	$21,150	4%
Limited 2.4L	$26,525	6%
Sport 2.0L Turbo	$28,575	6%
Hybrid Limited	$29,500	6%

Safety Checklist

Crash Tests:
Frontal . . . . Very Good
Side . . . . Average
Airbags:
Torso . . . . Front Pelvis/Torso from Seat
Pelvis . . . . Front Pelvis/Torso from Seat
Roll Sensing . . . . Yes
Knee Bolster . . . . Standard Driver
Crash Avoidance:
Collision Avoidance . . . . . Warning Only Optional
Blind Spot Detection . . . . Optional
Lane Keeping Assist . . . . None
Backup Camera . . . . None
Pedestrian Crash Avoidance . . . . None
General:
Auto. Crash Notification . . . Operator Assist.-Fee
Day Running Lamps . . . . Standard
Safety Belt/Restraint:
Dynamic Head Restraints . . . . None
Adjustable Belt . . . . Standard Front

Hyundai Sonata

Specifications

Drive	FWD
Engine	2.4-liter I4
Transmission	6-sp. Automatic
Tow Rating (lbs.)	Very Low-0
Head/Leg Room (in.)	Very Roomy-40.4/45.5
Interior Space (cu. ft.)	Roomy-106.1
Cargo Space (cu. ft.)	Cramped-16.3
Wheelbase/Length (in.)	110.4/191.1

*Crash test is for non-hybrid models only. For hybrid results see page 23.

Ratings—10 Best, 1 Worst

Combo Crash Tests	1
Safety Features	5
Rollover	3
Preventive Maintenance	4
Repair Costs	10
Warranty	10
Fuel Economy	5
Complaints	8
Insurance Costs	8
OVERALL RATING	**5**

Hyundai Tucson

Hyundai Tucson

At-a-Glance

Status/Year Series Started. Unchanged/2010
Twins . . . . Kia Sportage
Body Styles . . . . SUV
Seating 5
Anti-Theft Device . Std. Pass. Immobil. & Active Alarm
Parking Index Rating . . . . .Very Easy
Where Made. . . . . Ulsan, South Korea
Fuel Factor. . . . .
  MPG Rating (city/hwy) Average-21/28
  Driving Range (mi.) . . . . Very Short-362.0
  Fuel Type. . . . . .Regular
  Annual Fuel Cost . . . . Average-$1,775
  Gas Guzzler Tax . . . . .No
  Greenhouse Gas Emissions (tons/yr.). . Average-7.5
  Barrels of Oil Used per year High-13.7

How the Competition Rates

Competitors	Rating	Pg.
Ford Escape	5	138
Honda CR-V	6	151
Toyota RAV4	4	254

Price Range	Retail	Markup
GLS FWD	$21,500	4%
SE FWD	$23,550	4%
SE AWD	$25,050	4%
Limited AWD	$27,800	5%

Safety Checklist

Crash Tests:
  Frontal. . . . . .Very Poor
  Side. . . . . .Very Poor
Airbags:
  Torso . . . . .Front Pelvis/Torso from Seat
  Pelvis . . . . .Front Pelvis/Torso from Seat
  Roll Sensing. . . . . .Yes
  Knee Bolster . . . . None
Crash Avoidance:
  Collision Avoidance . . . . None
  Blind Spot Detection . . . . None
  Lane Keeping Assist . . . . None
  Backup Camera. . . . . Optional
  Pedestrian Crash Avoidance . . . . None
General:
  Auto. Crash Notification . . . Operator Assist.-Fee
  Day Running Lamps . . . . None
Safety Belt/Restraint:
  Dynamic Head Restraints . . . . . .Standard Front
  Adjustable Belt. . . . . .Standard Front

Hyundai Tucson

Specifications

Drive. . . . . FWD
Engine 2.4-liter I4
Transmission . . . . .6-sp. Automatic
Tow Rating (lbs.) . . . . Very Low-2000
Head/Leg Room (in.) Cramped-39.4/41.2
Interior Space (cu. ft.). Average-101.9
Cargo Space (cu. ft.) Roomy-25.7
Wheelbase/Length (in.) 103.9/173.2

Ratings—10 Best, 1 Worst

Combo Crash Tests	5
Safety Features	2
Rollover	7
Preventive Maintenance	5
Repair Costs	9
Warranty	10
Fuel Economy	9
Complaints	2
Insurance Costs	3
OVERALL RATING	**6**

Hyundai Veloster

Hyundai Veloster

At-a-Glance

Status/Year Series Started........ Unchanged/2012
Twins ....–
Body Styles .... Hatchback
Seating...................................4
Anti-Theft Device .Std. Pass. Immobil. & Active Alarm
Parking Index Rating ....Very Easy
Where Made............... Ulsan, South Korea
Fuel Factor...........................
  MPG Rating (city/hwy) .... Very Good-27/36
  Driving Range (mi.) Average-401.6
  Fuel Type........................Regular
  Annual Fuel Cost .... Very Low-$1,380
  Gas Guzzler Tax ....No
  Greenhouse Gas Emissions (tons/yr.)..... Low-6.0
  Barrels of Oil Used per year Average-11.0

How the Competition Rates

Competitors	Rating	Pg.
Chevrolet Sonic	9	119
Mini Cooper	–	211
Scion tC	5	236

Price Range	Retail	Markup
Base MT	$17,900	4%
RE:Flex AT	$21,850	4%
Turbo MT	$22,500	5%
Turbo AT	$23,500	5%

Safety Checklist

Crash Tests:
  Frontal......................... Average
  Side........................... Average
Airbags:
  Torso ....Front Pelvis/Torso from Seat
  Pelvis ....Front Pelvis/Torso from Seat
  Roll Sensing........................ No
  Knee Bolster .... None
Crash Avoidance:
  Collision Avoidance .... None
  Blind Spot Detection .... None
  Lane Keeping Assist .... None
  Backup Camera................... Standard
  Pedestrian Crash Avoidance .... None
General:
  Auto. Crash Notification...... Dial Assist.-Free
  Day Running Lamps .... Standard
Safety Belt/Restraint:
  Dynamic Head Restraints .... None
  Adjustable Belt.................... None

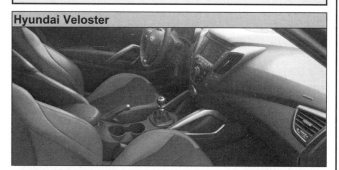

Hyundai Veloster

Specifications

Drive................................. FWD
Engine 1.6-liter I4
Transmission ....6-sp. Automatic
Tow Rating (lbs.) ....–
Head/Leg Room (in.) Roomy-39/43.9
Interior Space (cu. ft.).........Very Cramped-89.8
Cargo Space (cu. ft.) Cramped-15.5
Wheelbase/Length (in.) 104.3/166.1

Ratings—10 Best, 1 Worst

Combo Crash Tests	–
Safety Features	6
Rollover	7
Preventive Maintenance	8
Repair Costs	2
Warranty	7
Fuel Economy	5
Complaints	7
Insurance Costs	8
OVERALL RATING	**–**

Infiniti Q50

At-a-Glance

Status/Year Series Started........ Unchanged/2014
Twins ....–
Body Styles ....Sedan
Seating....................................5
Anti-Theft Device ...... Std. Pass. Immobil. & Alarm
Parking Index Rating .... Average
Where Made.................... Tochigi, Japan
Fuel Factor.............................
  MPG Rating (city/hwy).......Average-20/29
  Driving Range (mi.) Long-464.9
  Fuel Type......................Premium
  Annual Fuel Cost ....High-$2,064
  Gas Guzzler Tax ....No
  Greenhouse Gas Emissions (tons/yr.).....High-7.8
  Barrels of Oil Used per year High-14.3

How the Competition Rates

Competitors	Rating	Pg.
BMW 3 Series	9	94
Lexus IS	5	190
Lincoln MKZ	4	196

Price Range	Retail	Markup
3.7L	$37,150	8%
3.7L AWD	$38,950	8%
3.7 AWD Premium	$41,800	8%
Hybrid AWD	$48,600	8%

Infiniti Q50

Safety Checklist

Crash Tests:
  Frontal............................... –
  Sidel................................. –
Airbags:
  Torso ....Front Pelvis/Torso from Seat
  Pelvis ....Front Pelvis/Torso from Seat
  Roll Sensing.......................... No
  Knee Bolster .... None
Crash Avoidance:
  Collision Avoidance ...... Optional CIB & DBS
  Blind Spot Detection .... Optional
  Lane Keeping Assist .... Optional
  Backup Camera................... Standard
  Pedestrian Crash Avoidance .... None
General:
  Auto. Crash Notification ... Operator Assist.-Fee
  Day Running Lamps .... Standard
Safety Belt/Restraint:
  Dynamic Head Restraints .... None
  Adjustable Belt..............Standard Front

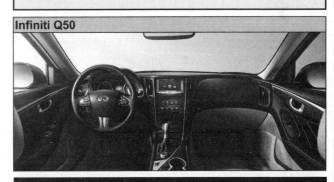

Infiniti Q50

Specifications

Drive................................RWD
Engine 3.7-liter V6
Transmission ....7-sp. Automatic
Tow Rating (lbs.) .... –
Head/Leg Room (in.) ...... Very Roomy-39.5/44.5
Interior Space (cu. ft.)..........Average-100
Cargo Space (cu. ft.) Cramped-13.5
Wheelbase/Length (in.) 112.2/188.3

Ratings—10 Best, 1 Worst

Combo Crash Tests	–
Safety Features	3
Rollover	8
Preventive Maintenance	8
Repair Costs	2
Warranty	7
Fuel Economy	4
Complaints	10
Insurance Costs	5
OVERALL RATING	**–**

Infiniti Q60

Infiniti Q60

Infiniti Q60

At-a-Glance

Status/Year Series Started	Unchanged/2007
Twins	–
Body Styles	Coupe, Convertible
Seating	4
Anti-Theft Device	Std. Pass. Immobil. & Alarm
Parking Index Rating	Easy
Where Made	Tochigi, Japan
Fuel Factor	
MPG Rating (city/hwy)	Poor-19/27
Driving Range (mi.)	Long-438.5
Fuel Type	Premium
Annual Fuel Cost	High-$2,189
Gas Guzzler Tax	No
Greenhouse Gas Emissions (tons/yr.)	High-8.2
Barrels of Oil Used per year	High-15.0

How the Competition Rates

Competitors	Rating	Pg.
BMW 4 Series	–	95
Lexus GS	–	188
Mercedes-Benz C-Class	–	203

Price Range

	Retail	Markup
Coupe Journey	$40,950	8%
Coupe AWD	$42,600	8%
Coupe Limited	$49,650	8%
IPL Convertible	$62,100	8%

Safety Checklist

Crash Tests:
Frontal . . . . –
Sidel . . . . –
Airbags:
Torso . . . . Front Pelvis/Torso from Seat
Pelvis . . . . Front Pelvis/Torso from Seat
Roll Sensing . . . . No
Knee Bolster . . . . None
Crash Avoidance:
Collision Avoidance . . . . None
Blind Spot Detection . . . . None
Lane Keeping Assist . . . . None
Backup Camera . . . . Standard
Pedestrian Crash Avoidance . . . . None
General:
Auto. Crash Notification . . . Operator Assist.-Fee
Day Running Lamps . . . . None
Safety Belt/Restraint:
Dynamic Head Restraints . . . . . . Standard Front
Adjustable Belt . . . . None

Infiniti Q60

Specifications

Drive	RWD
Engine	3.7-liter V6
Transmission	7-sp. Automatic
Tow Rating (lbs.)	–
Head/Leg Room (in.)	Roomy-39.4/43.8
Interior Space (cu. ft.)	Cramped-92.4
Cargo Space (cu. ft.)	Very Cramped-7.4
Wheelbase/Length (in.)	112.2/183.1

Ratings—10 Best, 1 Worst

Combo Crash Tests	–
Safety Features	6
Rollover	5
Preventive Maintenance	7
Repair Costs	1
Warranty	7
Fuel Economy	3
Complaints	2
Insurance Costs	5

OVERALL RATING — –

Infiniti Q70

Infiniti Q70

At-a-Glance

Status/Year Series Started Appearance Change/2011
Twins . . . .–
Body Styles . . . . .Sedan
Seating. 5
Anti-Theft Device . . . . . . Std. Pass. Immobil. & Alarm
Parking Index Rating . . . . Hard
Where Made. Tochigi, Japan
Fuel Factor. . . . .
 MPG Rating (city/hwy) Poor-18/24
 Driving Range (mi.) Average-405.6
 Fuel Type. . . . . .Premium
 Annual Fuel Cost . . . . Very High-$2,366
 Gas Guzzler Tax . . . . .No
 Greenhouse Gas Emissions (tons/yr.) High-9.0
 Barrels of Oil Used per year High-16.5

How the Competition Rates

Competitors	Rating	Pg.
BMW 5 Series	8	96
Lexus ES	7	187
Mercedes-Benz S-Class	–	210

Price Range	Retail	Markup
3.7L	$49,850	8%
3.7L AWD	$52,000	8%
Hybrid	$55,900	8%
5.6L AWD LWB	$67,050	8%

Safety Checklist

Crash Tests:
 Frontal. . . . .–
 Sidel . . . .–
Airbags:
 Torso . . . . .Front Pelvis/Torso from Seat
 Pelvis . . . . .Front Pelvis/Torso from Seat
 Roll Sensing. . . . . No
 Knee Bolster . . . . None
Crash Avoidance:
 Collision Avoidance . . . . . . Optional CIB & DBS
 Blind Spot Detection . . . . Optional
 Lane Keeping Assist . . . . None
 Backup Camera . . . . Standard
 Pedestrian Crash Avoidance . . . . None
General:
 Auto. Crash Notification . . . Operator Assist.-Fee
 Day Running Lamps . . . . Standard
Safety Belt/Restraint:
 Dynamic Head Restraints . . . . .Standard Front
 Adjustable Belt. . . . . .Standard Front

Infiniti Q70

Specifications

Drive. . . . . AWD
Engine 3.7-liter V6
Transmission . . . . .7-sp. Automatic
Tow Rating (lbs.) . . . . –
Head/Leg Room (in.) Roomy-39.1/44.4
Interior Space (cu. ft.). Average-103.6
Cargo Space (cu. ft.) Cramped-14.9
Wheelbase/Length (in.) 114.2/196.1

Ratings—10 Best, 1 Worst

Combo Crash Tests	–
Safety Features	8
Rollover	4
Preventive Maintenance	7
Repair Costs	1
Warranty	7
Fuel Economy	3
Complaints	1
Insurance Costs	8

OVERALL RATING — –

Infiniti QX60

Infiniti QX60

At-a-Glance

```
Status/Year Series Started........ Unchanged/2013
Twins . . . . . . . . . . . . . . . . . . . . . .Nissan Pathfinder
Body Styles . . . . . . . . . . . . . . . . . . . . . . . . . . SUV
Seating . . . . . . . . . . . . . . . . . . . . . . . . . . . . . .7
Anti-Theft Device . . . . . . Std. Pass. Immobil. & Alarm
Parking Index Rating . . . . . . . . . . . . . . . . . . . Hard
Where Made. . . . . . . . . . . . . . . . . . . . . Smyrna, TN
Fuel Factor. . . . . . . . . . . . . . . . . . . . . . . . . . . . .
  MPG Rating (city/hwy) . . . Poor-19/26
  Driving Range (mi.) . . . . . . . . . . Average-421.6
  Fuel Type. . . . . . . . . . . . . . . . . . . . . . .Premium
  Annual Fuel Cost . . . . . . . . . . . . . . . High-$2,220
  Gas Guzzler Tax . . . . . . . . . . . . . . . . . . . . . .No
  Greenhouse Gas Emissions (tons/yr.). . . . . High-8.2
  Barrels of Oil Used per year . . . . . . . . . . High-15.0
```

How the Competition Rates

Competitors	Rating	Pg.
Acura MDX	6	82
Buick Enclave	7	102
Hyundai Santa Fe	–	158

Price Range

	Retail	Markup
3.5L	$42,400	8%
3.5L AWD	$43,800	8%
Hybrid	$45,400	8%
Hybrid AWD	$46,800	8%

Safety Checklist

Crash Tests:
```
  Frontal. . . . . . . . . . . . . . . . . . . . . . . . . . . . .–
  Sidel . . . . . . . . . . . . . . . . . . . . . . . . . . . . . .–
```
Airbags:
```
  Torso . . . . . . . . . .Front Pelvis/Torso from Seat
  Pelvis . . . . . . . . . .Front Pelvis/Torso from Seat
  Roll Sensing. . . . . . . . . . . . . . . . . . . . . .Yes
  Knee Bolster . . . . . . . . . . . . . . . . . . . . None
```
Crash Avoidance:
```
  Collision Avoidance . . . . . . Optional CIB & DBS
  Blind Spot Detection . . . . . . . . . . . . . Optional
  Lane Keeping Assist . . . . . . . . . . . . . Optional
  Backup Camera . . . . . . . . . . . . . . . . Standard
  Pedestrian Crash Avoidance . . . . . . . . . . None
```
General:
```
  Auto. Crash Notification . . . Operator Assist.-Fee
  Day Running Lamps . . . . . . . . . . . . . . . None
```
Safety Belt/Restraint:
```
  Dynamic Head Restraints . . . . . . . . . . . None
  Adjustable Belt. . . . . . .Standard Front and Rear
```

Infiniti QX60

Specifications

```
Drive. . . . . . . . . . . . . . . . . . . . . . . . . . . . . . AWD
Engine . . . . . . . . . . . . . . . . . . . . . .3.5-liter V6
Transmission . . . . . . . . . . . . . . . .7-sp. Automatic
Tow Rating (lbs.) . . . . . . . . . . . . . . . . Low-5000
Head/Leg Room (in.) . . . . . . . . . Roomy-40.7/42.3
Interior Space (cu. ft.). . . . . . . . Very Roomy-149.8
Cargo Space (cu. ft.) . . . . . . . . . .Cramped-15.8
Wheelbase/Length (in.) . . . . . . . . .114.2/196.4
```

Ratings—10 Best, 1 Worst

Combo Crash Tests	–
Safety Features	6
Rollover	4
Preventive Maintenance	7
Repair Costs	1
Warranty	7
Fuel Economy	2
Complaints	10
Insurance Costs	5
OVERALL RATING	**–**

Infiniti QX70

Infiniti QX70

At-a-Glance

Status/Year Series Started. Unchanged/2009
Twins . . . .–
Body Styles . . . . SUV
Seating 5
Anti-Theft Device . . . . . . Std. Pass. Immobil. & Alarm
Parking Index Rating . . . . Average
Where Made. . . . . Tochigi, Japan
Fuel Factor . . . .
  MPG Rating (city/hwy) . . . . .Very Poor-16/22
  Driving Range (mi.) Long-434.1
  Fuel Type. . . . . .Premium
  Annual Fuel Cost . . . . Very High-$2,631
  Gas Guzzler Tax . . . . .No
  Greenhouse Gas Emissions (tons/yr.)Very High-10.0
  Barrels of Oil Used per year . . . . . . .Very High-18.3

How the Competition Rates

Competitors	Rating	Pg.
BMW X3	8	100
Mercedes-Benz M-Class	5	209
Porsche Cayenne	–	232

Price Range

	Retail	Markup
V6 RWD	$45,850	8%
V6 AWD	$47,300	8%

Safety Checklist

Crash Tests:
  Frontal . . . .–
  Sidel . . . .–
Airbags:
  Torso . . . . .Front Pelvis/Torso from Seat
  Pelvis . . . . .Front Pelvis/Torso from Seat
  Roll Sensing. . . . . .Yes
  Knee Bolster . . . . None
Crash Avoidance:
  Collision Avoidance . . . . Optional CIB
  Blind Spot Detection . . . . None
  Lane Keeping Assist . . . . None
  Backup Camera . . . . Standard
  Pedestrian Crash Avoidance . . . . None
General:
  Auto. Crash Notification . . . Operator Assist.-Fee
  Day Running Lamps . . . . None
Safety Belt/Restraint:
  Dynamic Head Restraints . . . . .Standard Front
  Adjustable Belt. . . . . .Standard Front

Infiniti QX70

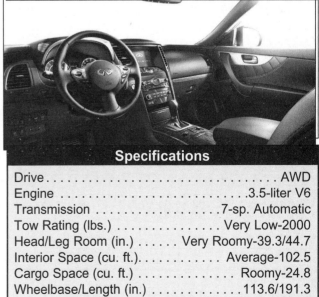

Specifications

Drive. . . . . .AWD
Engine 3.5-liter V6
Transmission . . . . .7-sp. Automatic
Tow Rating (lbs.) . . . . Very Low-2000
Head/Leg Room (in.) . . . . . . Very Roomy-39.3/44.7
Interior Space (cu. ft.). Average-102.5
Cargo Space (cu. ft.) Roomy-24.8
Wheelbase/Length (in.) 113.6/191.3

Ratings—10 Best, 1 Worst

Combo Crash Tests	–
Safety Features	8
Rollover	2
Preventive Maintenance	3
Repair Costs	3
Warranty	7
Fuel Economy	1
Complaints	10
Insurance Costs	8

OVERALL RATING	–

Infiniti QX80

Infiniti QX80

At-a-Glance

Status/Year Series Started Appearance Change/2011
Twins . . . .–
Body Styles . . . . SUV
Seating 7/8
Anti-Theft Device . . . . . . Std. Pass. Immobil. & Alarm
Parking Index Rating . . . . Very Hard
Where Made . . . . Kyushu, Japan
Fuel Factor . . . .
  MPG Rating (city/hwy) . . . . .Very Poor-14/20
  Driving Range (mi.) Average-420.8
  Fuel Type . . . . Premium
  Annual Fuel Cost . . . . Very High-$2,965
  Gas Guzzler Tax . . . . .No
  Greenhouse Gas Emissions (tons/yr.)Very High-11.2
  Barrels of Oil Used per year . . . . Very High-20.6

How the Competition Rates

Competitors	Rating	Pg.
Audi Q7	–	93
Lexus GX	–	189
Mercedes-Benz GL-Class	–	207

Price Range

	Retail	Markup
2WD	$63,250	8%
AWD	$66,350	8%

Safety Checklist

Crash Tests:
  Frontal . . . .–
  Sidel . . . .–
Airbags:
  Torso . . . . .Front Pelvis/Torso from Seat
  Pelvis . . . . .Front Pelvis/Torso from Seat
  Roll Sensing . . . . .Yes
  Knee Bolster . . . . None
Crash Avoidance:
  Collision Avoidance . . . . . . Optional CIB & DBS
  Blind Spot Detection . . . . Optional
  Lane Keeping Assist . . . . None
  Backup Camera . . . . Standard
  Pedestrian Crash Avoidance . . . . None
General:
  Auto. Crash Notification . . . Operator Assist.-Fee
  Day Running Lamps . . . . None
Safety Belt/Restraint:
  Dynamic Head Restraints . . . . . .Standard Front
  Adjustable Belt . . . . . . .Standard Front and Rear

Infiniti QX80

Specifications

Drive . . . . AWD
Engine 5.6-liter V8
Transmission . . . . .7-sp. Automatic
Tow Rating (lbs.) . . . . .Very High-8500
Head/Leg Room (in.) . . . . .Very Cramped-39.9/39.6
Interior Space (cu. ft.) . . . . Very Roomy-151.3
Cargo Space (cu. ft.) Average-16.6
Wheelbase/Length (in.) 121.1/208.9

Ratings—10 Best, 1 Worst

Combo Crash Tests	6
Safety Features	6
Rollover	3
Preventive Maintenance	5
Repair Costs	7
Warranty	5
Fuel Economy	5
Complaints	1
Insurance Costs	8
OVERALL RATING	**4**

Jeep Cherokee

Jeep Cherokee

At-a-Glance

Status/Year Series Started	Unchanged/2014
Twins	–
Body Styles	SUV
Seating	5
Anti-Theft Device	Std. Pass. Immobil. & Alarm
Parking Index Rating	Average
Where Made	Toledo, OH
Fuel Factor	
MPG Rating (city/hwy)	Average-21/28
Driving Range (mi.)	Short-376.2
Fuel Type	Regular
Annual Fuel Cost	Average-$1,775
Gas Guzzler Tax	No
Greenhouse Gas Emissions (tons/yr.)	Average-7.5
Barrels of Oil Used per year	High-13.7

How the Competition Rates

Competitors	Rating	Pg.
Ford Escape	5	138
Mazda CX-5	5	197
Toyota RAV4	4	254

Price Range

	Retail	Markup
Sport FWD	$22,995	2%
Latitude FWD	$24,595	3%
Trailhawk 4WD	$29,695	3%
Limited 4WD	$30,195	4%

Safety Checklist

Crash Tests:
Frontal......................Very Poor
Side.........................Very Good

Airbags:
Torso...........Front Pelvis/Torso from Seat
Pelvis......................Rear Pelvis
Roll Sensing...................Yes
Knee Bolster..............Standard Front

Crash Avoidance:
Collision Avoidance.....Warning Only Optional
Blind Spot Detection.............Standard
Lane Keeping Assist....Warning Only Optional
Backup Camera..................Standard
Pedestrian Crash Avoidance..........None

General:
Auto. Crash Notification..............None
Day Running Lamps.................None

Safety Belt/Restraint:
Dynamic Head Restraints..........None
Adjustable Belt..............Standard Front

Jeep Cherokee

Specifications

Drive	AWD
Engine	2.4-liter I4
Transmission	9-sp. Automatic
Tow Rating (lbs.)	Very Low-2000
Head/Leg Room (in.)	Cramped-39.4/41.1
Interior Space (cu. ft.)	Average-103.4
Cargo Space (cu. ft.)	Roomy-24.6
Wheelbase/Length (in.)	106.3/182

Ratings—10 Best, 1 Worst

Combo Crash Tests	–
Safety Features	5
Rollover	2
Preventive Maintenance	2
Repair Costs	9
Warranty	5
Fuel Economy	3
Complaints	4
Insurance Costs	8

OVERALL RATING — –

Jeep Compass

Jeep Compass

At-a-Glance

Status/Year Series Started	Unchanged/2007
Twins	–
Body Styles	SUV
Seating	5
Anti-Theft Device	Std. Pass. Immobil.
Parking Index Rating	Easy
Where Made	Belvedere, IL
Fuel Factor	
MPG Rating (city/hwy)	Poor-20/23
Driving Range (mi.)	Very Short-286.8
Fuel Type	Regular
Annual Fuel Cost	High-$1,976
Gas Guzzler Tax	No
Greenhouse Gas Emissions (tons/yr.)	High-8.6
Barrels of Oil Used per year	High-15.7

How the Competition Rates

Competitors	Rating	Pg.
Acura RDX	8	83
Ford Escape	5	138
Honda CR-V	6	151

Price Range

	Retail	Markup
Sport FWD	$18,795	1%
Latitude FWD	$22,595	3%
Latitude 4WD	$24,595	3%
Limited 4WD	$27,995	4%

Safety Checklist

Crash Tests:
Frontal . . . . –
Sidel . . . . –

Airbags:
Torso . . . . Front Pelvis/Torso from Seat
Pelvis . . . . Front Pelvis/Torso from Seat
Roll Sensing . . . . Yes
Knee Bolster . . . . None

Crash Avoidance:
Collision Avoidance . . . . None
Blind Spot Detection . . . . None
Lane Keeping Assist . . . . None
Backup Camera . . . . Standard
Pedestrian Crash Avoidance . . . . None

General:
Auto. Crash Notification . . . . None
Day Running Lamps . . . . None

Safety Belt/Restraint:
Dynamic Head Restraints . . . . . . Standard Front
Adjustable Belt . . . . Standard Front

Jeep Compass

Specifications

Drive	4WD
Engine	2.4-liter I4
Transmission	CVT
Tow Rating (lbs.)	Very Low-2000
Head/Leg Room (in.)	Average-40.7/40.6
Interior Space (cu. ft.)	Average-101.3
Cargo Space (cu. ft.)	Average-22.7
Wheelbase/Length (in.)	103.7/175.1

Ratings—10 Best, 1 Worst

Combo Crash Tests	6
Safety Features	7
Rollover	3
Preventive Maintenance	5
Repair Costs	7
Warranty	5
Fuel Economy	1
Complaints	1
Insurance Costs	8
OVERALL RATING	**3**

Jeep Grand Cherokee

At-a-Glance

Status/Year Series Started	Unchanged/2011
Twins	–
Body Styles	SUV
Seating	5
Anti-Theft Device	Std. Pass. Immobil. & Alarm
Parking Index Rating	Average
Where Made	Detroit, MI
Fuel Factor	
MPG Rating (city/hwy)	Very Poor-14/20
Driving Range (mi.)	Average-398.2
Fuel Type	Regular
Annual Fuel Cost	Very High-$2,595
Gas Guzzler Tax	No
Greenhouse Gas Emissions (tons/yr.)	Very High-11.3
Barrels of Oil Used per year	Very High-20.6

How the Competition Rates

Competitors	Rating	Pg.
Chevrolet Equinox	2	115
Ford Explorer	3	140
Honda Pilot	2	154

Price Range

Price Range	Retail	Markup
Laredo 2WD	$29,595	1%
Limited 2WD	$36,495	4%
Overland 4WD	$46,195	5%
SRT 4WD	$64,395	5%

Jeep Grand Cherokee

Safety Checklist

Crash Tests:
Frontal . . . . Good
Side . . . . Poor

Airbags:
Torso . . . . .Front Pelvis/Torso from Seat
Pelvis . . . . .Front Pelvis/Torso from Seat
Roll Sensing . . . . .Yes
Knee Bolster . . . . Standard Driver

Crash Avoidance:
Collision Avoidance . . . . .Warning Only Optional
Blind Spot Detection . . . . Standard
Lane Keeping Assist . . . . None
Backup Camera . . . . Standard
Pedestrian Crash Avoidance . . . . None

General:
Auto. Crash Notification . . . . None
Day Running Lamps . . . . None

Safety Belt/Restraint:
Dynamic Head Restraints . . . . . .Standard Front
Adjustable Belt . . . . .Standard Front

Jeep Grand Cherokee

Specifications

Drive	4WD
Engine	5.7-liter V8
Transmission	8-sp. Automatic
Tow Rating (lbs.)	Average-7200
Head/Leg Room (in.)	Cramped-39.9/40.3
Interior Space (cu. ft.)	Roomy-103.9
Cargo Space (cu. ft.)	Very Roomy-36.3
Wheelbase/Length (in.)	114.8/189.8

Ratings—10 Best, 1 Worst

Combo Crash Tests	–
Safety Features	4
Rollover	2
Preventive Maintenance	1
Repair Costs	10
Warranty	5
Fuel Economy	3
Complaints	3
Insurance Costs	5
OVERALL RATING	**–**

Jeep Patriot

Jeep Patriot

At-a-Glance

Status/Year Series Started	Unchanged/2007
Twins	–
Body Styles	SUV
Seating	5
Anti-Theft Device	Std. Pass. Immobil.
Parking Index Rating	Easy
Where Made	Belvedere, IL
Fuel Factor	
MPG Rating (city/hwy)	Poor-20/23
Driving Range (mi.)	Very Short-286.8
Fuel Type	Regular
Annual Fuel Cost	High-$1,976
Gas Guzzler Tax	No
Greenhouse Gas Emissions (tons/yr.)	High-8.6
Barrels of Oil Used per year	High-15.7

How the Competition Rates

Competitors	Rating	Pg.
Ford Escape	5	138
Mitsubishi Outlander Sport	4	216
Toyota RAV4	4	254

Price Range

	Retail	Markup
Sport FWD	$16,495	1%
Latitude FWD	$20,795	3%
Latitude 4WD	$24,095	4%
Limited 4WD	$26,495	4%

Safety Checklist

Crash Tests:
Frontal	–
Sidel	–

Airbags:
Torso	Front Pelvis/Torso from Seat
Pelvis	Front Pelvis/Torso from Seat
Roll Sensing	Yes
Knee Bolster	None

Crash Avoidance:
Collision Avoidance	None
Blind Spot Detection	None
Lane Keeping Assist	None
Backup Camera	None
Pedestrian Crash Avoidance	None

General:
Auto. Crash Notification	None
Day Running Lamps	None

Safety Belt/Restraint:
Dynamic Head Restraints	Standard Front
Adjustable Belt	Standard Front

Jeep Patriot

Specifications

Drive	4WD
Engine	2.4-liter I4
Transmission	CVT
Tow Rating (lbs.)	Very Low-2000
Head/Leg Room (in.)	Average-41/40.6
Interior Space (cu. ft.)	Roomy-104.4
Cargo Space (cu. ft.)	Roomy-23
Wheelbase/Length (in.)	103.7/173.8

Ratings—10 Best, 1 Worst

Combo Crash Tests	–
Safety Features	–
Rollover	2
Preventive Maintenance	–
Repair Costs	–
Warranty	5
Fuel Economy	–
Complaints	–
Insurance Costs	5

OVERALL RATING   –

Jeep Renegade

Jeep Renegade

Jeep Renegade

At-a-Glance

Status/Year Series Started	All New/2015
Twins	–
Body Styles	SUV
Seating	5
Anti-Theft Device	–
Parking Index Rating	Easy
Where Made	Melfi, Italy
Fuel Factor	
MPG Rating (city/hwy)	–
Driving Range (mi.)	–
Fuel Type	Regular
Annual Fuel Cost	–
Gas Guzzler Tax	No
Greenhouse Gas Emissions (tons/yr.)	–
Barrels of Oil Used per year	–

How the Competition Rates

Competitors	Rating	Pg.
Chevrolet Trax	7	124
Ford Edge	–	137
Nissan Juke	–	221

Price Range

	Retail	Markup

Safety Checklist

Crash Tests:
Frontal . . . . –
Sidel . . . . –

Airbags:
Torso . . . . *
Pelvis . . . . *
Roll Sensing. . . . . *
Knee Bolster . . . . *

Crash Avoidance:
Collision Avoidance . . . . *
Blind Spot Detection . . . . *
Lane Keeping Assist . . . . *
Backup Camera . . . . *
Pedestrian Crash Avoidance . . . . *

General:
Auto. Crash Notification . . . . *
Day Running Lamps . . . . *

Safety Belt/Restraint:
Dynamic Head Restraints . . . . *
Adjustable Belt . . . . *

Jeep Renegade

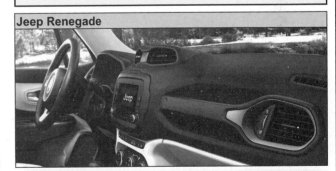

Specifications

Drive	4WD
Engine	1.4-liter I4
Transmission	6-sp. Manual
Tow Rating (lbs.)	Very Low-0
Head/Leg Room (in.)	Average-41.1/41.2
Interior Space (cu. ft.)	Average-100.1
Cargo Space (cu. ft.)	Average-18.5
Wheelbase/Length (in.)	101.2/166.6

Ratings—10 Best, 1 Worst	
Combo Crash Tests	–
Safety Features	1
Rollover	1
Preventive Maintenance	1
Repair Costs	9
Warranty	5
Fuel Economy	2
Complaints	1
Insurance Costs	8
OVERALL RATING	**–**

Jeep Wrangler

Jeep Wrangler

At-a-Glance

Status/Year Series Started	Unchanged/2007
Twins	–
Body Styles	SUV
Seating	4
Anti-Theft Device	Std. Pass. Immobil. & Alarm
Parking Index Rating	Very Easy
Where Made	Toledo, OH
Fuel Factor	
MPG Rating (city/hwy)	Very Poor-17/21
Driving Range (mi.)	Very Short-345.8
Fuel Type	Regular
Annual Fuel Cost	High-$2,258
Gas Guzzler Tax	No
Greenhouse Gas Emissions (tons/yr.)	Very High-10.0
Barrels of Oil Used per year	Very High-18.3

How the Competition Rates

Competitors	Rating	Pg.
Mitsubishi Outlander Sport	4	216
Nissan Xterra	–	231
Subaru Forester	2	240

Price Range

	Retail	Markup
Sport	$22,595	3%
Rubicon	$31,395	6%
Unlimited Sahara	$32,095	6%
Unlimited Rubicon	$35,195	6%

Safety Checklist

Crash Tests:
Frontal . . . . –
Sidel . . . . –
Airbags:
Torso . . . . Opt. Front Head/ Torso from Seat
Pelvis . . . . None
Roll Sensing . . . . No
Knee Bolster . . . . None
Crash Avoidance:
Collision Avoidance . . . . None
Blind Spot Detection . . . . None
Lane Keeping Assist . . . . None
Backup Camera . . . . None
Pedestrian Crash Avoidance . . . . None
General:
Auto. Crash Notification . . . . None
Day Running Lamps . . . . None
Safety Belt/Restraint:
Dynamic Head Restraints . . . . None
Adjustable Belt . . . . Standard Front

Jeep Wrangler

Specifications

Drive	4WD
Engine	3.6-liter V6
Transmission	5-sp. Automatic
Tow Rating (lbs.)	Very Low-2000
Head/Leg Room (in.)	Average-41.3/41
Interior Space (cu. ft.)	Very Cramped-88.4
Cargo Space (cu. ft.)	Very Cramped-12.8
Wheelbase/Length (in.)	95.4/152.8

Ratings—10 Best, 1 Worst

Combo Crash Tests	–
Safety Features	2
Rollover	7
Preventive Maintenance	8
Repair Costs	–
Warranty	10
Fuel Economy	4
Complaints	2
Insurance Costs	5
OVERALL RATING	**–**

Kia Cadenza

Kia Cadenza

At-a-Glance

Status/Year Series Started	Unchanged/2014
Twins	Hyundai Azera
Body Styles	Sedan
Seating	5
Anti-Theft Device	Std. Pass. Immobil. & Alarm
Parking Index Rating	Average
Where Made	Hwasung, South Korea
Fuel Factor	
MPG Rating (city/hwy)	Poor-19/28
Driving Range (mi.)	Average-410.9
Fuel Type	Regular
Annual Fuel Cost	Average-$1,890
Gas Guzzler Tax	No
Greenhouse Gas Emissions (tons/yr.)	High-8.2
Barrels of Oil Used per year	High-15.0

How the Competition Rates

Competitors	Rating	Pg.
Acura TLX	–	85
Honda Accord	7	148
Lexus ES	7	187

Price Range

Price Range	Retail	Markup
Premium	$34,900	8%
Limited	$43,800	8%

Safety Checklist

Crash Tests:

Frontal	–
Sidel	–

Airbags:

Torso	Front Pelvis/Torso from Seat
Pelvis	Rear Pelvis/Torso
Roll Sensing	No
Knee Bolster	None

Crash Avoidance:

Collision Avoidance	None
Blind Spot Detection	Optional
Lane Keeping Assist	Warning Only Optional
Backup Camera	Optional
Pedestrian Crash Avoidance	None

General:

Auto. Crash Notification	Dial Assist.-Free
Day Running Lamps	None

Safety Belt/Restraint:

Dynamic Head Restraints	None
Adjustable Belt	Standard Front

Specifications

Drive	FWD
Engine	3.3-liter V6
Transmission	6-sp. Automatic
Tow Rating (lbs.)	–
Head/Leg Room (in.)	Very Roomy-40/45.5
Interior Space (cu. ft.)	Roomy-106.8
Cargo Space (cu. ft.)	Cramped-15.9
Wheelbase/Length (in.)	112/195.5

Ratings—10 Best, 1 Worst

Combo Crash Tests	3
Safety Features	2
Rollover	7
Preventive Maintenance	8
Repair Costs	10
Warranty	10
Fuel Economy	8
Complaints	1
Insurance Costs	1
OVERALL RATING	**5**

Kia Forte

Kia Forte

At-a-Glance

Status/Year Series Started Unchanged/2014
Twins . . . . Hyundai Elantra
Body Styles . . . . Sedan, Hatchback
Seating 5
Anti-Theft Device . Std. Pass. Immobil. & Active Alarm
Parking Index Rating . . . . Easy
Where Made. . . . . Hwasung, South Korea
Fuel Factor . . . .
  MPG Rating (city/hwy) Good-25/36
  Driving Range (mi.) Short-382.6
  Fuel Type. . . . . .Regular
  Annual Fuel Cost . . . . Low-$1,449
  Gas Guzzler Tax . . . . .No
  Greenhouse Gas Emissions (tons/yr.) Low-6.2
  Barrels of Oil Used per year Average-11.4

How the Competition Rates

Competitors	Rating	Pg.
Chevrolet Cruze	8	114
Honda Civic	6	149
Subaru Impreza	4	241

Price Range

	Retail	Markup
LX Sedan MT	$15,890	2%
EX Sedan AT	$19,390	5%
SX Koup AT	$21,590	6%
SX Hatchback AT	$21,890	6%

Safety Checklist

Crash Tests:
  Frontal . . . . Poor
  Side . . . . Poor
Airbags:
  Torso . . . . .Front Pelvis/Torso from Seat
  Pelvis . . . . .Front Pelvis/Torso from Seat
  Roll Sensing. . . . . No
  Knee Bolster . . . . None
Crash Avoidance:
  Collision Avoidance . . . . None
  Blind Spot Detection . . . . None
  Lane Keeping Assist . . . . None
  Backup Camera . . . . Optional
  Pedestrian Crash Avoidance . . . . None
General:
  Auto. Crash Notification . . . . . . Dial Assist.-Free
  Day Running Lamps . . . . None
Safety Belt/Restraint:
  Dynamic Head Restraints . . . . None
  Adjustable Belt . . . . .Standard Front

Kia Forte

Specifications

Drive . . . . FWD
Engine 2.0-liter I4
Transmission . . . . .6-sp. Automatic
Tow Rating (lbs.) . . . . –
Head/Leg Room (in.) Average-39.1/42.2
Interior Space (cu. ft.). Cramped-96.2
Cargo Space (cu. ft.) Cramped-14.9
Wheelbase/Length (in.) 106.3/179.5

Ratings—10 Best, 1 Worst

Combo Crash Tests	6
Safety Features	2
Rollover	8
Preventive Maintenance	5
Repair Costs	10
Warranty	10
Fuel Economy	6
Complaints	6
Insurance Costs	1
OVERALL RATING	**7**

Kia Optima

Kia Optima

At-a-Glance

Status/Year Series Started........ Unchanged/2011
Twins . . . . –
Body Styles . . . . .Sedan
Seating 5
Anti-Theft Device . Std. Pass. Immobil. & Active Alarm
Parking Index Rating . . . . Easy
Where Made. . . . . West Point, GA
Fuel Factor . . . .
  MPG Rating (city/hwy) Average-23/34
  Driving Range (mi.) . . . . .Very Long-498.0
  Fuel Type. . . . . .Regular
  Annual Fuel Cost . . . . Low-$1,560
  Gas Guzzler Tax . . . . .No
  Greenhouse Gas Emissions (tons/yr.). . Average-6.7
  Barrels of Oil Used per year Average-12.2

How the Competition Rates

Competitors	Rating	Pg.
Honda Accord	7	148
Nissan Altima	5	218
Toyota Camry	7	248

Price Range

Price Range	Retail	Markup
LX	$21,500	4%
SX	$25,500	7%
EX Hybrid	$31,995	8%
SXL Turbo	$35,300	7%

Kia Optima

Safety Checklist

Crash Tests:
  Frontal. . . . . Good
  Side. . . . . .Very Poor

Airbags:
  Torso . . . . .Front Pelvis/Torso from Seat
  Pelvis . . . . .Front Pelvis/Torso from Seat
  Roll Sensing. . . . . No
  Knee Bolster . . . . None

Crash Avoidance:
  Collision Avoidance . . . . None
  Blind Spot Detection . . . . Optional
  Lane Keeping Assist . . . . None
  Backup Camera . . . . Optional
  Pedestrian Crash Avoidance . . . . None

General:
  Auto. Crash Notification . . . . . . Dial Assist.-Free
  Day Running Lamps . . . . None

Safety Belt/Restraint:
  Dynamic Head Restraints . . . . None
  Adjustable Belt. . . . . .Standard Front

Kia Optima

Specifications

Drive. . . . . FWD
Engine 2.4-liter I4
Transmission . . . . .6-sp. Automatic
Tow Rating (lbs.) . . . . –
Head/Leg Room (in.) . . . . .Very Roomy-40/45.5
Interior Space (cu. ft.). Roomy-117.6
Cargo Space (cu. ft.) Cramped-15.4
Wheelbase/Length (in.) 110/190.7

Ratings—10 Best, 1 Worst

Combo Crash Tests	1
Safety Features	1
Rollover	6
Preventive Maintenance	6
Repair Costs	10
Warranty	10
Fuel Economy	9
Complaints	9
Insurance Costs	1
OVERALL RATING	**5**

Kia Rio

Kia Rio

At-a-Glance

Status/Year Series Started	Unchanged/2012
Twins	Hyundai Accent
Body Styles	Sedan, Hatchback
Seating	5
Anti-Theft Device	Std. Pass. Immobil. & Active Alarm
Parking Index Rating	Very Easy
Where Made	Gwanmyeong, South Korea
Fuel Factor	
MPG Rating (city/hwy)	Very Good-27/37
Driving Range (mi.)	Very Short-350.4
Fuel Type	Regular
Annual Fuel Cost	Very Low-$1,366
Gas Guzzler Tax	No
Greenhouse Gas Emissions (tons/yr.)	Low-5.8
Barrels of Oil Used per year	Low-10.6

How the Competition Rates

Competitors	Rating	Pg.
Chevrolet Sonic	9	119
Ford Focus	–	144
Nissan Versa	2	230

Price Range

Price Range	Retail	Markup
LX Sedan MT	$13,900	2%
LX Hatchback AT	$15,240	3%
EX Sedan AT	$16,940	5%
SX Hatchback AT	$18,240	5%

Safety Checklist

Crash Tests:
Frontal....................Very Poor
Side.....................Very Poor*
Airbags:
Torso..........Front Pelvis/Torso from Seat
Pelvis..........Front Pelvis/Torso from Seat
Roll Sensing......................No
Knee Bolster....................None
Crash Avoidance:
Collision Avoidance................None
Blind Spot Detection..............None
Lane Keeping Assist...............None
Backup Camera.................Optional
Pedestrian Crash Avoidance..........None
General:
Auto. Crash Notification.............None
Day Running Lamps...............None
Safety Belt/Restraint:
Dynamic Head Restraints.............None
Adjustable Belt..............Standard Front

Kia Rio

Specifications

Drive	FWD
Engine	1.6-liter I4
Transmission	6-sp. Automatic
Tow Rating (lbs.)	–
Head/Leg Room (in.)	Roomy-40/43.8
Interior Space (cu. ft.)	Very Cramped-88.4
Cargo Space (cu. ft.)	Cramped-13.7
Wheelbase/Length (in.)	101.2/171.9

*Additional injury potential in side test. See footnote on page 20.

Ratings—10 Best, 1 Worst

Combo Crash Tests	–
Safety Features	6
Rollover	5
Preventive Maintenance	3
Repair Costs	8
Warranty	10
Fuel Economy	3
Complaints	–
Insurance Costs	5
OVERALL RATING	**–**

Kia Sedona

Kia Sedona

At-a-Glance

Status/Year Series Started	All New/2015
Twins	–
Body Styles	Minivan
Seating	7/8
Anti-Theft Device	Std. Pass. Immobil. & Active Alarm
Parking Index Rating	Hard
Where Made	West Point, GA
Fuel Factor	
MPG Rating (city/hwy)	Poor-18/24
Driving Range (mi.)	Long-427.9
Fuel Type	Regular
Annual Fuel Cost	High-$2,070
Gas Guzzler Tax	No
Greenhouse Gas Emissions (tons/yr.)	High-9.0
Barrels of Oil Used per year	High-16.5

How the Competition Rates

Competitors	Rating	Pg.
Honda Odyssey	7	153
Nissan Quest	–	226
Toyota Sequoia	–	255

Price Range

	Retail	Markup
L	$25,900	3%
EX	$32,100	6%
SX	$36,100	6%
SXL	$39,700	7%

Safety Checklist

Crash Tests:
Frontal .... –
Sidel .... –

Airbags:
Torso .... Front Pelvis/Torso from Seat
Pelvis .... Front Pelvis/Torso from Seat
Roll Sensing .... Yes
Knee Bolster .... None

Crash Avoidance:
Collision Avoidance .... Standard DBS
Blind Spot Detection .... Optional
Lane Keeping Assist .... Warning Only Optional
Backup Camera .... Optional
Pedestrian Crash Avoidance .... None

General:
Auto. Crash Notification ...... Dial Assist.-Free
Day Running Lamps .... None

Safety Belt/Restraint:
Dynamic Head Restraints .... None
Adjustable Belt .... Standard Front

Kia Sedona

Specifications

Drive	FWD
Engine	3.3-liter V6
Transmission	6-sp. Automatic
Tow Rating (lbs.)	Low-3500
Head/Leg Room (in.)	Roomy-39.8/43.1
Interior Space (cu. ft.)	–
Cargo Space (cu. ft.)	Very Roomy-33.9
Wheelbase/Length (in.)	120.5/201.4

Ratings—10 Best, 1 Worst

Combo Crash Tests	8
Safety Features	5
Rollover	3
Preventive Maintenance	4
Repair Costs	4
Warranty	10
Fuel Economy	4
Complaints	2
Insurance Costs	3
OVERALL RATING	**4**

Kia Sorento

Kia Sorento

At-a-Glance

Status/Year Series Started	Unchanged/2011
Twins	Hyundai Santa Fe Sport
Body Styles	SUV
Seating	5/7
Anti-Theft Device	Std. Pass. Immobil. & Active Alarm
Parking Index Rating	Easy
Where Made	West Point, GA
Fuel Factor	
MPG Rating (city/hwy)	Poor-20/27
Driving Range (mi.)	Short-394.6
Fuel Type	Regular
Annual Fuel Cost	Average-$1,855
Gas Guzzler Tax	No
Greenhouse Gas Emissions (tons/yr.)	High-7.8
Barrels of Oil Used per year	High-14.3

How the Competition Rates

Competitors	Rating	Pg.
Ford Edge	–	137
Nissan Rogue	2	227
Toyota Venza	3	259

Price Range

	Retail	Markup
LX FWD	$24,100	4%
LX AWD V6	$28,300	4%
SX AWD	$38,300	6%
Limited AWD	$41,700	6%

Safety Checklist

Crash Tests:
Frontal . . . . Very Good
Side . . . . Poor

Airbags:
Torso . . . . Front Pelvis/Torso from Seat
Pelvis . . . . Front Pelvis/Torso from Seat
Roll Sensing . . . . Yes
Knee Bolster . . . . None

Crash Avoidance:
Collision Avoidance . . . . None
Blind Spot Detection . . . . Optional
Lane Keeping Assist . . . . None
Backup Camera . . . . Optional
Pedestrian Crash Avoidance . . . . None

General:
Auto. Crash Notification . . . . . . Dial Assist.-Free
Day Running Lamps . . . . None

Safety Belt/Restraint:
Dynamic Head Restraints . . . . . .Standard Front
Adjustable Belt . . . . .Standard Front

Kia Sorento

Specifications

Drive	FWD
Engine	2.4-liter I4
Transmission	6-sp. Automatic
Tow Rating (lbs.)	Very Low-1650
Head/Leg Room (in.)	Cramped-39.2/41.3
Interior Space (cu. ft.)	Roomy-107.1
Cargo Space (cu. ft.)	Very Roomy-36.9
Wheelbase/Length (in.)	106.3/184.4

Ratings—10 Best, 1 Worst

Combo Crash Tests	9
Safety Features	4
Rollover	4
Preventive Maintenance	4
Repair Costs	9
Warranty	10
Fuel Economy	6
Complaints	3
Insurance Costs	3
OVERALL RATING	**7**

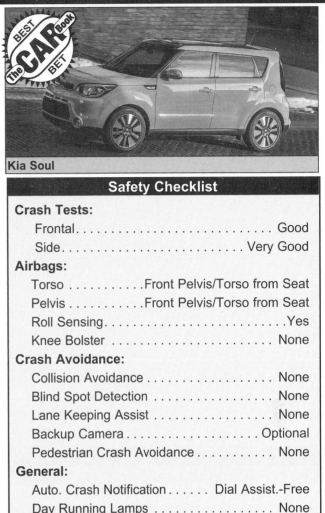

Kia Soul

Kia Soul

At-a-Glance

Status/Year Series Started	Unchanged/2014
Twins	–
Body Styles	Wagon
Seating	5
Anti-Theft Device	Std. Pass. Immobil. & Alarm
Parking Index Rating	Very Easy
Where Made	West Point, GA
Fuel Factor	
MPG Rating (city/hwy)	Average-23/31
Driving Range (mi.)	Short-369.5
Fuel Type	Regular
Annual Fuel Cost	Low-$1,614
Gas Guzzler Tax	No
Greenhouse Gas Emissions (tons/yr.)	Average-6.9
Barrels of Oil Used per year	Average-12.7

How the Competition Rates

Competitors	Rating	Pg.
Chevrolet Sonic	9	119
Mini Countryman	–	212
Scion xB	–	237

Price Range

	Retail	Markup
Base MT	$15,100	2%
+	$18,600	5%
!	$20,700	6%
EV+	$35,700	8%

Safety Checklist

Crash Tests:
Frontal	Good
Side	Very Good

Airbags:
Torso	Front Pelvis/Torso from Seat
Pelvis	Front Pelvis/Torso from Seat
Roll Sensing	Yes
Knee Bolster	None

Crash Avoidance:
Collision Avoidance	None
Blind Spot Detection	None
Lane Keeping Assist	None
Backup Camera	Optional
Pedestrian Crash Avoidance	None

General:
Auto. Crash Notification	Dial Assist.-Free
Day Running Lamps	None

Safety Belt/Restraint:
Dynamic Head Restraints	None
Adjustable Belt	Standard Front

Kia Soul

Specifications

Drive	FWD
Engine	2.0-liter I4
Transmission	6-sp. Automatic
Tow Rating (lbs.)	–
Head/Leg Room (in.)	Cramped-39.6/40.9
Interior Space (cu. ft.)	Average-101
Cargo Space (cu. ft.)	Roomy-24.2
Wheelbase/Length (in.)	101.2/163

Ratings—10 Best, 1 Worst

Combo Crash Tests	5
Safety Features	3
Rollover	3
Preventive Maintenance	4
Repair Costs	5
Warranty	10
Fuel Economy	5
Complaints	9
Insurance Costs	5
OVERALL RATING	**5**

Kia Sportage

At-a-Glance

Status/Year Series Started	Unchanged/2011
Twins	Hyundai Tucson
Body Styles	SUV
Seating	5
Anti-Theft Device	Std. Pass. Immobil. & Active Alarm
Parking Index Rating	Very Easy
Where Made	Gwangju, South Korea
Fuel Factor	
MPG Rating (city/hwy)	Average-21/28
Driving Range (mi.)	Very Short-343.1
Fuel Type	Regular
Annual Fuel Cost	Average-$1,775
Gas Guzzler Tax	No
Greenhouse Gas Emissions (tons/yr.)	Average-7.5
Barrels of Oil Used per year	High-13.7

How the Competition Rates

Competitors	Rating	Pg.
Ford Escape	5	138
Honda CR-V	6	151
Toyota RAV4	4	254

Price Range

Price Range	Retail	Markup
LX FWD	$21,750	4%
EX FWD	$25,150	6%
EX AWD	$26,650	6%
SX AWD	$29,600	7%

Kia Sportage

Safety Checklist

Crash Tests:
Frontal	Good
Side	Very Poor

Airbags:
Torso	Front Pelvis/Torso from Seat
Pelvis	Front Pelvis/Torso from Seat
Roll Sensing	No
Knee Bolster	None

Crash Avoidance:
Collision Avoidance	None
Blind Spot Detection	None
Lane Keeping Assist	None
Backup Camera	Optional
Pedestrian Crash Avoidance	None

General:
Auto. Crash Notification	Dial Assist.-Free
Day Running Lamps	Optional

Safety Belt/Restraint:
Dynamic Head Restraints	Standard Front
Adjustable Belt	Standard Front

Kia Sportage

Specifications

Drive	FWD
Engine	2.4-liter I4
Transmission	6-sp. Automaitc
Tow Rating (lbs.)	Very Low-2000
Head/Leg Room (in.)	Cramped-39.1/41.4
Interior Space (cu. ft.)	Average-100
Cargo Space (cu. ft.)	Roomy-26.1
Wheelbase/Length (in.)	103.9/174.8

Ratings—10 Best, 1 Worst

Combo Crash Tests	–
Safety Features	6
Rollover	2
Preventive Maintenance	5
Repair Costs	1
Warranty	3
Fuel Economy	1
Complaints	2
Insurance Costs	8
OVERALL RATING	**–**

Land Rover Range Rover

Land Rover Range Rover

At-a-Glance

Status/Year Series Started	Unchanged/2013
Twins	–
Body Styles	SUV
Seating	5
Anti-Theft Device	Std. Pass. Immobil. & Alarm
Parking Index Rating	Very Hard
Where Made	Solihull, England
Fuel Factor	
MPG Rating (city/hwy)	Very Poor-14/19
Driving Range (mi.)	Long-439.9
Fuel Type	Premium
Annual Fuel Cost	Very High-$3,022
Gas Guzzler Tax	No
Greenhouse Gas Emissions (tons/yr.)	Very High-11.3
Barrels of Oil Used per year	Very High-20.6

How the Competition Rates

Competitors	Rating	Pg.
Audi Q7	–	93
Lexus GX	–	189
Mercedes-Benz GL-Class	–	207

Price Range

Price Range	Retail	Markup
Base	$83,545	10%
HSE	$88,545	10%
Supercharged	$99,995	10%
Autobiography	$135,995	10%

Safety Checklist

Crash Tests:
Frontal	–
Sidel	–

Airbags:
Torso	Front Torso from Seat
Pelvis	None
Roll Sensing	Yes
Knee Bolster	None

Crash Avoidance:
Collision Avoidance	Std. DBS & Opt. CIB
Blind Spot Detection	Optional
Lane Keeping Assist	None
Backup Camera	Standard
Pedestrian Crash Avoidance	None

General:
Auto. Crash Notification	Dial Assist.-Free
Day Running Lamps	Standard

Safety Belt/Restraint:
Dynamic Head Restraints	None
Adjustable Belt	Standard Front

Land Rover Range Rover

Specifications

Drive	4WD
Engine	5.0-liter V8
Transmission	6-sp. Automatic
Tow Rating (lbs.)	High-7716
Head/Leg Room (in.)	Average-42.5/39.1
Interior Space (cu. ft.)	–
Cargo Space (cu. ft.)	Roomy-32.1
Wheelbase/Length (in.)	115/196.8

Land Rover Range Rover Evoque Small SUV

Land Rover Range Rover Evoque

Ratings—10 Best, 1 Worst

Combo Crash Tests	–
Safety Features	7
Rollover	4
Preventive Maintenance	10
Repair Costs	6
Warranty	3
Fuel Economy	5
Complaints	7
Insurance Costs	5
OVERALL RATING	**–**

Land Rover Range Rover Evoque

Land Rover Range Rover Evoque

At-a-Glance

Status/Year Series Started	Unchanged/2012
Twins	–
Body Styles	SUV
Seating	5
Anti-Theft Device	Std. Pass. Immobil. & Alarm
Parking Index Rating	Easy
Where Made	Halewood, England
Fuel Factor	
MPG Rating (city/hwy)	Average-21/30
Driving Range (mi.)	Long-448.9
Fuel Type	Premium
Annual Fuel Cost	High-$1,977
Gas Guzzler Tax	No
Greenhouse Gas Emissions (tons/yr.)	Average-7.5
Barrels of Oil Used per year	High-13.7

How the Competition Rates

Competitors	Rating	Pg.
Audi Q3	–	91
Lexus NX	–	191
Mercedes-Benz GLA-Class	–	206

Price Range

	Retail	Markup
Pure	$41,995	10%
Pure Premium 2 Door	$50,959	10%
Prestige	$56,295	10%
Dynamic 2 Door	$58,195	10%

Safety Checklist

Crash Tests:
Frontal . . . . –
Sidel . . . . –
Airbags:
Torso . . . . Front Torso from Seat
Pelvis . . . . None
Roll Sensing. . . . . .Yes
Knee Bolster . . . . Standard Driver
Crash Avoidance:
Collision Avoidance . . . . . . Std. DBS & Opt. CIB
Blind Spot Detection . . . . Optional
Lane Keeping Assist . . . . None
Backup Camera . . . . Standard
Pedestrian Crash Avoidance . . . . None
General:
Auto. Crash Notification . . . . . . Dial Assist.-Free
Day Running Lamps . . . . Standard
Safety Belt/Restraint:
Dynamic Head Restraints . . . . None
Adjustable Belt . . . . .Standard Front

Land Rover Range Rover Evoque

Specifications

Drive	4WD
Engine	2.0-liter I4
Transmission	9-sp. Automatic
Tow Rating (lbs.)	–
Head/Leg Room (in.)	Cramped-40.3/40.1
Interior Space (cu. ft.)	–
Cargo Space (cu. ft.)	Average-20.3
Wheelbase/Length (in.)	104.8/171.5

Ratings—10 Best, 1 Worst

Combo Crash Tests	–
Safety Features	6
Rollover	3
Preventive Maintenance	5
Repair Costs	1
Warranty	3
Fuel Economy	1
Complaints	10
Insurance Costs	5

OVERALL RATING — –

Land Rover Range Rover Sport

At-a-Glance

Status/Year Series Started	Unchanged/2014
Twins	–
Body Styles	SUV
Seating	5
Anti-Theft Device	Std. Pass. Immobil. & Alarm
Parking Index Rating	Very Hard
Where Made	Solihull, England
Fuel Factor	
MPG Rating (city/hwy)	Very Poor-14/19
Driving Range (mi.)	Long-439.9
Fuel Type	Premium
Annual Fuel Cost	Very High-$3,023
Gas Guzzler Tax	No
Greenhouse Gas Emissions (tons/yr.)	Very High-11.2
Barrels of Oil Used per year	Very High-20.6

How the Competition Rates

Competitors	Rating	Pg.
Acura MDX	6	82
Audi Q5	4	92
BMW X5	6	101

Price Range	Retail	Markup
SE	$63,495	10%
HSE	$68,495	10%
Supercharged	$79,995	10%
Autobiography	$93,295	10%

Land Rover Range Rover Sport

Safety Checklist

Crash Tests:
Frontal	–
Sidel	–

Airbags:
Torso	Front Torso from Seat
Pelvis	None
Roll Sensing	Yes
Knee Bolster	None

Crash Avoidance:
Collision Avoidance	Std. DBS & Opt. CIB
Blind Spot Detection	Optional
Lane Keeping Assist	None
Backup Camera	Standard
Pedestrian Crash Avoidance	None

General:
Auto. Crash Notification	Dial Assist.-Free
Day Running Lamps	Standard

Safety Belt/Restraint:
Dynamic Head Restraints	None
Adjustable Belt	Standard Front

Land Rover Range Rover Sport

Specifications

Drive	4WD
Engine	5.0-liter V8
Transmission	8-sp. Automatic
Tow Rating (lbs.)	High-7716
Head/Leg Room (in.)	Average-39.4/42.2
Interior Space (cu. ft.)	–
Cargo Space (cu. ft.)	Roomy-27.7
Wheelbase/Length (in.)	115.1/191.8

Ratings—10 Best, 1 Worst

Combo Crash Tests	–
Safety Features	5
Rollover	6
Preventive Maintenance	9
Repair Costs	2
Warranty	6
Fuel Economy	10
Complaints	6
Insurance Costs	3
OVERALL RATING	**–**

Lexus CT

Lexus CT

At-a-Glance

Status/Year Series Started	Unchanged/2011
Twins	–
Body Styles	Hatchback
Seating	5
Anti-Theft Device	Std. Pass. Immobil. & Alarm
Parking Index Rating	Easy
Where Made	Kyushu, Japan
Fuel Factor	
MPG Rating (city/hwy)	Very Good-43/40
Driving Range (mi.)	Very Long-495.0
Fuel Type	Regular
Annual Fuel Cost	Very Low-$1,009
Gas Guzzler Tax	No
Greenhouse Gas Emissions (tons/yr.)	Very Low-4.3
Barrels of Oil Used per year	Very Low-7.8

How the Competition Rates

Competitors	Rating	Pg.
Chevrolet Volt	8	125
Ford C-MAX	5	136
Toyota Prius	4	251

Price Range

	Retail	Markup
Hybrid	$32,050	5%

Safety Checklist

Crash Tests:
- Frontal . . . . –
- Sidel . . . . –

Airbags:
- Torso . . . . Front Pelvis/Torso from Seat
- Pelvis . . . . Front Pelvis/Torso from Seat
- Roll Sensing . . . . No
- Knee Bolster . . . . Standard Front

Crash Avoidance:
- Collision Avoidance . . . . . . Optional CIB & DBS
- Blind Spot Detection . . . . None
- Lane Keeping Assist . . . . None
- Backup Camera . . . . Optional
- Pedestrian Crash Avoidance . . . . None

General:
- Auto. Crash Notification . . . Operator Assist.-Fee
- Day Running Lamps . . . . Standard

Safety Belt/Restraint:
- Dynamic Head Restraints . . . . None
- Adjustable Belt . . . . Standard Front

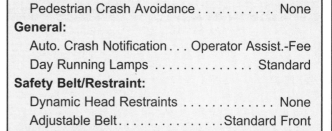
Lexus CT

Specifications

Drive	FWD
Engine	1.8-liter I4
Transmission	CVT
Tow Rating (lbs.)	–
Head/Leg Room (in.)	Cramped-38.3/42.1
Interior Space (cu. ft.)	Very Cramped-86.1
Cargo Space (cu. ft.)	Cramped-14.3
Wheelbase/Length (in.)	102.4/171.2

Ratings—10 Best, 1 Worst

Combo Crash Tests	6
Safety Features	9
Rollover	7
Preventive Maintenance	7
Repair Costs	1
Warranty	6
Fuel Economy	5
Complaints	9
Insurance Costs	5
OVERALL RATING	**7**

Lexus ES

Lexus ES

At-a-Glance

Status/Year Series Started. Unchanged/2013
Twins . . . . Toyota Avalon
Body Styles . . . . .Sedan
Seating 5
Anti-Theft Device . . . . . . Std. Pass. Immobil. & Alarm
Parking Index Rating . . . . Average
Where Made. . . . . Kyushu, Japan
Fuel Factor . . . .
  MPG Rating (city/hwy) Average-21/31
  Driving Range (mi.) Average-422.5
  Fuel Type. . . . . .Regular
  Annual Fuel Cost . . . . Average-$1,709
  Gas Guzzler Tax . . . . .No
  Greenhouse Gas Emissions (tons/yr.). . Average-7.5
  Barrels of Oil Used per year High-13.7

How the Competition Rates

Competitors	Rating	Pg.
Acura TLX	–	85
Infiniti Q70	–	165
Volkswagen Passat	5	265

Price Range	Retail	Markup
Sedan	$37,550	7%
Hybrid	$40,430	7%

Safety Checklist

Crash Tests:
  Frontal. . . . . Good
  Side. . . . . Average
Airbags:
  Torso . . . . Fr. & Rr. Pelvis/Torso from Seat
  Pelvis . . . . Fr. & Rr. Pelvis/Torso from Seat
  Roll Sensing. . . . . No
  Knee Bolster . . . . .Standard Front
Crash Avoidance:
  Collision Avoidance . . . . . . Optional CIB & DBS
  Blind Spot Detection . . . . Optional
  Lane Keeping Assist . . . .Warning Only Optional
  Backup Camera . . . . Standard
  Pedestrian Crash Avoidance . . . . None
General:
  Auto. Crash Notification . . . Operator Assist.-Fee
  Day Running Lamps . . . . Standard
Safety Belt/Restraint:
  Dynamic Head Restraints . . . . None
  Adjustable Belt. . . . . .Standard Front

Lexus ES

Specifications

Drive. . . . . .FWD
Engine .3.5-liter V6
Transmission . . . . .6-sp. Automatic
Tow Rating (lbs.) . . . . –
Head/Leg Room (in.) . . . . .Very Cramped-37.5/41.9
Interior Space (cu. ft.). Average-100.1
Cargo Space (cu. ft.) Cramped-15.2
Wheelbase/Length (in.) 111/192.7

Ratings—10 Best, 1 Worst

Combo Crash Tests	–
Safety Features	9
Rollover	7
Preventive Maintenance	8
Repair Costs	1
Warranty	6
Fuel Economy	4
Complaints	9
Insurance Costs	3
OVERALL RATING	**–**

Lexus GS

At-a-Glance

Status/Year Series Started. Unchanged/2012
Twins . . . .–
Body Styles . . . . .Sedan
Seating. 5
Anti-Theft Device . . . . . . Std. Pass. Immobil. & Alarm
Parking Index Rating . . . . Average
Where Made. . . . . Tahara, Japan
Fuel Factor. . . . .
  MPG Rating (city/hwy) Poor-19/29
  Driving Range (mi.) Short-391.3
  Fuel Type. . . . . .Premium
  Annual Fuel Cost . . . . High-$2,134
  Gas Guzzler Tax . . . . .No
  Greenhouse Gas Emissions (tons/yr.). High-7.8
  Barrels of Oil Used per year High-14.3

How the Competition Rates

Competitors	Rating	Pg.
Acura TLX	–	85
Audi A6	7	89
Hyundai Genesis	7	157

Price Range	Retail	Markup
Sedan	$48,600	8%
Sedan AWD	$50,850	8%
Hybrid	$61,330	8%

Lexus GS

Safety Checklist

Crash Tests:
  Frontal. . . . .–
  Sidel . . . .–
Airbags:
  Torso . . . . Fr. & Rr. Pelvis/Torso from Seat
  Pelvis . . . . Fr. & Rr. Pelvis/Torso from Seat
  Roll Sensing. . . . . No
  Knee Bolster . . . . .Standard Front
Crash Avoidance:
  Collision Avoidance . . . . . . Optional CIB & DBS
  Blind Spot Detection . . . . Optional
  Lane Keeping Assist . . . . Optional
  Backup Camera . . . . Standard
  Pedestrian Crash Avoidance . . . . None
General:
  Auto. Crash Notification . . . Operator Assist.-Fee
  Day Running Lamps . . . . Standard
Safety Belt/Restraint:
  Dynamic Head Restraints . . . . None
  Adjustable Belt. . . . . .Standard Front

Lexus GS

Specifications

Drive. . . . . .RWD
Engine 3.5-liter V6
Transmission . . . . .8-sp. Automatic
Tow Rating (lbs.) . . . . –
Head/Leg Room (in.) Cramped-38/42.3
Interior Space (cu. ft.). Average-99
Cargo Space (cu. ft.) Cramped-14.1
Wheelbase/Length (in.) 112.2/190.7

Ratings—10 Best, 1 Worst

Combo Crash Tests	–
Safety Features	10
Rollover	1
Preventive Maintenance	7
Repair Costs	3
Warranty	6
Fuel Economy	1
Complaints	8
Insurance Costs	8

OVERALL RATING — –

Lexus GX

Lexus GX

At-a-Glance

Status/Year Series Started. Unchanged/2003
Twins . . . . Toyota 4Runner
Body Styles . . . . SUV
Seating 7
Anti-Theft Device . . . . . . Std. Pass. Immobil. & Alarm
Parking Index Rating . . . . Very Hard
Where Made. . . . . Tahara, Japan
Fuel Factor . . . .
  MPG Rating (city/hwy) . . . . Very Poor-15/20
  Driving Range (mi.) Short-388.7
  Fuel Type. . . . . .Premium
  Annual Fuel Cost . . . . Very High-$2,840
  Gas Guzzler Tax . . . . .No
  Greenhouse Gas Emissions (tons/yr.)Very High-10.6
  Barrels of Oil Used per year . . . . Very High-19.4

How the Competition Rates

Competitors	Rating	Pg.
Audi Q7	–	93
Infiniti QX80	–	168
Mercedes-Benz GL-Class	–	207

Price Range

Price Range	Retail	Markup
4WD	$49,085	9%
4WD Luxury	$60,715	9%

Safety Checklist

Crash Tests:
  Frontal. . . . .–
  Sidel . . . .–
Airbags:
  Torso . . . . Fr. & Rr. Torso from Seat
  Pelvis . . . . .Front Pelvis/Torso from Seat
  Roll Sensing. . . . . .Yes
  Knee Bolster . . . . .Standard Front
Crash Avoidance:
  Collision Avoidance . . . . . . Optional CIB & DBS
  Blind Spot Detection . . . . Optional
  Lane Keeping Assist . . . . None
  Backup Camera. . . . . Standard
  Pedestrian Crash Avoidance . . . . None
General:
  Auto. Crash Notification . . . Operator Assist.-Fee
  Day Running Lamps . . . . Standard
Safety Belt/Restraint:
  Dynamic Head Restraints . . . . .Standard Front
  Adjustable Belt. . . . . . .Standard Front and Rear

Lexus GX

Specifications

Drive. 4WD
Engine 4.6-liter V8
Transmission . . . . .6-sp. Automatic
Tow Rating (lbs.) Average-6500
Head/Leg Room (in.) Cramped-38/41.7
Interior Space (cu. ft.). . . . . Very Roomy-129.7
Cargo Space (cu. ft.) . . . . . . .Very Cramped-11.6
Wheelbase/Length (in.) 109.8/192.1

Ratings—10 Best, 1 Worst

Combo Crash Tests	6
Safety Features	8
Rollover	8
Preventive Maintenance	7
Repair Costs	1
Warranty	6
Fuel Economy	5
Complaints	4
Insurance Costs	5
OVERALL RATING	**5**

Lexus IS

Lexus IS

At-a-Glance

Status/Year Series Started	Unchanged/2014
Twins	–
Body Styles	Sedan, Convertible
Seating	5
Anti-Theft Device	Std. Pass. Immobil. & Alarm
Parking Index Rating	Easy
Where Made	Kyushu, Japan / Tahara, Japan
Fuel Factor	
MPG Rating (city/hwy)	Average-21/30
Driving Range (mi.)	Average-422.4
Fuel Type	Premium
Annual Fuel Cost	High-$1,977
Gas Guzzler Tax	No
Greenhouse Gas Emissions (tons/yr.)	Average-7.5
Barrels of Oil Used per year	High-13.7

How the Competition Rates

Competitors	Rating	Pg.
Acura ILX	7	81
BMW 3 Series	9	94
Infiniti Q50	–	163

Price Range

	Retail	Markup
250 Sedan	$36,550	8%
350 Sedan AWD	$42,300	8%
350 Convertible	$47,240	8%
F	$63,350	8%

Safety Checklist

Crash Tests:
- Frontal ....Poor
- Side .... Very Good

Airbags:
- Torso .... Fr. & Rr. Pelvis/Torso from Seat
- Pelvis .... Fr. & Rr. Pelvis/Torso from Seat
- Roll Sensing .... No
- Knee Bolster ....Standard Front

Crash Avoidance:
- Collision Avoidance ...... Optional CIB & DBS
- Blind Spot Detection .... Optional
- Lane Keeping Assist ....Warning Only Optional
- Backup Camera................... Optional
- Pedestrian Crash Avoidance .... None

General:
- Auto. Crash Notification ... Operator Assist.-Fee
- Day Running Lamps .... Standard

Safety Belt/Restraint:
- Dynamic Head Restraints .... None
- Adjustable Belt..............Standard Front

Lexus IS

Specifications

Drive	RWD
Engine	2.5-liter V6
Transmission	6-sp. Automatic
Tow Rating (lbs.)	–
Head/Leg Room (in.)	Roomy-38.2/44.8
Interior Space (cu. ft.)	Very Cramped-90.2
Cargo Space (cu. ft.)	Cramped-13.8
Wheelbase/Length (in.)	110.2/183.7

Ratings—10 Best, 1 Worst

Combo Crash Tests	–
Safety Features	8
Rollover	3
Preventive Maintenance	–
Repair Costs	–
Warranty	6
Fuel Economy	5
Complaints	–
Insurance Costs	5

OVERALL RATING — –

Lexus NX

Lexus NX

At-a-Glance

Status/Year Series Started	All New/2015
Twins	Toyota RAV4
Body Styles	SUV
Seating	5
Anti-Theft Device	Std. Pass. Immobil. & Alarm
Parking Index Rating	Very Easy
Where Made	Kyushu, Japan
Fuel Factor	
MPG Rating (city/hwy)	Average-22/28
Driving Range (mi.)	Short-387.1
Fuel Type	Premium
Annual Fuel Cost	High-$1,971
Gas Guzzler Tax	No
Greenhouse Gas Emissions (tons/yr.)	Very Low-3.5
Barrels of Oil Used per year	High-13.7

How the Competition Rates

Competitors	Rating	Pg.
BMW X1	–	99
Lincoln MKC	5	193
Mercedes-Benz GLA-Class	–	206

Price Range

	Retail	Markup
Utility 2WD	$39,720	6%
Utility 4WD	$41,310	6%

Safety Checklist

Crash Tests:
Frontal . . . . –
Sidel . . . . –

Airbags:
Torso . . . . Front Pelvis/Torso from Seat
Pelvis . . . . Front Pelvis/Torso from Seat
Roll Sensing. . . . . .Yes
Knee Bolster . . . . .Standard Front

Crash Avoidance:
Collision Avoidance . . . . . . Optional CIB & DBS
Blind Spot Detection . . . . Optional
Lane Keeping Assist . . . . None
Backup Camera . . . . Standard
Pedestrian Crash Avoidance . . . . None

General:
Auto. Crash Notification . . . Operator Assist.-Fee
Day Running Lamps . . . . Standard

Safety Belt/Restraint:
Dynamic Head Restraints . . . . None
Adjustable Belt. . . . . .Standard Front

Lexus NX

Specifications

Drive	AWD
Engine	2.0-liter I4
Transmission	6-sp. Automatic
Tow Rating (lbs.)	Very Low-2000
Head/Leg Room (in.)	Cramped-38.2/42.8
Interior Space (cu. ft.)	Very Cramped-71.6
Cargo Space (cu. ft.)	Average-17.7
Wheelbase/Length (in.)	104.7/182.3

Ratings—10 Best, 1 Worst	
Combo Crash Tests	5
Safety Features	9
Rollover	3
Preventive Maintenance	6
Repair Costs	2
Warranty	6
Fuel Economy	3
Complaints	10
Insurance Costs	8
OVERALL RATING	**6**

Lexus RX

Lexus RX

At-a-Glance

Status/Year Series Started	Unchanged/2010
Twins	–
Body Styles	SUV
Seating	5
Anti-Theft Device	Std. Pass. Immobil. & Alarm
Parking Index Rating	Hard
Where Made	Kyushu, Japan / Cambridge, Ontario
Fuel Factor	
MPG Rating (city/hwy)	Poor-18/24
Driving Range (mi.)	Short-389.4
Fuel Type	Regular
Annual Fuel Cost	High-$2,070
Gas Guzzler Tax	No
Greenhouse Gas Emissions (tons/yr.)	High-9.0
Barrels of Oil Used per year	High-16.5

How the Competition Rates

Competitors	Rating	Pg.
Audi Q5	4	92
BMW X3	8	100
Mercedes-Benz GLK-Class	–	208

Price Range	Retail	Markup
350 Base FWD	$40,795	7%
350 Base AWD	$42,195	7%
350 F Sport AWD	$48,535	7%
450 Hybrid AWD	$48,845	6%

Safety Checklist

Crash Tests:
Frontal	Very Poor
Side	Very Good

Airbags:
Torso	Fr. & Rr. Torso from Seat
Pelvis	Front Pelvis/Torso from Seat
Roll Sensing	Yes
Knee Bolster	Standard Front

Crash Avoidance:
Collision Avoidance	Optional CIB & DBS
Blind Spot Detection	Optional
Lane Keeping Assist	None
Backup Camera	Optional
Pedestrian Crash Avoidance	None

General:
Auto. Crash Notification	Operator Assist.-Fee
Day Running Lamps	Standard

Safety Belt/Restraint:
Dynamic Head Restraints	Standard Front
Adjustable Belt	Standard Front

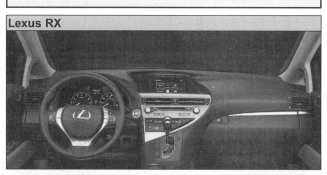
Lexus RX

Specifications

Drive	AWD
Engine	3.5-liter V6
Transmission	6-sp. Automatic
Tow Rating (lbs.)	Low-3500
Head/Leg Room (in.)	Average-39.1/43.1
Interior Space (cu. ft.)	Average-99.7
Cargo Space (cu. ft.)	Very Roomy-40
Wheelbase/Length (in.)	107.9/187.8

Ratings—10 Best, 1 Worst

Combo Crash Tests	3
Safety Features	8
Rollover	3
Preventive Maintenance	10
Repair Costs	–
Warranty	8
Fuel Economy	3
Complaints	–
Insurance Costs	5
OVERALL RATING	**5**

Lincoln MKC

Lincoln MKC

At-a-Glance

Status/Year Series Started. . . . . All New/2015
Twins . . . . .Ford Escape
Body Styles . . . . SUV
Seating 5
Anti-Theft Device . . . . . . Std. Pass. Immobil. & Alarm
Parking Index Rating . . . . Average
Where Made. . . . . Louisville, Kentucky
Fuel Factor . . . .
    MPG Rating (city/hwy) Poor-19/26
    Driving Range (mi.) . . . . Very Short-335.1
    Fuel Type. . . . . .Regular
    Annual Fuel Cost . . . . Average-$1,942
    Gas Guzzler Tax . . . . .No
    Greenhouse Gas Emissions (tons/yr.). High-8.2
    Barrels of Oil Used per year High-15.0

How the Competition Rates

Competitors	Rating	Pg.
Audi Q3	–	91
BMW X1	–	99
Lexus NX	–	191

Price Range	Retail	Markup
FWD	$33,100	5%
AWD	$35,595	5%

Safety Checklist

Crash Tests:
    Frontal. . . . . Poor
    Side. . . . . Poor*
Airbags:
    Torso . . . . .Front Pelvis/Torso from Seat
    Pelvis . . . . .Front Pelvis/Torso from Seat
    Roll Sensing. . . . . .Yes
    Knee Bolster . . . . Standard Driver
Crash Avoidance:
    Collision Avoidance . . . . .Warning Only Optional
    Blind Spot Detection . . . . Optional
    Lane Keeping Assist . . . . Optional
    Backup Camera. . . . . Standard
    Pedestrian Crash Avoidance . . . . None
General:
    Auto. Crash Notification. . . . . . Dial Assist.-Free
    Day Running Lamps . . . . Standard
Safety Belt/Restraint:
    Dynamic Head Restraints . . . . None
    Adjustable Belt. . . . . .Standard Front

Specifications

Drive. . . . . AWD
Engine 2.0-liter I5
Transmission . . . . .6-sp. Automatic
Tow Rating (lbs.) . . . . Very Low-2000
Head/Leg Room (in.) Average-39.6/42.8
Interior Space (cu. ft.). Average-97.9
Cargo Space (cu. ft.) Roomy-25.2
Wheelbase/Length (in.) 105.9/179.2

*Additional injury concerns. See page 25.

Ratings—10 Best, 1 Worst

Combo Crash Tests	7
Safety Features	5
Rollover	6
Preventive Maintenance	8
Repair Costs	2
Warranty	8
Fuel Economy	4
Complaints	5
Insurance Costs	3
OVERALL RATING	**5**

Lincoln MKS

Lincoln MKS

At-a-Glance

Status/Year Series Started	Unchanged/2009
Twins	–
Body Styles	Sedan
Seating	5
Anti-Theft Device	Std. Pass. Immobil. & Alarm
Parking Index Rating	Very Hard
Where Made	Chicago, IL
Fuel Factor	
MPG Rating (city/hwy)	Poor-19/28
Driving Range (mi.)	Average-422.0
Fuel Type	Regular
Annual Fuel Cost	Average-$1,890
Gas Guzzler Tax	No
Greenhouse Gas Emissions (tons/yr.)	High-8.2
Barrels of Oil Used per year	High-15.0

How the Competition Rates

Competitors	Rating	Pg.
Acura RLX	–	84
Chrysler 300	–	127
Lexus GS	–	188

Price Range

	Retail	Markup
FWD	$40,425	5%
AWD	$42,420	5%
Ecoboost AWD	$47,415	5%

Safety Checklist

Crash Tests:
Frontal	Very Good
Side	Poor

Airbags:
Torso	Front Torso from Seat
Pelvis	None
Roll Sensing	Yes
Knee Bolster	None

Crash Avoidance:
Collision Avoidance	Warning Only Optional
Blind Spot Detection	Optional
Lane Keeping Assist	Optional
Backup Camera	Standard
Pedestrian Crash Avoidance	None

General:
Auto. Crash Notification	Dial Assist.-Free
Day Running Lamps	None

Safety Belt/Restraint:
Dynamic Head Restraints	None
Adjustable Belt	Standard Front

Lincoln MKS

Specifications

Drive	FWD
Engine	3.7-liter V6
Transmission	6-sp. Automatic
Tow Rating (lbs.)	–
Head/Leg Room (in.)	Average-39.7/41.9
Interior Space (cu. ft.)	Roomy-105.8
Cargo Space (cu. ft.)	Average-19.2
Wheelbase/Length (in.)	112.9/205.6

Ratings—10 Best, 1 Worst

Combo Crash Tests	2
Safety Features	4
Rollover	5
Preventive Maintenance	9
Repair Costs	5
Warranty	8
Fuel Economy	2
Complaints	8
Insurance Costs	10
OVERALL RATING	**5**

Lincoln MKX

Lincoln MKX

At-a-Glance

Status/Year Series Started	Unchanged/2007
Twins	–
Body Styles	SUV
Seating	5
Anti-Theft Device	Std. Pass. Immobil. & Alarm
Parking Index Rating	Hard
Where Made	Oakland, Ontario
Fuel Factor	
MPG Rating (city/hwy)	Very Poor-17/23
Driving Range (mi.)	Short-369.8
Fuel Type	Regular
Annual Fuel Cost	High-$2,180
Gas Guzzler Tax	No
Greenhouse Gas Emissions (tons/yr.)	Very High-9.5
Barrels of Oil Used per year	Very High-17.3

How the Competition Rates

Competitors	Rating	Pg.
Acura MDX	6	82
Chevrolet Equinox	2	115
Infiniti QX70	–	167

Price Range	Retail	Markup
Base FWD	$39,795	5%
Base AWD	$41,745	5%
Elite AWD	$47,475	5%
Limited Edition AWD	$48,875	5%

Safety Checklist

Crash Tests:
Frontal . . . . Very Poor
Side . . . . Poor

Airbags:
Torso . . . . Front Torso from Seat
Pelvis . . . . None
Roll Sensing . . . . Yes
Knee Bolster . . . . None

Crash Avoidance:
Collision Avoidance . . . . . Warning Only Optional
Blind Spot Detection . . . . Optional
Lane Keeping Assist . . . . None
Backup Camera . . . . Optional
Pedestrian Crash Avoidance . . . . None

General:
Auto. Crash Notification . . . . . . Dial Assist.-Free
Day Running Lamps . . . . None

Safety Belt/Restraint:
Dynamic Head Restraints . . . . None
Adjustable Belt . . . . Standard Front

Lincoln MKX

Specifications

Drive	AWD
Engine	3.7-liter V6
Transmission	6-sp. Automatic
Tow Rating (lbs.)	Low-3500
Head/Leg Room (in.)	Average-40/42.4
Interior Space (cu. ft.)	Roomy-108.4
Cargo Space (cu. ft.)	Roomy-32.3
Wheelbase/Length (in.)	111.2/186.7

Ratings—10 Best, 1 Worst

Combo Crash Tests	6
Safety Features	6
Rollover	7
Preventive Maintenance	5
Repair Costs	1
Warranty	8
Fuel Economy	3
Complaints	5
Insurance Costs	5
OVERALL RATING	**4**

Lincoln MKZ

Lincoln MKZ

At-a-Glance

Status/Year Series Started......... Unchanged/2013
Twins .... Ford Fusion
Body Styles ....Sedan
Seating....................................5
Anti-Theft Device ...... Std. Pass. Immobil. & Alarm
Parking Index Rating .... Hard
Where Made.................Hermosillo, Mexico
Fuel Factor...............................
  MPG Rating (city/hwy)............Poor-18/27
  Driving Range (mi.) .... Very Short-349.4
  Fuel Type...........................Regular
  Annual Fuel Cost .... High-$1,983
  Gas Guzzler Tax ....No
  Greenhouse Gas Emissions (tons/yr.)..... High-8.1
  Barrels of Oil Used per year High-15.0

How the Competition Rates

Competitors	Rating	Pg.
BMW 3 Series	9	94
Buick Regal	6	105
Cadillac CTS	10	108

Price Range

Price Range	Retail	Markup
Hybrid	$35,190	5%
Base	$35,190	5%
Base AWD	$37,080	5%

Safety Checklist

Crash Tests:
  Frontal............................ Good
  Side.........................Very Poor
Airbags:
  Torso ....Front Pelvis/Torso from Seat
  Pelvis ....Front Pelvis/Torso from Seat
  Roll Sensing.......................... No
  Knee Bolster ....Standard Front
Crash Avoidance:
  Collision Avoidance .....Warning Only Optional
  Blind Spot Detection .... Optional
  Lane Keeping Assist .... Optional
  Backup Camera.................. Standard
  Pedestrian Crash Avoidance .... None
General:
  Auto. Crash Notification...... Dial Assist.-Free
  Day Running Lamps .... Standard
Safety Belt/Restraint:
  Dynamic Head Restraints .... None
  Adjustable Belt...............Standard Front

Specifications

Drive................................. FWD
Engine 3.7-liter V6
Transmission ....6-sp. Automatic
Tow Rating (lbs.) .... Very Low-1000
Head/Leg Room (in.) Average-37.9/44.3
Interior Space (cu. ft.)............Cramped-96.5
Cargo Space (cu. ft.) Cramped-15.4
Wheelbase/Length (in.) 112.2/194.1

Mazda CX-5

Ratings—10 Best, 1 Worst

Combo Crash Tests	9
Safety Features	5
Rollover	3
Preventive Maintenance	6
Repair Costs	10
Warranty	1
Fuel Economy	7
Complaints	2
Insurance Costs	3
OVERALL RATING	**5**

Mazda CX-5

Mazda CX-5

At-a-Glance

Status/Year Series Started	Unchanged/2013
Twins	–
Body Styles	SUV
Seating	5
Anti-Theft Device	Std. Pass. Immobil.
Parking Index Rating	Average
Where Made	Hiroshima, Japan
Fuel Factor	
MPG Rating (city/hwy)	Good-26/32
Driving Range (mi.)	Average-420.3
Fuel Type	Regular
Annual Fuel Cost	Low-$1,479
Gas Guzzler Tax	No
Greenhouse Gas Emissions (tons/yr.)	Low-6.2
Barrels of Oil Used per year	Average-11.4

How the Competition Rates

Competitors	Rating	Pg.
Buick Encore	10	103
Honda CR-V	6	151
Mitsubishi Outlander Sport	4	216

Price Range

	Retail	Markup
Sport FWD MT	$21,545	3%
Sport AWD AT	$24,195	3%
Touring AWD	$26,215	3%
Grand Touring AWD	$29,220	3%

Safety Checklist

Crash Tests:
Frontal	Very Good
Side	Good

Airbags:
Torso	Front Pelvis/Torso from Seat
Pelvis	Front Pelvis/Torso from Seat
Roll Sensing	Yes
Knee Bolster	None

Crash Avoidance:
Collision Avoidance	Optional CIB
Blind Spot Detection	Optional
Lane Keeping Assist	None
Backup Camera	Optional
Pedestrian Crash Avoidance	None

General:
Auto. Crash Notification	Dial Assist.-Free
Day Running Lamps	Standard

Safety Belt/Restraint:
Dynamic Head Restraints	None
Adjustable Belt	Standard Front

Mazda CX-5

Specifications

Drive	FWD
Engine	2.0-liter I4
Transmission	6-sp. Automatic
Tow Rating (lbs.)	Very Low-2000
Head/Leg Room (in.)	Average-40.1/41
Interior Space (cu. ft.)	Roomy-103.8
Cargo Space (cu. ft.)	Very Roomy-34.1
Wheelbase/Length (in.)	106.3/178.7

Mazda CX-9

Mazda CX-9

Ratings—10 Best, 1 Worst

Combo Crash Tests	1
Safety Features	4
Rollover	4
Preventive Maintenance	6
Repair Costs	5
Warranty	1
Fuel Economy	2
Complaints	6
Insurance Costs	8
OVERALL RATING	**1**

Mazda CX-9

At-a-Glance

Status/Year Series Started	Unchanged/2007
Twins	–
Body Styles	SUV
Seating	7
Anti-Theft Device	Std. Pass. Immobil. & Alarm
Parking Index Rating	Hard
Where Made	Hiroshima, Japan
Fuel Factor	
MPG Rating (city/hwy)	Very Poor-16/22
Driving Range (mi.)	Very Short-366.6
Fuel Type	Regular
Annual Fuel Cost	High-$2,302
Gas Guzzler Tax	No
Greenhouse Gas Emissions (tons/yr.)	Very High-10.0
Barrels of Oil Used per year	Very High-18.3

How the Competition Rates

Competitors	Rating	Pg.
Hyundai Santa Fe	–	158
Kia Sorento	4	180
Nissan Murano	–	224

Price Range

	Retail	Markup
Sport FWD	$29,985	6%
Touring FWD	$32,480	6%
Touring AWD	$34,070	6%
Grand Touring AWD	$36,625	6%

Safety Checklist

Crash Tests:
Frontal . . . . Very Poor
Sidel . . . . Very Poor

Airbags:
Torso . . . . Front Pelvis/Torso from Seat
Pelvis . . . . Front Pelvis/Torso from Seat
Roll Sensing . . . . Yes
Knee Bolster . . . . None

Crash Avoidance:
Collision Avoidance . . . . None
Blind Spot Detection . . . . Optional
Lane Keeping Assist . . . . None
Backup Camera . . . . Optional
Pedestrian Crash Avoidance . . . . None

General:
Auto. Crash Notification . . . . . . Dial Assist.-Free
Day Running Lamps . . . . Optional

Safety Belt/Restraint:
Dynamic Head Restraints . . . . None
Adjustable Belt . . . . Standard Front

Mazda CX-9

Specifications

Drive	AWD
Engine	3.7-liter V6
Transmission	6-sp. Automatic
Tow Rating (lbs.)	Low-3500
Head/Leg Room (in.)	Cramped-39.6/40.9
Interior Space (cu. ft.)	Very Roomy-139.4
Cargo Space (cu. ft.)	Average-17.2
Wheelbase/Length (in.)	113.2/200.6

Ratings—10 Best, 1 Worst

Combo Crash Tests	6
Safety Features	5
Rollover	7
Preventive Maintenance	5
Repair Costs	9
Warranty	1
Fuel Economy	9
Complaints	7
Insurance Costs	1
OVERALL RATING	**5**

Mazda3

Mazda3

At-a-Glance

Status/Year Series Started	Unchanged/2014
Twins	–
Body Styles	Sedan, Hatchback
Seating	5
Anti-Theft Device	Std. Pass. Immobil.
Parking Index Rating	Easy
Where Made	Hofu, Japan
Fuel Factor	
MPG Rating (city/hwy)	Very Good-30/41
Driving Range (mi.)	Long-450.4
Fuel Type	Regular
Annual Fuel Cost	Very Low-$1,230
Gas Guzzler Tax	No
Greenhouse Gas Emissions (tons/yr.)	Very Low-5.3
Barrels of Oil Used per year	Low-9.7

How the Competition Rates

Competitors	Rating	Pg.
Ford Focus	–	144
Mitsubishi Lancer	4	213
Volkswagen Jetta	5	264

Price Range	Retail	Markup
i Sedan MT	$16,945	3%
i Touring Sedan AT	$20,645	4%
s Touring Hatchback MT	$24,345	5%
s Grand Touring Hatchback AT	$26,595	5%

Safety Checklist

Crash Tests:
Frontal	Good
Side	Average

Airbags:
Torso	Front Pelvis/Torso from Seat
Pelvis	Front Pelvis/Torso from Seat
Roll Sensing	Yes
Knee Bolster	None

Crash Avoidance:
Collision Avoidance	Optional CIB
Blind Spot Detection	Optional
Lane Keeping Assist	None
Backup Camera	Optional
Pedestrian Crash Avoidance	None

General:
Auto. Crash Notification	Dial Assist.-Free
Day Running Lamps	Standard

Safety Belt/Restraint:
Dynamic Head Restraints	None
Adjustable Belt	Standard Front

Mazda3

Specifications

Drive	FWD
Engine	2.0-liter I4
Transmission	6-sp. Automatic
Tow Rating (lbs.)	–
Head/Leg Room (in.)	Cramped-38.6/42.2
Interior Space (cu. ft.)	Cramped-96.3
Cargo Space (cu. ft.)	Very Cramped-12.4
Wheelbase/Length (in.)	106.3/180.3

Mazda5

Ratings—10 Best, 1 Worst

Combo Crash Tests	–
Safety Features	1
Rollover	3
Preventive Maintenance	5
Repair Costs	8
Warranty	1
Fuel Economy	5
Complaints	6
Insurance Costs	5
OVERALL RATING	**–**

Mazda5

Safety Checklist

Crash Tests:
Frontal . . . . –
Sidel . . . . –

Airbags:
Torso . . . . Front Pelvis/Torso from Seat
Pelvis . . . . Front Pelvis/Torso from Seat
Roll Sensing . . . . No
Knee Bolster . . . . None

Crash Avoidance:
Collision Avoidance . . . . None
Blind Spot Detection . . . . None
Lane Keeping Assist . . . . None
Backup Camera . . . . None
Pedestrian Crash Avoidance . . . . None

General:
Auto. Crash Notification . . . . None
Day Running Lamps . . . . None

Safety Belt/Restraint:
Dynamic Head Restraints . . . . None
Adjustable Belt . . . . Standard Front

At-a-Glance

Status/Year Series Started Unchanged/2006
Twins . . . . –
Body Styles . . . . Minivan
Seating 5/7
Anti-Theft Device . . . . . . Std. Pass. Immobil. & Alarm
Parking Index Rating . . . . Easy
Where Made . . . . Hiroshima, Japan
Fuel Factor . . . .
  MPG Rating (city/hwy) Average-21/28
  Driving Range (mi.) Short-376.2
  Fuel Type . . . . Regular
  Annual Fuel Cost . . . . Average-$1,775
  Gas Guzzler Tax . . . . No
  Greenhouse Gas Emissions (tons/yr.) . . Average-7.5
  Barrels of Oil Used per year High-13.7

How the Competition Rates

Competitors	Rating	Pg.
Honda Odyssey	7	153
Subaru Forester	2	240
Toyota Prius V	8	253

Price Range

Price Range	Retail	Markup
Sport	$21,240	5%
Touring	$22,370	5%
Grand Touring	$24,770	5%

Mazda5

Specifications

Drive . . . . FWD
Engine 2.5-liter I4
Transmission . . . . 5-sp. Automatic
Tow Rating (lbs.) . . . . –
Head/Leg Room (in.) Average-40.7/40.7
Interior Space (cu. ft.) Average-97.7
Cargo Space (cu. ft.) . . . . Very Roomy-44.4
Wheelbase/Length (in.) 108.3/180.5

Mazda Mazda6

Ratings—10 Best, 1 Worst

Combo Crash Tests	6
Safety Features	3
Rollover	7
Preventive Maintenance	3
Repair Costs	10
Warranty	1
Fuel Economy	8
Complaints	2
Insurance Costs	5
OVERALL RATING	**4**

Mazda6

Mazda6

At-a-Glance

Status/Year Series Started. Unchanged/2014
Twins . . . . –
Body Styles . . . . Sedan
Seating 5
Anti-Theft Device . . . . . . Std. Pass. Immobil. & Alarm
Parking Index Rating . . . . Average
Where Made. Flat Rock, MI
Fuel Factor . . . .
 MPG Rating (city/hwy) Good-26/38
 Driving Range (mi.) . . . . .Very Long-497.0
 Fuel Type . . . . .Regular
 Annual Fuel Cost . . . . Very Low-$1,385
 Gas Guzzler Tax . . . . .No
 Greenhouse Gas Emissions (tons/yr.). Low-6.0
 Barrels of Oil Used per year Average-11.0

How the Competition Rates

Competitors	Rating	Pg.
Kia Optima	7	177
Nissan Altima	5	218
Toyota Camry	7	248

Price Range

	Retail	Markup
i Sport MT	$21,190	5%
i Sport AT	$22,895	5%
i Touring AT	$24,895	6%
i Grant Touring	$29,895	6%

Safety Checklist

Crash Tests:
 Frontal. . . . . Average
 Side. . . . . Good
Airbags:
 Torso . . . . .Front Pelvis/Torso from Seat
 Pelvis . . . . .Front Pelvis/Torso from Seat
 Roll Sensing. . . . . No
 Knee Bolster . . . . None
Crash Avoidance:
 Collision Avoidance . . . . Optional CIB
 Blind Spot Detection . . . . Optional
 Lane Keeping Assist . . . . None
 Backup Camera . . . . Optional
 Pedestrian Crash Avoidance . . . . None
General:
 Auto. Crash Notification . . . . . . Dial Assist.-Free
 Day Running Lamps . . . . Standard
Safety Belt/Restraint:
 Dynamic Head Restraints . . . . None
 Adjustable Belt . . . . .Standard Front

Mazda6

Specifications

Drive. . . . . FWD
Engine 2.5-liter I4
Transmission . . . . .6-sp. Automatic
Tow Rating (lbs.) . . . . –
Head/Leg Room (in.) Cramped-38.4/42.2
Interior Space (cu. ft.). Average-99.7
Cargo Space (cu. ft.). Cramped-14.8
Wheelbase/Length (in.) 111.4/191.5

Ratings—10 Best, 1 Worst

Combo Crash Tests	–
Safety Features	1
Rollover	10
Preventive Maintenance	5
Repair Costs	7
Warranty	1
Fuel Economy	5
Complaints	9
Insurance Costs	10
OVERALL RATING	–

Mazda MX-5 Miata

At-a-Glance

Status/Year Series Started. Unchanged/2006
Twins . . . . –
Body Styles . . . . Coupe, Convertible
Seating 2
Anti-Theft Device . . . . . . Std. Pass. Immobil. & Alarm
Parking Index Rating . . . . .Very Easy
Where Made. . . . . Hiroshima, Japan
Fuel Factor . . . .
  MPG Rating (city/hwy) Average-21/28
  Driving Range (mi.) . . . . Very Short-300.5
  Fuel Type . . . . .Regular
  Annual Fuel Cost . . . . Average-$1,775
  Gas Guzzler Tax . . . . .No
  Greenhouse Gas Emissions (tons/yr.) High-7.8
  Barrels of Oil Used per year High-14.3

How the Competition Rates

Competitors	Rating	Pg.
Nissan 370Z	–	217
Scion FR-S	3	235
Subaru BRZ	2	239

Price Range

	Retail	Markup
Sport MT	$23,970	6%
Club AT	$27,505	6%
Grand Touring Hardtop AT	$30,550	6%
25th Anniv. Ed. Hardtop AT	$32,655	6%

Mazda MX-5 Miata

Safety Checklist

Crash Tests:
  Frontal. . . . .–
  Sidel . . . .–
Airbags:
  Torso . . . . Front Head/Torso from Seat
  Pelvis . . . . None
  Roll Sensing. . . . . No
  Knee Bolster . . . . None
Crash Avoidance:
  Collision Avoidance . . . . None
  Blind Spot Detection . . . . None
  Lane Keeping Assist . . . . None
  Backup Camera. . . . . None
  Pedestrian Crash Avoidance . . . . None
General:
  Auto. Crash Notification . . . . None
  Day Running Lamps . . . . None
Safety Belt/Restraint:
  Dynamic Head Restraints . . . . None
  Adjustable Belt. None

Mazda MX-5 Miata

Specifications

Drive. . . . . .RWD
Engine 2.0-liter I4
Transmission . . . . .6-sp. Automatic
Tow Rating (lbs.) . . . . –
Head/Leg Room (in.) Cramped-37.4/43.1
Interior Space (cu. ft.). . . . . –
Cargo Space (cu. ft.) . . . . .Very Cramped-5.3
Wheelbase/Length (in.) 91.7/157.3

Ratings—10 Best, 1 Worst

Combo Crash Tests	–
Safety Features	10
Rollover	8
Preventive Maintenance	3
Repair Costs	3
Warranty	3
Fuel Economy	6
Complaints	–
Insurance Costs	8
OVERALL RATING	**–**

Mercedes-Benz C-Class

At-a-Glance

Status/Year Series Started. . . . . All New/2015
Twins . . . . –
Body Styles . . . . .Sedan, Coupe, Wagon
Seating 5
Anti-Theft Device . Std. Active Immobil. & Pass. Alarm
Parking Index Rating . . . . Average
Where Made. . . . . Tuscaloosa, AL
Fuel Factor . . . .
  MPG Rating (city/hwy) Average-22/31
  Driving Range (mi.) Long-455.5
  Fuel Type. . . . . .Premium
  Annual Fuel Cost . . . . Average-$1,896
  Gas Guzzler Tax . . . . .No
  Greenhouse Gas Emissions (tons/yr.). . Average-7.2
  Barrels of Oil Used per year High-13.2

How the Competition Rates

Competitors	Rating	Pg.
Audi A4	6	87
BMW 3 Series	9	94
Lexus IS	5	190

Price Range	Retail	Markup
C250	$38,200	8%
C350	$43,850	8%
C350 4Matic	$45,850	8%
C60 AMG	$62,750	8%

Mercedes-Benz C-Class

Safety Checklist

Crash Tests:
  Frontal. . . . . –
  Side. . . . .–
Airbags:
  Torso . . . . Fr. & Rr. Torso from Seat
  Pelvis . . . . None
  Roll Sensing. . . . . .Yes
  Knee Bolster . . . . Standard Driver
Crash Avoidance:
  Collision Avoidance . . . . . . Standard CIB & DBS
  Blind Spot Detection . . . . Optional
  Lane Keeping Assist . . . . Optional
  Backup Camera . . . . Optional
  Pedestrian Crash Avoidance . . . . Optional
General:
  Auto. Crash Notification . . . Operator Assist.-Fee
  Day Running Lamps . . . . Standard
Safety Belt/Restraint:
  Dynamic Head Restraints . . . . None
  Adjustable Belt. . . . . .Standard Front

Mercedes-Benz C-Class

Specifications

Drive. . . . . .RWD
Engine 2.0-liter I4
Transmission . . . . .7-sp. Automatic
Tow Rating (lbs.) . . . . –
Head/Leg Room (in.) . . . . .Very Cramped-37.1/41.7
Interior Space (cu. ft.). . . . . Very Cramped-81
Cargo Space (cu. ft.) . . . . .Very Cramped-12.8
Wheelbase/Length (in.) 111.8/184.5

Mercedes-Benz CLA-Class

Ratings—10 Best, 1 Worst

Combo Crash Tests	–
Safety Features	9
Rollover	7
Preventive Maintenance	2
Repair Costs	2
Warranty	3
Fuel Economy	8
Complaints	1
Insurance Costs	5
OVERALL RATING	–

Mercedes-Benz CLA-Class

At-a-Glance

Status/Year Series Started Unchanged/2014
Twins . . . . –
Body Styles . . . . .Coupe
Seating 5
Anti-Theft Device . Std. Active Immobil. & Pass. Alarm
Parking Index Rating . . . . Easy
Where Made . . . . Kecskemet, Hungary
Fuel Factor . . . .
  MPG Rating (city/hwy) Good-26/38
  Driving Range (mi.) Average-400.0
  Fuel Type . . . . .Premium
  Annual Fuel Cost . . . . Low-$1,583
  Gas Guzzler Tax . . . . .No
  Greenhouse Gas Emissions (tons/yr.) Low-6.1
  Barrels of Oil Used per year Average-11.0

How the Competition Rates

Competitors	Rating	Pg.
Acura ILX	7	81
Cadillac ATS	9	107
Infiniti Q50	–	163

Price Range	Retail	Markup
CLA250	$29,900	8%
CLA250 4Matic	$31,900	8%
CLA45 AMG	$47,450	8%

Mercedes-Benz CLA-Class

Safety Checklist

Crash Tests:
  Frontal . . . . –
  Sidel . . . . –
Airbags:
  Torso . . . . Fr. & Rr. Torso from Seat
  Pelvis . . . . None
  Roll Sensing . . . . .Yes
  Knee Bolster . . . . .Standard Front
Crash Avoidance:
  Collision Avoidance . . . . . .Standard CIB & DBS
  Blind Spot Detection . . . . Optional
  Lane Keeping Assist . . . .Warning Only Optional
  Backup Camera . . . . None
  Pedestrian Crash Avoidance . . . . None
General:
  Auto. Crash Notification . . . Operator Assist.-Fee
  Day Running Lamps . . . . Standard
Safety Belt/Restraint:
  Dynamic Head Restraints . . . . None
  Adjustable Belt . . . . .Standard Front

Mercedes-Benz CLA-Class

Specifications

Drive . . . . FWD
Engine 2.0-liter I4
Transmission . . . . .7-sp. Automatic
Tow Rating (lbs.) . . . . –
Head/Leg Room (in.) . . . . .Very Cramped-38.2/40.2
Interior Space (cu. ft.) . . . . Very Cramped-88
Cargo Space (cu. ft.) . . . . Very Cramped-13
Wheelbase/Length (in.) 106.3/182.3

Ratings—10 Best, 1 Worst

Combo Crash Tests	3
Safety Features	10
Rollover	8
Preventive Maintenance	2
Repair Costs	2
Warranty	3
Fuel Economy	5
Complaints	9
Insurance Costs	5
OVERALL RATING	**4**

Mercedes-Benz E-Class

Mercedes-Benz E-Class

At-a-Glance

Status/Year Series Started........	Unchanged/2010
Twins...........................	–
Body Styles	Sedan, Coupe, Wagon, Convertible
Seating..............	5
Anti-Theft Device .	Std. Active Immobil. & Pass. Alarm
Parking Index Rating............	Average
Where Made..............	Sindelfingen, Germany
Fuel Factor....................	
MPG Rating (city/hwy).........	Average-20/29
Driving Range (mi.)...........	Very Long-490.5
Fuel Type..................	Premium
Annual Fuel Cost............	High-$2,064
Gas Guzzler Tax............	No
Greenhouse Gas Emissions (tons/yr.).....	High-7.8
Barrels of Oil Used per year..........	High-14.3

How the Competition Rates

Competitors	Rating	Pg.
Audi A6	7	89
BMW 5 Series	8	96
Lexus GS	–	188

Price Range

	Retail	Markup
E250 Sport	$51,400	8%
E350 Luxury 4Matic	$54,400	8%
E400 Hybrid	$56,700	8%
E63 AMG S 4Matic	$102,370	8%

Safety Checklist

Crash Tests:
Frontal.........................Very Poor
Side.............................Average

Airbags:
Torso............. Fr. & Rr. Torso from Seat
Pelvis..............Front Pelvis from Seat
Roll Sensing..........................Yes
Knee Bolster.............. Standard Driver

Crash Avoidance:
Collision Avoidance......Standard CIB & DBS
Blind Spot Detection.............. Optional
Lane Keeping Assist.............. Optional
Backup Camera.................. Optional
Pedestrian Crash Avoidance......... Optional

General:
Auto. Crash Notification... Operator Assist.-Fee
Day Running Lamps.............. Standard

Safety Belt/Restraint:
Dynamic Head Restraints......Standard Front
Adjustable Belt.......Standard Front and Rear

Mercedes-Benz E-Class

Specifications

Drive.................................	RWD
Engine..........................	3.5-liter V6
Transmission...................	7-sp. Automatic
Tow Rating (lbs.)......................	–
Head/Leg Room (in.).....	Very Cramped-37.9/41.3
Interior Space (cu. ft.)..............	Average-98
Cargo Space (cu. ft.).........	Very Cramped-12.9
Wheelbase/Length (in.)..............	113.2/192.1

Mercedes-Benz GLA-Class   Small SUV

Ratings—10 Best, 1 Worst

Combo Crash Tests	–
Safety Features	9
Rollover	5
Preventive Maintenance	–
Repair Costs	–
Warranty	3
Fuel Economy	6
Complaints	–
Insurance Costs	5
OVERALL RATING	–

Mercedes-Benz GLA-Class

Mercedes-Benz GLA-Class

Mercedes-Benz GLA-Class

At-a-Glance

Status/Year Series Started. . . . . All New/2015
Twins . . . .–
Body Styles . . . . SUV
Seating 5
Anti-Theft Device . Std. Active Immobil. & Pass. Alarm
Parking Index Rating . . . . Average
Where Made. . . . . .Rastatt, Germany
Fuel Factor . . . .
MPG Rating (city/hwy) Average-24/32
Driving Range (mi.) Average-400.2
Fuel Type . . . . .Premium
Annual Fuel Cost . . . . Average-$1,775
Gas Guzzler Tax . . . . .No
Greenhouse Gas Emissions (tons/yr.). . Average-6.7
Barrels of Oil Used per year Average-12.2

How the Competition Rates

Competitors	Rating	Pg.
Audi Q3	–	91
Lexus NX	–	191
Porsche Macon	–	233

Price Range

Price Range	Retail	Markup
GLA250	$31,300	8%
GLA250 4Matic	$33,300	8%
GLA45 AMG 4Matic	$48,300	8%

Safety Checklist

Crash Tests:
Frontal. . . . .–
Sidel . . . .–
Airbags:
Torso . . . . Fr. & Rr. Torso from Seat
Pelvis . . . . None
Roll Sensing. . . . . .Yes
Knee Bolster . . . . .Standard Front
Crash Avoidance:
Collision Avoidance . . . . . . Standard CIB & DBS
Blind Spot Detection . . . . Optional
Lane Keeping Assist . . . .Warning Only Optional
Backup Camera . . . . Optional
Pedestrian Crash Avoidance . . . . None
General:
Auto. Crash Notification . . . Operator Assist.-Fee
Day Running Lamps . . . . Standard
Safety Belt/Restraint:
Dynamic Head Restraints . . . . None
Adjustable Belt. None

Mercedes-Benz GLA-Class

Specifications

Drive. . . . . .AWD
Engine 2.0-liter I4
Transmission . . . . .7-sp. Automatic
Tow Rating (lbs.) . . . .
Head/Leg Room (in.) Cramped-38.3/41.9
Interior Space (cu. ft.). . . . .
Cargo Space (cu. ft.) Average-17.2
Wheelbase/Length (in.) 106.3/173.9

Mercedes-Benz GL-Class Large SUV

Ratings—10 Best, 1 Worst

Combo Crash Tests	–
Safety Features	9
Rollover	2
Preventive Maintenance	2
Repair Costs	2
Warranty	3
Fuel Economy	2
Complaints	8
Insurance Costs	8
OVERALL RATING	**–**

Mercedes-Benz GL-Class

Mercedes-Benz GL-Class

At-a-Glance

Status/Year Series Started........ Unchanged/2007
Twins ....–
Body Styles .... SUV
Seating.....................................7
Anti-Theft Device . Std. Active Immobil. & Pass. Alarm
Parking Index Rating ....Very Hard
Where Made.................. Tuscaloosa, AL
Fuel Factor............................
  MPG Rating (city/hwy) ....Very Poor-17/21
  Driving Range (mi.) ....Very Long-490.9
  Fuel Type........................Premium
  Annual Fuel Cost .... Very High-$2,581
  Gas Guzzler Tax ....No
  Greenhouse Gas Emissions (tons/yr.)..... High-9.4
  Barrels of Oil Used per year ....Very High-17.3

How the Competition Rates

Competitors	Rating	Pg.
Audi Q7	–	93
Infiniti QX80	–	168
Lexus GX	–	189

Price Range	Retail	Markup
GL350	$63,600	8%
GL450	$65,200	8%
GL550	$89,950	8%
GL63 AMG	$119,450	8%

Safety Checklist

Crash Tests:
  Frontal.................................–
  Sidel ....–
Airbags:
  Torso .... Fr. & Rr. Torso from Seat
  Pelvis .... None
  Roll Sensing........................Yes
  Knee Bolster .... Standard Driver
Crash Avoidance:
  Collision Avoidance ...... Std. DBS & Opt. CIB
  Blind Spot Detection .... Optional
  Lane Keeping Assist .... Optional
  Backup Camera................... Standard
  Pedestrian Crash Avoidance .... None
General:
  Auto. Crash Notification... Operator Assist.-Fee
  Day Running Lamps .... Standard
Safety Belt/Restraint:
  Dynamic Head Restraints .... None
  Adjustable Belt...............Standard Front

Mercedes-Benz GL-Class

Specifications

Drive............................... 4WD
Engine 3.0-liter V6
Transmission ....7-sp. Automatic
Tow Rating (lbs.) High-7500
Head/Leg Room (in.) Average-41.2/40.3
Interior Space (cu. ft.)........ Very Roomy-127.6
Cargo Space (cu. ft.) Cramped-16
Wheelbase/Length (in.) 121.1/201.6

Ratings—10 Best, 1 Worst

Combo Crash Tests	–
Safety Features	9
Rollover	3
Preventive Maintenance	1
Repair Costs	2
Warranty	3
Fuel Economy	3
Complaints	3
Insurance Costs	5

OVERALL RATING   –

Mercedes-Benz GLK-Class

At-a-Glance

Status/Year Series Started........ Unchanged/2010
Twins . . . .–
Body Styles . . . . SUV
Seating 5
Anti-Theft Device . Std. Active Immobil. & Pass. Alarm
Parking Index Rating . . . . Average
Where Made. . . . . Bremen, Germany
Fuel Factor . . . .
  MPG Rating (city/hwy) Poor-18/25
  Driving Range (mi.) . . . . Very Short-358.4
  Fuel Type . . . . .Premium
  Annual Fuel Cost . . . . High-$2,330
  Gas Guzzler Tax . . . . .No
  Greenhouse Gas Emissions (tons/yr.). High-8.6
  Barrels of Oil Used per year High-15.7

How the Competition Rates

Competitors	Rating	Pg.
Audi Q5	4	92
BMW X3	8	100
Lexus RX	6	192

Price Range

Price Range	Retail	Markup
GLK350	$37,900	8%
GLK250 4Matic	$39,400	8%
GLK350 4Matic	$39,900	8%

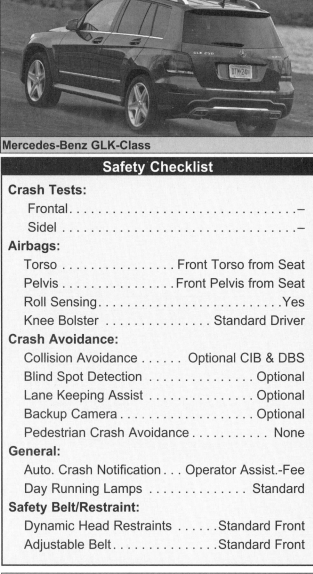

Mercedes-Benz GLK-Class

Safety Checklist

Crash Tests:
  Frontal. . . . .–
  Sidel . . . .–
Airbags:
  Torso . . . . Front Torso from Seat
  Pelvis . . . . .Front Pelvis from Seat
  Roll Sensing. . . . . .Yes
  Knee Bolster . . . . Standard Driver
Crash Avoidance:
  Collision Avoidance . . . . . . Optional CIB & DBS
  Blind Spot Detection . . . . Optional
  Lane Keeping Assist . . . . Optional
  Backup Camera . . . . Optional
  Pedestrian Crash Avoidance . . . . None
General:
  Auto. Crash Notification . . . Operator Assist.-Fee
  Day Running Lamps . . . . Standard
Safety Belt/Restraint:
  Dynamic Head Restraints . . . . . .Standard Front
  Adjustable Belt. . . . . .Standard Front

Mercedes-Benz GLK-Class

Specifications

Drive. 4WD
Engine 3.5-liter V6
Transmission . . . . .7-sp. Automatic
Tow Rating (lbs.) Low-3500
Head/Leg Room (in.) Cramped-39/41.4
Interior Space (cu. ft.). . . . . .Very Cramped-79.5
Cargo Space (cu. ft.) Cramped-16.5
Wheelbase/Length (in.) 108.5/178.3

Ratings—10 Best, 1 Worst

Combo Crash Tests	10
Safety Features	9
Rollover	3
Preventive Maintenance	1
Repair Costs	1
Warranty	3
Fuel Economy	2
Complaints	10
Insurance Costs	5
OVERALL RATING	**5**

Mercedes-Benz M-Class

Mercedes-Benz M-Class

At-a-Glance

Status/Year Series Started	Unchanged/2012
Twins	–
Body Styles	SUV
Seating	5
Anti-Theft Device	Std. Active Immobil. & Pass. Alarm
Parking Index Rating	Hard
Where Made	Tuscaloosa, AL
Fuel Factor	
MPG Rating (city/hwy)	Very Poor-17/22
Driving Range (mi.)	Long-465.8
Fuel Type	Premium
Annual Fuel Cost	Very High-$2,534
Gas Guzzler Tax	No
Greenhouse Gas Emissions (tons/yr.)	High-9.4
Barrels of Oil Used per year	Very High-17.3

How the Competition Rates

Competitors	Rating	Pg.
Audi Q5	4	92
BMW X5	6	101
Volvo XC60	9	270

Price Range	Retail	Markup
ML250	$49,800	8%
ML350 4Matic	$50,800	8%
ML400 4Matic	$62,900	8%
ML63 AMG	$98,400	8%

Safety Checklist

Crash Tests:
Frontal	Very Good
Side	Very Good

Airbags:
Torso	Fr. & Rr. Pelvis/Torso from Seat
Pelvis	Fr. & Rr. Pelvis/Torso from Seat
Roll Sensing	Yes
Knee Bolster	Standard Driver

Crash Avoidance:
Collision Avoidance	Std. DBS & Opt. CIB
Blind Spot Detection	Optional
Lane Keeping Assist	Optional
Backup Camera	Optional
Pedestrian Crash Avoidance	None

General:
Auto. Crash Notification	Operator Assist.-Fee
Day Running Lamps	Standard

Safety Belt/Restraint:
Dynamic Head Restraints	None
Adjustable Belt	Standard Front

Mercedes-Benz M-Class

Specifications

Drive	4WD
Engine	3.5-liter V6
Transmission	7-sp. Automatic
Tow Rating (lbs.)	Average-7200
Head/Leg Room (in.)	Cramped-40.4/40.33
Interior Space (cu. ft.)	Very Roomy-123.2
Cargo Space (cu. ft.)	Very Roomy-38.2
Wheelbase/Length (in.)	114.8/189.1

Ratings—10 Best, 1 Worst

Combo Crash Tests	–
Safety Features	10
Rollover	8
Preventive Maintenance	2
Repair Costs	1
Warranty	3
Fuel Economy	3
Complaints	7
Insurance Costs	1
OVERALL RATING	**–**

Mercedes-Benz S-Class

At-a-Glance

Status/Year Series Started	Unchanged/2014
Twins	–
Body Styles	Sedan, Coupe
Seating	5
Anti-Theft Device	
Parking Index Rating	Very Hard
Where Made	Sindelfingen, Germany
Fuel Factor	
MPG Rating (city/hwy)	Poor-17/26
Driving Range (mi.)	Long-424.9
Fuel Type	Premium
Annual Fuel Cost	Very High-$2,383
Gas Guzzler Tax	No
Greenhouse Gas Emissions (tons/yr.)	High-9.0
Barrels of Oil Used per year	High-16.5

How the Competition Rates

Competitors	Rating	Pg.
Acura RLX	–	84
BMW 7 Series	–	98
Cadillac XTS	9	110

Price Range

Price Range	Retail	Markup
S550	$94,400	8%
S550 4Matic	$97,400	8%
S600	$166,900	8%
S65 AMG	$222,000	8%

Mercedes-Benz S-Class

Safety Checklist

Crash Tests:
Frontal . . . .–
Side . . . .–

Airbags:
Torso . . . . Fr. & Rr. Torso from Seat
Pelvis . . . . None
Roll Sensing . . . . .Yes
Knee Bolster . . . . Standard Front

Crash Avoidance:
Collision Avoidance . . . . . . Standard CIB & DBS
Blind Spot Detection . . . . Optional
Lane Keeping Assist . . . . Optional
Backup Camera . . . . Standard
Pedestrian Crash Avoidance . . . . Optional

General:
Auto. Crash Notification . . . Operator Assist.-Fee
Day Running Lamps . . . . Standard

Safety Belt/Restraint:
Dynamic Head Restraints . . . . None
Adjustable Belt . . . . .Standard Front

Mercedes-Benz S-Class

Specifications

Drive	RWD
Engine	4.7-liter V8
Transmission	7-sp. Automatic
Tow Rating (lbs.)	–
Head/Leg Room (in.)	Average-39.7/41.4
Interior Space (cu. ft.)	Roomy-112
Cargo Space (cu. ft.)	Cramped-16.5
Wheelbase/Length (in.)	124.6/206.5

Ratings—10 Best, 1 Worst

Combo Crash Tests	–
Safety Features	2
Rollover	7
Preventive Maintenance	10
Repair Costs	4
Warranty	9
Fuel Economy	9
Complaints	4
Insurance Costs	5
OVERALL RATING	**–**

Mini Cooper

Mini Cooper

At-a-Glance

Status/Year Series Started. Unchanged/2014
Twins . . . . –
Body Styles . . . . Hatchback
Seating 4
Anti-Theft Device . . . . Std. Passive Alarm Only
Parking Index Rating . . . . .Very Easy
Where Made. . . . . .Oxford, England
Fuel Factor . . . .
  MPG Rating (city/hwy) . . . . Very Good-28/37
  Driving Range (mi.) . . . . Very Short-364.7
  Fuel Type . . . . .Premium
  Annual Fuel Cost . . . . Low-$1,526
  Gas Guzzler Tax . . . . .No
  Greenhouse Gas Emissions (tons/yr.). Low-5.8
  Barrels of Oil Used per year Low-10.6

How the Competition Rates

Competitors	Rating	Pg.
Kia Soul	7	181
Scion xB	–	237
Volkswagen Beetle	3	261

Price Range

Price Range	Retail	Markup
Base Hatchback	$20,450	9%
S Coupe	$25,300	9%
S Convertible	$28,700	9%
John Cooper Works Roadster	$36,250	9%

Safety Checklist

Crash Tests:
  Frontal. . . . .–
  Side. . . . .–
Airbags:
  Torso . . . . Front Head/Torso from Seat
  Pelvis . . . . None
  Roll Sensing. . . . . No
  Knee Bolster . . . . None
Crash Avoidance:
  Collision Avoidance . . . . . . Optional CIB & DBS
  Blind Spot Detection . . . . None
  Lane Keeping Assist . . . . None
  Backup Camera . . . . None
  Pedestrian Crash Avoidance . . . . Optional
General:
  Auto. Crash Notification . . . . None
  Day Running Lamps . . . . Standard
Safety Belt/Restraint:
  Dynamic Head Restraints . . . . None
  Adjustable Belt. . . . . None

Mini Cooper

Specifications

Drive. . . . . .FWD
Engine 1.5-liter I3
Transmission . . . . .6-sp. Automatic
Tow Rating (lbs.) . . . . –
Head/Leg Room (in.) Average-40.3/41.4
Interior Space (cu. ft.). . . . . Very Cramped-80
Cargo Space (cu. ft.) . . . . .Very Cramped-8.7
Wheelbase/Length (in.) 98.2/151.1

Ratings—10 Best, 1 Worst

Combo Crash Tests	–
Safety Features	2
Rollover	5
Preventive Maintenance	10
Repair Costs	6
Warranty	9
Fuel Economy	8
Complaints	10
Insurance Costs	5
OVERALL RATING	**–**

Mini Countryman

Mini Countryman

At-a-Glance

Status/Year Series Started........ Unchanged/2012
Twins . . . . –
Body Styles . . . . Hatchback
Seating 5
Anti-Theft Device . . . . Std. Passive Alarm Only
Parking Index Rating . . . . Easy
Where Made. . . . . Oxford, England
Fuel Factor . . . .
  MPG Rating (city/hwy) Good-27/34
  Driving Range (mi.) . . . . Very Short-369.0
  Fuel Type . . . . .Premium
  Annual Fuel Cost . . . . Low-$1,613
  Gas Guzzler Tax . . . . .No
  Greenhouse Gas Emissions (tons/yr.) Low-6.0
  Barrels of Oil Used per year Average-11.0

How the Competition Rates

Competitors	Rating	Pg.
Kia Soul	7	181
Nissan Juke	–	221
Subaru Impreza	4	241

Price Range

Price Range	Retail	Markup
Base	$22,750	9%
S	$26,100	9%
S ALL4	$27,850	9%
John Cooper Works ALL4	$35,350	9%

Safety Checklist

Crash Tests:
  Frontal . . . . –
  Side . . . . –
Airbags:
  Torso . . . . Front Torso from Seat
  Pelvis . . . . None
  Roll Sensing. . . . . .Yes
  Knee Bolster . . . . Standard Passenger
Crash Avoidance:
  Collision Avoidance . . . . None
  Blind Spot Detection . . . . None
  Lane Keeping Assist . . . . None
  Backup Camera . . . . None
  Pedestrian Crash Avoidance . . . . None
General:
  Auto. Crash Notification . . . . None
  Day Running Lamps . . . . Standard
Safety Belt/Restraint:
  Dynamic Head Restraints . . . . None
  Adjustable Belt . . . . None

Mini Countryman

Specifications

Drive . . . . .FWD
Engine 1.6-liter I4
Transmission . . . . .6-sp. Manual
Tow Rating (lbs.) . . . . –
Head/Leg Room (in.) Cramped-39.9/40.4
Interior Space (cu. ft.). . . . . Very Cramped-87
Cargo Space (cu. ft.) Average-17.5
Wheelbase/Length (in.) 102.2/162.2

Ratings—10 Best, 1 Worst

Combo Crash Tests	2
Safety Features	2
Rollover	6
Preventive Maintenance	9
Repair Costs	5
Warranty	4
Fuel Economy	8
Complaints	5
Insurance Costs	1
OVERALL RATING	**2**

Mitsubishi Lancer

At-a-Glance

Status/Year Series Started	Unchanged/2008
Twins	–
Body Styles	Sedan
Seating	5
Anti-Theft Device	Std. Pass. Immobil. & Alarm
Parking Index Rating	Very Easy
Where Made	Mizushima, Japan
Fuel Factor	
MPG Rating (city/hwy)	Good-26/34
Driving Range (mi.)	Long-450.7
Fuel Type	Regular
Annual Fuel Cost	Low-$1,444
Gas Guzzler Tax	No
Greenhouse Gas Emissions (tons/yr.)	Low-6.2
Barrels of Oil Used per year	Average-11.4

How the Competition Rates

Competitors	Rating	Pg.
Honda Civic	6	149
Mazda Mazda3	5	199
Subaru Impreza	4	241

Price Range	Retail	Markup
ES MT	$17,395	4%
GT AT	$21,595	4%
Ralliart AWD	$29,495	4%
Evolution MR Touring AWD	$40,995	5%

Mitsubishi Lancer

Safety Checklist

Crash Tests:
Frontal	Poor
Side	Very Poor

Airbags:
Torso	Front Pelvis/Torso from Seat
Pelvis	Front Pelvis/Torso from Seat
Roll Sensing	No
Knee Bolster	Standard Driver

Crash Avoidance:
Collision Avoidance	None
Blind Spot Detection	None
Lane Keeping Assist	None
Backup Camera	None
Pedestrian Crash Avoidance	None

General:
Auto. Crash Notification	None
Day Running Lamps	Optional

Safety Belt/Restraint:
Dynamic Head Restraints	None
Adjustable Belt	Standard Front

Mitsubishi Lancer

Specifications

Drive	FWD
Engine	2.0-liter I4
Transmission	CVT
Tow Rating (lbs.)	–
Head/Leg Room (in.)	Average-39.6/42.3
Interior Space (cu. ft.)	Cramped-93.5
Cargo Space (cu. ft.)	Very Cramped-12.3
Wheelbase/Length (in.)	103.7/180

Ratings—10 Best, 1 Worst

Combo Crash Tests	2
Safety Features	2
Rollover	3
Preventive Maintenance	–
Repair Costs	–
Warranty	10
Fuel Economy	10
Complaints	6
Insurance Costs	3
OVERALL RATING	**3**

Mitsubishi Mirage

Mitsubishi Mirage

At-a-Glance

Status/Year Series Started Unchanged/2014
Twins . . . . –
Body Styles . . . . Hatchback
Seating 5
Anti-Theft Device . Std. Pass. Immobil. & Active Alarm
Parking Index Rating . . . . .Very Easy
Where Made. . . . . .Laem Chabang, Thailand
Fuel Factor . . . .
　MPG Rating (city/hwy) . . . . Very Good-37/44
　Driving Range (mi.) . . . . Very Short-366.6
　Fuel Type. . . . . .Regular
　Annual Fuel Cost . . . . Very Low-$1,053
　Gas Guzzler Tax . . . . .No
　Greenhouse Gas Emissions (tons/yr.). Very Low-4.5
　Barrels of Oil Used per year . . . . Very Low-8.2

How the Competition Rates

Competitors	Rating	Pg.
Ford Fiesta	2	142
Nissan Versa	2	230
Toyota Yaris	5	260

Price Range	Retail	Markup
DE MT	$12,995	2%
DE AT	$14,095	2%
ES MT	$14,295	2%
ES AT	$15,395	2%

Safety Checklist

Crash Tests:
　Frontal. . . . . .Poor
　Side. . . . . .Very Poor
Airbags:
　Torso . . . . .Front Pelvis/Torso from Seat
　Pelvis . . . . .Front Pelvis/Torso from Seat
　Roll Sensing. . . . . No
　Knee Bolster . . . . Standard Driver
Crash Avoidance:
　Collision Avoidance . . . . None
　Blind Spot Detection . . . . None
　Lane Keeping Assist . . . . None
　Backup Camera . . . . Optional
　Pedestrian Crash Avoidance . . . . None
General:
　Auto. Crash Notification . . . . None
　Day Running Lamps . . . . None
Safety Belt/Restraint:
　Dynamic Head Restraints . . . . None
　Adjustable Belt. . . . . .Standard Front

Mitsubishi Mirage

Specifications

Drive. . . . . FWD
Engine 1.2-liter I3
Transmission . . . . .CVT
Tow Rating (lbs.) . . . . –
Head/Leg Room (in.) Cramped-39.1/41.7
Interior Space (cu. ft.). . . . . .Very Cramped-86.1
Cargo Space (cu. ft.) Average-17.2
Wheelbase/Length (in.) 96.5/148.8

Ratings—10 Best, 1 Worst

Combo Crash Tests	5
Safety Features	6
Rollover	3
Preventive Maintenance	4
Repair Costs	7
Warranty	10
Fuel Economy	6
Complaints	1
Insurance Costs	3
OVERALL RATING	**4**

Mitsubishi Outlander

Mitsubishi Outlander

At-a-Glance

Status/Year Series Started Appearance Change/2014
Twins . . . . –
Body Styles . . . . SUV
Seating 7
Anti-Theft Device . . . . . . Std. Pass. Immobil. & Alarm
Parking Index Rating . . . . Easy
Where Made. . . . Mizushima, Japan / Okazaki, Japan
Fuel Factor . . . .
  MPG Rating (city/hwy) Average-24/29
  Driving Range (mi.) Average-411.1
  Fuel Type . . . . .Regular
  Annual Fuel Cost . . . . Low-$1,614
  Gas Guzzler Tax . . . . .No
  Greenhouse Gas Emissions (tons/yr.) . . Average-6.9
  Barrels of Oil Used per year Average-12.7

How the Competition Rates

Competitors	Rating	Pg.
Hyundai Santa Fe	–	158
Nissan Pathfinder	–	225
Toyota Highlander	7	250

Price Range	Retail	Markup
ES 2WD	$23,195	3%
SE 2WD	$24,195	3%
SE AWD	$26,195	3%
GT AWD	$28,195	3%

Safety Checklist

Crash Tests:
  Frontal . . . . Average
  Side . . . . .Poor
Airbags:
  Torso . . . . .Front Pelvis/Torso from Seat
  Pelvis . . . . .Front Pelvis/Torso from Seat
  Roll Sensing. . . . . .Yes
  Knee Bolster . . . . Standard Driver
Crash Avoidance:
  Collision Avoidance . . . . . . Optional CIB & DBS
  Blind Spot Detection . . . . None
  Lane Keeping Assist . . . .Warning Only Optional
  Backup Camera . . . . Optional
  Pedestrian Crash Avoidance . . . . None
General:
  Auto. Crash Notification . . . . None
  Day Running Lamps . . . . None
Safety Belt/Restraint:
  Dynamic Head Restraints . . . . None
  Adjustable Belt . . . . .Standard Front

Mitsubishi Outlander

Specifications

Drive 4WD
Engine 2.4-liter I4
Transmission . . . . .CVT
Tow Rating (lbs.) . . . . Very Low-1500
Head/Leg Room (in.) Average-40.6/40.9
Interior Space (cu. ft.). . . . . Very Roomy-128.2
Cargo Space (cu. ft.) . . . . . .Very Cramped-10.3
Wheelbase/Length (in.) 105.1/183.3

Mitsubishi Outlander Sport

Small SUV

Ratings—10 Best, 1 Worst

Combo Crash Tests	4
Safety Features	4
Rollover	2
Preventive Maintenance	6
Repair Costs	3
Warranty	10
Fuel Economy	7
Complaints	10
Insurance Costs	1
OVERALL RATING	**4**

Mitsubishi Outlander Sport

Mitsubishi Outlander Sport

At-a-Glance

Status/Year Series Started. Unchanged/2013
Twins . . . . –
Body Styles . . . . SUV
Seating 5
Anti-Theft Device . . . . . . Std. Pass. Immobil. & Alarm
Parking Index Rating . . . . .Very Easy
Where Made. .Normal, IL
Fuel Factor . . . .
  MPG Rating (city/hwy) Good-25/32
  Driving Range (mi.) Average-424.3
  Fuel Type . . . . .Regular
  Annual Fuel Cost . . . . Low-$1,514
  Gas Guzzler Tax . . . . .No
  Greenhouse Gas Emissions (tons/yr.). Low-6.4
  Barrels of Oil Used per year Average-11.8

How the Competition Rates

Competitors	Rating	Pg.
Acura RDX	8	83
Hyundai Santa Fe Sport	7	159
Jeep Cherokee	4	169

Price Range

Price Range	Retail	Markup
ES 2WD MT	$19,595	3%
ES 2WD AT	$20,795	3%
ES 4WD	$22,195	3%
SE 4WD	$24,195	3%

Safety Checklist

Crash Tests:
  Frontal. . . . . Average
  Side. . . . . .Poor
Airbags:
  Torso . . . . .Front Pelvis/Torso from Seat
  Pelvis . . . . .Front Pelvis/Torso from Seat
  Roll Sensing. . . . . .Yes
  Knee Bolster . . . . Standard Driver
Crash Avoidance:
  Collision Avoidance . . . . None
  Blind Spot Detection . . . . None
  Lane Keeping Assist . . . . None
  Backup Camera . . . . Optional
  Pedestrian Crash Avoidance . . . . None
General:
  Auto. Crash Notification . . . . None
  Day Running Lamps . . . . Optional
Safety Belt/Restraint:
  Dynamic Head Restraints . . . . None
  Adjustable Belt . . . . .Standard Front

Mitsubishi Outlander Sport

Specifications

Drive. . . . . FWD
Engine 2.0-liter I4
Transmission . . . . .CVT
Tow Rating (lbs.) . . . . –
Head/Leg Room (in.) Cramped-39.4/41.6
Interior Space (cu. ft.). Cramped-97.5
Cargo Space (cu. ft.) Average-21.7
Wheelbase/Length (in.) 105.1/169.1

216

Ratings—10 Best, 1 Worst

Combo Crash Tests	–
Safety Features	2
Rollover	10
Preventive Maintenance	1
Repair Costs	3
Warranty	1
Fuel Economy	3
Complaints	6
Insurance Costs	5
OVERALL RATING	**–**

Nissan 370Z

Nissan 370Z

At-a-Glance

Status/Year Series Started	Unchanged/2010
Twins	–
Body Styles	Coupe, Convertible
Seating	2
Anti-Theft Device	Std. Pass. Immobil. & Alarm
Parking Index Rating	Very Easy
Where Made	Tochigi, Japan
Fuel Factor	
MPG Rating (city/hwy)	Poor-19/26
Driving Range (mi.)	Average-410.8
Fuel Type	Premium
Annual Fuel Cost	High-$2,220
Gas Guzzler Tax	No
Greenhouse Gas Emissions (tons/yr.)	Average-7.6
Barrels of Oil Used per year	High-15.7

How the Competition Rates

Competitors	Rating	Pg.
Mazda MX-5 Miata	–	202
Scion FR-S	3	235
Subaru BRZ	2	239

Price Range

	Retail	Markup
Base Coupe MT	$29,990	10%
Sport Tech Coupe AT	$38,370	10%
Nismo Tech Coupe AT	$46,790	10%
Touring Sport Roadster AT	$49,400	10%

Safety Checklist

Crash Tests:
Frontal . . . . –
Side . . . . –

Airbags:
Torso . . . . Front Pelvis/Torso from Seat
Pelvis . . . . Front Pelvis/Torso from Seat
Roll Sensing . . . . No
Knee Bolster . . . . None

Crash Avoidance:
Collision Avoidance . . . . None
Blind Spot Detection . . . . None
Lane Keeping Assist . . . . None
Backup Camera . . . . Optional
Pedestrian Crash Avoidance . . . . None

General:
Auto. Crash Notification . . . . None
Day Running Lamps . . . . Standard

Safety Belt/Restraint:
Dynamic Head Restraints . . . . . . Standard Front
Adjustable Belt . . . . None

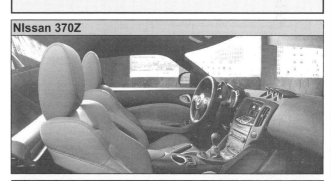

Nissan 370Z

Specifications

Drive	RWD
Engine	3.7-liter V6
Transmission	7-sp. Automatic
Tow Rating (lbs.)	Very Low-0
Head/Leg Room (in.)	Average-38.2/42.9
Interior Space (cu. ft.)	Very Cramped-51.6
Cargo Space (cu. ft.)	Very Cramped-6.9
Wheelbase/Length (in.)	100.4/167.5

Ratings—10 Best, 1 Worst

Combo Crash Tests	6
Safety Features	4
Rollover	7
Preventive Maintenance	8
Repair Costs	8
Warranty	1
Fuel Economy	9
Complaints	3
Insurance Costs	1
OVERALL RATING	**5**

Nissan Altima

Nissan Altima

At-a-Glance

Status/Year Series Started........ Unchanged/2013
Twins . . . . –
Body Styles . . . . .Sedan
Seating 5
Anti-Theft Device . . . . . . Std. Pass. Immobil. & Alarm
Parking Index Rating . . . . Easy
Where Made. . . . . Smyrna, TN / Canton, MS
Fuel Factor . . . .
  MPG Rating (city/hwy) . . . . Very Good-27/38
  Driving Range (mi.) . . . . .Very Long-558.8
  Fuel Type. . . . . .Regular
  Annual Fuel Cost . . . . Very Low-$1,352
  Gas Guzzler Tax . . . . .No
  Greenhouse Gas Emissions (tons/yr.). Low-5.8
  Barrels of Oil Used per year Low-10.6

How the Competition Rates

Competitors	Rating	Pg.
Honda Accord	7	148
Kia Optima	7	177
Toyota Camry	7	248

Price Range

Price Range	Retail	Markup
Base	$22,300	7%
S 2.5L	$22,560	7%
SV 3.5L	$29,830	9%
SL 3.5L	$31,950	9%

Safety Checklist

Crash Tests:
  Frontal. . . . . Very Good
  Side. . . . . .Very Poor
Airbags:
  Torso . . . . .Front Pelvis/Torso from Seat
  Pelvis . . . . .Front Pelvis/Torso from Seat
  Roll Sensing. . . . . .Yes
  Knee Bolster . . . . None
Crash Avoidance:
  Collision Avoidance . . . . None
  Blind Spot Detection . . . . Optional
  Lane Keeping Assist . . . .Warning Only Optional
  Backup Camera . . . . Optional
  Pedestrian Crash Avoidance . . . . None
General:
  Auto. Crash Notification . . . . None
  Day Running Lamps . . . . None
Safety Belt/Restraint:
  Dynamic Head Restraints . . . . None
  Adjustable Belt. . . . . .Standard Front

Nissan Altima

Specifications

Drive. . . . . FWD
Engine 2.5-liter I4
Transmission . . . . .6-sp. Automatic
Tow Rating (lbs.) . . . . –
Head/Leg Room (in.) . . . . Very Roomy-40/45
Interior Space (cu. ft.). Average-101.9
Cargo Space (cu. ft.) Cramped-15.4
Wheelbase/Length (in.) 109.3/191.5

Ratings—10 Best, 1 Worst

Combo Crash Tests	–
Safety Features	2
Rollover	1
Preventive Maintenance	3
Repair Costs	4
Warranty	1
Fuel Economy	1
Complaints	3
Insurance Costs	8

OVERALL RATING — –

Nissan Armada

Nissan Armada

At-a-Glance

Status/Year Series Started. Unchanged/2004
Twins . . . . –
Body Styles . . . . SUV
Seating 7/8
Anti-Theft Device . . . . . . Std. Pass. Immobil. & Alarm
Parking Index Rating . . . . Very Hard
Where Made. Canton, MS
Fuel Factor . . . .
  MPG Rating (city/hwy) . . . . .Very Poor-13/19
  Driving Range (mi.) Long-424.3
  Fuel Type . . . . .Regular
  Annual Fuel Cost . . . . Very High-$2,771
  Gas Guzzler Tax . . . . .No
  Greenhouse Gas Emissions (tons/yr.)Very High-12.0
  Barrels of Oil Used per year . . . . . . .Very High-22.0

How the Competition Rates

Competitors	Rating	Pg.
Chevrolet Suburban	5	121
Ford Expedition	7	139
Toyota Sequoia	–	255

Price Range

Price Range	Retail	Markup
SV 2WD	$38,060	10%
SL 2WD	$43,150	10%
SL 4WD	$46,050	10%
Platinum 4WD	$53,330	10%

Safety Checklist

Crash Tests:
  Frontal. . . . .–
  Side. . . . .–
Airbags:
  Torso . . . . .Front Pelvis/Torso from Seat
  Pelvis . . . . .Front Pelvis/Torso from Seat
  Roll Sensing. . . . . No
  Knee Bolster . . . . None
Crash Avoidance:
  Collision Avoidance . . . . None
  Blind Spot Detection . . . . None
  Lane Keeping Assist . . . . None
  Backup Camera . . . . Optional
  Pedestrian Crash Avoidance . . . . None
General:
  Auto. Crash Notification . . . . None
  Day Running Lamps . . . . None
Safety Belt/Restraint:
  Dynamic Head Restraints . . . . . .Standard Front
  Adjustable Belt . . . . . . .Standard Front and Rear

Nissan Armada

Specifications

Drive . . . . RWD
Engine 5.6-liter V8
Transmission . . . . .5-sp. Automatic
Tow Rating (lbs.) High-8200
Head/Leg Room (in.) Roomy-41/41.8
Interior Space (cu. ft.). . . . . –
Cargo Space (cu. ft.) Average-20
Wheelbase/Length (in.) 123.2/207.7

Ratings—10 Best, 1 Worst

Combo Crash Tests	–
Safety Features	4
Rollover	2
Preventive Maintenance	3
Repair Costs	8
Warranty	1
Fuel Economy	1
Complaints	6
Insurance Costs	5

OVERALL RATING	–

Nissan Frontier

Nissan Frontier

At-a-Glance

Status/Year Series Started. Unchanged/2005
Twins . . . . –
Body Styles . . . . Pickup
Seating. 5
Anti-Theft Device . . . . . . Std. Pass. Immobil. & Alarm
Parking Index Rating . . . . .Very Hard
Where Made. . . . . Canton, MS
Fuel Factor. . . . .
  MPG Rating (city/hwy) . . . . .Very Poor-15/21
  Driving Range (mi.) . . . . Very Short-363.2
  Fuel Type. . . . . .Regular
  Annual Fuel Cost . . . . Very High-$2,440
  Gas Guzzler Tax . . . . .No
  Greenhouse Gas Emissions (tons/yr.)Very High-10.5
  Barrels of Oil Used per year . . . . Very High-19.4

How the Competition Rates

Competitors	Rating	Pg.
Chevrolet Colorado	–	112
GMC Canyon	–	112
Toyota Tacoma	1	257

Price Range	Retail	Markup
S King Cab I4 2WD MT	$17,990	5%
SV Crew Cab V6 2WD AT	$25,350	7%
PRO-4X Crew Cab 4WD AT	$32,560	8%
SL Crew Cab 4WD AT	$35,260	8%

Safety Checklist

Crash Tests:
  Frontal. . . . .–
  Side. . . . .–
Airbags:
  Torso . . . . .Front Pelvis/Torso from Seat
  Pelvis . . . . .Front Pelvis/Torso from Seat
  Roll Sensing. . . . . .Yes
  Knee Bolster . . . . None
Crash Avoidance:
  Collision Avoidance . . . . None
  Blind Spot Detection . . . . None
  Lane Keeping Assist . . . . None
  Backup Camera . . . . Optional
  Pedestrian Crash Avoidance . . . . None
General:
  Auto. Crash Notification . . . . None
  Day Running Lamps . . . . None
Safety Belt/Restraint:
  Dynamic Head Restraints . . . . . .Standard Front
  Adjustable Belt. . . . . .Standard Front

Nissan Frontier

Specifications

Drive. 4WD
Engine 4.0-liter V6
Transmission . . . . .5-sp. Automatic
Tow Rating (lbs.) Average-6300
Head/Leg Room (in.) Average-39.7/42.4
Interior Space (cu. ft.). . . . . . . .Very Cramped-87.7
Cargo Space (cu. ft.) Roomy-33.5
Wheelbase/Length (in.) 125.9/205.5

Ratings—10 Best, 1 Worst

Combo Crash Tests	–
Safety Features	3
Rollover	4
Preventive Maintenance	7
Repair Costs	6
Warranty	1
Fuel Economy	7
Complaints	9
Insurance Costs	5
OVERALL RATING	**–**

Nissan Juke

Nissan Juke

At-a-Glance

Status/Year Series Started Appearance Change/2011
Twins . . . . –
Body Styles . . . . SUV
Seating 5
Anti-Theft Device . . . . . . Std. Pass. Immobil. & Alarm
Parking Index Rating . . . . .Very Easy
Where Made. . . . . Oppama, Japan
Fuel Factor. . . . .
    MPG Rating (city/hwy) Good-26/31
    Driving Range (mi.) . . . . Very Short-330.8
    Fuel Type. . . . . .Premium
    Annual Fuel Cost . . . . Average-$1,712
    Gas Guzzler Tax . . . . .No
    Greenhouse Gas Emissions (tons/yr.) Low-6.5
    Barrels of Oil Used per year Average-11.8

How the Competition Rates

Competitors	Rating	Pg.
Ford Escape	5	138
Kia Soul	7	181
Mitsubishi Outlander Sport	4	216

Price Range

	Retail	Markup
S FWD	$20,250	5%
SV FWD	$22,300	5%
SL AWD	$26,940	6%
NISMO RS AWD	$30,020	6%

Safety Checklist

Crash Tests:
    Frontal. . . . .–
    Side. . . . .–
Airbags:
    Torso . . . . .Front Pelvis/Torso from Seat
    Pelvis . . . . .Front Pelvis/Torso from Seat
    Roll Sensing. . . . . No
    Knee Bolster . . . . None
Crash Avoidance:
    Collision Avoidance . . . . None
    Blind Spot Detection . . . . Optional
    Lane Keeping Assist . . . . None
    Backup Camera . . . . Optional
    Pedestrian Crash Avoidance . . . . None
General:
    Auto. Crash Notification . . . . None
    Day Running Lamps . . . . None
Safety Belt/Restraint:
    Dynamic Head Restraints . . . . . .Standard Front
    Adjustable Belt. . . . . .Standard Front

Nissan Juke

Specifications

Drive. . . . . AWD
Engine 1.6-liter I4
Transmission . . . . .CVT
Tow Rating (lbs.) . . . . –
Head/Leg Room (in.) Average-39.6/42.1
Interior Space (cu. ft.). . . . . Very Cramped-87
Cargo Space (cu. ft.) . . . . .Very Cramped-10.5
Wheelbase/Length (in.) 99.6/162.4

Ratings—10 Best, 1 Worst

Combo Crash Tests	1
Safety Features	2
Rollover	7
Preventive Maintenance	7
Repair Costs	4
Warranty	1
Fuel Economy	10
Complaints	2
Insurance Costs	8
OVERALL RATING	**2**

Nissan Leaf

Nissan Leaf

At-a-Glance

Status/Year Series Started........ Unchanged/2011
Twins ....–
Body Styles .... Hatchback
Seating 5
Anti-Theft Device ...... Std. Pass. Immobil. & Alarm
Parking Index Rating ....Very Easy
Where Made...................... Smyrna, TN
Fuel Factor ....
  MPG Rating (city/hwy) .... Very Good-126/101
  Driving Range (mi.) ....Very Short-84
  Fuel Type......................... Electricity
  Annual Fuel Cost ....Very Low-$370
  Gas Guzzler Tax ....No
  Greenhouse Gas Emissions (tons/yr.). Very Low-3.1
  Barrels of Oil Used per year .... Very Low-0.2

How the Competition Rates

Competitors	Rating	Pg.
Chevrolet Volt	8	125
Ford C-MAX	5	136
Toyota Prius	4	251

Price Range	Retail	Markup
S	$29,010	7%
SV	$32,000	7%
SL	$35,120	7%

Safety Checklist

Crash Tests:
  Frontal.........................Very Poor
  Side............................Very Poor
Airbags:
  Torso ....Front Pelvis/Torso from Seat
  Pelvis ....Front Pelvis/Torso from Seat
  Roll Sensing......................... No
  Knee Bolster .... None
Crash Avoidance:
  Collision Avoidance .... None
  Blind Spot Detection .... None
  Lane Keeping Assist .... None
  Backup Camera.................. Standard
  Pedestrian Crash Avoidance .... None
General:
  Auto. Crash Notification.............. None
  Day Running Lamps .... None
Safety Belt/Restraint:
  Dynamic Head Restraints .... None
  Adjustable Belt...............Standard Front

Nissan Leaf

Specifications

Drive................................... FWD
Engine .... Electric
Transmission ....-
Tow Rating (lbs.) .... Very Low-0
Head/Leg Room (in.) Roomy-41.2/42.1
Interior Space (cu. ft.)............Cramped-92.4
Cargo Space (cu. ft.) Roomy-24
Wheelbase/Length (in.) 106.3/175

Ratings—10 Best, 1 Worst

Combo Crash Tests	1
Safety Features	1
Rollover	8
Preventive Maintenance	6
Repair Costs	6
Warranty	1
Fuel Economy	3
Complaints	7
Insurance Costs	3
OVERALL RATING	**1**

Nissan Maxima

Nissan Maxima

At-a-Glance

Status/Year Series Started........ Unchanged/2009
Twins .... –
Body Styles .... Sedan
Seating 5
Anti-Theft Device ...... Std. Pass. Immobil. & Alarm
Parking Index Rating .... Average
Where Made............................ Smyrna, TN
Fuel Factor...............................
 MPG Rating (city/hwy) Poor-19/26
 Driving Range (mi.) Long-432.4
 Fuel Type............................ Premium
 Annual Fuel Cost .... High-$2,220
 Gas Guzzler Tax ....No
 Greenhouse Gas Emissions (tons/yr.).. Average-7.3
 Barrels of Oil Used per year High-15.0

How the Competition Rates

Competitors	Rating	Pg.
Chevrolet Malibu	7	117
Ford Fusion	4	145
Honda Accord	7	148

Price Range	Retail	Markup
S	$31,200	9%
SV	$34,290	9%

Safety Checklist

Crash Tests:
 Frontal.........................Very Poor
 Side..........................Very Poor
Airbags:
 Torso ....Front Pelvis/Torso from Seat
 Pelvis ....Front Pelvis/Torso from Seat
 Roll Sensing........................ No
 Knee Bolster .... None
Crash Avoidance:
 Collision Avoidance .... None
 Blind Spot Detection .... None
 Lane Keeping Assist .... None
 Backup Camera................... Optional
 Pedestrian Crash Avoidance .... None
General:
 Auto. Crash Notification............. None
 Day Running Lamps .... None
Safety Belt/Restraint:
 Dynamic Head Restraints .... None
 Adjustable Belt..............Standard Front

Nissan Maxima

Specifications

Drive................................. FWD
Engine 3.5-liter V6
Transmission ....CVT
Tow Rating (lbs.) .... –
Head/Leg Room (in.) Average-38.5/43.8
Interior Space (cu. ft.)...........Cramped-95.8
Cargo Space (cu. ft.) Cramped-14.2
Wheelbase/Length (in.).......109.3/190.6

Ratings—10 Best, 1 Worst

Combo Crash Tests	–
Safety Features	7
Rollover	4
Preventive Maintenance	1
Repair Costs	6
Warranty	1
Fuel Economy	5
Complaints	–
Insurance Costs	10

OVERALL RATING	–

Nissan Murano

At-a-Glance

Status/Year Series Started	All New/2015
Twins	–
Body Styles	SUV
Seating	5
Anti-Theft Device	Std. Pass. Immobil. & Alarm
Parking Index Rating	Hard
Where Made	Canton, MS
Fuel Factor	
MPG Rating (city/hwy)	Average-21/28
Driving Range (mi.)	Long-449.6
Fuel Type	Regular
Annual Fuel Cost	Average-$1,775
Gas Guzzler Tax	No
Greenhouse Gas Emissions (tons/yr.)	Average-7.5
Barrels of Oil Used per year	High-13.7

How the Competition Rates

Competitors	Rating	Pg.
Chevrolet Equinox	2	115
Ford Explorer	3	140
Honda Pilot	2	154

Price Range

	Retail	Markup
S FWD	$29,560	9%
SV FWD	$32,620	9%
SL AWD	$38,550	9%
Platinum AWD	$40,600	9%

Nissan Murano

Safety Checklist

Crash Tests:
- Frontal . . . . –
- Side . . . . –

Airbags:
- Torso . . . . Front Pelvis/Torso from Seat
- Pelvis . . . . Front Pelvis/Torso from Seat
- Roll Sensing . . . . Yes
- Knee Bolster . . . . Standard Driver

Crash Avoidance:
- Collision Avoidance . . . . . . Optional CIB & DBS
- Blind Spot Detection . . . . Optional
- Lane Keeping Assist . . . . None
- Backup Camera . . . . Standard
- Pedestrian Crash Avoidance . . . . None

General:
- Auto. Crash Notification . . . . None
- Day Running Lamps . . . . Standard

Safety Belt/Restraint:
- Dynamic Head Restraints . . . . None
- Adjustable Belt . . . . Standard Front

Nissan Murano

Specifications

Drive	AWD
Engine	3.5-liter V6
Transmission	CVT
Tow Rating (lbs.)	Very Low-1500
Head/Leg Room (in.)	Cramped-39.9/40.5
Interior Space (cu. ft.)	Roomy-108.1
Cargo Space (cu. ft.)	Very Roomy-39.6
Wheelbase/Length (in.)	111.2/192.4

Ratings—10 Best, 1 Worst

Combo Crash Tests	–
Safety Features	4
Rollover	3
Preventive Maintenance	7
Repair Costs	6
Warranty	1
Fuel Economy	3
Complaints	1
Insurance Costs	10

OVERALL RATING —

Nissan Pathfinder

Nissan Pathfinder

At-a-Glance

Status/Year Series Started	Unchanged/2013
Twins	Infiniti QX60
Body Styles	SUV
Seating	7
Anti-Theft Device	Std. Pass. Immobil. & Alarm
Parking Index Rating	Hard
Where Made	Smyrna, TN
Fuel Factor	
MPG Rating (city/hwy)	Poor-19/26
Driving Range (mi.)	Average-421.6
Fuel Type	Regular
Annual Fuel Cost	Average-$1,942
Gas Guzzler Tax	No
Greenhouse Gas Emissions (tons/yr.)	High-8.2
Barrels of Oil Used per year	High-15.0

How the Competition Rates

Competitors	Rating	Pg.
Buick Enclave	7	102
Chevrolet Traverse	7	123
Toyota Highlander	7	250

Price Range	Retail	Markup
S 2WD	$29,510	7%
SV 2WD	$32,810	9%
SL 4WD	$37,750	9%
Platinum 4WD	$43,100	9%

Safety Checklist

Crash Tests:
Frontal	–
Side	–

Airbags:
Torso	Front Pelvis/Torso from Seat
Pelvis	Front Pelvis/Torso from Seat
Roll Sensing	Yes
Knee Bolster	None

Crash Avoidance:
Collision Avoidance	None
Blind Spot Detection	Optional
Lane Keeping Assist	None
Backup Camera	Optional
Pedestrian Crash Avoidance	None

General:
Auto. Crash Notification	None
Day Running Lamps	None

Safety Belt/Restraint:
Dynamic Head Restraints	None
Adjustable Belt	Standard Front and Rear

Specifications

Drive	4WD
Engine	3.5-liter V6
Transmission	CVT
Tow Rating (lbs.)	Low-5000
Head/Leg Room (in.)	Roomy-41.1/42.3
Interior Space (cu. ft.)	Very Roomy-157.8
Cargo Space (cu. ft.)	Cramped-16
Wheelbase/Length (in.)	114.2/197.2

Ratings—10 Best, 1 Worst

Combo Crash Tests	–
Safety Features	3
Rollover	3
Preventive Maintenance	1
Repair Costs	6
Warranty	1
Fuel Economy	4
Complaints	4
Insurance Costs	5
OVERALL RATING	**–**

Nissan Quest

Nissan Quest

At-a-Glance

Status/Year Series Started	Unchanged/2011
Twins	–
Body Styles	Minivan
Seating	7/8
Anti-Theft Device	Std. Pass. Immobil. & Alarm
Parking Index Rating	Average
Where Made	Kyushu, Japan
Fuel Factor	
MPG Rating (city/hwy)	Poor-20/27
Driving Range (mi.)	Long-452.8
Fuel Type	Regular
Annual Fuel Cost	Average-$1,855
Gas Guzzler Tax	No
Greenhouse Gas Emissions (tons/yr.)	High-8.2
Barrels of Oil Used per year	High-15.0

How the Competition Rates

Competitors	Rating	Pg.
Chrysler Town and Country	3	128
Honda Odyssey	7	153
Toyota Sienna	3	256

Price Range

	Retail	Markup
S	$26,530	7%
SV	$30,280	9%
SL	$34,060	9%
Platinum	$43,180	9%

Safety Checklist

Crash Tests:
Frontal . . . . –
Side . . . . –

Airbags:
Torso . . . . Front Pelvis/Torso from Seat
Pelvis . . . . Front Pelvis/Torso from Seat
Roll Sensing . . . . No
Knee Bolster . . . . No

Crash Avoidance:
Collision Avoidance . . . . None
Blind Spot Detection . . . . Optional
Lane Keeping Assist . . . . None
Backup Camera . . . . Optional
Pedestrian Crash Avoidance . . . . None

General:
Auto. Crash Notification . . . . None
Day Running Lamps . . . . None

Safety Belt/Restraint:
Dynamic Head Restraints . . . . . . Standard Front
Adjustable Belt . . . . Standard Front and Rear

Nissan Quest

Specifications

Drive	FWD
Engine	3.5-liter V6
Transmission	CVT
Tow Rating (lbs.)	Low-3500
Head/Leg Room (in.)	Very Roomy-42.1/43.8
Interior Space (cu. ft.)	Very Roomy-177.8
Cargo Space (cu. ft.)	Very Roomy-37.1
Wheelbase/Length (in.)	118.1/200.8

Ratings—10 Best, 1 Worst

Combo Crash Tests	1
Safety Features	6
Rollover	3
Preventive Maintenance	7
Repair Costs	4
Warranty	1
Fuel Economy	7
Complaints	8
Insurance Costs	5
OVERALL RATING	**2**

Nissan Rogue

Nissan Rogue

At-a-Glance

Status/Year Series Started	Unchanged/2014
Twins	–
Body Styles	SUV
Seating	5/7
Anti-Theft Device	Std. Pass. Immobil. & Alarm
Parking Index Rating	Average
Where Made	Smyrna, TN
Fuel Factor	
MPG Rating (city/hwy)	Good-25/32
Driving Range (mi.)	Average-402.1
Fuel Type	Regular
Annual Fuel Cost	Low-$1,514
Gas Guzzler Tax	No
Greenhouse Gas Emissions (tons/yr.)	Low-6.4
Barrels of Oil Used per year	Average-11.8

How the Competition Rates

Competitors	Rating	Pg.
Kia Sorento	4	180
Toyota Venza	3	259
Volvo XC60	9	270

Price Range

	Retail	Markup
S FWD	$22,790	5%
SV FWD	$24,490	5%
SV AWD	$25,840	5%
SL AWD	$29,630	5%

Safety Checklist

Crash Tests:
Frontal...........................Very Poor
Side............................Very Poor

Airbags:
Torso...........Front Pelvis/Torso from Seat
Pelvis..........Front Pelvis/Torso from Seat
Roll Sensing..........................Yes
Knee Bolster.......................None

Crash Avoidance:
Collision Avoidance.....Warning Only Optional
Blind Spot Detection...............Optional
Lane Keeping Assist....Warning Only Optional
Backup Camera..................Standard
Pedestrian Crash Avoidance...........None

General:
Auto. Crash Notification..............None
Day Running Lamps.............Standard

Safety Belt/Restraint:
Dynamic Head Restraints.............None
Adjustable Belt...............Standard Front

Nissan Rogue

Specifications

Drive	AWD
Engine	2.5-liter I4
Transmission	CVT
Tow Rating (lbs.)	Very Low-1000
Head/Leg Room (in.)	Very Roomy-41.6/43
Interior Space (cu. ft.)	Roomy-105.8
Cargo Space (cu. ft.)	Very Cramped-9.4
Wheelbase/Length (in.)	106.5/182.3

Ratings—10 Best, 1 Worst

Combo Crash Tests	–
Safety Features	1
Rollover	6
Preventive Maintenance	7
Repair Costs	9
Warranty	1
Fuel Economy	9
Complaints	6
Insurance Costs	5

OVERALL RATING   –

Nissan Sentra

At-a-Glance

Status/Year Series Started	Unchanged/2013
Twins	–
Body Styles	Sedan
Seating	5
Anti-Theft Device	Std. Pass. Immobil. & Alarm
Parking Index Rating	Easy
Where Made	Aguascalientes, Mexico / Kyushu, Japan
Fuel Factor	
MPG Rating (city/hwy)	Very Good-30/39
Driving Range (mi.)	Long-441.9
Fuel Type	Regular
Annual Fuel Cost	Very Low-$1,254
Gas Guzzler Tax	No
Greenhouse Gas Emissions (tons/yr.)	Very Low-5.3
Barrels of Oil Used per year	Low-9.7

How the Competition Rates

Competitors	Rating	Pg.
Chevrolet Cruze	8	114
Honda Civic	6	149
Toyota Corolla	8	249

Price Range

Price Range	Retail	Markup
S MT	$15,990	4%
SV	$17,490	7%
SR	$18,690	7%
SL	$19,590	7%

Nissan Sentra

Safety Checklist

Crash Tests:
Frontal.................................–
Side..................................–
Airbags:
Torso ....Front Pelvis/Torso from Seat
Pelvis ....Front Pelvis/Torso from Seat
Roll Sensing............................No
Knee Bolster ....None
Crash Avoidance:
Collision Avoidance ....None
Blind Spot Detection ....None
Lane Keeping Assist ....None
Backup Camera....................Optional
Pedestrian Crash Avoidance ....None
General:
Auto. Crash Notification..............None
Day Running Lamps ....None
Safety Belt/Restraint:
Dynamic Head Restraints ....None
Adjustable Belt.............Standard Front

Nissan Sentra

Specifications

Drive	FWD
Engine	2.0-liter I4
Transmission	CVT
Tow Rating (lbs.)	–
Head/Leg Room (in.)	Average-39.4/42.5
Interior Space (cu. ft.)	Cramped-95.9
Cargo Space (cu. ft.)	Cramped-15.1
Wheelbase/Length (in.)	106.3/182.1

Nissan Titan

Ratings—10 Best, 1 Worst

Combo Crash Tests	–
Safety Features	4
Rollover	2
Preventive Maintenance	3
Repair Costs	5
Warranty	1
Fuel Economy	1
Complaints	4
Insurance Costs	5
OVERALL RATING	**–**

Nissan Titan

Nissan Titan

At-a-Glance

Status/Year Series Started	Unchanged/2004
Twins	–
Body Styles	Pickup
Seating	5
Anti-Theft Device	Std. Pass. Immobil. & Alarm
Parking Index Rating	Very Hard
Where Made	Canton, MS
Fuel Factor	
MPG Rating (city/hwy)	Very Poor-12/17
Driving Range (mi.)	Short-387.3
Fuel Type	Regular
Annual Fuel Cost	Very High-$3,036
Gas Guzzler Tax	No
Greenhouse Gas Emissions (tons/yr.)	Very High-13.1
Barrels of Oil Used per year	Very High-23.5

How the Competition Rates

Competitors	Rating	Pg.
Chevrolet Silverado	7	118
Ford F-150	–	141
Toyota Tundra	3	258

Price Range	Retail	Markup
S King Cab 2WD	$29,270	10%
SV King Cab 4WD	$34,550	10%
PRO-4X Crew Cab 4WD	$39,690	10%
SL Crew Cab 4WD	$43,190	10%

Safety Checklist

Crash Tests:
Frontal . . . . –
Side . . . . –

Airbags:
Torso . . . . Front Pelvis/Torso from Seat
Pelvis . . . . Front Pelvis/Torso from Seat
Roll Sensing . . . . Yes
Knee Bolster . . . . None

Crash Avoidance:
Collision Avoidance . . . . None
Blind Spot Detection . . . . None
Lane Keeping Assist . . . . None
Backup Camera . . . . Optional
Pedestrian Crash Avoidance . . . . None

General:
Auto. Crash Notification . . . . None
Day Running Lamps . . . . None

Safety Belt/Restraint:
Dynamic Head Restraints . . . . . . Standard Front
Adjustable Belt . . . . Standard Front

Nissan Titan

Specifications

Drive	4WD
Engine	5.6-liter V8
Transmission	5-sp. Automatic
Tow Rating (lbs.)	High-7400
Head/Leg Room (in.)	Roomy-41/41.8
Interior Space (cu. ft.)	Roomy-112.8
Cargo Space (cu. ft.)	Very Roomy-58.1
Wheelbase/Length (in.)	139.8/224.6

Nissan Versa

Ratings—10 Best, 1 Worst	
Combo Crash Tests	1*
Safety Features	1
Rollover	4
Preventive Maintenance	8
Repair Costs	10
Warranty	1
Fuel Economy	9
Complaints	7
Insurance Costs	1
OVERALL RATING	**2**

Nissan Versa

At-a-Glance

Status/Year Series Started Appearance Change/2006
Twins . . . . –
Body Styles . . . . Sedan, Hatchback
Seating 4
Anti-Theft Device . . . . Std. Pass. Immobil.
Parking Index Rating . . . . .Very Easy
Where Made Aguascalientes, Mexico / Kyushu, Japan
Fuel Factor . . . .
  MPG Rating (city/hwy) . . . . Very Good-31/40
  Driving Range (mi.) Short-372.5
  Fuel Type . . . . .Regular
  Annual Fuel Cost . . . . Very Low-$1,217
  Gas Guzzler Tax . . . . .No
  Greenhouse Gas Emissions (tons/yr.). Very Low-5.1
  Barrels of Oil Used per year Low-9.4

How the Competition Rates

Competitors	Rating	Pg.
Hyundai Accent	5	155
Kia Forte	5	176
Toyota Yaris	5	260

Price Range	Retail	Markup
S MT	$11,990	4%
S Plus	$13,990	4%
SL Hatchback	$16,330	4%
SL	$16,890	4%

Safety Checklist

Crash Tests:
  Frontal. . . . . .Very Poor
  Side. . . . . .Very Poor
Airbags:
  Torso . . . . .Front Pelvis/Torso from Seat
  Pelvis . . . . .Front Pelvis/Torso from Seat
  Roll Sensing. . . . . No
  Knee Bolster . . . . None
Crash Avoidance:
  Collision Avoidance . . . . None
  Blind Spot Detection . . . . None
  Lane Keeping Assist . . . . None
  Backup Camera . . . . Optional
  Pedestrian Crash Avoidance . . . . None
General:
  Auto. Crash Notification . . . . None
  Day Running Lamps . . . . None
Safety Belt/Restraint:
  Dynamic Head Restraints . . . . None
  Adjustable Belt . . . . .Standard Front

Nissan Versa

Specifications

Drive . . . . FWD
Engine 1.6-liter I4
Transmission . . . . .CVT
Tow Rating (lbs.) . . . . –
Head/Leg Room (in.) Average-39.8/41.8
Interior Space (cu. ft.). . . . . .Very Cramped-90.2
Cargo Space (cu. ft.) Cramped-14.9
Wheelbase/Length (in.) 102.4/175.4

*Crash test is for sedan only. For Versa Note results see page 20.

Ratings—10 Best, 1 Worst

Combo Crash Tests	–
Safety Features	4
Rollover	1
Preventive Maintenance	3
Repair Costs	8
Warranty	1
Fuel Economy	1
Complaints	3
Insurance Costs	10

OVERALL RATING — –

Nissan Xterra

Nissan Xterra

At-a-Glance

Status/Year Series Started	Unchanged/2005
Twins	–
Body Styles	SUV
Seating	5
Anti-Theft Device	Std. Pass. Immobil. & Alarm
Parking Index Rating	Easy
Where Made	Canton, MS
Fuel Factor	
MPG Rating (city/hwy)	Very Poor-15/20
Driving Range (mi.)	Very Short-356.6
Fuel Type	Regular
Annual Fuel Cost	Very High-$2,485
Gas Guzzler Tax	No
Greenhouse Gas Emissions (tons/yr.)	Very High-10.6
Barrels of Oil Used per year	Very High-19.4

How the Competition Rates

Competitors	Rating	Pg.
Ford Explorer	3	140
Honda Pilot	2	154
Jeep Wrangler	–	174

Price Range

	Retail	Markup
X 2WD AT	$23,660	6%
S 2WD AT	$25,670	6%
S 4WD AT	$27,720	6%
PRO-4X 4WD AT	$31,640	7%

Safety Checklist

Crash Tests:
Frontal .... –
Side .... –

Airbags:
Torso .... Front Pelvis/Torso from Seat
Pelvis .... Front Pelvis/Torso from Seat
Roll Sensing .... Yes
Knee Bolster .... None

Crash Avoidance:
Collision Avoidance .... None
Blind Spot Detection .... None
Lane Keeping Assist .... None
Backup Camera .... Optional
Pedestrian Crash Avoidance .... None

General:
Auto. Crash Notification .... None
Day Running Lamps .... None

Safety Belt/Restraint:
Dynamic Head Restraints ......Standard Front
Adjustable Belt.......Standard Front and Rear

Nissan Xterra

Specifications

Drive	4WD
Engine	4.0-liter V6
Transmission	5-sp. Automatic
Tow Rating (lbs.)	Low-5000
Head/Leg Room (in.)	Average-39.9/42.4
Interior Space (cu. ft.)	Average-99.8
Cargo Space (cu. ft.)	Very Roomy-36.3
Wheelbase/Length (in.)	106.3/178.7

Ratings—10 Best, 1 Worst

Combo Crash Tests	–
Safety Features	5
Rollover	4
Preventive Maintenance	3
Repair Costs	2
Warranty	5
Fuel Economy	2
Complaints	9
Insurance Costs	8
OVERALL RATING	–

Porsche Cayenne

Porsche Cayenne

At-a-Glance

Status/Year Series Started Appearance Change/2011
Twins . . . . Volkswagen Touareg
Body Styles . . . . SUV
Seating 5
Anti-Theft Device . Std. Pass. Immobil. & Active Alarm
Parking Index Rating . . . . Hard
Where Made . Bratislava, Slovakia / Leipzig, Germany
Fuel Factor . . . .
  MPG Rating (city/hwy) . . . . .Very Poor-17/24
  Driving Range (mi.) . . . . .Very Long-516.6
  Fuel Type . . . . .Premium
  Annual Fuel Cost . . . . Very High-$2,452
  Gas Guzzler Tax . . . . .No
  Greenhouse Gas Emissions (tons/yr.) High-9.0
  Barrels of Oil Used per year High-16.5

How the Competition Rates

Competitors	Rating	Pg.
BMW X5	6	101
Land Rover Range Rover Sport	–	185
Mercedes-Benz GLK-Class	–	208

Price Range

	Retail	Markup
Diesel	$61,700	10%
S	$74,100	10%
S E-Hybrid	$76,400	10%
Turbo	$113,600	10%

Safety Checklist

Crash Tests:
  Frontal . . . .–
  Side . . . .–
Airbags:
  Torso . . . . Fr. & Rr. Torso from Seat
  Pelvis . . . . None
  Roll Sensing . . . . .Yes
  Knee Bolster . . . . Standard Driver
Crash Avoidance:
  Collision Avoidance . . . . .Optional DBS
  Blind Spot Detection . . . . Optional
  Lane Keeping Assist . . . . None
  Backup Camera . . . . Optional
  Pedestrian Crash Avoidance . . . . None
General:
  Auto. Crash Notification . . . . None
  Day Running Lamps . . . . Standard
Safety Belt/Restraint:
  Dynamic Head Restraints . . . . None
  Adjustable Belt . . . . .Standard Front

Porsche Cayenne

Specifications

Drive . . . . AWD
Engine 3.6-liter V6
Transmission . . . . .8-sp. Automatic
Tow Rating (lbs.) High-7716
Head/Leg Room (in.) . . . . –
Interior Space (cu. ft.) . . . . –
Cargo Space (cu. ft.) Roomy-23.66
Wheelbase/Length (in.) 114/191.1

Ratings—10 Best, 1 Worst

Combo Crash Tests	–
Safety Features	7
Rollover	5
Preventive Maintenance	–
Repair Costs	–
Warranty	5
Fuel Economy	2
Complaints	–
Insurance Costs	5
OVERALL RATING	–

Porsche Macan

Porsche Macan

At-a-Glance

Status/Year Series Started	All New/2015
Twins	–
Body Styles	SUV
Seating	5
Anti-Theft Device	Std. Pass. Immobil. & Active Alarm
Parking Index Rating	Hard
Where Made	Leipzig, Germany
Fuel Factor	
MPG Rating (city/hwy)	Very Poor-17/23
Driving Range (mi.)	Short-381.4
Fuel Type	Premium
Annual Fuel Cost	Very High-$2,492
Gas Guzzler Tax	No
Greenhouse Gas Emissions (tons/yr.)	Very High-9.5
Barrels of Oil Used per year	Very High-17.3

How the Competition Rates

Competitors	Rating	Pg.
Audi Q3	–	91
BMW X1	–	99
Mercedes-Benz GLA-Class	–	206

Price Range

	Retail	Markup
S	$49,900	10%
Turbo	$72,300	10%

Safety Checklist

Crash Tests:
Frontal............................... –
Side................................. –

Airbags:
Torso .... Fr. & Rr. Torso from Seat
Pelvis .... None
Roll Sensing......................... Yes
Knee Bolster .... Standard Front

Crash Avoidance:
Collision Avoidance .... Optional DBS
Blind Spot Detection .... Optional
Lane Keeping Assist .... Optional
Backup Camera .... Optional
Pedestrian Crash Avoidance .... None

General:
Auto. Crash Notification .... None
Day Running Lamps .... Standard

Safety Belt/Restraint:
Dynamic Head Restraints .... None
Adjustable Belt.............. Standard Front

Porsche Macan

Specifications

Drive	AWD
Engine	3.0-liter V6
Transmission	7-sp. Automatic
Tow Rating (lbs.)	Low-4409
Head/Leg Room (in.)	–
Interior Space (cu. ft.)	–
Cargo Space (cu. ft.)	Average-17.7
Wheelbase/Length (in.)	110.51/184.29

Ratings—10 Best, 1 Worst	
Combo Crash Tests	6*
Safety Features	4
Rollover	2
Preventive Maintenance	5
Repair Costs	10
Warranty	5
Fuel Economy	1
Complaints	3
Insurance Costs	5
OVERALL RATING	**3**

Ram 1500

Ram 1500

At-a-Glance

Status/Year Series Started	Unchanged/2009
Twins	–
Body Styles	Pickup
Seating	5/6
Anti-Theft Device	Std. Pass. Immobil. & Alarm
Parking Index Rating	Very Hard
Where Made	Warren, MI / Saltillo, Mexico
Fuel Factor	
MPG Rating (city/hwy)	Very Poor-13/19
Driving Range (mi.)	Short-394.0
Fuel Type	Regular
Annual Fuel Cost	Very High-$2,771
Gas Guzzler Tax	No
Greenhouse Gas Emissions (tons/yr.)	Very High-12.0
Barrels of Oil Used per year	Very High-22.0

How the Competition Rates

Competitors	Rating	Pg.
Chevrolet Silverado	7	118
Ford F-150	–	141
Nissan Titan	–	229

Price Range

	Retail	Markup
Tradesman Reg. Cab 2WD	$24,610	7%
SLT Quad Cab 2WD	$33,040	7%
Sport Crew Cab 4WD	$43,415	9%
Laramie Longhorn Crew Cab 4WD	$49,630	9%

Safety Checklist

Crash Tests:
Frontal	Poor
Side	Good

Airbags:
Torso	Front Pelvis/Torso from Seat
Pelvis	Front Pelvis/Torso from Seat
Roll Sensing	Yes
Knee Bolster	None

Crash Avoidance:
Collision Avoidance	None
Blind Spot Detection	None
Lane Keeping Assist	None
Backup Camera	Standard
Pedestrian Crash Avoidance	None

General:
Auto. Crash Notification	None
Day Running Lamps	None

Safety Belt/Restraint:
Dynamic Head Restraints	None
Adjustable Belt	Standard Front

Ram 1500

Specifications

Drive	4WD
Engine	5.7-liter V8
Transmission	6-sp. Automatic
Tow Rating (lbs.)	Very High-8807
Head/Leg Room (in.)	Average-41/41
Interior Space (cu. ft.)	Roomy-116.6
Cargo Space (cu. ft.)	Very Roomy-57.5
Wheelbase/Length (in.)	140.5/229

*Crash test is for 1500 Quad and Regular Cab only. For 1500 Crew Cab results see page 27.

Ratings—10 Best, 1 Worst

Combo Crash Tests	4
Safety Features	1
Rollover	10
Preventive Maintenance	6
Repair Costs	5
Warranty	2
Fuel Economy	7
Complaints	8
Insurance Costs	1
OVERALL RATING	**3**

Scion FR-S

Scion FR-S

At-a-Glance

Status/Year Series Started	Unchanged/2013
Twins	Subaru BRZ
Body Styles	Coupe
Seating	4
Anti-Theft Device	Std. Pass. Immobil.
Parking Index Rating	Very Easy
Where Made	Gunma, Japan
Fuel Factor	
MPG Rating (city/hwy)	Good-25/34
Driving Range (mi.)	Short-374.6
Fuel Type	Premium
Annual Fuel Cost	Average-$1,691
Gas Guzzler Tax	No
Greenhouse Gas Emissions (tons/yr.)	Low-6.4
Barrels of Oil Used per year	Average-11.8

How the Competition Rates

Competitors	Rating	Pg.
Mazda MX-5 Miata	–	202
Nissan 370Z	–	217
Subaru BRZ	2	239

Price Range

	Retail	Markup
Base MT	$24,900	5%
Base AT	$26,000	5%
Release Series 1.0 MT	$29,990	5%
Release Series 1.0 AT	$31,090	5%

Safety Checklist

Crash Tests:
Frontal . . . . Average
Side . . . . Very Poor

Airbags:
Torso . . . . .Front Pelvis/Torso from Seat
Pelvis . . . . .Front Pelvis/Torso from Seat
Roll Sensing. . . . . No
Knee Bolster . . . . None

Crash Avoidance:
Collision Avoidance . . . . None
Blind Spot Detection . . . . None
Lane Keeping Assist . . . . None
Backup Camera . . . . None
Pedestrian Crash Avoidance . . . . None

General:
Auto. Crash Notification . . . . None
Day Running Lamps . . . . Standard

Safety Belt/Restraint:
Dynamic Head Restraints . . . . None
Adjustable Belt. None

Scion FR-S

Specifications

Drive	RWD
Engine	2.0-liter I4
Transmission	6-sp. Automatic
Tow Rating (lbs.)	–
Head/Leg Room (in.)	Very Cramped-37.1/41.9
Interior Space (cu. ft.)	Very Cramped-76.5
Cargo Space (cu. ft.)	Very Cramped-6.9
Wheelbase/Length (in.)	101.2/166.7

Ratings—10 Best, 1 Worst

Combo Crash Tests	6
Safety Features	2
Rollover	7
Preventive Maintenance	10
Repair Costs	6
Warranty	2
Fuel Economy	6
Complaints	10
Insurance Costs	1
OVERALL RATING	**5**

Scion tC

Scion tC

Scion tC

At-a-Glance

Status/Year Series Started Unchanged/2011
Twins . . . . –
Body Styles . . . . .Coupe
Seating 5
Anti-Theft Device . . . . Std. Pass. Immobil.
Parking Index Rating . . . . Easy
Where Made. . . . . .Tsutsumi, Japan
Fuel Factor . . . .
  MPG Rating (city/hwy) Average-23/31
  Driving Range (mi.) Short-377.3
  Fuel Type . . . . .Regular
  Annual Fuel Cost . . . . Low-$1,614
  Gas Guzzler Tax . . . . .No
  Greenhouse Gas Emissions (tons/yr.). . Average-6.9
  Barrels of Oil Used per year Average-12.7

How the Competition Rates

Competitors	Rating	Pg.
Mazda Mazda3	5	199
Mitsubishi Lancer	4	213
Subaru Impreza	4	241

Price Range

Price Range	Retail	Markup
MT	$19,210	5%
AT	$20,360	5%

Safety Checklist

Crash Tests:
  Frontal. . . . . Average
  Side. . . . . Good
Airbags:
  Torso . . . . .Front Pelvis/Torso from Seat
  Pelvis . . . . .Front Pelvis/Torso from Seat
  Roll Sensing. . . . . No
  Knee Bolster . . . . .Standard Front
Crash Avoidance:
  Collision Avoidance . . . . None
  Blind Spot Detection . . . . None
  Lane Keeping Assist . . . . None
  Backup Camera. None
  Pedestrian Crash Avoidance . . . . None
General:
  Auto. Crash Notification . . . . None
  Day Running Lamps . . . . None
Safety Belt/Restraint:
  Dynamic Head Restraints . . . . . .Standard Front
  Adjustable Belt . . . . None

Scion tC

Specifications

Drive. . . . . FWD
Engine 2.5-liter I4
Transmission . . . . .6-sp. Automatic
Tow Rating (lbs.) . . . . –
Head/Leg Room (in.) . . . . .Very Cramped-37.7/41.8
Interior Space (cu. ft.). . . . . .Very Cramped-88.4
Cargo Space (cu. ft.) . . . . Very Roomy-34.5
Wheelbase/Length (in.) 106.3/176.6

Ratings—10 Best, 1 Worst

Combo Crash Tests	–
Safety Features	1
Rollover	4
Preventive Maintenance	7
Repair Costs	8
Warranty	2
Fuel Economy	5
Complaints	8
Insurance Costs	1
OVERALL RATING	**–**

Scion xB

Scion xB

At-a-Glance

Status/Year Series Started	Unchanged/2008
Twins	–
Body Styles	Hatchback
Seating	5
Anti-Theft Device	None
Parking Index Rating	Very Easy
Where Made	Iwata, Japan
Fuel Factor	
MPG Rating (city/hwy)	Average-22/28
Driving Range (mi.)	Very Short-340.9
Fuel Type	Regular
Annual Fuel Cost	Average-$1,725
Gas Guzzler Tax	No
Greenhouse Gas Emissions (tons/yr.)	Average-7.5
Barrels of Oil Used per year	High-13.7

How the Competition Rates

Competitors	Rating	Pg.
Kia Soul	7	181
Mini Countryman	–	212
Toyota Yaris	5	260

Price Range	Retail	Markup
MT	$16,970	5%
AT	$17,920	5%

Safety Checklist

Crash Tests:
Frontal . . . . –
Side . . . . –
Airbags:
Torso . . . . Front Pelvis/Torso from Seat
Pelvis . . . . .Front Pelvis/Torso from Seat
Roll Sensing . . . . No
Knee Bolster . . . . None
Crash Avoidance:
Collision Avoidance . . . . None
Blind Spot Detection . . . . None
Lane Keeping Assist . . . . None
Backup Camera . . . . None
Pedestrian Crash Avoidance . . . . None
General:
Auto. Crash Notification . . . . None
Day Running Lamps . . . . None
Safety Belt/Restraint:
Dynamic Head Restraints . . . . None
Adjustable Belt . . . . Standard Front

Scion xB

Specifications

Drive	FWD
Engine	2.4-liter I4
Transmission	4-sp. Automatic
Tow Rating (lbs.)	–
Head/Leg Room (in.)	Cramped-40/40.7
Interior Space (cu. ft.)	Average-100.8
Cargo Space (cu. ft.)	Very Cramped-11.6
Wheelbase/Length (in.)	102.4/168.1

Ratings—10 Best, 1 Worst

Combo Crash Tests	–
Safety Features	1
Rollover	4
Preventive Maintenance	3
Repair Costs	4
Warranty	3
Fuel Economy	10
Complaints	5
Insurance Costs	5
OVERALL RATING	**–**

Smart ForTwo

Smart ForTwo

At-a-Glance

Status/Year Series Started. Unchanged/2008
Twins . . . . –
Body Styles . . . . Hatchback
Seating 2
Anti-Theft Device . Std. Active Immobil. & Pass. Alarm
Parking Index Rating . . . . .Very Easy
Where Made. . . . . .Hambach, France
Fuel Factor . . . .
  MPG Rating (city/hwy) . . . . Very Good-34/38
  Driving Range (mi.) . . . . Very Short-310.5
  Fuel Type. . . . . .Premium
  Annual Fuel Cost . . . . Very Low-$1,344
  Gas Guzzler Tax . . . . .No
  Greenhouse Gas Emissions (tons/yr.). Very Low-5.0
  Barrels of Oil Used per year Low-9.1

How the Competition Rates

Competitors	Rating	Pg.
Fiat 500	2	134
Mini Cooper	–	211
Mitsubishi Mirage	3	214

Price Range

Price Range	Retail	Markup
pure	$13,270	8%
passion Coupe	$14,930	8%
passion Cabriolet	$17,930	8%
Electric Coupe	$25,000	8%

Safety Checklist

Crash Tests:
  Frontal. . . . . –
  Side. . . . . –
Airbags:
  Torso . . . . Front Torso from Seat
  Pelvis . . . . None
  Roll Sensing. . . . . No
  Knee Bolster . . . . .Standard Front
Crash Avoidance:
  Collision Avoidance . . . . None
  Blind Spot Detection . . . . None
  Lane Keeping Assist . . . . None
  Backup Camera . . . . None
  Pedestrian Crash Avoidance . . . . None
General:
  Auto. Crash Notification . . . . None
  Day Running Lamps . . . . Optional
Safety Belt/Restraint:
  Dynamic Head Restraints . . . . None
  Adjustable Belt . . . . None

Smart ForTwo

Specifications

Drive. . . . . .RWD
Engine 1.0-liter I3
Transmission . . . . .5-sp. Automatic
Tow Rating (lbs.) . . . . Very Low-0
Head/Leg Room (in.) Cramped-39.7/41.2
Interior Space (cu. ft.). . . . . .Very Cramped-45.4
Cargo Space (cu. ft.) . . . . Very Cramped-12
Wheelbase/Length (in.) 73.5/106.1

Ratings—10 Best, 1 Worst

Combo Crash Tests	4
Safety Features	1
Rollover	10
Preventive Maintenance	4
Repair Costs	7
Warranty	2
Fuel Economy	7
Complaints	3
Insurance Costs	1
OVERALL RATING	**2**

Subaru BRZ

Subaru BRZ

At-a-Glance

Status/Year Series Started	Unchanged/2013
Twins	Scion FR-S
Body Styles	Coupe
Seating	4
Anti-Theft Device	Std. Pass. Immobil. & Opt. Pass. Alarm
Parking Index Rating	Very Easy
Where Made	Gunma, Japan
Fuel Factor	
MPG Rating (city/hwy)	Good-25/34
Driving Range (mi.)	Short-374.6
Fuel Type	Premium
Annual Fuel Cost	Average-$1,691
Gas Guzzler Tax	No
Greenhouse Gas Emissions (tons/yr.)	Low-6.4
Barrels of Oil Used per year	Average-11.8

How the Competition Rates

Competitors	Rating	Pg.
Mazda MX-5 Miata	–	202
Nissan 370Z	–	217
Scion FR-S	3	235

Price Range

Price Range	Retail	Markup
Premium MT	$25,695	5%
Limited MT	$27,695	5%
Limited AT	$28,795	5%
Series Blue MT	$29,490	5%

Subaru BRZ

Safety Checklist

Crash Tests:

Frontal	Average
Side	Very Poor

Airbags:

Torso	Front Pelvis/Torso from Seat
Pelvis	Front Pelvis/Torso from Seat
Roll Sensing	No
Knee Bolster	None

Crash Avoidance:

Collision Avoidance	None
Blind Spot Detection	None
Lane Keeping Assist	None
Backup Camera	None
Pedestrian Crash Avoidance	None

General:

Auto. Crash Notification	None
Day Running Lamps	Standard

Safety Belt/Restraint:

Dynamic Head Restraints	None
Adjustable Belt	None

Subaru BRZ

Specifications

Drive	RWD
Engine	2.0-liter I4
Transmission	6-sp. Automatic
Tow Rating (lbs.)	–
Head/Leg Room (in.)	Very Cramped-37.1/41.9
Interior Space (cu. ft.)	Very Cramped-76.5
Cargo Space (cu. ft.)	Very Cramped-6.9
Wheelbase/Length (in.)	101.2/166.7

Ratings—10 Best, 1 Worst

Combo Crash Tests	6
Safety Features	8
Rollover	3
Preventive Maintenance	3
Repair Costs	7
Warranty	2
Fuel Economy	6
Complaints	3
Insurance Costs	1
OVERALL RATING	**2**

Subaru Forester

Subaru Forester

At-a-Glance

Status/Year Series Started........ Unchanged/2014
Twins ....–
Body Styles .... SUV
Seating....................................... 5
Anti-Theft Device . Std. Pass. Immobil. & Active Alarm
Parking Index Rating .... Very Easy
Where Made........................Lafayette, IN
Fuel Factor..................................
  MPG Rating (city/hwy) Average-24/32
  Driving Range (mi.) Long-430.0
  Fuel Type............................Regular
  Annual Fuel Cost .... Low-$1,553
  Gas Guzzler Tax ....No
  Greenhouse Gas Emissions (tons/yr.).. Average-6.6
  Barrels of Oil Used per year Average-12.2

How the Competition Rates

Competitors	Rating	Pg.
Hyundai Tucson	5	161
Mazda CX-5	5	197
Toyota RAV4	4	254

Price Range	Retail	Markup
2.5i MT	$22,195	6%
2.5i Premium AT	$25,095	6%
2.5i Touring	$30,095	7%
2.0 XT Touring	$33,095	7%

Safety Checklist

Crash Tests:
  Frontal............................Poor
  Side............................ Very Good
Airbags:
  Torso ....Front Pelvis/Torso from Seat
  Pelvis ....Front Pelvis/Torso from Seat
  Roll Sensing..........................Yes
  Knee Bolster .... Standard Driver
Crash Avoidance:
  Collision Avoidance ...... Optional CIB & DBS
  Blind Spot Detection .... None
  Lane Keeping Assist ....Warning Only Optional
  Backup Camera.................. Standard
  Pedestrian Crash Avoidance .... Optional
General:
  Auto. Crash Notification.............. None
  Day Running Lamps .... Standard
Safety Belt/Restraint:
  Dynamic Head Restraints .... None
  Adjustable Belt..............Standard Front

Subaru Forester

Specifications

Drive...................................AWD
Engine 2.5-liter I4
Transmission ....CVT
Tow Rating (lbs.) .... Very Low-1500
Head/Leg Room (in.) ....Very Roomy-41.4/43
Interior Space (cu. ft.)............. Roomy-113.1
Cargo Space (cu. ft.) .... Very Roomy-34.4
Wheelbase/Length (in.) 103.9/180.9

Subaru Impreza

Ratings—10 Best, 1 Worst

Combo Crash Tests	4
Safety Features	5
Rollover	8
Preventive Maintenance	4
Repair Costs	7
Warranty	2
Fuel Economy	9
Complaints	7
Insurance Costs	1
OVERALL RATING	**4**

Subaru Impreza

Subaru Impreza

At-a-Glance

Status/Year Series Started........ Unchanged/2012
Twins . . . . –
Body Styles . . . . Sedan, Hatchback
Seating 5
Anti-Theft Device . Std. Pass. Immobil. & Active Alarm
Parking Index Rating . . . . .Very Easy
Where Made. . . . . Gunma, Japan
Fuel Factor . . . .
  MPG Rating (city/hwy) . . . . Very Good-28/37
  Driving Range (mi.) Long-455.9
  Fuel Type . . . . .Regular
  Annual Fuel Cost . . . . Very Low-$1,335
  Gas Guzzler Tax . . . . .No
  Greenhouse Gas Emissions (tons/yr.) Low-5.8
  Barrels of Oil Used per year Low-10.6

How the Competition Rates

Competitors	Rating	Pg.
Dodge Dart	5	131
Honda Civic	6	149
Mitsubishi Lancer	4	213

Price Range

	Retail	Markup
2.0i Sedan MT	$18,195	5%
2.0i Premium Hatchback AT	$21,495	5%
2.0i Limited Sedan	$22,295	6%
2.0i Sport Limited Hatchback	$24,090	6%

Safety Checklist

Crash Tests:
  Frontal. . . . . .Very Poor
  Side. . . . . Good
Airbags:
  Torso . . . . .Front Pelvis/Torso from Seat
  Pelvis . . . . .Front Pelvis/Torso from Seat
  Roll Sensing. . . . . No
  Knee Bolster . . . . Standard Driver
Crash Avoidance:
  Collision Avoidance . . . . . . Optional CIB & DBS
  Blind Spot Detection . . . . None
  Lane Keeping Assist . . . .Warning Only Optional
  Backup Camera . . . . Standard
  Pedestrian Crash Avoidance . . . . Optional
General:
  Auto. Crash Notification . . . . None
  Day Running Lamps . . . . Standard
Safety Belt/Restraint:
  Dynamic Head Restraints . . . . None
  Adjustable Belt . . . . .Standard Front

Subaru Impreza

Specifications

Drive. . . . . AWD
Engine 2.0-liter I4
Transmission . . . . .CVT
Tow Rating (lbs.) . . . . –
Head/Leg Room (in.) Roomy-39.8/43.5
Interior Space (cu. ft.). Cramped-96.9
Cargo Space (cu. ft.) . . . . Very Cramped-12
Wheelbase/Length (in.) 104.1/180.5

Ratings—10 Best, 1 Worst

Combo Crash Tests	10
Safety Features	8
Rollover	8
Preventive Maintenance	2
Repair Costs	8
Warranty	2
Fuel Economy	8
Complaints	–
Insurance Costs	1
OVERALL RATING	**7**

Subaru Legacy

Subaru Legacy

At-a-Glance

Status/Year Series Started	All New/2015
Twins	–
Body Styles	Sedan
Seating	5
Anti-Theft Device	Std. Pass. Immobil. & Active Alarm
Parking Index Rating	Average
Where Made	Lafayette, IN
Fuel Factor	
MPG Rating (city/hwy)	Good-26/36
Driving Range (mi.)	Very Long-549.7
Fuel Type	Regular
Annual Fuel Cost	Very Low-$1,413
Gas Guzzler Tax	No
Greenhouse Gas Emissions (tons/yr.)	Low-6.0
Barrels of Oil Used per year	Average-11.0

How the Competition Rates

Competitors	Rating	Pg.
Ford Fusion	4	145
Kia Optima	7	177
Mazda Mazda6	4	201

Price Range

	Retail	Markup
Base	$21,695	6%
Premium	$23,495	6%
Limited	$26,495	6%
3.6R Limited	$29,959	8%

Subaru Legacy

Safety Checklist

Crash Tests:
Frontal......................... Very Good
Side........................... Very Good
Airbags:
Torso ....Front Pelvis/Torso from Seat
Pelvis ....Front Pelvis/Torso from Seat
Roll Sensing...........................Yes
Knee Bolster .... None
Crash Avoidance:
Collision Avoidance ...... Optional CIB & DBS
Blind Spot Detection .... Optional
Lane Keeping Assist ....Warning Only Optional
Backup Camera................... Standard
Pedestrian Crash Avoidance .... Optional
General:
Auto. Crash Notification.............. None
Day Running Lamps .... Standard
Safety Belt/Restraint:
Dynamic Head Restraints .... None
Adjustable Belt...............Standard Front

Subaru Legacy

Specifications

Drive	AWD
Engine	2.5-liter I4
Transmission	6-sp. Automatic
Tow Rating (lbs.)	–
Head/Leg Room (in.)	Roomy-40/42.9
Interior Space (cu. ft.)	Roomy-104.6
Cargo Space (cu. ft.)	Cramped-15
Wheelbase/Length (in.)	108.3/188.8

Subaru Outback

Ratings—10 Best, 1 Worst

Combo Crash Tests	10
Safety Features	8
Rollover	3
Preventive Maintenance	2
Repair Costs	8
Warranty	2
Fuel Economy	7
Complaints	–
Insurance Costs	5
OVERALL RATING	**7**

Subaru Outback

At-a-Glance

Status/Year Series Started. . . . . All New/2015
Twins . . . . –
Body Styles . . . . Wagon
Seating 5
Anti-Theft Device . Std. Pass. Immobil. & Active Alarm
Parking Index Rating . . . . Easy
Where Made. .Lafayette, IN
Fuel Factor . . . .
  MPG Rating (city/hwy) Good-25/33
  Driving Range (mi.) . . . . .Very Long-519.1
  Fuel Type. . . . . .Regular
  Annual Fuel Cost . . . . Low-$1,496
  Gas Guzzler Tax . . . . .No
  Greenhouse Gas Emissions (tons/yr.) Low-6.4
  Barrels of Oil Used per year Average-11.8

How the Competition Rates

Competitors	Rating	Pg.
Toyota Venza	3	259
Volkswagen Jetta	5	264
Volvo V60	–	269

Price Range

	Retail	Markup
Base	$24,895	6%
Premium	$26,995	6%
Limited	$29,995	7%
3.6R Limited	$32,995	7%

Safety Checklist

Crash Tests:
  Frontal. . . . . Very Good
  Side. . . . . Very Good
Airbags:
  Torso . . . . .Front Pelvis/Torso from Seat
  Pelvis . . . . .Front Pelvis/Torso from Seat
  Roll Sensing. . . . . .Yes
  Knee Bolster . . . . None
Crash Avoidance:
  Collision Avoidance . . . . . . Optional CIB & DBS
  Blind Spot Detection . . . . Optional
  Lane Keeping Assist . . . .Warning Only Optional
  Backup Camera . . . . Standard
  Pedestrian Crash Avoidance . . . . Optional
General:
  Auto. Crash Notification . . . . None
  Day Running Lamps . . . . Standard
Safety Belt/Restraint:
  Dynamic Head Restraints . . . . None
  Adjustable Belt. . . . . .Standard Front

Subaru Outback

Specifications

Drive. . . . . AWD
Engine 2.5-liter I4
Transmission . . . . .6-sp. Automatic
Tow Rating (lbs.) . . . . Very Low-2700
Head/Leg Room (in.) Roomy-40.8/42.9
Interior Space (cu. ft.). Roomy-108.1
Cargo Space (cu. ft.) . . . . Very Roomy-35.5
Wheelbase/Length (in.) 108.1/189.6

Subaru XV Crosstrek

Ratings—10 Best, 1 Worst

Combo Crash Tests	5
Safety Features	8
Rollover	4
Preventive Maintenance	4
Repair Costs	7
Warranty	2
Fuel Economy	8
Complaints	9
Insurance Costs	3
OVERALL RATING	**5**

Subaru XV Crosstrek

Safety Checklist

Crash Tests:
Frontal . . . . Average
Side . . . . Poor
Airbags:
Torso . . . . .Front Pelvis/Torso from Seat
Pelvis . . . . .Front Pelvis/Torso from Seat
Roll Sensing . . . . .Yes
Knee Bolster . . . . Standard Driver
Crash Avoidance:
Collision Avoidance . . . . . . Optional CIB & DBS
Blind Spot Detection . . . . None
Lane Keeping Assist . . . .Warning Only Optional
Backup Camera . . . . Standard
Pedestrian Crash Avoidance . . . . Optional
General:
Auto. Crash Notification . . . . None
Day Running Lamps . . . . Standard
Safety Belt/Restraint:
Dynamic Head Restraints . . . . None
Adjustable Belt . . . . .Standard Front

At-a-Glance

Status/Year Series Started Unchanged/2013
Twins . . . . –
Body Styles . . . . SUV
Seating 5
Anti-Theft Device . Std. Pass. Immobil. & Active Alarm
Parking Index Rating . . . . .Very Easy
Where Made . . . . Gunma, Japan
Fuel Factor . . . .
 MPG Rating (city/hwy) Good-26/34
 Driving Range (mi.) Long-462.4
 Fuel Type . . . . .Regular
 Annual Fuel Cost . . . . Low-$1,444
 Gas Guzzler Tax . . . . .No
 Greenhouse Gas Emissions (tons/yr.) Low-6.2
 Barrels of Oil Used per year Average-11.4

Subaru XV Crosstrek

How the Competition Rates

Competitors	Rating	Pg.
Jeep Renegade	–	173
Kia Soul	7	181
Nissan Juke	–	221

Price Range

Price Range	Retail	Markup
Premium MT	$21,995	5%
Premium AT w/Nav	$24,295	6%
Limited w/Moon&Nav	$26,595	6%
Hybrid Touring	$29,295	5%

Specifications

Drive . . . . .AWD
Engine 2.0-liter I4
Transmission . . . . .CVT
Tow Rating (lbs.) . . . . –
Head/Leg Room (in.) Roomy-39.8/43.5
Interior Space (cu. ft.) Cramped-97.5
Cargo Space (cu. ft.) Average-22.3
Wheelbase/Length (in.) 103.7/175.2

Tesla Model S

Ratings—10 Best, 1 Worst

Combo Crash Tests	9
Safety Features	10
Rollover	10
Preventive Maintenance	–
Repair Costs	–
Warranty	8
Fuel Economy	10
Complaints	–
Insurance Costs	5
OVERALL RATING	**10**

Tesla Model S

Tesla Model S

At-a-Glance

Status/Year Series Started. Unchanged/2015
Twins . . . . –
Body Styles . . . . Sedan
Seating 5
Anti-Theft Device . . . . Std. Passive Alarm Only
Parking Index Rating . . . . Hard
Where Made. Fremont, CA
Fuel Factor . . . .
  MPG Rating (city/hwy) . . . . Very Good-88/90
  Driving Range (mi.) . . . . Very Short-265
  Fuel Type . . . . Electricity
  Annual Fuel Cost . . . . Very Low-$472
  Gas Guzzler Tax . . . . No
  Greenhouse Gas Emissions (tons/yr.). Very Low-4.1
  Barrels of Oil Used per year . . . . Very Low-0.2

How the Competition Rates

Competitors	Rating	Pg.
Chevrolet Volt	8	125
Lexus ES	7	187
Nissan Leaf	2	222

Price Range

	Retail	Markup
60 kWh	$71,070	0%
85 kWh	$81,070	0%
85 kWh Performance	$105,670	0%

Safety Checklist

Crash Tests:
  Frontal. . . . . Good
  Side. . . . . Very Good
Airbags:
  Torso . . . . Front Pelvis/Torso from Seat
  Pelvis . . . . Front Pelvis/Torso from Seat
  Roll Sensing. . . . . Yes
  Knee Bolster . . . . Standard Front
Crash Avoidance:
  Collision Avoidance . . . . . . Standard CIB & DBS
  Blind Spot Detection . . . . Standard
  Lane Keeping Assist . . . . Optional
  Backup Camera . . . . Standard
  Pedestrian Crash Avoidance . . . . None
General:
  Auto. Crash Notification . . . . None
  Day Running Lamps . . . . Standard
Safety Belt/Restraint:
  Dynamic Head Restraints . . . . None
  Adjustable Belt . . . . None

Tesla Model S

Specifications

Drive . . . . RWD
Engine . . . . Electric
Transmission . . . . –
Tow Rating (lbs.) . . . . –
Head/Leg Room (in.) Average-38.8/42.7
Interior Space (cu. ft.). Cramped-94
Cargo Space (cu. ft.) Roomy-31.6
Wheelbase/Length (in.) 116.5/196

Ratings—10 Best, 1 Worst

Combo Crash Tests	2
Safety Features	7
Rollover	1
Preventive Maintenance	9
Repair Costs	4
Warranty	2
Fuel Economy	2
Complaints	10
Insurance Costs	10
OVERALL RATING	**3**

Toyota 4Runner

Toyota 4Runner

At-a-Glance

Status/Year Series Started	Unchanged/2006
Twins	Lexus GX
Body Styles	SUV
Seating	5/7
Anti-Theft Device	Std. Pass. Immobil.
Parking Index Rating	Average
Where Made	Tahara, Japan
Fuel Factor	
MPG Rating (city/hwy)	Very Poor-17/21
Driving Range (mi.)	Long-427.7
Fuel Type	Regular
Annual Fuel Cost	High-$2,258
Gas Guzzler Tax	No
Greenhouse Gas Emissions (tons/yr.)	Very High-10.0
Barrels of Oil Used per year	Very High-18.3

How the Competition Rates

Competitors	Rating	Pg.
Chevrolet Tahoe	6	122
Ford Expedition	7	139
Nissan Armada	–	219

Price Range	Retail	Markup
SR5 2WD	$33,010	9%
SR5 Premium 4WD	$37,625	9%
Trail Edition Prem 4WD	$38,655	9%
Limited 4WD	$43,420	9%

Safety Checklist

Crash Tests:
Frontal . . . . .Very Poor
Side . . . . Poor

Airbags:
Torso . . . . Front Pelvis/Torso from Seat
Pelvis . . . . Front Pelvis/Torso from Seat
Roll Sensing . . . . .Yes
Knee Bolster . . . . .Standard Front

Crash Avoidance:
Collision Avoidance . . . . None
Blind Spot Detection . . . . None
Lane Keeping Assist . . . . None
Backup Camera . . . . Standard
Pedestrian Crash Avoidance . . . . None

General:
Auto. Crash Notification . . . Operator Assist.-Fee
Day Running Lamps . . . . Standard

Safety Belt/Restraint:
Dynamic Head Restraints . . . . . .Standard Front
Adjustable Belt . . . . .Standard Front

Toyota 4Runner

Specifications

Drive	4WD
Engine	4.0-liter V6
Transmission	5-sp. Automatic
Tow Rating (lbs.)	Low-4700
Head/Leg Room (in.)	Cramped-39.3/41.7
Interior Space (cu. ft.)	Very Roomy-128
Cargo Space (cu. ft.)	Very Cramped-9
Wheelbase/Length (in.)	109.8/190.2

Ratings—10 Best, 1 Worst

Combo Crash Tests	7
Safety Features	8
Rollover	7
Preventive Maintenance	8
Repair Costs	4
Warranty	2
Fuel Economy	5
Complaints	4
Insurance Costs	8
OVERALL RATING	**7**

Toyota Avalon

Toyota Avalon

At-a-Glance

Status/Year Series Started........ Unchanged/2013
Twins .... Lexus ES
Body Styles ....Sedan
Seating 5
Anti-Theft Device ...... Std. Pass. Immobil. & Alarm
Parking Index Rating .... Average
Where Made...................Georgetown, KY
Fuel Factor...............................
  MPG Rating (city/hwy) Average-21/31
  Driving Range (mi.) Average-417.6
  Fuel Type...........................Regular
  Annual Fuel Cost .... Average-$1,709
  Gas Guzzler Tax ....No
  Greenhouse Gas Emissions (tons/yr.).. Average-7.5
  Barrels of Oil Used per year High-13.7

How the Competition Rates

Competitors	Rating	Pg.
Chevrolet Impala	6	116
Ford Taurus	4	147
Hyundai Genesis	7	157

Price Range

Price Range	Retail	Markup
XLE	$32,285	11%
XLE Premium	$34,140	11%
XLE Touring Sport	$37,170	11%
Limited Hybrid	$41,700	11%

Safety Checklist

Crash Tests:
  Frontal......................... Average
  Side..................... Good
Airbags:
  Torso .... Fr. & Rr. Pelvis/Torso from Seat
  Pelvis .... Fr. & Rr. Pelvis/Torso from Seat
  Roll Sensing.......................... No
  Knee Bolster ....Standard Front
Crash Avoidance:
  Collision Avoidance ...... Optional CIB & DBS
  Blind Spot Detection .... Optional
  Lane Keeping Assist .... None
  Backup Camera.................. Standard
  Pedestrian Crash Avoidance .... None
General:
  Auto. Crash Notification ... Operator Assist.-Fee
  Day Running Lamps .... Standard
Safety Belt/Restraint:
  Dynamic Head Restraints .... None
  Adjustable Belt..............Standard Front

Toyota Avalon

Specifications

Drive................................. FWD
Engine 3.5-liter V6
Transmission ....6-sp. Automatic
Tow Rating (lbs.) .... Very Low-1000
Head/Leg Room (in.) Cramped-37.6/42.1
Interior Space (cu. ft.)........... Roomy-103.63
Cargo Space (cu. ft.) Cramped-16
Wheelbase/Length (in.) 111/195.3

Toyota Camry

Ratings—10 Best, 1 Worst

Combo Crash Tests	7
Safety Features	10
Rollover	7
Preventive Maintenance	8
Repair Costs	4
Warranty	2
Fuel Economy	8
Complaints	7
Insurance Costs	3
OVERALL RATING	**7**

Toyota Camry

At-a-Glance

Status/Year Series Started Appearance Change/2012
Twins . . . . –
Body Styles . . . . .Sedan
Seating 5
Anti-Theft Device. .Std. Pass. Immobil. & Opt. Pass. Alarm
Parking Index Rating . . . . Average
Where Made. . . . . .Georgetown, KY
Fuel Factor . . . .
  MPG Rating (city/hwy) Good-25/35
  Driving Range (mi.) . . . . .Very Long-487.7
  Fuel Type. . . . . .Regular
  Annual Fuel Cost . . . . Low-$1,464
  Gas Guzzler Tax . . . . .No
  Greenhouse Gas Emissions (tons/yr.). Low-6.4
  Barrels of Oil Used per year Average-11.8

How the Competition Rates

Competitors	Rating	Pg.
Ford Fusion	4	145
Honda Accord	7	148
Subaru Legacy	7	242

Price Range

	Retail	Markup
LE	$22,970	9%
XSE	$26,150	10%
XLE Hybrid	$29,980	9%
XLE V6	$31,370	10%

Safety Checklist

Crash Tests:
  Frontal . . . . Average
  Side . . . . Good
Airbags:
  Torso . . . . Fr. & Rr. Pelvis/Torso from Seat
  Pelvis . . . . Fr. & Rr. Pelvis/Torso from Seat
  Roll Sensing. . . . . .Yes
  Knee Bolster . . . . .Standard Front
Crash Avoidance:
  Collision Avoidance . . . . . . Optional CIB & DBS
  Blind Spot Detection . . . . Optional
  Lane Keeping Assist . . . .Warning Only Optional
  Backup Camera . . . . Standard
  Pedestrian Crash Avoidance . . . . None
General:
  Auto. Crash Notification . . . Operator Assist.-Fee
  Day Running Lamps . . . . Standard
Safety Belt/Restraint:
  Dynamic Head Restraints . . . . None
  Adjustable Belt . . . . .Standard Front

Toyota Camry

Specifications

Drive . . . . FWD
Engine 2.5-liter I4
Transmission . . . . .6-sp. Automatic
Tow Rating (lbs.) . . . . Very Low-0
Head/Leg Room (in.) Cramped-38.8/41.6
Interior Space (cu. ft.). Average-102.7
Cargo Space (cu. ft.) Cramped-15.4
Wheelbase/Length (in.) 109.3/190.9

Toyota Corolla Compact

Ratings—10 Best, 1 Worst

Combo Crash Tests	8
Safety Features	2
Rollover	6
Preventive Maintenance	10
Repair Costs	9
Warranty	2
Fuel Economy	9
Complaints	9
Insurance Costs	1
OVERALL RATING	**8**

Toyota Corolla

Toyota Corolla

At-a-Glance

Status/Year Series Started	Unchanged/2014
Twins	–
Body Styles	Sedan
Seating	5
Anti-Theft Device	Std. Pass. Immobil.
Parking Index Rating	Easy
Where Made	Tupelo, MS
Fuel Factor	
MPG Rating (city/hwy)	Very Good-27/36
Driving Range (mi.)	Average-401.6
Fuel Type	Regular
Annual Fuel Cost	Very Low-$1,380
Gas Guzzler Tax	No
Greenhouse Gas Emissions (tons/yr.)	Low-5.8
Barrels of Oil Used per year	Low-10.6

How the Competition Rates

Competitors	Rating	Pg.
Chevrolet Cruze	8	114
Honda Civic	6	149
Nissan Sentra	–	228

Price Range

	Retail	Markup
L MT	$16,900	6%
LE	$18,515	8%
LE Eco Plus	$19,615	8%
S Premium	$22,905	8%

Safety Checklist

Crash Tests:
Frontal	Good
Side	Very Good

Airbags:
Torso	Front Pelvis/Torso from Seat
Pelvis	Front Pelvis/Torso from Seat
Roll Sensing	No
Knee Bolster	Standard Driver

Crash Avoidance:
Collision Avoidance	None
Blind Spot Detection	None
Lane Keeping Assist	None
Backup Camera	Optional
Pedestrian Crash Avoidance	None

General:
Auto. Crash Notification	None
Day Running Lamps	Standard

Safety Belt/Restraint:
Dynamic Head Restraints	None
Adjustable Belt	Standard Front

Toyota Corolla

Specifications

Drive	FWD
Engine	1.8-liter I4
Transmission	4-sp. Automatic
Tow Rating (lbs.)	Very Low-0
Head/Leg Room (in.)	Cramped-38.3/42.3
Interior Space (cu. ft.)	Cramped-97.5
Cargo Space (cu. ft.)	Very Cramped-13
Wheelbase/Length (in.)	106.3/182.6

Ratings—10 Best, 1 Worst

Combo Crash Tests	9
Safety Features	8
Rollover	3
Preventive Maintenance	9
Repair Costs	2
Warranty	2
Fuel Economy	3
Complaints	10
Insurance Costs	8
OVERALL RATING	**7**

Toyota Highlander

Toyota Highlander

Safety Checklist

Crash Tests:
Frontal . . . . Good
Side . . . . Very Good
Airbags:
Torso . . . . Front Pelvis/Torso from Seat
Pelvis . . . . Front Pelvis/Torso from Seat
Roll Sensing . . . . Yes
Knee Bolster . . . . Standard Driver
Crash Avoidance:
Collision Avoidance . . . . . . Optional CIB & DBS
Blind Spot Detection . . . . Optional
Lane Keeping Assist . . . . Warning Only Optional
Backup Camera . . . . Standard
Pedestrian Crash Avoidance . . . . None
General:
Auto. Crash Notification . . . Operator Assist.-Fee
Day Running Lamps . . . . Standard
Safety Belt/Restraint:
Dynamic Head Restraints . . . . None
Adjustable Belt . . . . Standard Front

At-a-Glance

Status/Year Series Started Unchanged/2014
Twins . . . . –
Body Styles . . . . SUV
Seating 7/8
Anti-Theft Device Std. Pass. Immobil. & Opt. Pass. Alarm
Parking Index Rating . . . . Hard
Where Made . . . . Princeton, IN
Fuel Factor . . . .
  MPG Rating (city/hwy) Poor-18/24
  Driving Range (mi.) Short-389.4
  Fuel Type . . . . Regular
  Annual Fuel Cost . . . . High-$2,070
  Gas Guzzler Tax . . . . No
  Greenhouse Gas Emissions (tons/yr.) High-9.0
  Barrels of Oil Used per year High-16.5

Toyota Highlander

How the Competition Rates

Competitors	Rating	Pg.
Buick Enclave	7	102
Chevrolet Traverse	7	123
Nissan Pathfinder	–	225

Price Range

	Retail	Markup
LE I4 FWD	$29,415	10%
LE Plus AWD	$34,400	10%
Limited AWD	$41,300	10%
Hybrid LTD Platinum	$49,990	10%

Specifications

Drive . . . . AWD
Engine 3.5-liter V6
Transmission . . . . 6-sp. Automatic
Tow Rating (lbs.) . . . . Very Low-2000
Head/Leg Room (in.) . . . . . . Very Roomy-40.7/44.2
Interior Space (cu. ft.) . . . . Very Roomy-144.9
Cargo Space (cu. ft.) Cramped-13.8
Wheelbase/Length (in.) 109.8/191.1

Ratings—10 Best, 1 Worst	
Combo Crash Tests	4
Safety Features	5
Rollover	6
Preventive Maintenance	10
Repair Costs	6
Warranty	2
Fuel Economy	10
Complaints	2
Insurance Costs	3
OVERALL RATING	**4**

Toyota Prius

Toyota Prius

At-a-Glance

Status/Year Series Started	Unchanged/2010
Twins	–
Body Styles	Hatchback
Seating	5
Anti-Theft Device	Std. Pass. Immobil.
Parking Index Rating	Very Easy
Where Made	Tsutsumi, Japan
Fuel Factor	
MPG Rating (city/hwy)	Very Good-51/48
Driving Range (mi.)	Very Long-590.3
Fuel Type	Regular
Annual Fuel Cost	Very Low-$846
Gas Guzzler Tax	No
Greenhouse Gas Emissions (tons/yr.)	Very Low-3.6
Barrels of Oil Used per year	Very Low-6.6

How the Competition Rates

Competitors	Rating	Pg.
Chevrolet Volt	8	125
Ford C-MAX	5	136
Lexus CT	–	186

Price Range	Retail	Markup
One	$23,215	5%
Three	$25,765	7%
Five	$30,005	7%
Plug-In Hybrid Adv.	$34,905	4%

Safety Checklist

Crash Tests:
Frontal . . . . Poor
Side . . . . Average
Airbags:
Torso . . . . Front Torso from Seat
Pelvis . . . . None
Roll Sensing . . . . No
Knee Bolster . . . . Standard Driver
Crash Avoidance:
Collision Avoidance . . . . . . Optional CIB & DBS
Blind Spot Detection . . . . None
Lane Keeping Assist . . . . Optional
Backup Camera . . . . Optional
Pedestrian Crash Avoidance . . . . None
General:
Auto. Crash Notification . . . Operator Assist.-Fee
Day Running Lamps . . . . Standard
Safety Belt/Restraint:
Dynamic Head Restraints . . . . . . Standard Front
Adjustable Belt . . . . Standard Front

Toyota Prius

Specifications

Drive	FWD
Engine	1.8-liter I4
Transmission	CVT
Tow Rating (lbs.)	–
Head/Leg Room (in.)	Average-38.6/42.5
Interior Space (cu. ft.)	Cramped-93.7
Cargo Space (cu. ft.)	Average-21.6
Wheelbase/Length (in.)	106.3/176.4

Ratings—10 Best, 1 Worst

Combo Crash Tests	2
Safety Features	2
Rollover	6
Preventive Maintenance	9
Repair Costs	9
Warranty	2
Fuel Economy	10
Complaints	10
Insurance Costs	3
OVERALL RATING	**5**

Toyota Prius C

Toyota Prius C

Toyota Prius C

At-a-Glance

Status/Year Series Started Appearance Change/2013
Twins . . . . –
Body Styles . . . . Hatchback
Seating 5
Anti-Theft Device . . . . . .Optional Pass. Immobil. Only
Parking Index Rating . . . . .Very Easy
Where Made. . . . . .Iwata, Japan
Fuel Factor. . . . .
  MPG Rating (city/hwy) . . . . Very Good-53/46
  Driving Range (mi.) . . . . .Very Long-471.2
  Fuel Type. . . . . .Regular
  Annual Fuel Cost . . . . Very Low-$846
  Gas Guzzler Tax . . . . .No
  Greenhouse Gas Emissions (tons/yr.). Very Low-3.6
  Barrels of Oil Used per year . . . . Very Low-6.6

How the Competition Rates

Competitors	Rating	Pg.
Chevrolet Sonic	9	119
Ford C-MAX	5	136
Nissan Leaf	2	222

Price Range	Retail	Markup
One	$19,540	5%
Two	$20,340	6%
Three	$21,765	7%
Four	$24,475	7%

Safety Checklist

Crash Tests:
  Frontal. . . . . .Poor
  Side. . . . . Very Poor*
Airbags:
  Torso . . . . .Front Pelvis/Torso from Seat
  Pelvis . . . . .Front Pelvis/Torso from Seat
  Roll Sensing. . . . . No
  Knee Bolster . . . . Standard Driver
Crash Avoidance:
  Collision Avoidance . . . . None
  Blind Spot Detection . . . . None
  Lane Keeping Assist . . . . None
  Backup Camera . . . . Optional
  Pedestrian Crash Avoidance . . . . None
General:
  Auto. Crash Notification . . . . None
  Day Running Lamps . . . . Standard
Safety Belt/Restraint:
  Dynamic Head Restraints . . . . None
  Adjustable Belt. . . . . None

Toyota Prius C

Specifications

Drive. . . . . FWD
Engine 1.5-liter I4
Transmission . . . . .CVT
Tow Rating (lbs.) . . . . –
Head/Leg Room (in.) Cramped-38.6/41.7
Interior Space (cu. ft.). . . . . . . .Very Cramped-87.4
Cargo Space (cu. ft.) Average-17.1
Wheelbase/Length (in.) 100.4/157.3

*Additional injury potential in side test. See footnote on page 20.

Ratings—10 Best, 1 Worst	
Combo Crash Tests	7
Safety Features	5
Rollover	5
Preventive Maintenance	10
Repair Costs	6
Warranty	2
Fuel Economy	10
Complaints	9
Insurance Costs	5
OVERALL RATING	**8**

Toyota Prius V

Toyota Prius V

At-a-Glance

Status/Year Series Started Appearance Change/2013	
Twins	–
Body Styles	Wagon
Seating	5
Anti-Theft Device	Std. Pass. Immobil.
Parking Index Rating	Easy
Where Made	Tsutsumi, Japan
Fuel Factor	
MPG Rating (city/hwy)	Very Good-44/40
Driving Range (mi.)	Very Long-501.1
Fuel Type	Regular
Annual Fuel Cost	Very Low-$997
Gas Guzzler Tax	No
Greenhouse Gas Emissions (tons/yr.)	Very Low-4.3
Barrels of Oil Used per year	Very Low-7.8

How the Competition Rates

Competitors	Rating	Pg.
Ford C-MAX	5	136
Lexus CT	–	186
Mazda Mazda5	–	200

Price Range	Retail	Markup
Two	$26,675	7%
Three	$28,060	7%
Four	$29,695	7%
Five	$30,935	7%

Safety Checklist

Crash Tests:
Frontal . . . . Poor
Side . . . . Very Good

Airbags:
Torso . . . . Front Pelvis/Torso from Seat
Pelvis . . . . Front Pelvis/Torso from Seat
Roll Sensing . . . . No
Knee Bolster . . . . Standard Driver

Crash Avoidance:
Collision Avoidance . . . . . . Optional CIB & DBS
Blind Spot Detection . . . . None
Lane Keeping Assist . . . . Warning Only Optional
Backup Camera . . . . Standard
Pedestrian Crash Avoidance . . . . None

General:
Auto. Crash Notification . . . Operator Assist.-Fee
Day Running Lamps . . . . Standard

Safety Belt/Restraint:
Dynamic Head Restraints . . . . None
Adjustable Belt . . . . Standard Front

Toyota Prius V

Specifications

Drive	FWD
Engine	1.8-liter I4
Transmission	CVT
Tow Rating (lbs.)	–
Head/Leg Room (in.)	Cramped-39.6/41.3
Interior Space (cu. ft.)	Cramped-97.2
Cargo Space (cu. ft.)	Very Roomy-34.3
Wheelbase/Length (in.)	109.4/182.3

Ratings—10 Best, 1 Worst

Combo Crash Tests	4
Safety Features	6
Rollover	3
Preventive Maintenance	8
Repair Costs	3
Warranty	2
Fuel Economy	5
Complaints	9
Insurance Costs	8
OVERALL RATING	**4**

Toyota RAV4

Toyota RAV4

At-a-Glance

Status/Year Series Started	Unchanged/2013
Twins	Lexus NX
Body Styles	SUV
Seating	5
Anti-Theft Device	Std. Pass. Immobil.
Parking Index Rating	Very Easy
Where Made	Woodstock, Ontario / Tahara, Japan
Fuel Factor	
MPG Rating (city/hwy)	Average-22/29
Driving Range (mi.)	Short-392.4
Fuel Type	Regular
Annual Fuel Cost	Average-$1,701
Gas Guzzler Tax	No
Greenhouse Gas Emissions (tons/yr.)	Average-7.2
Barrels of Oil Used per year	High-13.2

How the Competition Rates

Competitors	Rating	Pg.
Ford Escape	5	138
Honda CR-V	6	151
Hyundai Tucson	5	161

Price Range

	Retail	Markup
LE 2WD	$23,680	7%
LE AWD	$25,080	7%
XLE AWD	$26,640	7%
Limited AWD	$29,850	7%

Safety Checklist

Crash Tests:
Frontal	Very Poor
Side	Good

Airbags:
Torso	Front Pelvis/Torso from Seat
Pelvis	Front Pelvis/Torso from Seat
Roll Sensing	Yes
Knee Bolster	Standard Driver

Crash Avoidance:
Collision Avoidance	Warning Only Optional
Blind Spot Detection	Optional
Lane Keeping Assist	Warning Only Optional
Backup Camera	Optional
Pedestrian Crash Avoidance	None

General:
Auto. Crash Notification	None
Day Running Lamps	Standard

Safety Belt/Restraint:
Dynamic Head Restraints	None
Adjustable Belt	Standard Front

Toyota RAV4

Specifications

Drive	AWD
Engine	2.5-liter I4
Transmission	6-sp. Automatic
Tow Rating (lbs.)	Very Low-1500
Head/Leg Room (in.)	Average-39.8/42.6
Interior Space (cu. ft.)	Average-101.9
Cargo Space (cu. ft.)	Very Roomy-38.4
Wheelbase/Length (in.)	104.7/179.9

Ratings—10 Best, 1 Worst

Combo Crash Tests	–
Safety Features	6
Rollover	2
Preventive Maintenance	9
Repair Costs	3
Warranty	2
Fuel Economy	1
Complaints	8
Insurance Costs	10

OVERALL RATING —

Toyota Sequoia

Toyota Sequoia

At-a-Glance

Status/Year Series Started	Unchanged/2008
Twins	–
Body Styles	SUV
Seating	8
Anti-Theft Device	Std. Pass. Immobil. & Alarm
Parking Index Rating	Very Hard
Where Made	Princeton, IN
Fuel Factor	
MPG Rating (city/hwy)	Very Poor-13/17
Driving Range (mi.)	Short-383.8
Fuel Type	Regular
Annual Fuel Cost	Very High-$2,888
Gas Guzzler Tax	No
Greenhouse Gas Emissions (tons/yr.)	Very High-12.8
Barrels of Oil Used per year	Very High-23.5

How the Competition Rates

Competitors	Rating	Pg.
Chevrolet Tahoe	6	122
Dodge Durango	2	132
Nissan Armada	–	219

Price Range	Retail	Markup
SR5 2WD	$44,395	10%
Limited 2WD	$53,355	10%
Limited 4WD	$56,580	10%
Platinum 4WD	$64,320	10%

Safety Checklist

Crash Tests:
Frontal . . . . –
Side . . . . –

Airbags:
Torso . . . . .Front Pelvis/Torso from Seat
Pelvis . . . . .Front Pelvis/Torso from Seat
Roll Sensing . . . . .Yes
Knee Bolster . . . . .Standard Front

Crash Avoidance:
Collision Avoidance . . . . None
Blind Spot Detection . . . . Optional
Lane Keeping Assist . . . . None
Backup Camera . . . . Standard
Pedestrian Crash Avoidance . . . . None

General:
Auto. Crash Notification . . . . None
Day Running Lamps . . . . Optional

Safety Belt/Restraint:
Dynamic Head Restraints . . . . None
Adjustable Belt . . . . . . .Standard Front and Rear

Toyota Sequoia

Specifications

Drive	4WD
Engine	5.7-liter V8
Transmission	6-sp. Automatic
Tow Rating (lbs.)	Average-7100
Head/Leg Room (in.)	Very Cramped-34.8/42.5
Interior Space (cu. ft.)	–
Cargo Space (cu. ft.)	Average-18.9
Wheelbase/Length (in.)	122/205.1

Toyota Sienna

Ratings—10 Best, 1 Worst

Combo Crash Tests	4
Safety Features	8
Rollover	5
Preventive Maintenance	7
Repair Costs	3
Warranty	2
Fuel Economy	3
Complaints	4
Insurance Costs	8
OVERALL RATING	**3**

Toyota Sienna

At-a-Glance

Status/Year Series Started Appearance Change/2004
Twins . . . . –
Body Styles . . . . .Minivan
Seating 7/8
Anti-Theft Device . Std. Pass. Immobil. & Opt. Pass. Alarm
Parking Index Rating . . . . Hard
Where Made. . . . . Princeton, IN
Fuel Factor. . . . .
  MPG Rating (city/hwy) Poor-18/25
  Driving Range (mi.) Average-411.9
  Fuel Type. . . . . .Regular
  Annual Fuel Cost . . . . High-$2,039
  Gas Guzzler Tax . . . . .No
  Greenhouse Gas Emissions (tons/yr.). High-8.6
  Barrels of Oil Used per year High-15.7

How the Competition Rates

Competitors	Rating	Pg.
Honda Odyssey	7	153
Kia Sedona	–	179
Nissan Quest	–	226

Price Range	Retail	Markup
L FWD	$28,600	8%
SE FWD	$34,900	8%
XLE Premium FWD	$38,355	9%
LTD Premium AWD	$46,150	9%

Safety Checklist

Crash Tests:
  Frontal. . . . . .Very Poor
  Side. . . . . Good
Airbags:
  Torso . . . . .Front Pelvis/Torso from Seat
  Pelvis . . . . .Front Pelvis/Torso from Seat
  Roll Sensing. . . . . .Yes
  Knee Bolster . . . . Standard Driver
Crash Avoidance:
  Collision Avoidance . . . . . . Optional CIB & DBS
  Blind Spot Detection . . . . Optional
  Lane Keeping Assist . . . . None
  Backup Camera . . . . Standard
  Pedestrian Crash Avoidance . . . . None
General:
  Auto. Crash Notification . . . Operator Assist.-Fee
  Day Running Lamps . . . . Optional
Safety Belt/Restraint:
  Dynamic Head Restraints . . . . . .Standard Front
  Adjustable Belt. . . . . . .Standard Front and Rear

Toyota Sienna

Specifications

Drive. . . . . FWD
Engine 3.5-liter V6
Transmission . . . . .6-sp. Automatic
Tow Rating (lbs.) Low-3500
Head/Leg Room (in.) Average-41/40.5
Interior Space (cu. ft.). . . . . Very Roomy-164.4
Cargo Space (cu. ft.) . . . . Very Roomy-39.1
Wheelbase/Length (in.) 119.3/200.2

Toyota Tacoma Compact Pickup

Ratings—10 Best, 1 Worst

Combo Crash Tests	1*
Safety Features	4
Rollover	2
Preventive Maintenance	9
Repair Costs	6
Warranty	2
Fuel Economy	2
Complaints	8
Insurance Costs	5
OVERALL RATING	**1**

Toyota Tacoma

Toyota Tacoma

At-a-Glance

Status/Year Series Started........ Unchanged/2009
Twins . . . .–
Body Styles . . . . Pickup
Seating 5
Anti-Theft Device . . . . . . Opt. Pass. Immobil. & Alarm
Parking Index Rating . . . . Very Hard
Where Made. . . . . San Antonio, TX / Tijuana, Mexico
Fuel Factor . . . .
  MPG Rating (city/hwy) . . . . Very Poor-16/21
  Driving Range (mi.) Short-378.1
  Fuel Type . . . . .Regular
  Annual Fuel Cost . . . . Very High-$2,343
  Gas Guzzler Tax . . . . .No
  Greenhouse Gas Emissions (tons/yr.)Very High-10.0
  Barrels of Oil Used per year . . . . Very High-18.3

How the Competition Rates

Competitors	Rating	Pg.
Chevrolet Colorado	–	112
GMC Acadia	6	-
Nissan Frontier	–	220

Price Range

	Retail	Markup
Base Access Cab 2WD MT	$20,765	7%
Prerunner Access Cab 2WD AT	$22,325	7%
Base Dbl. Cab 4WD V6 AT	$28,035	8%
TRD Pro Dbl. Cab 4WD V6 AT	$37,415	8%

Safety Checklist

Crash Tests:
  Frontal. . . . . .Very Poor
  Side. . . . . .Very Poor
Airbags:
  Torso . . . . Front Torso from Seat
  Pelvis . . . . None
  Roll Sensing. . . . . .Yes
  Knee Bolster . . . . None
Crash Avoidance:
  Collision Avoidance . . . . None
  Blind Spot Detection . . . . None
  Lane Keeping Assist . . . . None
  Backup Camera . . . . Optional
  Pedestrian Crash Avoidance . . . . None
General:
  Auto. Crash Notification . . . . None
  Day Running Lamps . . . . Standard
Safety Belt/Restraint:
  Dynamic Head Restraints . . . . . .Standard Front
  Adjustable Belt. . . . . .Standard Front

Toyota Tacoma

Specifications

Drive. 4WD
Engine 4.0-liter V6
Transmission . . . . .5-sp. Automatic
Tow Rating (lbs.) Average-6500
Head/Leg Room (in.) Average-40.2/41.7
Interior Space (cu. ft.). . . . . –
Cargo Space (cu. ft.) Roomy-33.54
Wheelbase/Length (in.) 127.4/208.1

*Crash test is for Regular Cab only. For Crew Cab results see page 27.

Ratings—10 Best, 1 Worst

Combo Crash Tests	5*
Safety Features	6
Rollover	2
Preventive Maintenance	9
Repair Costs	3
Warranty	2
Fuel Economy	1
Complaints	9
Insurance Costs	5
OVERALL RATING	**3**

Toyota Tundra

Toyota Tundra

At-a-Glance

Status/Year Series Started	Unchanged/2007
Twins	–
Body Styles	Pickup
Seating	5/6
Anti-Theft Device	Std. Pass. Immobil. & Opt. Pass. Alarm
Parking Index Rating	Very Hard
Where Made	San Antonio, TX
Fuel Factor	
MPG Rating (city/hwy)	Very Poor-13/17
Driving Range (mi.)	Short-383.8
Fuel Type	Regular
Annual Fuel Cost	Very High-$2,888
Gas Guzzler Tax	No
Greenhouse Gas Emissions (tons/yr.)	Very High-12.0
Barrels of Oil Used per year	Very High-22.0

How the Competition Rates

Competitors	Rating	Pg.
Chevrolet Silverado	7	118
Ford F-150	–	141
Nissan Titan	–	229

Price Range

Price Range	Retail	Markup
SR Reg. Cab 2WD 5.7 V8	$29,120	8%
SR5 Dbl. Cab 4WD 5.7 V8	$34,710	8%
Limited Crew Max 4WD 5.7 V8	$42,550	8%
1794 Edition Crew Max 5.7 V8	$47,975	8%

Safety Checklist

Crash Tests:
Frontal .... Very Poor
Side .... Very Good

Airbags:
Torso .... Front Pelvis/Torso from Seat
Pelvis .... Front Pelvis/Torso from Seat
Roll Sensing .... Yes
Knee Bolster .... Standard Front

Crash Avoidance:
Collision Avoidance .... None
Blind Spot Detection .... Optional
Lane Keeping Assist .... None
Backup Camera .... Standard
Pedestrian Crash Avoidance .... None

General:
Auto. Crash Notification .... None
Day Running Lamps .... Optional

Safety Belt/Restraint:
Dynamic Head Restraints .... None
Adjustable Belt .... Standard Front and Rear

Toyota Tundra

Specifications

Drive	4WD
Engine	5.7-liter V8
Transmission	6-sp. Automatic
Tow Rating (lbs.)	Very High-10000
Head/Leg Room (in.)	Average-39.7/42.5
Interior Space (cu. ft.)	–
Cargo Space (cu. ft.)	Very Roomy-67.1
Wheelbase/Length (in.)	145.7/228.9

*Crash test is for Crew Cab only.

Ratings—10 Best, 1 Worst	
Combo Crash Tests	6
Safety Features	2
Rollover	4
Preventive Maintenance	6
Repair Costs	4
Warranty	2
Fuel Economy	4
Complaints	8
Insurance Costs	5
OVERALL RATING	**3**

Toyota Venza

Toyota Venza

At-a-Glance

Status/Year Series Started	Unchanged/2009
Twins	–
Body Styles	SUV
Seating	5
Anti-Theft Device	Std. Pass. Immobil. & Opt. Pass. Alarm
Parking Index Rating	Very Hard
Where Made	Georgetown, KY
Fuel Factor	
MPG Rating (city/hwy)	Poor-20/26
Driving Range (mi.)	Short-395.0
Fuel Type	Regular
Annual Fuel Cost	Average-$1,881
Gas Guzzler Tax	No
Greenhouse Gas Emissions (tons/yr.)	High-7.8
Barrels of Oil Used per year	High-14.3

How the Competition Rates

Competitors	Rating	Pg.
Chevrolet Equinox	2	115
Honda Crosstour	–	150
Nissan Murano	–	224

Price Range	Retail	Markup
LE FWD	$28,915	9%
XLE FWD	$31,960	10%
XLE AWD	$33,410	10%
Limited V6 AWD	$39,790	10%

Safety Checklist

Crash Tests:
Frontal	Average
Side	Average

Airbags:
Torso	Front Torso from Seat
Pelvis	None
Roll Sensing	No
Knee Bolster	Standard Driver

Crash Avoidance:
Collision Avoidance	None
Blind Spot Detection	None
Lane Keeping Assist	None
Backup Camera	Optional
Pedestrian Crash Avoidance	None

General:
Auto. Crash Notification	None
Day Running Lamps	Standard

Safety Belt/Restraint:
Dynamic Head Restraints	Standard Front
Adjustable Belt	Standard Front

Toyota Venza

Specifications

Drive	FWD
Engine	2.7-liter I4
Transmission	6-sp. Automatic
Tow Rating (lbs.)	Very Low-1000
Head/Leg Room (in.)	Cramped-39.6/40.2
Interior Space (cu. ft.)	Roomy-108
Cargo Space (cu. ft.)	Very Roomy-36.2
Wheelbase/Length (in.)	109.3/189

Ratings—10 Best, 1 Worst

Combo Crash Tests	3
Safety Features	1
Rollover	5
Preventive Maintenance	10
Repair Costs	10
Warranty	2
Fuel Economy	9
Complaints	10
Insurance Costs	3
OVERALL RATING	**5**

Toyota Yaris

Toyota Yaris

Toyota Yaris

At-a-Glance

Status/Year Series Started Appearance Change/2012
Twins . . . . –
Body Styles . . . . Hatchback
Seating 5
Anti-Theft Device . . . . Std. Pass. Immobil.
Parking Index Rating . . . . .Very Easy
Where Made. .Iwata, Japan
Fuel Factor . . . .
  MPG Rating (city/hwy) . . . . Very Good-30/36
  Driving Range (mi.) . . . . Very Short-360.0
  Fuel Type . . . . .Regular
  Annual Fuel Cost . . . . Very Low-$1,295
  Gas Guzzler Tax . . . . .No
  Greenhouse Gas Emissions (tons/yr.). Low-5.6
  Barrels of Oil Used per year Low-10.3

How the Competition Rates

Competitors	Rating	Pg.
Chevrolet Sonic	9	119
Kia Rio	5	178
Nissan Versa	2	230

Price Range

Price Range	Retail	Markup
L 2 Door MT	$14,845	4%
L 4 Door AT	$15,945	4%
LE 4 Door	$16,880	4%
SE 4 Door	$17,620	4%

Safety Checklist

Crash Tests:
  Frontal. . . . . .Poor
  Side. . . . . .Poor
Airbags:
  Torso . . . . .Front Pelvis/Torso from Seat
  Pelvis . . . . .Front Pelvis/Torso from Seat
  Roll Sensing. . . . . No
  Knee Bolster . . . . Standard Driver
Crash Avoidance:
  Collision Avoidance . . . . None
  Blind Spot Detection . . . . None
  Lane Keeping Assist . . . . None
  Backup Camera . . . . None
  Pedestrian Crash Avoidance . . . . None
General:
  Auto. Crash Notification . . . . None
  Day Running Lamps . . . . Optional
Safety Belt/Restraint:
  Dynamic Head Restraints . . . . None
  Adjustable Belt. . . . . None

Toyota Yaris

Toyota Yaris

Specifications

Drive . . . . FWD
Engine 1.5-liter I4
Transmission . . . . .4-sp. Automatic
Tow Rating (lbs.) . . . . –
Head/Leg Room (in.) Cramped-39.3/40.6
Interior Space (cu. ft.). . . . . .Very Cramped-85.1
Cargo Space (cu. ft.) Cramped-15.6
Wheelbase/Length (in.) 98.8/155.5

Ratings—10 Best, 1 Worst

Combo Crash Tests	4
Safety Features	2
Rollover	7
Preventive Maintenance	6
Repair Costs	5
Warranty	4
Fuel Economy	7
Complaints	5
Insurance Costs	3
OVERALL RATING	**3**

Volkswagen Beetle

Volkswagen Beetle

At-a-Glance

Status/Year Series Started........ Unchanged/2012
Twins ....–
Body Styles .... Hatchback, Convertible
Seating....................................4
Anti-Theft Device ...... Std. Pass. Immobil. & Alarm
Parking Index Rating ....Very Easy
Where Made................. Hai Phong, Vietnam
Fuel Factor...................................
  MPG Rating (city/hwy) Good-25/33
  Driving Range (mi.) Average-406.9
  Fuel Type.........................Regular
  Annual Fuel Cost .... Low-$1,496
  Gas Guzzler Tax ....No
  Greenhouse Gas Emissions (tons/yr.) Low-6.5
  Barrels of Oil Used per year Average-11.8

How the Competition Rates

Competitors	Rating	Pg.
Chevrolet Sonic	9	119
Fiat 500	2	134
Mini Cooper	–	211

Price Range

	Retail	Markup
1.8T MT	$20,470	4%
1.8T w/Sunroof AT	$25,095	4%
R-Line MT	$25,195	4%
R-Line w/Sunroof AT	$31,625	4%

Safety Checklist

Crash Tests:
  Frontal............................Poor
  Side............................ Average
Airbags:
  Torso .... Front Head/Torso from Seat
  Pelvis .... None
  Roll Sensing......................... No
  Knee Bolster .... None
Crash Avoidance:
  Collision Avoidance .... None
  Blind Spot Detection .... Optional
  Lane Keeping Assist .... None
  Backup Camera................... Optional
  Pedestrian Crash Avoidance .... None
General:
  Auto. Crash Notification... Operator Assist.-Fee
  Day Running Lamps .... Standard
Safety Belt/Restraint:
  Dynamic Head Restraints .... None
  Adjustable Belt...................... None

Volkswagen Beetle

Specifications

Drive................................. FWD
Engine 1.8-liter I4
Transmission ....6-sp. Automatic
Tow Rating (lbs.) ....–
Head/Leg Room (in.) Cramped-39.4/41.3
Interior Space (cu. ft.)........Very Cramped-85.1
Cargo Space (cu. ft.) Cramped-15.4
Wheelbase/Length (in.) 100/168.4

Ratings—10 Best, 1 Worst

Combo Crash Tests	–
Safety Features	3
Rollover	8
Preventive Maintenance	4
Repair Costs	5
Warranty	4
Fuel Economy	6
Complaints	6
Insurance Costs	5
OVERALL RATING	**–**

Volkswagen CC

Volkswagen CC

Safety Checklist

Crash Tests:
Frontal . . . . –
Side . . . . –

Airbags:
Torso . . . . .Front Pelvis/Torso from Seat
Pelvis . . . . .Front Pelvis/Torso from Seat
Roll Sensing. . . . . No
Knee Bolster . . . . None

Crash Avoidance:
Collision Avoidance . . . . None
Blind Spot Detection . . . . None
Lane Keeping Assist . . . . None
Backup Camera . . . . Standard
Pedestrian Crash Avoidance . . . . None

General:
Auto. Crash Notification . . . Operator Assist.-Fee
Day Running Lamps . . . . Standard

Safety Belt/Restraint:
Dynamic Head Restraints . . . . None
Adjustable Belt. . . . . .Standard Front

At-a-Glance

Status/Year Series Started. Unchanged/2009
Twins . . . . –
Body Styles . . . . .Coupe
Seating 5
Anti-Theft Device . . . . . . Std. Pass. Immobil. & Alarm
Parking Index Rating . . . . Average
Where Made. . . . . .Emden, Germany
Fuel Factor . . . .
  MPG Rating (city/hwy) Average-22/31
  Driving Range (mi.) . . . . .Very Long-468.2
  Fuel Type. .Premium
  Annual Fuel Cost . . . . Average-$1,896
  Gas Guzzler Tax .No
  Greenhouse Gas Emissions (tons/yr.) . . Average-7.2
  Barrels of Oil Used per year High-13.2

How the Competition Rates

Competitors	Rating	Pg.
Acura TLX	–	85
Mercedes-Benz CLA-Class	–	204
Subaru Legacy	7	242

Price Range

	Retail	Markup
Sport MT	$32,685	4%
R-Line AT	$35,025	4%
Executive	$37,705	4%
VR6 4Motion	$43,140	4%

Volkswagen CC

Specifications

Drive. . . . . FWD
Engine 2.0-liter I4
Transmission . . . . .6-sp. Automatic
Tow Rating (lbs.) . . . . –
Head/Leg Room (in.) . . . . .Very Cramped-37.4/41.6
Interior Space (cu. ft.). Cramped-93.6
Cargo Space (cu. ft.) Cramped-13.2
Wheelbase/Length (in.) 106.7/189.1

Ratings—10 Best, 1 Worst

Combo Crash Tests	–
Safety Features	3
Rollover	7
Preventive Maintenance	6
Repair Costs	8
Warranty	4
Fuel Economy	8
Complaints	–
Insurance Costs	3
OVERALL RATING	**–**

Volkswagen Golf

Volkswagen Golf

At-a-Glance

Status/Year Series Started	All New/2015
Twins	Audi A3
Body Styles	Hatchback
Seating	5
Anti-Theft Device	Std. Pass. Immobil. & Alarm
Parking Index Rating	Very Easy
Where Made	Wolfsburg, Germany / Puebla, Mexico
Fuel Factor	
MPG Rating (city/hwy)	Good-26/36
Driving Range (mi.)	Short-392.2
Fuel Type	Regular
Annual Fuel Cost	Very Low-$1,413
Gas Guzzler Tax	No
Greenhouse Gas Emissions (tons/yr.)	Low-6.2
Barrels of Oil Used per year	Average-11.4

How the Competition Rates

Competitors	Rating	Pg.
Chevrolet Sonic	9	119
Mazda Mazda3	5	199
Subaru Impreza	4	241

Price Range

	Retail	Markup
Launch Edition 2 Door MT	$17,995	4%
S 2 Door AT	$20,295	4%
TDI S AT	$23,095	4%
TDI SEL AT	$29,095	4%

Safety Checklist

Crash Tests:
- Frontal . . . . –
- Side . . . . –

Airbags:
- Torso . . . . Front Pelvis/Torso from Seat
- Pelvis . . . . Front Pelvis/Torso from Seat
- Roll Sensing . . . . No
- Knee Bolster . . . . None

Crash Avoidance:
- Collision Avoidance . . . . . Warning Only Optional
- Blind Spot Detection . . . . None
- Lane Keeping Assist . . . . None
- Backup Camera . . . . Optional
- Pedestrian Crash Avoidance . . . . None

General:
- Auto. Crash Notification . . . Operator Assist.-Fee
- Day Running Lamps . . . . Standard

Safety Belt/Restraint:
- Dynamic Head Restraints . . . . None
- Adjustable Belt . . . . Standard Front

Volkswagen Golf

Specifications

Drive	FWD
Engine	1.8-liter I4
Transmission	6-sp. Automatic
Tow Rating (lbs.)	–
Head/Leg Room (in.)	Very Cramped-38.4/41.2
Interior Space (cu. ft.)	Cramped-93.5
Cargo Space (cu. ft.)	Average-22.8
Wheelbase/Length (in.)	103.8/167.5

Ratings—10 Best, 1 Worst

Combo Crash Tests	7
Safety Features	5
Rollover	7
Preventive Maintenance	5
Repair Costs	5
Warranty	4
Fuel Economy	6
Complaints	5
Insurance Costs	3
OVERALL RATING	**5**

Volkswagen Jetta

Volkswagen Jetta

Volkswagen Jetta

At-a-Glance

Status/Year Series Started Appearance Change/2011
Twins . . . . –
Body Styles . . . . Sedan, Wagon
Seating 5
Anti-Theft Device . . . . . . Std. Pass. Immobil. & Alarm
Parking Index Rating . . . . Easy
Where Made. . . . . .Puebla, Mexico
Fuel Factor . . . .
  MPG Rating (city/hwy) Average-23/34
  Driving Range (mi.) Short-390.3
  Fuel Type. .Regular
  Annual Fuel Cost . . . . Low-$1,560
  Gas Guzzler Tax . . . . .No
  Greenhouse Gas Emissions (tons/yr.). . Average-6.9
  Barrels of Oil Used per year Average-12.7

How the Competition Rates

Competitors	Rating	Pg.
Ford Focus	–	144
Nissan Sentra	–	228
Toyota Corolla	8	249

Price Range	Retail	Markup
2.0L S MT	$17,325	4%
1.8T SE AT	$20,095	4%
TDI AT	$22,740	4%
Hybrid SEL Premium	$31,670	4%

Safety Checklist

Crash Tests:
  Frontal. . . . . Average
  Side. . . . . Very Good
Airbags:
  Torso . . . . .Front Pelvis/Torso from Seat
  Pelvis . . . . .Front Pelvis/Torso from Seat
  Roll Sensing. . . . . .Yes
  Knee Bolster . . . . None
Crash Avoidance:
  Collision Avoidance . . . . .Warning Only Optional
  Blind Spot Detection . . . . Optional
  Lane Keeping Assist . . . . None
  Backup Camera . . . . Optional
  Pedestrian Crash Avoidance . . . . None
General:
  Auto. Crash Notification . . . Operator Assist.-Fee
  Day Running Lamps . . . . Standard
Safety Belt/Restraint:
  Dynamic Head Restraints . . . . None
  Adjustable Belt. . . . . .Standard Front

Volkswagen Jetta

Specifications

Drive. . . . . .FWD
Engine 2.0-liter I4
Transmission . . . . .6-sp. Automatic
Tow Rating (lbs.) . . . . –
Head/Leg Room (in.) . . . . .Very Cramped-38.2/41.2
Interior Space (cu. ft.). Cramped-94.1
Cargo Space (cu. ft.) Cramped-15.7
Wheelbase/Length (in.) 104.4/183.3

Volkswagen Passat

Ratings—10 Best, 1 Worst	
Combo Crash Tests	8
Safety Features	2
Rollover	7
Preventive Maintenance	6
Repair Costs	4
Warranty	4
Fuel Economy	7
Complaints	4
Insurance Costs	3
OVERALL RATING	**5**

Volkswagen Passat

Volkswagen Passat

At-a-Glance

Status/Year Series Started	Unchanged/2012
Twins	–
Body Styles	Sedan
Seating	5
Anti-Theft Device	Std. Pass. Immobil. & Alarm
Parking Index Rating	Average
Where Made	Chattanooga, TN
Fuel Factor	
MPG Rating (city/hwy)	Good-24/36
Driving Range (mi.)	Very Long-522.4
Fuel Type	Regular
Annual Fuel Cost	Low-$1,487
Gas Guzzler Tax	No
Greenhouse Gas Emissions (tons/yr.)	Low-6.4
Barrels of Oil Used per year	Average-11.8

How the Competition Rates

Competitors	Rating	Pg.
Acura TLX	–	85
Ford Fusion	4	145
Volvo S60	10	268

Price Range	Retail	Markup
S 1.8T MT	$21,120	4%
Wolfsburg	$24,135	4%
SE TDI	$26,825	4%
SEL Premium 3.6L	$35,660	4%

Safety Checklist

Crash Tests:
Frontal . . . . Very Good
Side . . . . Poor

Airbags:
Torso . . . . Front Pelvis/Torso from Seat
Pelvis . . . . Front Pelvis/Torso from Seat
Roll Sensing . . . . No
Knee Bolster . . . . None

Crash Avoidance:
Collision Avoidance . . . . None
Blind Spot Detection . . . . None
Lane Keeping Assist . . . . None
Backup Camera . . . . Optional
Pedestrian Crash Avoidance . . . . None

General:
Auto. Crash Notification . . . Operator Assist.-Fee
Day Running Lamps . . . . Standard

Safety Belt/Restraint:
Dynamic Head Restraints . . . . None
Adjustable Belt . . . . Standard Front

Volkswagen Passat

Specifications

Drive	FWD
Engine	1.8-liter I4
Transmission	6-sp. Automatic
Tow Rating (lbs.)	–
Head/Leg Room (in.)	Cramped-38.3/42.4
Interior Space (cu. ft.)	Average-102
Cargo Space (cu. ft.)	Cramped-15.9
Wheelbase/Length (in.)	110.4/191.6

Volkswagen Tiguan   Small SUV

Volkswagen Tiguan

Ratings—10 Best, 1 Worst

Combo Crash Tests	2
Safety Features	4
Rollover	3
Preventive Maintenance	4
Repair Costs	5
Warranty	4
Fuel Economy	4
Complaints	3
Insurance Costs	8
OVERALL RATING	**1**

Volkswagen Tiguan

Safety Checklist

Crash Tests:
Frontal . . . . Very Poor
Side . . . . Poor

Airbags:
Torso . . . . Front Pelvis/Torso from Seat
Pelvis . . . . Front Pelvis/Torso from Seat
Roll Sensing . . . . Yes
Knee Bolster . . . . None

Crash Avoidance:
Collision Avoidance . . . . None
Blind Spot Detection . . . . None
Lane Keeping Assist . . . . None
Backup Camera . . . . Optional
Pedestrian Crash Avoidance . . . . None

General:
Auto. Crash Notification . . . Operator Assist.-Fee
Day Running Lamps . . . . Standard

Safety Belt/Restraint:
Dynamic Head Restraints . . . . None
Adjustable Belt . . . . Standard Front

At-a-Glance

Status/Year Series Started Unchanged/2009
Twins . . . . Audi Q3
Body Styles . . . . SUV
Seating 5
Anti-Theft Device . . . . . . Std. Pass. Immobil. & Alarm
Parking Index Rating . . . . Average
Where Made . . . Wolfsburg, Germany / Kaluga, Russia
Fuel Factor . . . .
   MPG Rating (city/hwy) Poor-21/26
   Driving Range (mi.) Short-388.5
   Fuel Type . . . . Premium
   Annual Fuel Cost . . . . High-$2,087
   Gas Guzzler Tax . . . . No
   Greenhouse Gas Emissions (tons/yr.) High-7.8
   Barrels of Oil Used per year High-14.3

How the Competition Rates

Competitors	Rating	Pg.
Ford Escape	5	138
Lexus NX	–	191
Toyota RAV4	4	254

Price Range

	Retail	Markup
S	$25,998	4%
SE 4Motion	$29,925	4%
SEL	$33,255	4%
R-Line 4Motion	$39,235	4%

Volkswagen Tiguan

Specifications

Drive . . . . FWD
Engine 2.0-liter I4
Transmission . . . . 6-sp. Automatic
Tow Rating (lbs.) . . . . Very Low-2200
Head/Leg Room (in.) . . . . . Very Cramped-39.1/40.1
Interior Space (cu. ft.) Cramped-95.4
Cargo Space (cu. ft.) Roomy-23.8
Wheelbase/Length (in.) 102.5/174.5

Ratings—10 Best, 1 Worst

Combo Crash Tests	–
Safety Features	6
Rollover	3
Preventive Maintenance	4
Repair Costs	2
Warranty	4
Fuel Economy	2
Complaints	3
Insurance Costs	5
OVERALL RATING	**–**

Volkswagen Touareg

Volkswagen Touareg

At-a-Glance

Status/Year Series Started Appearance Change/2011
Twins . . . . .Porsche Cayenne
Body Styles . . . . SUV
Seating 5
Anti-Theft Device . . . . . . Std. Pass. Immobil. & Alarm
Parking Index Rating . . . . Hard
Where Made. . . Bratislava, Slovakia / Kaluga, Russia
Fuel Factor . . . .
 MPG Rating (city/hwy) . . . . .Very Poor-17/23
 Driving Range (mi.) . . . . .Very Long-508.5
 Fuel Type . . . . .Premium
 Annual Fuel Cost . . . . .Very High-$2,492
 Gas Guzzler Tax . . . . .No
 Greenhouse Gas Emissions (tons/yr.). High-9.4
 Barrels of Oil Used per year . . . . . . .Very High-17.3

How the Competition Rates

Competitors	Rating	Pg.
Acura MDX	6	82
BMW X5	6	101
Volvo XC60	9	270

Price Range	Retail	Markup
Sport VR6	$44,570	5%
Lux TDI	$55,550	5%
X TDI	$56,170	5%
Hybrid	$64,745	5%

Safety Checklist

Crash Tests:
 Frontal . . . .–
 Side . . . .–
Airbags:
 Torso . . . . .Front Pelvis/Torso from Seat
 Pelvis . . . . .Front Pelvis/Torso from Seat
 Roll Sensing. . . . . .Yes
 Knee Bolster . . . . None
Crash Avoidance:
 Collision Avoidance . . . . . . Optional CIB & DBS
 Blind Spot Detection . . . . Optional
 Lane Keeping Assist . . . . None
 Backup Camera . . . . Optional
 Pedestrian Crash Avoidance . . . . None
General:
 Auto. Crash Notification . . . . None
 Day Running Lamps . . . . Standard
Safety Belt/Restraint:
 Dynamic Head Restraints . . . . None
 Adjustable Belt . . . . .Standard Front

Volkswagen Touareg

Specifications

Drive . . . . AWD
Engine 3.6-liter V6
Transmission . . . . .8-sp. Automatic
Tow Rating (lbs.) High-7716
Head/Leg Room (in.) Cramped-39.6/41.4
Interior Space (cu. ft.). Average-103.6
Cargo Space (cu. ft.) Roomy-32.1
Wheelbase/Length (in.) 113.9/188.8

Ratings—10 Best, 1 Worst

Combo Crash Tests	9
Safety Features	10
Rollover	8
Preventive Maintenance	9
Repair Costs	7
Warranty	8
Fuel Economy	8
Complaints	7
Insurance Costs	5
OVERALL RATING	**10**

Volvo S60

Volvo S60

Volvo S60

Safety Checklist

Crash Tests:
Frontal . . . . Very Good
Side . . . . Average

Airbags:
Torso . . . Front Pelvis/Torso/Shoulder from Seat
Pelvis . . . . Front Pelvis/Torso from Seat
Roll Sensing . . . . .Yes
Knee Bolster . . . . None

Crash Avoidance:
Collision Avoidance . . . . . . Standard CIB & DBS
Blind Spot Detection . . . . Optional
Lane Keeping Assist . . . . Optional
Backup Camera . . . . Optional
Pedestrian Crash Avoidance . . . . Optional

General:
Auto. Crash Notification . . Operator Assist.- Free
Day Running Lamps . . . . Standard

Safety Belt/Restraint:
Dynamic Head Restraints . . . . None
Adjustable Belt . . . . .Standard Front

At-a-Glance

Status/Year Series Started Unchanged/2011
Twins . . . . –
Body Styles . . . . .Sedan
Seating 5
Anti-Theft Device . Std. Pass. Immobil. & Active Alarm
Parking Index Rating . . . . Average
Where Made . . . . Ghent, Belgium
Fuel Factor . . . .
  MPG Rating (city/hwy) Good-25/37
  Driving Range (mi.) . . . . .Very Long-521.0
  Fuel Type . . . . .Regular
  Annual Fuel Cost . . . . Low-$1,434
  Gas Guzzler Tax . . . . .No
  Greenhouse Gas Emissions (tons/yr.) Low-6.2
  Barrels of Oil Used per year Average-11.4

Volvo S60

How the Competition Rates

Competitors	Rating	Pg.
Acura TLX	–	85
Audi A6	7	89
Subaru Legacy	7	242

Specifications

Drive . . . . FWD
Engine 2.0-liter I4
Transmission . . . . .8-sp. Automatic
Tow Rating (lbs.) . . . . –
Head/Leg Room (in.) Average-39.3/41.9
Interior Space (cu. ft.) Cramped-92
Cargo Space (cu. ft.) . . . . Very Cramped-12
Wheelbase/Length (in.) 109.3/182.5

Price Range

Price Range	Retail	Markup
T5 FWD	$33,750	6%
T5 Premier AWD	$37,850	6%
T6 Platinum FWD	$42,750	6%
T6 R Design Platinum AWD	$46,950	6%

Ratings—10 Best, 1 Worst

Combo Crash Tests	–
Safety Features	10
Rollover	7
Preventive Maintenance	–
Repair Costs	–
Warranty	8
Fuel Economy	8
Complaints	–
Insurance Costs	5

OVERALL RATING   –

Volvo V60

At-a-Glance

Status/Year Series Started	All New/2015
Twins	–
Body Styles	Wagon
Seating	5
Anti-Theft Device	Std. Pass. Immobil. & Active Alarm
Parking Index Rating	Average
Where Made	Torslanda, Sweden
Fuel Factor	
MPG Rating (city/hwy)	Good-25/37
Driving Range (mi.)	Very Long-521.0
Fuel Type	Regular
Annual Fuel Cost	Low-$1,434
Gas Guzzler Tax	No
Greenhouse Gas Emissions (tons/yr.)	Low-6.2
Barrels of Oil Used per year	Average-11.4

How the Competition Rates

Competitors	Rating	Pg.
Subaru Outback	7	243
Toyota Prius V	8	253
Volkswagen Jetta	5	264

Price Range

	Retail	Markup
T5 FWD	$35,570	6%
T5 Premier AWD	$39,150	6%
T5 Platinum FWD	$41,300	6%
T6 R-Design Platinum AWD	$48,550	6%

Volvo V60

Safety Checklist

Crash Tests:
Frontal . . . . –
Side . . . . –
Airbags:
Torso . . . Front Pelvis/Torso/Shoulder from Seat
Pelvis . . . . Front Pelvis/Torso from Seat
Roll Sensing . . . . Yes
Knee Bolster . . . . None
Crash Avoidance:
Collision Avoidance . . . . . . Standard CIB & DBS
Blind Spot Detection . . . . Optional
Lane Keeping Assist . . . . Optional
Backup Camera . . . . Optional
Pedestrian Crash Avoidance . . . . Optional
General:
Auto. Crash Notification . . Operator Assist.- Free
Day Running Lamps . . . . Standard
Safety Belt/Restraint:
Dynamic Head Restraints . . . . None
Adjustable Belt . . . . Standard Front

Volvo V60

Specifications

Drive	FWD
Engine	2.0-liter I4
Transmission	8-sp. Automatic
Tow Rating (lbs.)	Low-3500
Head/Leg Room (in.)	Cramped-38.7/41.9
Interior Space (cu. ft.)	Cramped-92
Cargo Space (cu. ft.)	Roomy-28
Wheelbase/Length (in.)	109.3/182.5

Ratings—10 Best, 1 Worst

Combo Crash Tests	9
Safety Features	9
Rollover	3
Preventive Maintenance	9
Repair Costs	7
Warranty	8
Fuel Economy	2
Complaints	6
Insurance Costs	10
OVERALL RATING	**9**

Volvo XC60

Volvo XC60

At-a-Glance

Status/Year Series Started........ Unchanged/2009
Twins . . . . –
Body Styles . . . . SUV
Seating 5
Anti-Theft Device . Std. Pass. Immobil. & Active Alarm
Parking Index Rating . . . . Average
Where Made. . . . . Ghent, Belgium
Fuel Factor. . . . .
  MPG Rating (city/hwy) . . . . .Very Poor-17/24
  Driving Range (mi.) . . . . Very Short-362.0
  Fuel Type. . . . . .Regular
  Annual Fuel Cost . . . . High-$2,146
  Gas Guzzler Tax . . . . .No
  Greenhouse Gas Emissions (tons/yr.) High-9.0
  Barrels of Oil Used per year High-16.5

How the Competition Rates

Competitors	Rating	Pg.
Audi Q5	4	92
BMW X5	6	101
Mercedes-Benz M-Class	5	209

Price Range	Retail	Markup
T5 FWD	$36,200	6%
T5 Platinum AWD	$45,200	6%
T6 R AWD	$46,650	6%
T6 R Platinum AWD	$50,750	6%

Safety Checklist

Crash Tests:
  Frontal. . . . . Very Good
  Side. . . . . Good
Airbags:
  Torso . . . Front Pelvis/Torso/Shoulder from Seat
  Pelvis . . . . .Front Pelvis/Torso from Seat
  Roll Sensing. . . . . .Yes
  Knee Bolster . . . . None
Crash Avoidance:
  Collision Avoidance . . . . . . .Standard CIB & DBS
  Blind Spot Detection . . . . Optional
  Lane Keeping Assist . . . .Warning Only Optional
  Backup Camera . . . . Optional
  Pedestrian Crash Avoidance . . . . Optional
General:
  Auto. Crash Notification . . . Operator Assist.-Fee
  Day Running Lamps . . . . Standard
Safety Belt/Restraint:
  Dynamic Head Restraints . . . . None
  Adjustable Belt. . . . . .Standard Front

Volvo XC60

Specifications

Drive. . . . . AWD
Engine 3.0-liter I6
Transmission . . . . .6-sp. Automatic
Tow Rating (lbs.) Low-3500
Head/Leg Room (in.) Cramped-39.1/41.2
Interior Space (cu. ft.). Average-99
Cargo Space (cu. ft.) Roomy-30.8
Wheelbase/Length (in.) 109.2/182.8